W9-BTS-850

SWORD
Scrapbook I

SWORD of the LORD
PUBLISHERS
P.O.BOX 1099, MURFREESBORO, TN 37133

Copyright 1969, by
Sword of the Lord Publishers

ISBN 0-87398-787-X

PRINTED IN U.S.A.

INTRODUCTION

We believe that more preachers get sermon outlines, illustrations, bits of wisdom from THE SWORD OF THE LORD than from any other Christian magazine published. And among the treasures published through the years are bits of wisdom, sweet devotional pieces, charming illustrations and quotations, from a thousand sources. Here, then, are jewels of wit, pearls of devotion, diamonds of spiritual wisdom, culled from some 1,700 issues of this Christian paper, THE SWORD OF THE LORD, in 34 years. What a refreshing of heart they give to the reader! What a treasury of apt sayings, of pertinent illustrations, of wise counsel is here!

> A smile, a tear, a chuckle,
>   An amen or "wow" now and then,
> From the pleasantry, counsel or warning,
>   As this scrapbook tells about sin.
>
> Convictions and holy arousement,
>   Some laughter and sweet content,
> Should come to the one perusing,
>   The harvest of blessings here sent.

How many items? Hundreds, hundreds, hundreds! — 1,034!

Every preacher, every Sunday school teacher, every after-dinner speaker, will find here hundreds of things he will want to quote to brighten a message or emphasize a truth. Many a family gathered together in the evening will read some of these blessed stories or quotations aloud.

Here is collected much of the wisdom from great men through the years.

To Miss Viola Walden, editorial assistant, we offer our sincere thanks for long, long hours of labor, selecting, classifying, and indexing these scraps for the Scrapbook. Then an artist friend, Mr. Bill Bickford, was employed to lay out, page by page, all the wealth of good things, and to illustrate many items.

We hope that these attractive pages will prove to be, as the advertisements say about a certain brand of potato chips: "You can't eat only one!"

If some will be strengthened, if many will be cheered and comforted, and if others will spend here many a happy hour, we shall be repaid indeed for the toil and time in sending out this Sword of the Lord Scrapbook.

And may the dear Lord Jesus Christ our Saviour bless every reader.

John R. Rice, Founder
THE SWORD OF THE LORD

Ten Men in a Row

By Ester De La Cruz
as told to Elsie V. Gleason,
Anoka, Minn.

Back of our home in the Philippines during World War II was the place where the Japanese tortured and killed their victims. We could hear the screams of the tortured day and night. They liked to throw the babies in the air and catch them on the point of a sword, and the things they devised to torture adults were unthinkable.

Twice my father had been taken by enemy officers and had been returned to us as a result of my mother's prayers.

The third time the officer said, "He has been returned to you two times — but don't you ever think he will be spared the third time. This time he dies."

"If you don't believe in prayer, get out of here," Mother told him. The officer left, taking my father with him.

Mother put us five children to bed on our grass mats. Then she began her prayer vigil in behalf of our father. At four a.m., she woke us saying, "The burden has become so heavy I cannot bear it alone. Get up and help me pray for your father."

We gathered in a circle around Mother, with the two-month-old baby on the floor in the centre. While we were praying we heard footsteps. We were sure the officer was coming for us, and Mother threw her arms around us as far as she could reach.

Suddenly she said, "Those are your father's footsteps!"

"Are you safe?" he asked, pulling the bamboo door back. We lit the lamp and saw his white shirt splattered with blood from those who had stood near him.

"I understand now why they let me go," he said soberly. "You were praying."

He told us that he had been the last in a row of ten men. A man had gone down the row, slashing off the heads of each with a sword.

"He raised his sword when he came to me, and just as he was ready to bring it down the officer in charge suddenly screamed, 'Stop!' Then that officer roared at me, 'Go home. *Quick, get out of here.* Go home.'

"Then he dived at me, grabbed my arm and propelled me toward the gate and past the guard as fast as he could — and here I am."

That had been what was happening at the time Mother was so burdened that she got us up to pray.

We do not know what the officer experienced to make him change the order — but we do know *why*.

—The Pentecostal Evangel

The saints should never be dismay'd,
Nor sink in hopeless fear!
For when they least expect His aid,
The Saviour will appear.

Wait for His seasonable aid,
And though it tarry, wait;
The promise may be long delay'd
But cannot come too late.
—Cowper.

THERE ARE NO TRAFFIC JAMS ON THE STRAIGHT AND NARROW WAY.

QUALITY FIRST
The bull bellows loudest;
The cow gives the milk.
A butterfly is beautiful;
The worm spins the silk.
And barreled goods are valued
By the contents (not the keg).
The rooster does the crowing;
It's the hen that lays the egg.

Mrs. William

The Devil is not afraid of the Bible that has dust on it.
—Anonymous.

"Do Not Stem Revival's Tide!"
"Has my brother ought against me?
Have I wronged him in the past?
Have I harbored unkind mem'ries?
Have I false aspersions cast?
Have I treated him with coldness?
Passed him by—the other side?
Then, forgive me, oh! my brother,
Do not stem Revival's Tide."

Bible Reading

Take one book at a time. Don't be in a hurry. Read a book over, over and over. God will give light. The sixty-six books are sixty-six battering rams for Christians to conquer Satan with. So we shall slay and conquer. Try different ways of studying the Bible till you succeed. My wife wanted me to like tomatoes. I tried them raw, with vinegar, with sugar, and cooked, but I could not eat them. At last she thought of another way, and succeeded, and I thought it the best vegetable in the world.—Moody.

"On Being Behind With One's Reading"

Junior bit the meter man.
Junior kicked the cook
Junior's antisocial now
(According to the book)

Junior smashed the clock and lamp.
Junior hacked the tree.
(Destructive trends are treated
in chapters two and three)

Junior threw his milk at mom.
Junior screamed for more.
(Notes on self-assertiveness
are found in chapter 4.)

Junior tossed his shoes and socks
out into the rain.
(Negation, that, and normal—
disregard the stain.)

Junior got in Grandpops room
Tore up his fishing line.
That's to gain attention
(See page 89.)

Grandpop seized a slipper and
Yanked junior 'cross his knee
(Grandpa hasn't read a book
since 1893.)

Selected

The Artist and the . . . . . . Gipsy Girl

Many years ago in the old city of Dusseldorf, a town of Rhenish Prussia, there dwelt an artist by the name of Stenburg. A Roman Catholic, he had been taught their doctrines, but knew nothing of Christ as his own Saviour from the guilt and power of sin. He had been engaged to paint a great picture of the crucifixion, and this he was doing—not from any real love to Christ or faith in Him, but for money and fame. But in mercy God brought this man to know the wondrous love which led Jesus Christ to suffer that awful death of the cross; and how this was done this story will tell.

One beautiful spring morning Stenburg was seeking recreation in the forest near Dusseldorf when he came upon a gipsy girl plaiting straw baskets. She was gifted with more than the usual beauty of her race, and Stenburg was so impressed by it, that he determined to engage her as a model for a picture of a Spanish dancing-girl. So he bargained with Pepita, for that was her name, to come thrice a week to his studio to pose as a model.

At the appointed hour she arrived; and as her great eyes roved round the studio she was full of wonder, while looking at the pictures. The large one (the crucifixion) caught her eye. Gazing at it intently, she asked in an awed voice, pointing to the figure in the center, "Who is that?"

"The Christ," answered Stenburg carelessly.

"What is being done to Him?"

"They are crucifying Him."

"Who are those about Him with the bad faces?"

"Now, look here," said the artist, "I cannot talk. You have nothing to do but stand as I tell you." The girl dared not speak again, but she continued to gaze and wonder.

Every time she came to the studio, the fascination of the picture grew upon her. Then again she ventured to ask a question, for she longed to learn more of its meaning.

"Why did they crucify Him? Was He bad, very bad?"

"No, very good."

That was all she learned at one interview, but it added a little to her knowledge of that wonderful scene.

At last, seeing she was so anxious to know the meaning of the picture, Stenburg one day said, "Listen: I will tell you once for all; and then ask no more questions;" and he told her the story of the cross—new to Pepita, though so old to the artist that it had ceased to touch him. He could paint that dying agony, and not a nerve of his quiver; but the thought of it wrung her heart. Tears filled her eyes, and she could hardly control her emotion.

Pepita's last visit to the studio had come. She stood before the great picture, loth to leave it. "Come," said the artist, "here is your money, and a gold piece over."

"Thanks, Master." Then, again turning to the picture, said: "You must love Him very much when He has done all that for you; do you not?"

Stenburg could not answer. Pepita with a sad heart went back to her people. But her words pierced Stenburg like an arrow. God's Spirit sent the gipsy girl's words home to his heart. He could not forget them. "All that for you," rang in his ears. He became restless and sad. He knew he did not love the crucified One; and Rome can give no real rest to the troubled heart. Her votaries rarely know the peace of God.

Some time after this Stenburg was led to follow a few poor people who gathered in a retired place to hear the Bible read and the gospel preached. There for the first time he met those who had a living faith, and heard the simple gospel. He was made to realize why Christ hung upon the cross for sinners; that he was a sinner, and therefore Christ was there for him, bearing his sins. Thus God led the artist to the knowledge of salvation and he began to know the love of Christ and could say, "He loved me, and gave Himself for me."

And now he longed to make that wondrous love known to others; but how could he do it? Suddenly it flashed upon him. He could paint. His brush could tell out the love of Christ. Praying for God's help in the work, he painted as never before, and the picture was placed among other paintings in the famous gallery of Dusseldorf. Underneath he placed the words—

"All this I did for thee; what hast thou done for Me?"

Eternity alone will tell how many were led to Christ by the words and the painting.

One day Stenburg saw a poorly-dressed girl weeping bitterly as she stood by the picture. It was Pepita.

"O master! If He had but loved me so!" she cried.

Then the artist told her how He did die for her, poor gipsy girl though she was, as much as for the rich and great. Stenburg did not weary now of answering all her eager questions. He was as anxious to tell as she to hear of the love of Christ; and as it was presented to her, she received it, and went from that room a sinner saved, rejoicing in that wonderful love. Thus the Lord used Pepita's words to bring the artist to Himself, and then used the artist's words by which to reveal Himself to her.

Months afterward Stenburg was suddenly called one night by a dark-looking stranger to visit a dying person. Following his guide through the streets into the country, and then beyond into the deep forest, at last they came to a few poor tents in a sheltered spot. In one of these he found Pepita dying in poverty, but happy in the precious love of Christ. He saw her die praising her Saviour for His love, knowing that He had taken all her sins away, and that she was going into His blessed presence to be forever with Him.

Long after this, when the artist, too, had gone to be with the Lord, a wealthy young nobleman found his way into the picture-gallery, and as he gazed upon the picture and the words underneath it, God there and then spoke to his heart. It was Count Zinzendorf, who from that day became an earnest Christian, and also became the father of the Moravian missions by means of which God led thousands of souls to Himself. Such are the wonderful ways of God!

The Diary of a Bible — Was It Yours?

January 15—Been resting quietly for a week. The first few nights after the first of this year my owner read me regularly, but he has forgotten me, I guess.

February 2—Clean-up. I was dusted with other things and put back in my place.

February 12—Owner used me last night for a short time after dinner, looking up a few references. Went to Sunday School.

March 7—Clean-up. I am dusted and in my old place again. I have been down in the lower hall since my trip to Sunday School.

April 12—Busy day. Owner led league meeting and had to look up references. He had an awful time finding one, though it was right there in its place all the time.

May 5—In Grandma's lap all afternoon. She is here on a visit. She let a teardrop fall on Colossians 2:5-7.

May 6—In Grandma's lap again this afternoon. She spent most of her time on I Corinthians 13 and the last four verses of the 15th chapter.

May 7, 8, 9—In Grandma's lap every afternoon now. It's a comfortable spot. Sometimes she reads me and sometimes she talk to me.

May 10—Grandma gone. Back in the old place. She kissed me good-bye.

June 3—Had a couple of four-leaved clovers stuck in me today.

July 1—Packed in a trunk with clothes and other things. Off on a vacation, I guess.

July 7—Still in the trunk.

July 10—Still in the trunk, though nearly everything else has been taken out.

July 15—Home again and in my old place. It was quite a journey, but I do not see why I went.

August 1—Rather stuffy and hot, I have two magazines, a novel, and an old hat on top of me. Wish they would take them off.

August 12—Clean-up. Dusted and set right again.

August 20—Used by Mary a few moments today. She was writing a letter to a friend whose brother had died, and wanted an appropriate verse.

August 31—Clean-up again.

Why Abraham Lincoln Refused to Drink or Smoke

One day Lincoln was riding in a stage coach, as they rode in those days, in company with a Kentucky colonel. After riding a number of miles together the colonel took a bottle of whiskey out of his pocket and said, "Mr. Lincoln, won't you take a drink with me?"

"No, Colonel, thank you," replied Mr. Lincoln. "I never drink whisky."

They rode along together for a number of miles more, visiting very pleasantly, when the gentleman from Kentucky reached into his pocket and brought out some cigars, saying: "Now Mr. Lincoln, if you won't take a drink with me, won't you take a smoke with me? For here are some of Kentucky's finest cigars."

"Now, Colonel," said Mr. Lincoln, "you are such a fine, agreeable man to travel with, maybe I ought to take a smoke with you. But before I do so, let me tell you a story, an experience I had when a boy.

"My mother called me to her bed one day when I was about nine years old. She was sick—very sick—and she said to me, 'Abey, the doctor tells me I am not going to get well. I want you to promise me before I go that you will never use whisky nor tobacco as long as you live.' And I promised my mother I never would. Up to this hour, Colonel, I have kept that promise. Now would you advise me to break that promise to my dear mother and take a smoke with you?"

The Colonel put his hand gently on Mr. Lincoln's shoulder and said with a voice trembling with emotion: "No, Mr. Lincoln, I wouldn't have you do it for the world. It was one of the best promises you ever made. I would give a thousand dollars today if I had made my mother a promise like that and had kept it as you have done."

There is scarcely a man or woman in this country today but what believes that Abraham Lincoln's keeping his promise to his mother helped to make him the great and good and loved man that he was.—Western Recorder

Red Stains

Three ghosts met upon a lonesome road
And spake each to one another,
How came that red stain upon your mouth?
From eating of forbidden fruit,
  Brother, my brother.

Three ghosts met upon a windy road
And spake each to one another,
How came that burn upon your foot?
I stamped a neighbor's hearthflame out,
  Brother, my brother.

Three ghosts met upon a darkened road
And spake each to one another,
How came that red stain upon your
      hand no dust nor ash may cover?
From breaking of a woman's heart,
  Brother, my brother.

(Author unknown)

A FAMILY WON BY A SMILE

When I asked Mr. Moody what he thought of Spurgeon, he said:

"He is a perpetual stream of Christian sunlight. One Sunday morning in London," continued Mr. Moody, "Spurgeon said to me, just before he commenced his sermon: 'Moody, I want you to notice that family there in one of the front seats, and when we go home I want to tell you their story.'

"When we got home," said Moody, "I asked him for the story, and he said:

"'All that family were won by a smile.'

"'Why,' said I, 'how's that?'

"'Well,' said he, 'as I was walking down a street one day, I saw a child at a window; it smiled, and I smiled, and we bowed. It was the same the second time; I bowed, she bowed. It was not long before there was another child, and I had got in a habit of looking and bowing, and pretty soon the group grew, and at last, as I went by, a lady was with them. I didn't know what to do. I didn't want to bow to her, but I knew the children expected it, and so I bowed to them all. And the mother saw I was a minister, because I carried a Bible every Sunday morning. So the children followed me the next Sunday and found I was a minister. And they thought I was the greatest preacher, and their parents must hear me. A minister who is kind to a child and gives him a pat on the head, why, the children will think he is the greatest preacher in the world. Kindness goes a great way. And, finally, the father and mother and five children were converted, and they are going to join our church next Sunday.'

"Won to Christ by a smile!" said Moody. "We must get the wrinkles out of our brows, and we must have smiling faces, if we want to succeed in our work of love."

A lady was mailing a gift of a Bible to a relative. The postal clerk examined the heavy package and inquired if it contained anything breakable. "Nothing," the lady told him, "but the Ten Commandments."

What's the Matter With Mrs. Craig?

The following news items appeared in the Nashville Banner, June 19, 1956:

PORTER, Okla. [(AP)]—Mrs. Ella Craig, age 81, hasn't missed Sunday School attendance in 1,040 Sundays— a perfect record for 20 years.

1. Doesn't Mrs. Craig ever have company on Sunday to keep her away from church?

2. Doesn't she ever go anywhere on Saturday night and get up tired on Sunday morning?

3. Doesn't she ever have headaches, colds, nervous spells, tired feelings, poor breakfast, sudden calls out of town, business trips, Sunday picnics, or any trouble of any kind?

4. Doesn't she have any friends at all— friends who invite her to a week end trip to the sea shore or mountains?

5. Doesn't she ever sleep late on Sunday mornings?

6. Doesn't it ever rain or snow on Sunday mornings?

7. Doesn't she ever get her feelings hurt by somebody in church?

8. Doesn't she ever get mad at the preacher or Sunday School teacher?

9. Doesn't she have a radio or television so she can listen to "some mighty good sermons from out of town?"

What's the matter with Mrs. Craig?

A Humble Answer

How a soft answer can turn away wrath, as well as dissatisfaction, is illustrated in the following anecdote of the late President Wayland. Deacon Moses Pond went to Dr. Wayland once with the complaint that the preaching did not edify him. "I'm sorry," said the pastor; "I know that they are poor sermons. I wish I could make them better. Come, let us pray that I may be able to do so." The deacon, telling the story, used to say, "Dr. Wayland prayed and I prayed; he cried and I cried. But I have thought a hundred times that it was strange that he did not turn me out of the house. I tell you there never was a better man nor a greater preacher than Dr. Wayland."

There is a story of an Arab who said at night, "I will loose my camel and trust in God to find it." But a wiser one said, "Tie your camel and trust in God." Prayer and care should go together.

—*Christian Safeguard.*

Grimaldi, the celebrated clown, went to a physician to obtain a cure for his depressed spirit. The physician did not know who the patient was, and thinking he only needed a little amusement, said to him, "For medicine, go and hear Grimaldi." "But, doctor," was the answer, "I am Grimaldi."

—Selected.

Man on His Knees

In the early days of the Republic, a stranger once asked at Congress how he could distinguish Washington.

He was told, "You can easily distinguish him when Congress goes to prayer. Washington is the gentleman who kneels."

MAKES YOU FEEL BETTER

"I wish I could sing; I think I'd feel 'weller' then," said a seven-year-old lad in Bellevue Hospital in New York while a surgeon was examining him for injuries sustained in a fall into a twelve-foot-deep excavation.

"All right, laddie, you may sing if you will sing something nice," said the kind-hearted Dr. McLean. The little fellow began to sing in a high, clear soprano, "Nearer, My God, to Thee." As the childish notes rang out, nurses, doctors, and attendants from various parts of the hospital began to steal into the room until there were fully a hundred present.

"Well, I guess you're all right, little man," said the doctor as he finished his examination; "I can't find any broken bones."

"I guess it was the singing that fixed me," replied the boy. "I always sing when I feel bad."

If all of us would do as this chap did --sing when we "feel bad," we would certainly "feel 'weller!'"

Time to Resign

On an American troopship, the soldiers crowded around their chaplain asking, "Do you believe in Hell?" "I do not." "Well, then, will you please resign, for if there is no hell, we do not need you, and if there is a Hell, we do not wish to be led astray."

—*Christian Beacon*

He placed me in a little cage
Away from gardens fair;
But I must sing the sweetest song
Because He placed me there.
Not beat my wings against the gate,
If it's my Maker's will,
But rise my voice to Heaven's gate
And sing the louder still.

—Selected.

Doctrines and Duties

Some of our hearers do not desire to hear the whole counsel of God. They have their favorite doctrines, and would have us silent on all besides. Many are like the Scotch woman who, after hearing a sermon, said, "It was very well if it hadna been for the trash of duties at the HINNER end."—*Spurgeon.*

9

Opened Windows

One of the statements most commonly made is that tithing was intended for the Jew only and does not apply to the Christian living under grace. If this were true, then our Lord would not have said of tithing: "These ought ye to have done" (Matt. 23:23; Luke 11:42).

Our heavenly Father does not promise wealth to every one who tithes, but He does promise to "open the windows of heaven and pour you out a blessing that there shall not be room enough to receive it." Take Him at His word today.

Dr. S. D. Gordon wrote he could never forget his mother's paraphrase of Malachi 3:10. The verse begins: "Bring ye the whole tithe in" and ends, "I will pour" the blessing out till you'll be embarrassed for space. Her paraphrase was this: "Give all He asks: take all He promises."

Tithing pays rich dividends in the home, at school, in business, in the pulpit, on the mission field; in fact, in every walk of life.
--Tither

Laying or Lying?

Two men got into an animated argument over which is right, grammatically, to say, "The hen is setting," or "The hen is sitting." Each contended that he was right, and both showed a ready disposition to prove he was right with fistic blows. Finally reason obtained. They agreed to go to Farmer Brown, and put the question to him. Hearing the matter, Farmer Brown guffawed heartily. Then, he said rather contemptuously, "Men, when I see a hen in such a position on a nest, I don't ask whether she is sitting, or setting. I only ask, 'Is she LAYING, or is she LYING?'"

W. B. Knight

When You Pray

Long prayers and long sermons tend to quench the fire instead of kindling it. Brethren, in all things has our Lord Jesus given us the best example—also in regard to praying. When with His disciples, His prayers were of medium length. In the midst of a large crowd, as at Lazarus' grave and the feeding of the five thousand, His prayer was short. When He was alone with His Father—in the Garden or on the Mount—then He prayed all night.

So ought ye also to do, dear brethren. Among God's children, make your prayer medium long, as Jesus did when He was about to be crucified. When in a crowd or with the sick or dying or the unfortunate, short. When you are alone with your Father in your secret closet, pray as long as you please.—C. H. Spurgeon.

TOO BUSY TO LOVE

A father and his young daughter were great friends and much in each other's company. Then the father noted a change in his daughter. If he went for a walk, she excused herself from going. He grieved about it, but could not understand. When his birthday came, she presented him with a pair of exquisitely worked slippers, saying, "I have made them for you." Then he understood what had been the matter for the past three months, and he said, "My darling, I like these slippers very much, but next time buy the slippers and let me have you all the days. I would rather have my child than anything she can make for me."

Some of us are so busy for the Lord that He cannot get much of us. To us He would say, "I know your works, your labor, your patience, but I miss the first love."
--G. Campbell Morgan

THE GIRL

Little Girls are the nicest things that happen to people. They are born with a little bit of angel-shine about them and though it wears thin sometimes, there is always enough left to lasso your heart—even when they are sitting in the mud, or crying temperamental tears, or parading up the street in Mother's best clothes.

A little girl can be sweeter (and badder) oftener than anyone else in the world. She can jitter around; and stomp, and make funny noises that frazzle your nerves yet just when you open your mouth, she stands there demure with that special look in her eyes. A girl is Innocence playing in the mud, Beauty standing on its head, and Motherhood dragging a doll by the foot.

Girls are available in five colors—black, white, red, yellow, or brown, yet Mother Nature always manages to select your favorite color when you place your order. They disprove the law of supply and demand—there are millions of little girls, but each is as precious as rubies.

God borrows from many creatures to make a little girl. He uses the song of a bird, the squeal of a pig, the stubbornness of a mule, the antics of a monkey, the spryness of a grasshopper, the curiosity of a cat, the speed of a gazelle, the slyness of a fox, the softness of a kitten, and to top it all off, He adds the mysterious mind of a woman.

A little girl likes new shoes, pretty dresses, small animals, first grade, noisemakers, the girl next door, dolls, make-believe. Mother's high heels, ice cream, kitchens, coloring books, cans of water, going visiting, and tea parties. She doesn't care so much for visitors, large dogs, hand-me-downs, straight chairs, vegetables, snow suits, or staying in the front yard. She is loudest when you are thinking, the prettiest when she has provoked you, the busiest at bedtime and the quietest when you want to show her off.

Who else can cause you more grief, joy, irritation, satisfaction, embarrassment, and genuine delight than this combination of Eve, Salome, and Florence Nightingale? She can muss up your home, your hair, and your dignity—spend your money, your time, and your temper—then just when your patience is ready to crack, her sunshine peeks through and you've lost again.

Yes, she is a nerve-racking nuisance, just a noisy bundle of mischief. But when your dreams tumble down and the world is a mess—when it seems you are pretty much of a fool after all—she can make you a king when she climbs on your knee and whispers, "I love you best of all!" (—Author unknown) ★

THE BOY

Between the innocence of babyhood and the dignity of manhood we find a delightful creature called a boy. Boys come in assorted sizes, weights, and colors, but all boys have the same creed: To enjoy every second of every minute of every hour of every day and to protest noisily (their only weapon) when the last minute has come and the adult males pack them off to bed at night.

Boys are found everywhere—on top of, underneath, inside of, climbing on, swinging from, running around, or jumping to. Mothers love them, little girls hate them, older sisters and brothers tolerate them, adults ignore them, and Heaven protects them. A boy is Truth with dirt on its face, Beauty with a cut on its finger, Wisdom with bubble gum in its hair, and the Hope of the future with a frog in its pocket.

When you are busy, a boy is an inconsiderate, bothersome, intruding jangle of noise. When you want him to make a good impression, his brain turns to jelly or else he becomes a savage, sadistic, jungle creature bent on destroying the world and himself with it.

A boy is a composite—he has the appetite of a horse, the energy of a pocketsize atomic bomb, the curiosity of a cat, the lungs of a dictator, the imagination of a Paul Bunyan, the shyness of a violet, the audacity of a steel trap, the enthusiasm of a fire cracker, and when he makes something he has five thumbs on each hand.

He likes ice cream, knives, saws, Christmas, the boy across the street, woods, water (in its natural habitat), large animals, Dad, trains, Saturday mornings and fire engines. He's not much for school, company, books without pictures, music lessons, neckties, barbers, girls, overcoats, adults, or bedtime.

Nobody else is so early to rise, or so late to supper. Nobody else gets so much fun out of trees, dogs, and breezes. Nobody else can cram into one pocket a rusty knife, a half-eaten apple, 3 feet of string, an empty plastic sack, 2 gum drops, 6 pennies, a sling shot, a chunk of unknown substance, and a genuine super-sonic code ring with a secret compartment.

A boy is a magical creature—you can lock him out of your workshop, but you can't lock him out of your heart. You can get him out of your study, but you can't get him out of your mind. Might as well give up—he is your captor, your jailer and your boss—a freckled-face, pint-sized, cat-chasing bundle of noise. But when you come home at night with only the shattered pieces of your hopes and dreams, he can mend them like new with the two magic words—"Hi Dad!" (—Author unknown) ★

11

The First Settler's Story

By Will Carleton; Died 1912

It ain't the funniest thing a man can do —
Existing in a country when it's new;
Nature, who moved in first — a good long while —
Has things already somewhat her own style,
And she don't want her woodland splendors battered,
Her rustic furniture broke up and scattered,
Her paintings, which long years ago were done
By that old splendid artist-king, the sun,
Torn down and dragged into civilization's gutter,
Or sold to purchase settler's bread and butter.
She don't want things exposed from porch to closet,
And so she kind o' nags the man who does it.
She carries in her pockets bags of seeds,
As general agent of the thriftiest weeds;
She sends her blackbirds, in the early morn,
To superintend his fields of planted corn;
She gives him rain past any duck's desire —
Then, maybe, several weeks of quiet fire;
She sails mosquitoes — leeches perched on wings —
To poison him with blood-devouring stings;
She loves her ague muscle to display,
And shake him up, say every other day;
With thoughtful, conscientious care she makes
Those travelin' poison-bottles, rattlesnakes;
She finds time, 'mongst her other family cares,
To keep in stock good wildcats, wolves and bears.

Well, when I first infested this retreat,
Things to my view seemed frightful incomplete,
But I had come with heart-thrift in my song,
And brought my wife and plunder right along.
I hadn't a round-trip ticket to go back,
And if I had, there wasn't no railroad track,
And drivin' East was what I couldn't endure,
I hadn't started on a circular tour.
My girl-wife was brave as she was good,
And helped me every way she could;
She seemed to take to every rough old tree,
As sing'lar as when first she took to me.
She kep' our little log house neat as wax,
And once I caught her foolin' with my axe.
She learned a hundred masculine things to do;
She aimed a shotgun pretty middlin' true,
Although in spite of my expressed desire,
She always shut her eyes before she'd fire.
She hadn't the muscle (though she *had* the heart)
In outdoor life to take an active part;
Though in our firm of Duty and Endeavor
She wasn't no silent partner whatsoever.
When I was loggin', burnin', choppin' wood,
She'd linger round and help me all she could,
And kep' me fresh-ambitious all the while,
And lifted tons just with her voice and smile.
With no desire my glory for to rob,
She used to stan' around and boss the job;
And when first-class success my hands befell,
Would proudly say, "*We* did that pretty well."
She was delicious, both to hear and see —
That pretty wife-girl that kep' house for me.

Well, neighborhoods meant counties in those days,
The roads didn't have accommodatin' ways;
And maybe weeks would pass before she'd see —
And much less talk with — anyone but me.
The Indians sometimes showed their sun-baked faces,
But they didn't teem with conversational graces.
Some ideas from the birds and trees she stole,
But 'twasn't like talking with a human soul.
And finally I thought that I could trace
A half heart-hunger peering from her face.

Then she would drive it back and shut the door;
Of course that only made me see it more.
'Twas hard to see her give her life to mine,
Making a steady effort not to pine;
'Twas hard to hear that laugh bloom out each minute,
And recognize the seeds of sorrow in it.
No misery makes a close observer mourn
Like hopeless grief with hopeful courage borne;
There's nothing sets the sympathies to paining
Like a complaining woman uncomplaining.
It always draws my breath out into sighs
To see a brave look in a woman's eyes.
Well, she went on, as plucky as could be,
Fighting the foe she thought I did not see,
And using her heart-horticultural powers
To turn that forest to a bed of flowers.
You cannot check an unadmitted sigh,
And so I had to soothe her on the sly,
And secretly to help her bear her load;
And soon it came to be an up-hill road.
Hard work bears hard upon the average pulse,
Even with satisfactory results,
But when effects are scarce, the heavy strain
Falls dead and solid on the heart and brain,
And when we're bothered, it will oft occur
We seek blame-timber, and I lit on her,
And looked at her with daily lessening favor,
For what I knew she couldn't help, to save her.
And Discord, when once he'd called and seen us,
Came round quite often and edged in between us.

One night, when I'd come home unusual late,
Too hungry and too tired to feel first-rate,
Her supper struck me wrong, though I'll allow
She hadn't much to strike with anyhow.
And when I went to milk the cows, and found
They'd wandered from their usual feeding ground
And maybe'd left a few long miles behind them,
Which I must copy, if I meant to find 'em,
Flash-quick the stay-chains of my temper broke,
And in a trice, these hot words I had spoke,
"You ought to've kept the animals in view,
And drove 'em in, you'd nothing else to do,
The heft of all our work on me must fall;
You just lie around and let me do it all."
That speech — it hadn't been gone a half a minute
Before I saw the cold, black poison in it;
And I'd have given all I had, and more,
To've only safely got it back in-door.
I'm now what most folks "well-to-do" would call;
I feel to-day as if I'd give it all,
Provided I through fifty years might reach,
And kill and bury that half-minute speech.

She handed back no words as I could hear,
She didn't frown, she didn't shed a tear;
Half-proud, half-crushed, she stood and looked me o'er
Like someone she had never seen before!
But such a sudden anguish-lit surprise
I never viewed before in human eyes.
I've seen it oft enough since in a dream;
It sometimes wakes me like a midnight scream.

Next morning, when, stone-faced, but heavy-hearted,
With dinner pail and sharpened axe, I started
Away for my day's work, she watched the door,
And followed me half way to it or more,
And I was just a-turning round at this,
A-asking for my usual goodbye kiss,
But on her lip I saw a proudish curve,
And in her eyes a shadow of reserve;

And she had shown, perhaps half-unawares,
Some little independent breakfast airs.
And so the usual parting didn't occur,
Although her eyes invited me to her,
Or rather, half-invited me, for she
Didn't advertise to furnish kisses free.
You always had — that is, I had — to pay
Full market price, and go more'n half the way.
So, with a short "Goodbye," I shut the door,
And left her as I never had before.
But when at noon my lunch I came to eat,
Put up by her so delicately neat,
Choicer, somewhat, than yesterday's had been,
And some fresh, sweet-eyed pansies she'd put in.
"Tender and pleasant thoughts," I knew they meant,
It seemed as if her kiss with me she'd sent.
Then I became once more her humble lover,
And said, "To-night I'll ask forgiveness of her."

I went home over-early on that eve,
Having contrived to make myself believe
By various signs I kind o' knew and guessed
A thunder storm was coming from the west.
"Tis strange when one sly reason fills the heart,
How many honest ones will take its part.
A dozen first-class reasons said 'twas right
That I should strike home early on that night.
Half out of breath, the cabin door I swung,
With tender heart-words trembling on my tongue.
But all within was desolate and bare;
My house had lost its soul, she was not there!
A pencilled note was on the table spread,
And these are something like the words it said:
"The cows have strayed away again I fear,
I watched them pretty close, don't scold me, dear,
And where they are, I think I nearly know,
I heard the bell not very long ago.
I've hunted for them all the afternoon,
I'll try once more. I think I'll find them soon.
Dear, if a burden I have been to you,
And haven't helped you as I ought to do,
Let old-time memories my forgiveness plead,
I've tried to do my best, I have indeed.
Darling, piece out with love the strength I lack,
And have kind words for me when I get back."
Scarce did I give this message sight and tongue, —
Some swift-blown raindrops to the window clung,
And from the clouds a low deep growl proceeded,
My thunder storm had come, now 'twasn't needed.

I rushed out-door. The air was stained with black;
Night had come early on the storm-cloud's back,
And everything kept dimming to the sight,
Save when the clouds threw their electric light,
When, for a flash, so clean-cut was the view,
I'd think I saw her, knowing it wasn't true.
Through my small clearing dashed wide sheets of spray,
As if the ocean-waves had lost their way;
Scarcely a pause the thunder battle made
In the bold clamor of its cannonade.

And she, while I was sheltered dry and warm,
Was somewhere in the clutches of this storm.
She who, when storm-frights found her at her best,
Had always hid her white face on my breast.
My dog, who'd skirmished round me all the day,
Now crouched and whimpering in a corner lay.
I dragged him by the collar to the wall,
I pressed his quivering muzzle to a shawl.
"Track her, old boy!" I shouted, and he whined,
Matched eyes with me as if to read my mind,
Then with a yell went tearing through the wood;
I followed him as faithful as I could.
No pleasure trip was that, through flood and flame,
We raced with death, we hunted noble game.

All night we dragged the woods without avail,
The ground got drenched, we could not keep the trail.
Three times again my cabin home I found,
Half-hoping she might be there safe and sound.
But each time it was an unavailing care.
My house had lost its soul, she was not there.
When climbing the wet trees, next morning sun
Laughed at the ruin that the night had done,
Bleeding and drenched, by toil and sorrow spent,
Back to what used to be my home I went.
But as I neared our little clearing ground —
Listen! I heard the cowbell's tinkling sound,
The cabin door was just a bit ajar.
It gleamed upon my glad eyes like a star.
"Brave heart," I said, "for such a fragile form!
She made them guide her homeward through the storm."
Such pangs of joy I never felt before,
"You've come!" I shouted, and rushed through the door.
Yes, she had come — and gone again. She lay
With all her young life crushed and wrenched away.
Lay, the heart-ruins of our home among,
Not far from where I killed her with my tongue.
The rain drops glittered 'mid her hair's long strands,
The forest thorns had torn her feet and hands,
And 'midst the tears — brave tears — that one could trace
Upon the pale but sweetly resolute face,
I once again the mournful words could read,
"I've tried to do my best, I have indeed."

And now I'm mostly done, my story's o'er,
Part of it never breathed the air before.
'Tisn't ever usual, it must be allowed,
To volunteer heart history to a crowd,
And scatter 'mongst them confidential tears,
But you'll protect an old man with his years.
And whosoever this story's voice may reach,
This is the sermon I would have it preach:
Boys flying kites haul in their white-winged birds,
You can't do that way when you're flying words.
"Careful with fire" is good advice we know,
"Careful with words" is ten times doubly so.
Thoughts unexpressed may sometimes fall back dead,
But God himself can't kill them when they're said.
You have my life-grief, do not think a minute,
'Twas told to take up time, there's business in it.
It sheds advice, whoe'er will take and live it
Is welcome to the pain it costs to give it.

Claims of Children

Socrates once said, "Could I climb to the highest place in Athens, I would lift my voice and proclaim—Fellow-citizens, why do ye turn and scrape every stone to gather wealth, and take so little care of your children, to whom one day you must relinquish it all?"—Family Circle.

Having listened to more profanity than he could endure, a man turned to the swearer and asked, "How much does Satan pay you for such profanity?" When told he received nothing, the man continued, "You certainly work cheap for a thing which destroys character and makes you less than a gentleman."

HE WHO DOES NOT FORGIVE OTHERS BURNS BEFORE HIM THE BRIDGE TO GOD'S FORGIVENESS.

W. B. Knight

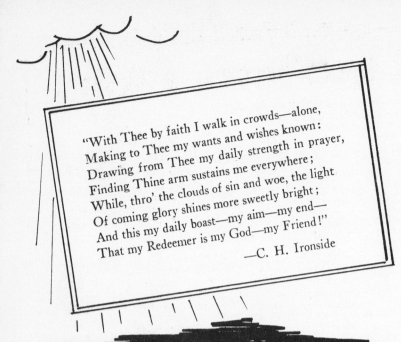

"With Thee by faith I walk in crowds—alone,
Making to Thee my wants and wishes known:
Drawing from Thee my daily strength in prayer,
Finding Thine arm sustains me everywhere;
While, thro' the clouds of sin and woe, the light
Of coming glory shines more sweetly bright;
And this my daily boast—my aim—my end—
That my Redeemer is my God—my Friend!"

—C. H. Ironside

The Time Is Short

The time is short!
If thou wouldst work for God
it must be now;
If thou wouldst win the gar-
land for thy brow,
Redeem the time.

With His reward
He comes; He tarries not; His
day is near;
When men least look for Him
will He be here;
Prepare for Him!

—H. Bonar

You must do as well as ever
you can whatever God gives
you to do; that is the best
possible preparation for what
He may want you to do next.
—Thomas Chalmers.

John Wesley's Advice

Believe evil of no one, and put the best construction on everything.

Speak evil of no one; keep your thoughts to yourself till you come to the person concerned.

If you see what you think wrong in a person, tell him plainly.

Be serious; let your motto be "Holiness to the Lord." Avoid all lightness, jesting, and foolish talking.

Be diligent; never while away time, nor spend more time than is necessary in unprofitable talk or occupation.

Converse sparingly and cautiously with the opposite sex.

Beware of all affectation, and preach the gospel as the servants of all.

You have nothing to do but to . . . spend and be spent in the work of the Lord.

Be punctual; do everything exactly at the time.

Be ashamed of nothing but sin; not of cleaning your own boots or your neighbor's or such things.

In all things act not according to your own will. Employ your time according to your profession in preaching, reading, meditating, and prayer.

What Think Ye Of Christ?

B. C. Downs

Pilate, what do you think of this man? "I find no fault in Him at all."

Judas? "I have sinned in that I have betrayed the innocent blood."

Centurion, what is your testimony concerning this One? "Truly, this was the Son of God."

Demos, what is your word? "This was the Son of God."

John the Baptist? "Behold the Son of God that taketh away the sin of the world."

And John? "He is the Bright and Morning Star."

Peter? "Thou art the Christ, the Son of the Living God."

Thomas, What is your testimony? "My Lord and my God."

Paul, what do you think of Christ, "I count all things loss for the excellency of the knowledge of Christ Jesus, my Lord."

Angels in heaven, what is your testimony? "Unto you is born a Saviour, which is Christ the Lord."

And our **Heavenly Father?** "This is My beloved Son in Whom I am well pleased."

Paul said, "I am an apostle by the will of God." Paul was a success. God called him. He answered God's call and did what God told him to do. God has a plan for every surrendered person. We have said over and over to our Bob Jones University students that life is not divided into the secular and the sacred. Any job to which God calls a man and which the man does under divine direction and for the glory of God is a sacred job. God is not looking for big people as the world looks for big people. He is looking for surrendered people. He wants people who will fit into His plans and do what He wants done. This is the only secret of success and is also the secret of happiness. Everything that God ever made, that does what God made it to do, is happy. He made the birds for the air and the fish for the sea; and the birds sing in the air because they are where they belong, and fish play in the water because they are where God meant them to be. People who go to Hell will be intruders, for Hell was not made for man. It was made for the Devil and his angels. There is no happiness outside the directive will of God for a human life. There may be hardships along the road of God's purpose for an individual, but a Christian can glory in tribulation, because he has in his heart a peace which the world cannot give and the world cannot take away—Bob Jones, Sr.

"Like Father, Like Son!"

It was Sunday morning. A father sat in his easy chair reading the Sunday newspaper. Then he said to his boy, "Put down that funny paper. Get ready for Sunday school." "Daddy, aren't you going with me?" "No, I'm not going with you, but I want you to hurry up and get ready." "Daddy, did you go to Sunday school when you were a little boy like me?" "Certainly I did. I went every Sunday," said the father. Said the little fellow as he walked sadly away, "I bet it won't do me any good, either!"—*Baptist Standard*

Criminals are home-grown.
—J. Edgar Hoover

THE SHEPHERD PSALM

The 23rd Psalm has been a source of comfort to myriads of people in life and death. Consider the following outline, and allow the Psalm to become a source of life and comfort to you, regardless of your circumstances and surroundings.

The Lord is my Shepherd
—Perfect Saviour.

I shall not want
—Perfect Salvation.

He maketh me to lie down in green pastures
—Perfect Rest.

He leadeth me beside the still waters
—Perfect Refreshment.

He restoreth my soul
—Perfect Restoration.

He leadeth me in paths of righteousness
—Perfect Guidance.

I will fear no evil
—Perfection Protection.

Thou art with me
—Perfect Company.

Thy rod and Thy staff
—Perfect Comfort.

Thou preparest a table
—Perfect Provision

Thou anointest my head
—Perfect Consecration.

My cup runneth over
—Perfect Joy.

Goodness and mercy shall follow me
—Perfect Care.

I will dwell . . . forever
—Perfect Destiny.

Christian Victory

A Dance Becomes a Revival

It was a Saturday night in an inn on the road through the Cumberland Mountains in the spring of 1820. A crowd of the settlers from the vicinity were gathering for the Saturday night dance. All was jollity as the company took off their wraps, the floor was cleared, and the old fiddler tuned up his fiddle. In a far corner of the room sat Peter Cartwright, prominent Methodist circuit-rider of Kentucky. On his way home from the General Conference in Baltimore night had overtaken him near this inn. The host had warned him of the dance and said that he could not promise him much quiet for rest. However, since the next inn was seven miles farther on, and it was now dark and the road strange and dangerous, he had decided to stay.

As Cartwright sat as inconspicuously as possible in his corner he was pleased to note that the company was quite respectable and that little drinking was going on. However, as the music struck up and the dance began he felt very much out of place. Methodists were opposed to such worldly amusements, but the public room of the inn was the only room heated and lighted and he must stay or go to bed.

As he sat meditating he resolved to find some way to invite all of these people to a service the next day. As he was about to approach the host and ask permission to use this room for the service he was surprised to see the most beautiful young lady in the room approaching him gaily with an inviting smile on her face. She paused in front of him and with a graceful bow addressed him.

"Sir," she said, "you should not be sitting here all by yourself. We are a friendly people and would like to have you enjoy the evening with us. Come and dance this dance with me."

For an instant Peter was taken aback. He did not know what to do. Then he resolved on a desperate experiment. He arose and bowed to the young lady. She moved to his right side. He grasped her right hand with his and they moved to the middle of the floor. All of the company seemed pleased and with smiles all around made place for them. The fiddler was about to strike up, but holding up his hand to restrain him Peter quietly addressed the whole group.

"Friends," he said, "I am grateful for the kind way in which you have all received me. I am thankful to this charming young lady for her courtesy. However, for many years I have never undertaken any matter of importance without asking the blessing of God upon it. So now I desire to ask God's blessing upon this kind and beautiful young lady, and upon all of you people who have treated me so kindly. Let us all kneel down and pray."

Quickly Peter dropped to his knees and started to pray. His fair partner tried to get away but he held on to her right hand tightly and she too fell upon her knees. At first all of the company were astonished and stood looking on in amazement. Then some knelt. Others stood watching. Some fled out of the door. Meanwhile the preacher prayed with all of his might for the whole company and that the converting power of God would fall upon all of them.

As Cartwright prayed some began to weep and some to pray aloud to God for mercy. His prayer concluded, the preacher arose and began to exhort the whole group to turn to Christ for salvation.

As a result of this daring venture of Peter Cartwright 32 people were organized into a church with the landlord of the inn as leader.

The great artist Leonardo da Vinci once took a friend to view his greatest masterpiece, "The Last Supper." His friend remarked, "The most striking thing in the picture is the cup." The famous artist took his brush, and with one strike wiped out the cup, as he said, "Nothing in my painting shall attract more attention than the face of my Master!"

—Selected

15

Is Abortion Murder?

By Samuel Voisard

A mother stepped into the doctor's office carrying a bright and beautiful baby a year old. Seating herself near her family physician, she said, "Doctor, I want you to help me out of trouble. My baby is only one year old, and I have conceived again, and I do not want to have children so close together."

"What do you expect me to do?" asked the physician.

"Oh, anything to get rid of it for me," she replied.

After thinking seriously for a moment the doctor said, "I think I can suggest a better method of helping you out. If you object to having two children so near together, the best way would be to kill the one on your lap, and let the other one come on. It is easy to get at the one on your lap, and it makes no difference to me which one I kill for you. Besides, it might be dangerous for you if I undertook to kill the younger one."

As the doctor finished speaking he reached for a knife, and continued by asking the mother to lay the baby out on her lap, and turn her head the other way.

The woman almost fainted away as she jumped from her chair, and uttered one word, "Murderer!"

A few words of explanation from the doctor soon convinced the mother that his offer to commit murder was no worse than her request for the destruction of the unborn child. In either case it would be murder. The only difference would be in the age of the victim. —*Old Faith Contender*

Universal Depravity

When Chicago was a small town, it was incorporated and made a city. There was one clause in the new law that no man should be a policeman who was not a certain height—five feet six inches, let us say. When the commissioners got into power, they advertised for men as candidates, and in the advertisement they stated that no man need apply who could not bring good credentials to recommend him. I remember going past the office one day, and there was a crowd of them waiting to get in. They quite blocked up the side of the street; and they were comparing notes as to their chances of success. One says to another, "I have got a good letter of recommendation from the mayor, and one from the supreme judge." Another says, "And I have got a good letter from Senator So-and-so. I'm sure to get in." The two men come on together, and lay their letters down on the commissioners' desk. "Well," say the officials, "you have certainly a good many letters but we won't read them till we measure you." Ah! they forgot all about that. So the first man is measured, and he is only five feet. "No chance for you sir; the law says the men must be five feet six inches, and you don't come up to the standard." The other says, "Well, my chance is a good deal better than his. I'm a good bit taller than he is"—he begins to measure himself by the other man. That is what people are always doing, measuring themselves by others. Measure yourselves by the law of God, or by the Son of God Himself; and if you do that, you will find you have come short. He goes up to have the officers, and they measure him; he is five feet five inches and nine-tenths of an inch. "No good," they tell him; "you're not up to the standard." "But I'm only one-tenth of an inch short," he remonstrates. "It's no matter," they say; "There's no difference." He goes with the man who was five feet. One comes short six inches, and the other only one-tenth of an inch, but the law cannot be changed. And the law of God is, that no man shall go into the kingdom of Heaven with one sin on him. He that has broken the least law is guilty of all.—Moody.

Good Old Days!

They may cause a smile but the following office rules that were in effect in 1872 in the establishment of Zachary U. Geiger are certainly based on good sound principles:

1. Office employees will daily sweep the floors, dust the furniture, shelves, and showcases.

2. Each day fill lamps, clean chimneys, and trim wicks. Wash the windows once a week.

3. Each clerk will bring in a bucket of water and a scuttle of coal for the day's business.

4. Make your pens carefully. You may whittle your nibs to your individual taste.

5. This office will open at 7:00 a.m. and close at 9:00 p.m. daily, except on the Sabbath, on which day it will remain closed. Each employee is expected to spend the Sabbath Day by attending church and contributing liberally to the cause of the Lord.

6. Men employees will be given an evening off each week for courting purposes, or two evenings a week if they go regularly to church.

7. After an employee has spent 13 hours of labor in the office, he should spend the time reading the Bible and other good books while contemplating the glories and building up of the Kingdom.

8. Every employee should lay aside from each pay a goodly sum of his earnings, so that he will not become a burden upon the charity of his betters.

9. The employee who has performed his labors faithfully and without fault for a period of five years in my service, and who had been thrifty and attentive to his religious duties, is looked upon by his fellowmen as a substantial and law-abiding citizen, will be given an increase of five cents per day in his pay, providing a just return in profits from the business permits it.

To one who asked George Muller the secret of his service, he replied: "There was a day when I *died*," and as he spoke he bent lower, until he almost reached the floor. Continuing, he added, "*Died* to George Muller, his opinions, preferences, tastes and will; *died* to the world, its approval or censure; *died* to the approval or blame even of my brethren or friends; and since then I have studied only to show myself approved unto God."

The Lawyer Was Too Busy!

When I was assistant pastor of the large First Baptist Church in Plainview, Texas, I was made financial secretary of the church. A lawyer for many years had had the financial secretary to write a check for $5 on the first of each month on him. He always honored the check. But after one or two months I was so grieved at his indifference that I could not write the check. When his checks came at the end of the month and he discovered that he had not given a penny to the Lord's cause because I had not written the check, he was embarrassed and troubled. "Go ahead and write a check on me every month for $5," he said. "I want the church to have the money. I do not begrudge it at all. I am just too busy to take time to write a check and mail it in, and I don't want to have to think about it every month," said he.

But I answered, "If you are too busy to write a check for God, you are too busy. If you can't take time and thought to personally attend to this matter, I do not believe that God wants your money." I told him that God was not poor, that God did not need his measly $5, but in His gracious providence has allowed us Christians the joy of giving and having a part in His work.

I thought then and think now that it is disgraceful for any Christian not to have time to look after the Lord's work and give personal attention to getting out the Gospel.

John R. Rice

"There are deep things of God. Push out from shore.

Hast thou found much? Give thanks and look for more,

Dost fear the generous Giver to offend?

Then know His store of bounty hath no end.

He doth not need to be implored or teased;

The more we take, the better He is pleased."

Beside the common inheritance of the land, there are some special possessions.

—A. B. Simpson

TEN COMMANDMENTS

Thou shalt not have another God but me.
Thou shalt not to an image bow the knee.
Thoul shalt not take the name of God in vain.
See that the Sabbath thou do not profane.
Honor thy father and thy mother too.
In act, or thought, see thou no murder do.
From fornication keep thy body clean.
Thou shalt not steal, though thou be very mean.
Bear no false witness; keep thee without spot.
What is thy neighbor's, see thou covet not.

John Bunyan.

HYPOCRISY

The man who says he is kept away from religion by hypocrites is not influenced by them anywhere else.

Businss is full of them, but if he sees a chance at making money he does not stop for that.

Society is crowded with them, and yet he never thinks of becoming a hermit.

Married life is full of them, but that doesn't make him remain a bachelor.

Hell is full of them, and yet he doesn't do a thing to keep himself from going there.

He wants to have you think that he is trying to avoid the society of hypocrites, and yet he takes not a single step toward Heaven, the only place where no hypocrites can go!—Selected.

"A RASCAL"

A man once said to Sam Jones, the evangelist, "Mr. Jones, the church has put my assessment too high."

"How much do you pay?" the evangelist inquired.

"Five dollars a year."

"Well," replied Mr. Jones, "how long have you been converted?"

"About four years."

"What did you do before you were converted?"

"I was a drunkard."

"How much did you spend for drink?"
"About $250 a year."

"How much were you worth?"

"I had nothing of my own. I rented land and plowed with a steer."

"What have you now?"

"I have a good plantation and a span of horses."

"Well," said the evangelist, emphatically, "you paid the Devil $250 a year for the privilege of plowing with a steer on rented land, and now you don't want to give God, who saved you, five dollars a year for the privilege of plowing with horses on your own plantation. You're a rascal from the crown of your head to the sole of your foot."

17

Mean Mother

I had the meanest mother in the whole world. While other children ate candy for breakfast, I had to have cereal, eggs or toast. When others had cokes and candy for lunch, I had to eat a sandwich. As you guess, my supper was different from other children's also.

But at least I wasn't alone in my suffering. My sister and two brothers had the same MEAN MOTHER AS I DID.

My mother insisted upon knowing where we were at all times—you'd think we were on a CHAIN GANG. She had to know who our friends were and what we were doing. She insisted if we said we'd be gone an hour that we be gone one hour or less—not one hour and a minute. I am nearly ashamed to admit it, but she actually struck us. Not once, but each time we did as we pleased. Can you imagine someone actually hitting a child just because he disobeyed?

NOW YOU CAN BEGIN TO SEE HOW MEAN SHE REALLY WAS.

While the other girls were wearing miniskirts and smoking cigarettes we had to be little grandmas and were called OLD FASHIONED. Mother would not even let us go to the DRIVE-IN MOVIES. How could she be so MEAN!

My mother was a complete failure as a mother. None of us has ever been arrested, divorced or beaten his mate. Each of my brothers served his time in the service of this country. And whom do we have to blame for the terrible way we turned out? You're right—OUR MEAN MOTHER.

Look what all we missed. We never got to march in a PROTEST PARADE, nor to take part in a RIOT, burn DRAFT CARDS, and a million and one things that other children did.

She forced us to grow up into GOD-FEARING, EDUCATED, HONEST ADULTS.

Using this as a background, I am trying to raise my three children. I stand a little taller and I am filled with pride when my children call me MEAN.

The worst is yet to come. We had to be in bed by nine each night and up early the next morning. We couldn't sleep till noon like our friends. So while they slept, my mother actually had the nerve to break the CHILD-LABOR LAW. She made us work. We had to wash dishes, make beds, learn to cook and all sorts of cruel things. I believe she lay awake at night thinking up MEAN THINGS to do to us.

She always insisted upon our telling the truth, the whole truth and nothing but the truth, even if it KILLED us, and it nearly did.

By the time we were teen-agers, she was wiser—and our life became even more unbearable. None of this tooting of the car horn by the boys for us to come running.

She embarrassed us no end by making our dates and friends come to the door to get us. I forgot to mention, while my friends were dating at the mature age of 12 and 13, my old, mean MOTHER refused to let me date until the age of 15 and 18. Fifteen, that is, if you dated only to a school function. And that was maybe twice a year.

A Useless Christian

I ONCE ASKED A LADY TO GO AND SPEAK TO A WOMAN WHO SAT WEEPING, ABOUT HER SOUL. "OH!" SAID THE LADY, "I AM AFRAID I AM NOT QUALIFIED FOR THE WORK; PLEASE SEND SOMEONE ELSE." "HOW LONG," I SAID, "HAVE YOU BEEN A CHRISTIAN?" "TWENTY YEARS." TWENTY YEARS ON THE LORD'S SIDE, AND NOT QUALIFIED TO POINT A SOUL TO CHRIST! I AM AFRAID THERE WILL BE A GOOD MANY STARLESS CROWNS IN THE GLORY.—Moody.

Last night my little boy came to me, confessed some childish wrong, and, kneeling at my knee, prayed with tear-filled eyes: "O Lord, make me a man like Daddy—wise and strong. I know you can." That night while he slept, I knelt beside his bed, confessed my sins, and prayed with low-bowed head: "O God, make me a child like my child here; guileless, trusting Thee with faith sincere."—Selected.

I BELIEVE THAT IF THERE IS ONE THING WHICH PIERCES THE MASTER'S HEART WITH UNUTTERABLE GRIEF, IT IS NOT THE WORLD'S INIQUITY, BUT THE CHURCH'S INDIFFERENCE.—F. B. MEYER.

Light

A sluttish housemaid, when scolded for the untidiness of the chambers, exclaimed, "I'm sure the rooms would be clean enough if it were not for the nasty sun which is always showing the dirty corners." Thus do men revile the Gospel because it reveals their own sin. Thus all agitations for reforms in Church and State are opposed, and all manner of mischief attributed to them as if they created the evils which they bring to light. The lover of the right courts anything which may manifest the wrong, but those who love evil have never a good word for those disturbing beams of truth which show up the filthy corners of their hearts and lives.

—Charles Spurgeon

I have seen the Christian man in the depths of poverty, when he lived from hand to mouth, and scarcely knew where he should find the next meal, still with his mind unruffled, calm and quiet. If he had been as rich as an Indian prince, yet could he not have had less care. If he had been told that his bread should always come to his door, and the stream which ran hard by should never dry; if he had been quite sure that ravens would bring him bread and meat in the morning, and again in the evening—he would not have been one wit more calm. There is his neighbor on the other side of the street not half so poor, but wearied from morning till night, working his fingers to the bone, bringing himself to the grave with anxiety.—Spurgeon.

On the day of Pentecost the people were together with one accord. They had been in a prayer meeting; and they all believed what the Lord Jesus Christ, who was God manifest in the flesh, had told them. He told them to go to Jerusalem and wait and that He would pray the Father to send another Comforter. These were orthodox Christians. They were united on the Word of God. The Lord Jesus Christ kept His word. He prayed the Father and the Holy Ghost came down.

—Bob Jones, Sr.

HEALTH IS A BLESSING
By Horace Mohler

The angel touched my arm and spoke,
 And startled by his voice, I woke.
"Get up," he said, "there comes the sun—
 Another day has just begun!"
And with this most unsavory warning
I realized that it was morning.

I frowned and cried: "O bitter cup!
 I am so tired of getting up!
Oh, how I long for that glad day
 When you'll no longer come and say:
'The sun is up, the day is dawning;
Now rise and shine, for it is morning!' "

"Perhaps," said he, "you'll come along
 And let me show you that vast throng,
That multitude who can but lay
 And keep their beds day after day?"
"Oh, no," said I, "I'll not be going!"
But through the air we soon were flowing.

In one swift flash 'mid groans and glooms
I looked into ten thousand rooms,
Where lay the sick, the halt, the blind—

The weak and suffering of mankind.
I saw their months and years of lying,
I saw their tears, and heard their sighing.

In horror I recoiled and said:
 "What endless years they spend abed!
How tired and tedious their days,
 Their nights what long and bitter maze!"
I heard the little children crying,
I saw the gasping of the dying.

In tears I thought it could not be,
 That these were bound, and I was free.
I cried, "O Lord, forgive my pleas
 To lie in bed and take my ease!"
I felt a touch—I had been dreaming—
There stood my angel friend abeaming!

"Get up!" said he. "There is the sun;
 Another day has just begun.
There are so many things to do,
 And so I came to waken you!"
With happy shout my room resounding,
I leaped into the day rebounding!

"Be Sure!"

The man who once most wisely said, "Be sure you're right, then go ahead," might as well have added this, to wit: "Be sure you're wrong before you quit."—*Selected*

SOMEONE SAYS, "I AM NOT READY TO TAKE A STAND JUST NOW." I HAVE A CONTEMPT FOR A MAN WHO KNOWS WHAT THE RIGHT STAND IS BUT HAS NOT ENOUGH COURAGE TO TAKE A STAND.—DR. BOB JONES, SR.

Henry Clay said: "A wise mother and good books enabled me to succeed in life. She was very poor, but never too poor to buy books for her children. It is a mean sort of poverty that starves the mind to feed the body."

An Open Letter to God

DEAR GOD:

I'm sorry You made Sunday where You did. You see it's like this—we could attend church more regularly if Your day came at some other time. You have chosen a day that comes at the end of a hard week, and we are all tired out. Not only that, but it is the day following Saturday night.

Saturday evening, You know, is one time we feel we should enjoy ourselves, so we go to the movies or a party, and often it is after midnight when we reach home. It is almost impossible to get up on Sunday morning. You have chosen the very day we want to sleep late, and it makes it mighty hard to get the children off to Sunday School, and especially when they leave it is so early.

THEN THERE ARE dishes to wash, and we always have some things we just have to wash out. I mean no disrespect, dear God, but You must realize that You have picked the day on which we have the biggest dinner. Not only that, but the Church has fixed the hour of worship at the very time we must be preparing dinner.

Then, too. You must think of John. He is cooped up in his office all week, and Sunday morning is the only time he has to tinker with the car and to mow the lawn. When he gets into his old clothes and his hands are all greasy You could not expect him to put his work aside and go off to church.

I AM TELLING You these things, dear God, because I want You to get our viewpoint. It is not our fault that we are unable to get to church on Sunday mornings. We would like to go, and we know we should go, and need to go. But it must be clear to You that the reason we cannot go is because You have chosen the wrong day. If You will select another day we shall be glad to go to church and Sunday School more faithfully.

Sincerely yours,
I. M. BUSY

The Boy With 14,000 Sins

"Do you know how many sins you have?" I asked a lad of fourteen, whom I knew, at the close of a Sunday afternoon service.

"No," he replied; "I have never thought about it."

"Well, suppose we try to find out. Do you think you have committed three sins a day—one of thought, one of word, and one of deed?"

"Oh, I expect lots more than that," he said.

"Well, then, we shall be quite safe in saying that you have committed three sins a day. How many is that for a year?"

He was not very quick at mental arithmetic, so I helped him, and we discovered that he must have been guilty of more than one thousand sins a year.

"One thousand sins a year, Jimmy," I said. "How many sins have you?"

"Fourteen thousand," he said, under his breath, and as the thought gripped him it made him gasp.

"Jimmy," I said, "that's all I want to say to you today. Fourteen thousands sins, think of that!"

Jimmy told his chums, and they laughed; it was a rare joke they thought, and Jimmy joined in the

$$3 \times 364 = 1092$$
$$14 \times 1092 = 15288$$
SINS

laughter. But when he got into bed that night he did not laugh. It seemed as though someone came close to him and whispered in his ear, "Fourteen thousand sins, Jimmy, think of that!" He bore it as long as he could, and at last he crept out of his bed in search of his father, and told him his trouble. "I have at least fourteen thousand sins," he said, "and I don't know what to do with them."

His father knew, and he told his boy again of Christ Jesus who came into the world to save sinners. He told him that though all are like sheep that have gone astray, and have gone their own way (Isa. 53:6), the Lord laid upon Jesus, our great Saviour, the sins of us all. He showed him from the pages of the Bible that if we confess our sins, the blood of Jesus Christ, God's Son, will cleanse us from all sin (I John 1:7), and that God says of all who come to the Lord Jesus and accept His sacrifice, "Their sins and iniquities will I remember no more."—Heb. 10:17.

Jimmy saw it all, and believed it, and went back to his bed a relieved and happy lad. The following Thursday he met me with a smiling face, and said, "They are all gone, sir."

"What are all gone?" I asked him.

"All the fourteen thousand sins," he answered and then he told me all about it. That was a happy day for him.

Uplift, or Upset?

From the autobiography of the late Dr. Clarence E. Macartney we share the following humorous tale.

Two men were passing through a field in the country when they were charged by a bull. They started for the nearest fence; but it was soon apparent that they could not make it before the bull would be upon them. One said to the other, "Put up a prayer, John. We're in for it!"

But John answered, "I can't. I never made a public prayer in my life."

"But you must," said his companion, "the bull will soon be upon us. Pray, John, and pray quickly!"

"All right," said John, "I'll give you the only prayer I know, the one my father used to repeat at the table: 'O Lord, for what we are about to receive, make us truly thankful.'"

In the circumstances of life—whether it be an uplift or an upset, can we truly say, "Lord, I am thankful"?

Carrying Brother

The crossing was muddy, the street
    was wide
And water was running on either
    side;
The wind whistled past with a bit-
    ter moan
As I wended my weary way alone.
In crossing the street I chanced
    to pass
A boy in the arms of a wee, tod-
    dling lass—
"Isn't he heavy, my sweet little
    mother?"
"Oh, no," she replied, "he's my
    baby brother."
Thy load may be heavy, thy road
    may be long,
The winds of adversity bitter and
    strong,
But the way will seem brighter if
    ye love one another,
The burden will be light if ye carry
    a brother.   —*Selected*

Gratitude

*There is a very touching lit-
tle story told of a poor woman
with two children who had
not a bed for them to lie upon
and scarcely any clothes to
cover them. In the depth of
winter they were nearly froz-
en, and the mother took the
door of a cellar off the hinges
and set it up before the corner where they crouched down
to sleep, that some of the
draft and cold might be kept
from them. One of the children whispered to her, when
she complained of how badly
off they were, "Mother, what
do those dear little children
do who have no cellar door to
put up in front of them?"
Even there, you see, the little
heart found cause for thank-
fulness.—Charles Spurgeon.*

To Mothers

Now I lay me down to sleep—
    Don't want to sleep, I want to think.
    I didn't mean to spill that ink;
I only meant to softly creep
    Under the desk an' be a bear—
    'Taint 'bout the spanking that I care.

'F she'd only let me 'splain and tell
    Just how it was an accident,
    An' that I never truly meant
An' never saw it 'til it fell.
    I feel a whole lot worse'n her;
    I'm sorry, an' I said I were.

I s'pose if I'd just cried a lot
    An' choked all up like sister does,
    An' acted sadder than I wuz,
An' sobbed 'bout the "naughty spot,"
    She'd said: "He shan't be whipped, he shan't,"
    And kissed me—but, somehow, I can't.

But I don't think it's fair a bit,
    That when she talks and talks at you
    An' you wait patient till she's through,
An' start to tell your side of it,
    She says: "Now that'll do, my son,
    I've heard enough!"—'fore you've begun.

'F I should die before I wake—
    Maybe I ain't got any soul;
    Maybe there's only just a hole
Where 't ought to be—there's such an ache
    Down there somewhere! She seemed to think
    That I just loved to spill that ink!

—Author unknown

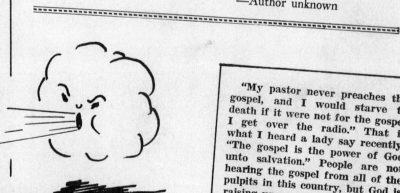

"The time consumed between
the opportunity to do right and the
doing of the right is often spent
trying to justify doing wrong."—
Jack Hyles

Measured by the best standards of
pedagogy, Jesus was the greatest teacher
in the world:
    He knew His subject;
    He knew His pupils:
    He lived what He taught.
            —Dr. Bob Jones, Sr.

"My pastor never preaches the
gospel, and I would starve to
death if it were not for the gospel
I get over the radio." That is
what I heard a lady say recently.
"The gospel is the power of God
unto salvation." People are not
hearing the gospel from all of the
pulpits in this country, but God is
raising up men to preach the gospel over the radio. Millions of people daily are hearing the message.
—Bob Jones, Sr.

If your lips would keep from slips,
    Five things observe with care;
Of whom you speak, to whom you speak,
    And how and when and where.

Meet the "Tator" Family

THIS IS DICK-TATOR:

He is the daddy, self-appointed leader of the church, heads all committees, feels very important, he just dictates, never works.

THIS IS EMMY-TATOR:

She is the mother, never has any thoughts of her own, just imitates, always seconds the motion of someone else. She is active in all phases of church work, just imitating.

THIS IS HEZY-TATOR:

He is the oldest son, goes to college. When he is asked to do anything, he just hesitates. He feels he isn't qualified to do any job, always too busy doing something else. He just hesitates out of doing anything.

THIS IS CARMEN-TATOR:

She is the daughter, sits on the back row of Sunday School, Church and Training Union, commenting on everything and everybody.

THIS IS SPEC-TATOR:

He is in high school. When asked to take part on programs or at parties, he says, no, he will just watch. He never takes part, he just spectates.

THIS IS GRANDMA AGI-TATOR:

This is the oldest member of the family, grandma agitator. She's been in the church 40 years, doesn't believe in any changes at all, is against anything new for the church, believes in doing it the same old way, continually agitating the whole church, keeps things stirred up.

AND THIS IS SWEET-TATOR:

This is the ideal member of the church . . . takes part and supports the whole church program, never says no, generous with time and talents. NEVER DICTATES, IMITATES, HESITATES, COMMENTATES or AGITATES the real CHRISTIANS of our church. Which "Tator" are you?

—Baptist Outlook

Mayo on Alcohol
A REMARKABLE STATEMENT FROM A REMARKABLE MAN

We publish the following statement by Dr. Charles H. Mayo by special permission from the Mayo family, Rochester, Minnesota.

In addressing a large convention of boys, Dr. Mayo said in part:

"You can get along with a wooden leg, but you can't get along with a wooden head. The physical value of man is not so much. Man, as analyzed in our laboratories, is worth about ninety-eight cents; seven bars of soap, lime enough to whitewash a chicken coop, phosphorous enough to cover the heads of a thousand matches. This is not very much you see. It is the brain that counts. But in order that your brain may be kept clear you must keep your body fit and well. That cannot be done if one drinks liquor. A man who has to drag around a habit that is a danger and a menace to society ought to go off to the woods and live alone. We do not tolerate the obvious use of morphine or cocaine or opium, and we should not tolerate intoxicating liquor because I tell you these things are what break down the command of the individual over his own life and his own destiny. Through alcohol a man loses his co-ordination. That is why liquor is no advantage to the brain. You hear people tell how they had their wits quickened for the first half-hour by liquor, but they don't tell you how later their bodies could not act in co-ordination with their brain."

—From Temperance Trumpet

22

To an Aged Sick Person

The following letter was written by Charles H. Spurgeon to a very close friend:

Westwood,
June 12, 1884

Dear Friend,

I casually heard from Mr. Abraham that you were ill, but I had no idea that it was a serious matter; but Mr. Rochfort has kindly given me further news. I feel very sad about it, but I am sure you do not. The loss will be ours, and Heaven and you will gain.

Dear loving brother, you have nothing now to do but to go Home; and what a Home! You will be quite at home where all is love, for you have lived in that blessed element, and are filled with it. I shall soon come hobbling after you, and shall find you out. We are bound to gravitate to each other whether here or in Glory. We love the same Lord, and the same blessed truth.

May the everlasting arms be underneath you! I breathe for you a loving, tender prayer, — 'Lord, comfort Thy dear servant, and when he departs, may it be across a dried-up river into the land of living fountains!'

I am fifty next Thursday, and you are near your Jubilee. In this we are alike; but Jesus is the highest joy. Into the Father's hands I commit you, 'until the day break, and the shadows flee away.'

Your loving brother,
C. H. SPURGEON

Children to Be Reared for Heaven

There was a mother lay dying, some time ago, and she requested her children to be brought to her bedside. The eldest one came in first, and putting her loving hands on his head, she gave him a mother's parting message. Then came another, and then another. To all of them she gave her parting message, until the last — the seventh one, an infant — was brought in. She was so young she could not understand the message of love; so the mother gave it to her husband for her, and then she took the child to her bosom, and kissed it, and caressed it, until her time was almost up. Then, turning to her husband, she said: "I charge you to bring all these children home to heaven with you."—Moody.

The Best Robe

The best robe that God has to give is waiting for the sinner. Yonder is the prodigal in the distance in rags. He has been away in the far country, and has spent his substance in riotous living: now he is a beggar. Will his father receive him? If so, it will be as a servant—at least so the prodigal reasons.

There he is now drawing near to his father's house. Servants may not know him, but the father knows him; and while his boy is still a long way off, he runs to meet him. Then the wanderer begins his little speech, every word of which he had prepared beforehand. But he gets only the length of the first sentence, when his father interrupts him—with a kiss, and turning round to his astonished servant, he says, "Bring forth the best robe."

There were doubtless many robes in that mansion; but the long-lost wanderer was to have the best. What a time of rejoicing they had over him who was "lost and is found," who "was dead and is alive again." Is it different with our Father in Heaven? No. He gives like a king. He gives the best robe. Yonder poor sinner has been constrained by grace to say, "I will arise." He is coming. His back is upon sin and the world, and his face is looking Heavenwards. Will God receive him? Not a doubt of it. He has seen the returning one while yet a long way off, and now he meets him with the kiss of redeeming love; and astonished angels hear the command given, "Bring forth the best robe."

This is how God deals with the awakened sinner. He could give ten thousand other robes, but He gives the best—a better even than angels wear—"Even the righteousness of God which is by faith of Jesus Christ unto all and upon all them that believe" (Rom. 3:22). Are *you* covered by it? Have you fled for refuge? Are you safe beneath the shelter of the blood of Christ?

—Selected

He Is Risen

I was standing before the window of an art store where a picture of the Crucifixion of our Lord was on exhibition. As I gazed, I was conscious of the approach of another, and turning, beheld a little lad gazing also intently at this picture. Noticing that this mite of humanity was a sort of street arab, I thought I would speak to him; so I asked, pointing to the picture, "Do you know who He is?"

"Yes," came the quick response; "that's our Saviour," with a mingled look of pity and surprise that I should not know what the picture represented.

With an evident desire to enlighten me further, he continued, after a pause: "Them's the soldiers, the Roman soldiers, and," with a long drawn sigh, "that woman crying there is His mother."

He waited, apparently for me to question him further, then thrust his hands in his pockets, and with a reverent and subdued voice and tear-stained face added, "They killed Him, mister. Yes, sir, they killed Him."

I looked at the little, dirty, ragged fellow and asked, "Where did you learn this?"

He replied, "At the Mission Sunday School."

Full of thoughts regarding the benefits of Mission Sunday Schools, I turned and resumed my walk, leaving the little lad still looking at the picture. I had not walked a block when I heard his childish treble calling, "Mister! say, mister!" I turned. He was running toward me but paused; then up went his little hand, and with a triumphant sound in his voice and now radiant face, he said, "I wanted to tell you: HE ROSE AGAIN."

His message delivered, he smiled, waved his hand, turned, and went his way, feeling, I presume, that as he had been enlightened, he had done his duty in enlightening another. What a challenge to everyone of us?—*R. A. Torrey.*

"How Heavy Is Sin? ?"

A flippant youth asked a preacher, "You say that unsaved people carry a weight of sin. I feel nothing. *How heavy is sin?* Is it ten pounds? Eighty pounds?" The preacher replied by asking the youth, "If you laid a four hundred pound weight on a corpse, would it feel the load?" The youth replied, "It would feel nothing, because it is dead." The preacher concluded, "That spirit, too, is indeed dead which feels no load of sin or is indifferent to its burden and flippant about its presence." The youth was silenced! !

The marks on the grave of a guide who died while climbing the Alps were: "He died climbing." On the tomb of a Christian astronomer were these words (by his partner): "We have gazed too long at the stars together to be afraid of the night."

Facts About Personal SOUL WINNING

By John R. Rice

1. IT IS THE WAY MOST ARE WON

A famous preacher, Dr. Charles Gallaudet Trumbell, said he had preached for years to great congregations, for 20 years had written weekly to and edited a religious paper which had some of the time a circulation of 100,000 copies, and was the author of 30 books, but that in this time he had won more people to Christ in private conversation than in sermon, or print, as far as he knew. The late Dr. C. A. Dixon said the same thing. Some preachers think that the public expounding of the Word to crowds is the main thing. Not so. Preaching the Gospel is the main thing, and every Christian can do that with one hearer. Great preachers must be great personal soul winners. And those who are saved in public service without private help are few.

2. EVERY CHRISTIAN CAN DO IT

Yes, every Christian can win souls, if he will pay the price. The Bible does not leave the preaching to preachers. Deacons also preached in public. John 15 is to every Christian. Matthew 28:19, 20, is to all. It doesn't take worldly wisdom, nor gift of speech, nor special training. It just takes a broken heart and Holy Spirit power, thank God. It can be done anywhere. I have seen people saved in church, at home, by a well, two in an orchard, and at least 20 by the roadside, some in my car, one on an interurban car, several in hospitals, 50 in jails, one walking down Main Street in Fort Worth, one on the top of a barn, one Methodist at a baptizing, even. I have seen them saved in a crowd or alone. Mothers, fathers, brother, sister, sweethearts, teachers, and rank strangers can win them. Sometimes just tears will decide it. More often a verse of Scripture. Many, many times just the touch of a hand turns a man to Christ. All can win souls.

3. IT COSTS SOMETHING

A woman once said to an evangelist, "Oh, I would give the world if I could win souls as you do!"

"That's just what it cost me," answered the soul winner.

Soul winning costs something. It cannot be done best and most without deep knowledge of God's Word and experience. It cannot be done at all without surrender to God and Holy Spirit leadership. It costs time, tears, labor and sacrifice to become an artist, and soul winning is the finest of arts. Thank God, this is the one artistic possibility born in us all, but at the second birth.

Great soul winners are men of burdened hearts, single purpose, secret vigil, and unreserved surrender. Oh, it costs! It cost Jesus Bethlehem and Gethsemane and Calvary—betrayal and blood, torture and tears. It costs, but thank God, it pays more than it costs.

4. IT IS CONTAGIOUS

One example is worth a thousand arguments. Let a fellow but try this blessed business of winning souls, and others see that people want to be saved, see that it is not natural ability, but Holy Spirit leadership, and humble surrender to God that gets results, and they will try it. The way to learn to preach is to preach, and the way to learn to win souls is to get at it. How preachers should set the holy example of personal approach to individuals! How we should hold up the personal work of Jesus and of Paul, His great apostle! How we should pray for an irresistible epidemic of individuals seeking individuals, like that which modern times has seen in Wales and Korea, and that in Russia since the beginning of the war. It will take examples, examples from the ministry especially, but also from the ranks of businessmen, women, and young people to start a revival of personal seeking and winning the lost in private and in public services outside the pulpit. Soul winning is contagious.

5. IT WILL KEEP THE CHRISTIAN RIGHT

The monks who spent their days in prayer and self-affliction were not near to God's heart and plan. A preacher who preaches to crowds and lives in pleasant places among generous and kindly people, is often not right with God, nor happy, nor victorious. I know; I have been there. But the man who has had the continuous evidence of God's blessing on his ministry in personally winning the lost, may be sure he is on the right track. How often I have tried to preach when words were hollow, the sky was brass, and weighty words went from a cold heart to colder ears. How often the Book had no message, and there was no joy in prayer. How often the weight of a service was breaking my heart and I had no victory for the sermon. Then I have slipped away to a neighbor, or more often among boys and girls, privately sought the appointed one with the hungry heart, and told again the sweet story that lived again in my heart with the telling, saw tears flow, heard the great confession, felt the angels rejoicing again. Then I have gone again to public ministry and found that the Holy One had taken an ember from dead ashes in my heart, lighted a coal from The Book of God and fanned it with His Heavenly Presence to a holy, blessed flame.

O brethren, personal, earnest, heartbroken seeking of the lost by us preachers, not as preachers but as Christians, will fix our ministry, will fix our temptations, will fix our prayers, as nothing else will, because God will see to it that we can win souls only in proportion as we are right. Soul winning both gains and proves the abiding Holy Spirit.

Young Christian, what about worldly amusements? Is it hard to give them up? Soul winning will take away their charm. Jesus said "Every branch that beareth fruit, he purgeth it that it may bring forth more fruit." Do you have trouble remembering prayer? Get a sinning, helpless, hopeless, hungry lost world on your heart, and go fishing for men with tears, and you cannot help praying. Soul winning will keep the Christian right.

6. IT IS THE HIGHEST JOY

"They that sow in tears shall reap in joy." A Christian's best joy does not come when he is saved, but when he helps someone else to the Saviour. The soul winner has the joy of God's favor, of the saved one's gratitude, and Holy Spirit abiding. Clothes wear out, money disappears, land doesn't go to Heaven, a night of pleasure is gone in the morning, but souls won will be in Heaven to meet and shine "as the stars for ever and ever" (Daniel 12:3).

Christians, the personal seeking, wooing, winning of Christ's lost sheep is God's balm of Gilead to restless, worrying unhappy hearts. To win souls is the greatest glory to Jesus, the greatest gain in Heaven, the greatest growth to the winner, and the highest joy on earth.

Why not right now, before you lay this paper down, open your heart and ask God to make you a compassionate winner of lost men. Nothing else on earth pays in such coin.

Now I will glory in the cross,
For this I count the world but
    dross.
There I with Christ was crucified,
His death is mine; with Him I
    died;
And while I live my song shall be,
No longer I, but Christ in me.
—H. A. Ironside

The noted Dr. T. DeWitt Talmage said: "We are speeding toward the last hour of our earthly residence. When I see the sunset I say: "One day less to live." When I close this Bible Sunday night, I say: "Another Lord's day departed." When I bury a friend, I say: "Another earthly attraction gone forever."

Can we not learn, like tired children, to fall into Everlasting Arms and rest, not in what we know, but in what we trust?—S. A. Eliot.

Out of Bounds

The old shepherd who offered prayer in a Welsh revival meeting put it exactly right when he lamented his backslidings in these words: "Lord, I got among the thorns and briars, and was scratched and torn and bleeding; but, Lord, it is only fair to say that it was not on Thy ground; I had wandered out of Thy pasture."
—Lawson

MEN ARE FOUR

Men are four:
He who knows and knows he
    knows—
    He is wise—follow him.
He who knows, and knows not he
    knows—
    He is asleep—wake him.
He who knows not, and knows not
    he knows not—
    He is a fool—shun him.
He who knows not and knows he
    knows not,—
    He is a child—teach him.
—Arabian Proverb.

SCARRED

The shame He suffered left its
    brand
In gaping wound in either hand;
Sin's penalty He deigned to meet
Has torn and scarred His blessed
    feet;
The condemnation by Him borne
Marred His brow with print of
    thorn.
Trespass and guilt for which He
    died
Have marked Him with a riven
    side.

Mine was the shame, the penalty;
The sin was mine; it was for me
He felt the nails, the thorns, the
    spear.
For love of me the scars appear
In hands and feet and side and
    brow.
Beholding them I can but bow
Myself a living sacrifice
To Him who paid so dear a price.
—Bob Jones, Jr.

When I first began preaching, I remember how I wept from the beginning to the end of my sermons. I was embarrassed about it. This was wholly unlike the college debating, the commencement addresses and other public speaking which I had been accustomed to doing. The tears flowed down my cheeks almost continually, and I was so broken up that sometimes I could scarcely talk. Then I grew ashamed of my tears and longed to speak more logically. As I recall, I asked the Lord to give me better control of myself as I preached. My tears soon vanished and I found I had only the dry husk of preaching left. Then I begged God to give me again the broken heart, the concern, even if it meant tears in public and a trembling voice. I feel the same need today. We preachers ought to cry out like Jeremiah, "Oh, that my head were waters, and mine eyes a fountain of tears, that I might weep day and night for the slain of the daughter of my people!" (Jer. 9:1).

John R. Rice

*Today, a full century after the death
of Abraham Lincoln, he is still greatly honored
and remembered as . . .*

The Praying President

By Gordon Lindsay

"Can we have a Christian president?" I believe that we can if America will pray.

In the winter of 1857-58, we are told that the greatest revival in American history took place, due in a great part to the efforts of Charles G. Finney. One man who traveled through the country said that he found a prayer meeting two thousand miles long. In Finney's autobiography we are told that at the height of the visitation some 50,000 a week were converted. This revival came just before the great judgment of the Civil War. But God raised up a praying president—Abraham Lincoln—and our nation was saved. The story of how Abraham Lincoln became the Christian president has not often been told, but is most assuredly true.

The mother of Abraham Lincoln was a woman of superior character for her time and surroundings. She had attended a school in Virginia, and was intellectually above those around her. She was especially devoted in her Christian life, striving to live up to the teachings of the Bible, which was her daily companion. She sought to follow the scriptural injunction, "Train up a child in the way he should go: and when he is old, he will not depart from it." On Sunday she would read those Bible stories so interesting to all children, and then she would pray with her family. She impressed her own ideals and convictions of righteousness indelibly upon her son, and her earnest prayers made a lifelong impression upon his young mind; for he said after he became president, speaking of his mother: "I remember her prayers, and they have always followed me. They have clung to me all my life."

Mother's Death

When Abe was nine years old, his mother died on October 5, 1818. A friend present at the time says: "The mother knew she was going to die, and called her children (Abe and Sarah) to her bedside. She was very weak, and the children leaned over while she gave her last message. Placing her feeble hand on little Abe's head, she told him to be kind and good to his father and sister; to both she said, 'Be good to one another,' expressing a hope that they might live as they had been taught by her, to love their kindred and worship God."

Little did this mother, "dying amid the miserable surroundings of a home in the wilderness," dream that her name, Nancy Hanks Lincoln, was to become important through the ragged, barefoot, hapless lad who gazed with wondering eyes upon this strange transition. Earth's noblest crown has been wreathed about her memory, and never more beautifully told than in these words: "Though of lowly birth, the victim of poverty and hard usage, she takes a place in history as the mother of a son who liberated a race of men."

The effect of this mother's prayers, teachings, and dying benediction may best be told by her own son, after he became known and loved the world over: "All that I am, all that I hope to be, I owe to my angel mother—blessings on her memory."

The books to which young Lincoln had access were few, but they were the best. The first was the Bible. He kept it within easy reach, and read it over and over again. He could repeat much of it from memory. His mind was saturated with its precepts and his heart was filled with its truths. The second book which he read was Bunyan's *Pilgrim's Progress*, which his father borrowed for him.

The Period of Doubt and Uncertainty

There was a time in his life when Abraham Lincoln wrestled with doubt and uncertainty. In his searchings for truth he came under the powerful influence of a distinguished preacher and profound thinker, the Rev. James Smith, D. D., who was pastor of the Presbyterian Church of Springfield, Illinois. Rev. Smith related the following:

"Mr. Lincoln, at the time of my coming to Springfield, had no denominational preferences and when his wife changed to the Presbyterian Church, he attended with her." In the latter part of 1849, death came to his second son, and Mr. Smith was asked to take charge of the funeral. At that time it seemed that Lincoln was much depressed and downcast as the result of the death of his son. His views seemed confused, and as those of a deist. Nevertheless, the minister found that he had been a constant reader of the Bible. Mr. Lincoln then unbosomed his doubts, struggles and unrest of his soul. Rev. Smith, after giving him some instructions on the right attitude required for impartial investigation, then placed his book, *The Christian's Defense,* in his hands. Mr. Lincoln took the book and for a number of weeks, as a lawyer, examined and weighed the evidence. While he was investigating, the pastor prayed that the Spirit of Truth might lead him.

When Mr. Lincoln had concluded his examination, he came forth, his doubts scattered to the winds and his reason convinced by the arguments in the support of the inspired and infallible authority of the Old and New Testaments. He was a convinced believer in God, in His providential government, in Christ being the Way, the Truth, and the Life. From then on Mr. Lincoln attended church regularly, even the prayer meetings and the revival meetings.

Farewell Speech at Springfield

In Lincoln's farewell speech at Springfield, Illinois, just before he left for Washington, the man shows his reliance on God:

"Today I leave you. I go to assume a task more difficult than that which devolved upon General Washington. Unless the great God who assisted him shall be with and aid me, I must fail; but if the same Omniscient Mind and Almighty Arm that directed and protected him shall guide and support me, I shall not fail—I shall succeed. Let us all pray that the God of our fathers may not forsake us now. To Him I commend you all. Permit me to ask that with equal sincerity and faith you will invoke His wisdom and guidance for me."

The First National Fast Day During the Civil War

That "Mr. Lincoln was profoundly and intensely religious" is shown in his proclamations of days of fasting, prayer, and thanksgiving. The first proclamation of a national fast day was issued August 12, 1861, part of which follows:

"Whereas it is fit and becoming in all people, at all times, to acknowledge and revere the supreme government of God; to bow in humble submission to His chastise-

ments; to confess and deplore their sins and transgressions, in the full conviction that the fear of the Lord is the beginning of wisdom; and to pray for His mercy—to pray that we may be spared further punishment though most justly deserved; that our arms may be blessed and made effectual for the establishment of law, order, and peace, throughout the wide extent of our country. . . .

"Therefore, I, Abraham Lincoln, President of the United States, do appoint the last Thursday of September next as a day of humiliation, prayer, and fasting for all the people of the nation."

His Great Sorrow

Thursday, February 20, 1862, Mr. Lincoln experienced what perhaps was the greatest sorrow of his life in the death of his little boy, Willie. He was filled with the deepest sadness and melancholy. Mrs. Lincoln became alarmed for his health. Dr. Francis Vinton, an acquaintance of the family, was in Washington and was invited to visit the White House. Observing the deep grief of the president, Dr. Vinton told him it was sinful to grieve in such a way, and unworthy of a believer in the Christian religion. The scene is described as follows:

"Your son," said Dr. Vinton, "is alive in paradise. Do you remember that passage in the Gospels, 'God is not a God of the dead, but of the living: for all live unto him'?" As Mr. Lincoln caught the words, "Your son is alive," he started from his seat as one aroused from a stupor, and exclaimed, "Alive! Alive! Surely you mock me!" "No sir; believe me," replied Dr. Vinton. "It is a most comforting doctrine of the church, founded upon the words of Christ Himself." Mr. Lincoln threw his arm around Dr. Vinton's neck, laid his head upon his breast, and sobbed aloud, "Alive? Alive?" Dr. Vinton, greatly moved, said: "My dear sir, believe this, for it is God's most precious truth. Seek not your son among the dead; he is not there; he lives today in paradise! Think of the full import of the words I have quoted. The Sadducees, when they questioned Jesus, had no other conception than that Abraham, Isaac, and Jacob were dead and buried. Mark the reply: 'Now that the dead are raised, even Moses showed at the bush when he called the Lord the God of Abraham, the God of Isaac, and the God of Jacob. For He is not the God of the dead, but of the living, for all live unto Him!' "

Dr. Vinton told Lincoln that he had a sermon on the subject. Mr. Lincoln asked him to send it to him as soon as possible, and thanked him repeatedly for his cheering and hopeful words. When

Lincoln received the sermon he read it over and over, and had a copy made for his own private use. A member of the family said that Mr. Lincoln's views in relation to spiritual things seemed changed from that hour.

A Praying President

On July 4, 1863, just 87 years to a day after the signing of the Declaration of Independence, came the great victories of Vicksburg and Gettysburg. A well-authenticated incident told by General James F. Rusling and General Daniel Sickles of Lincoln's prayers in connection with these victories comes to us.

"General James F. Rusling, of Trenton, New Jersey, relates a significant conversation which he heard on Sunday, July 5, 1863, in the room in Washington where General Sickles lay wounded, just after the great victory at Gettysburg. In reply to a question from General Sickles whether or not the President was anxious about the battle at Gettysburg, Lincoln gravely said, 'No, I was not; some of my Cabinet and many others in Washington were, but I had no fears.'

"General Sickles inquired how this was and seemed curious about it. Mr. Lincoln hesitated, but finally replied: 'Well, I will tell you how it was. In the pinch of your campaign up there, when everybody seemed panic-stricken, and nobody could tell what was going to happen, oppressed by the gravity of our affairs, I went to my room one day, and I locked the door, and got down on my knees before Almighty God, and prayed to Him mightily for victory at Gettysburg. I told Him that this was His war, and our cause His cause, but we couldn't stand another Fredericksburg or Chancellorsville. And I then and there made a solemn vow to Almighty God that if He would stand by our boys at Gettysburg, I would stand by Him. And He did stand by you boys, and I will stand by Him. And after that (I don't know how it was, and I can't explain it), soon a sweet comfort crept into my soul that God Almighty had taken the whole business into His own hands and that things would go all right at Gettysburg. And that is why I had no fears about you.' Asked concerning Vicksburg, the news of which victory had not yet reached him, he said, 'I have been praying for Vicksburg also, and believe our Heavenly Father is going to give us a victory there, too.' General Rosling says that Mr. Lincoln spoke 'solemnly and pathetically, as if from the depth of his heart,' and that his manner was deeply touching."

Immortal Words

In that remarkable and ever-memorable second inaugural address, delivered at Washington,

March 4, 1865, just six weeks before his death, he gave utterance to these sublime and immortal words:

"Both read the same Bible, and pray to the same God; and each invokes His aid against the other. It may seem strange that any man should dare to ask a just God's assistance in wringing their bread from the sweat of other men's faces; but let us judge not, that we be not judged. The prayers of both could not be answered —that of neither has been answered fully.

"The Almighty has His own purposes. 'Woe unto the world because of offenses! for it must needs be that offenses come; but woe to that man by whom the offense cometh.' If we shall suppose that American slavery is one of those offenses which, in the providence of God, must need come, but which, having continued through His appointed time, He now wills to remove, and that He gives to both North and South this terrible war, as the woe to those whom the offense came, shall we discern therein any departure from those divine attributes which the believers in a living God always ascribe to Him? Fondly do we hope—fervently do we pray—that this mighty scourge of war may speedily pass away.

Yet, if God wills that it continue until all the wealth piled by the bondman's two hundred and fifty years of unrequited toil shall be sunk, and until every drop of blood drawn with the lash shall be paid with another drawn with the sword, as was said three thousand years ago, so still it must be said, 'The judgments of the Lord are true and righteous altogether.'

"With malice toward none; with charity for all; with firmness in the right, as God gives us to see the right, let us strive on to finish the work we are in; to bind up the nation's wounds; to care for him who shall have borne the battle, and for his widow, and his orphan—to do all which may achieve and cherish a just and a lasting peace among ourselves, and with all nations."

These words show the President still untouched by resentment, still brotherly in his feelings toward the enemies of the government, and still profoundly conscious of the overruling power of Providence in national affairs. Well has it been said that it was a paper whose Christian sentiment and whose reverent and pious spirit has no parallel among the state papers of the American Presidents. "His mind and soul has reached the full development in a religious life so unusually intense and absorbing that it could not otherwise than utter itself in the grand sentences of his last address to the people. The knowledge had come, and the faith had come, and the charity had come, and with all had come the love of God."

Last Days

The last days of Lincoln were marked by events revealing the spiritual maturity of his life. When he went to Richmond after Lee had evacuated it, an old Negro caught sight of him and said, "Bless de Lawd, dere is de great Messiah. I knowed him as soon as I seed him." He and others fell at Mr. Lincoln's feet and kissed them. But the President restrained them and said, "Don't kneel to me. That is not right. You must kneel to God only, and thank Him for the liberty you will hereafter enjoy."

When news came of the capitulation of Lee, at the suggestion of the President, all the cabinet dropped on their knees and offered, in silence and tears, their humble and heartfelt acknowledgements to the Almighty for the triumph He had granted the national cause.

The last Act of Congress signed by him was the one requiring that the motto, "In God we trust," should forever be inscribed on our national coins.

His last public speech, on April 11, 1865, spoke of a call for national thanksgiving.

His last recorded words were his wish that after he had completed his time of office he might visit the Holy Land and see the places "hallowed by the footsteps of the Saviour."

—From the Voice of the Nazerene, *The Universal Challenger*

Don't Let Brother Brimstone Get You!

A modern fable tells about how his Satanic Majesty solved the problem of the loss of patronage in his Infernal Domain. It seems that he found there were still many "prospects" on the Earth Plane. But why weren't they coming to him?

After cudgeling his brain until both horns hurt, he decided he'd use Earth's method for solving problems. He'd have a contest. So . . . he gathered all his little Imps together and explained the problem. "One week from today," he growled, "we will meet together right here . . . and the one who has the best solution to the problem of our lack of business will receive an asbestos helmet and a gold pitchfork."

Since the prizes offered were so attractive, the little Imps of Satan diligently picked their own and each other's brains all week. Came the Big Day, and many were the suggestions offered, but Brother Brimstone won the prize. What was unique about his Big Idea? Listen!

"First," chortled Brimstone, "we will pick out a nice, juicy prospect. Then we will put our arm around his shoulder and say, "Tell me, Mr. Smith, how would you like to go to Heaven when you die?" Naturally he'll say yes, so then we proceed. 'Then here's what you'll have to do: Stop that heavy drinking and carousing, stay away from your neighbor's wife. . . .'" He was interrupted by a clamor from the rest of the Imps.

"Whose side are you on . . . anyhow?" they screamed.

But Brother Brimstone had anticipated their clamor. He held up one front hoof to quiet them. "Hear me out," he smiled, "I then whisper in his ear: 'But you don't have to start doing those things right now . . . just SOME MORE CONVENIENT TIME!'"

It is seldom a "convenient time" to do the things that will lead us to greater success. But, haven't you noticed that those who get ahead have a knack of doing things BEFORE THEY ARE READY?—Western Voice.

God In Human Shoes

By Rev. J. L. H. Hawkins
Elmendorf, Texas

(Excerpt of a sermon preached at First Baptist Church, Elmendorf, Texas, and published by request.)

Text: Matthew 3:11; John 1:36. Recently I have read *The Robe* by Lloyd C. Douglas, a story purporting to show what became of the robe of Jesus for which the soldiers cast lots. The claims of this novel are, of course, visionary and without foundation, as are the claims of Catholicism, that the robe fell upon Peter at Rome. No one can prove that Peter was ever at Rome and any sane mind knows that it is very improbable that this robe ever reached Rome.

But intriguing as might be the speculations on what became of the robe of Jesus, I am far more interested in the shoes that He wore. John the Baptist was also. The first thing that he ever spoke of Jesus was about His shoes—"whose shoes I am not worthy to bear."

The Apostle John never spoke of the robe of Jesus, but he did "stand looking upon Jesus as He walked," and he said that he was not worthy to unlace His shoe strings. (John 1:27).

Jesus was a normal child, and no doubt wore shoes about His home and they appealed to Him just as your shoes appealed to you when you were a child. He made tracks in those shoes running errands and obeying His parents. He used His shoes going to church. He walked over sixty miles to church once each year and back home again. He went in shoes each Sabbath to the Synagogue to worship God. He walked in shoes from His home to Jordan to be baptised of John in Jordan (Matt. 3:13). In those shoes Jesus walked

to the wilderness to be tempted of the Devil (Matt. 4:1). He walked in those shoes to His task in Judea, in Galilee, in Perea. He walked in those shoes up the mountain to pray and in the valley to labor, in the country and in the cities doing good (Matt. 9:35).

Among the erring He walked to guide them to the right; among the sick and needy to heal and to bless (John 5:1-9). Out into the dark and to Gethsemane. Then, "he went a little farther," even to Calvary. There they pierced His hands and His heart, and His feet, His hands to do, His heart to love, His feet to go.

"Looking upon Jesus as he walked"—What stately steps! What dignity of action! What grace of motion! What lofty strides! What intelligent destiny expressed in His walk! What surety and poise and purpose in His victorious stride! He walked with a divine purpose, with divine mission and accomplishment. No staggering doubt as to what; no tottering of fear as to results, "He walked"....

Foot prints of Jesus that make the pathway glow,
We will follow the steps of Jesus wher-e'er they go.

God's Word has much to say about feet and walking. Isaiah says, "How beautiful upon the mountain are the feet of those who bring glad tidings" (Isa. 52:7).

We are told in Daniel about three faithful men who were bound and cast into the fiery furnace and a king exclaiming, "Lo, I see four men loose, walking in the midst of the fire, and they have no hurt." Paul speaks of "the steps of that faith of Abraham," and again, "We walk by

faith"; and yet again he says, "Abraham went out"; "The steps of a good man are ordered by the Lord."

There are more commands in the Word of God to "Go" than there are invitations to "Come." "Go, ye, therefore."

Jesus washed the feet of His disciples that they might be clean to "go after that which was lost."

God wants shoes, shoes, shoes! Big shoes, little shoes, high heeled shoes, low heeled shoes! Shoes in which He may place feet to go after the lost of the world.

A time ago a young father came running to me crying, "Oh, Edna is dead, come quickly. Our precious little girl is dead." I ran with him to his home and there upon the bed lay the lifeless form of his ten year old daughter. No one knew why but she was gone. The father and mother and I stood by the bed heart broken. I prayed. Just then the mother wailed out and stooped for two little shoes placed under the bed the night before as the little one had prepared for sleep. The mother hugged them to her breast and patted them. Then, holding them out to her husband she said, "Frank, we are going to follow these shoes to Heaven."

We have been calling for "bundles for Britain," I appeal for "Shoes for the Saviour." Will you give Him yours? Your feet must be in them, else He cannot use them. Your shoes will exactly fit His feet if He has your feet.

Can you and will you say,

I'll go where you want me to go, dear Lord,
O'er mountain or plain or sea;
I'll say what you want me to say, dear Lord,
I'll be what you want me to be.

"The beginning of anxiety is the end of faith, and the beginning of true faith is the end of anxiety."—George Mueller.

Have courage for the great sorrows of life and patience for the small ones; and when you have laboriously accomplished your daily task, go to sleep in peace. God is awake.—Victor Hugo.

LET DOGS DELIGHT TO BARK AND BITE
FOR GOD HATH MADE THEM SO;
LET BEARS AND LIONS GROWL AND FIGHT,
FOR 'TIS THEIR NATURE TOO.
—WATTS

Years ago I was in a revival campaign in a country community in West Texas. In a daytime service I set out to teach people gathered under a brush arbor that God demanded first place in everything, that He wanted tithes and offerings from the loving and believing hearts of His people. Present in the service that day was a dear country preacher, Brother Kuykendal. He was then, and had been for years, county missionary in Palo Pinto county, preaching in churchless communities, building up weak churches, selling and giving away Gospel literature as a rural missionary. He asked if he might tell how God had dealt with him about tithing. I gladly asked him to proceed. He arose and told his story about like this.

"Some years ago when I was county missionary of this county the famous Baptist businessman, H. Z. Duke, who founded the Duke and Ayers Nickel Stores over a wide area, came to this county and, speaking as a Christian layman, urged the men and women everywhere to try God and see if He would not make good His promises to bless them in material things when they gave tithes and offerings to His cause. After Mr. Duke had spoken in one community, I took him in my buggy to another community. Mr. Duke said to me, 'Brother Kuykendal, do you believe in tithing?'

" 'I certainly do,' I said. 'I believe in tithing and I preach it myself.'

" 'But, Brother Kuykendal, do you *practice* tithing?'

"Sadly I had to answer, 'No, I do not. I believe in tithing, but I cannot practice it. You see, I have thirteen children at home. Every meal fifteen of us sit down at the table. I receive only $125 a month, $1500 a year as salary. I have to maintain my own horse and buggy for constant travelling. It is just impossible to take care of all the needs of a family of fifteen out of $125 a month and have money left to tithe. So I believe in tithing, and I preach it, but I cannot practice it.'

"Mr. Duke was a very kindly man. He said, 'Brother Kuykendal, would you like to tithe? Would you tithe if I would back you up financially so you could be sure you would not lose by it?'

" 'Nothing would please me more,' I said.

"So Mr. Duke made me the following proposition:

" 'I want you to set out to give God at least $12.50 every month, as soon as you get your salary. Then as you feel led, you may give more. I promise you that if you need help, I will give it. Simply write me a letter and say, "Brother Duke, I am giving a tithe, but I miss the money. I need it for my family. I have given this year so much." I promise you that I will send you a check by return mail. Are you willing to try tithing on that basis?'

30

"I hesitated a moment, moved with emotion, and Brother Duke said, 'I have thirty-two stores. I have plenty of money to make good my promise. I will be glad to do it. Will you risk me and start tithing on my simple promise that I will make good any amount you have given, any time that you find you miss it and need it? Will you trust me about it?'

"I gladly accepted his offer. I said, 'Yes, Brother Duke, I have long wanted to tithe, but I felt I simply could not do it. Now, thank God, I can tithe and I will be glad to. And I will not feel like a hypocrite when I tell others they ought to tithe.'

"So I started tithing for the first time in my life. Every month I took out first of all one-tenth of my salary and gave it to the Lord's cause; then, as I felt led, I gave more. In the back of my mind I always had this thought, 'Mr. Duke promised me that he would make it up any time I need it. He will send me the money if I simply ask him for it.'

"But a strange thing happened. It seemed our money went farther than before. I would preach in some country community and somebody would tie a crate of chickens on the back of my buggy. Somebody would put a ham under the seat. Or a godly woman would put some home-canned fruit in my buggy.

"A neighbor farmer said, 'Brother Kuykendal, God has blessed me so that I cannot get all my corn in the crib this year. I have a big wagon load extra that I cannot keep. May I put it in your crib for your buggy horse?'

"Another neighbor drove over with a great hay wagon full of hay for the cow.

"It was very strange, but that year we had no doctor bills. The children's clothes seemed not to wear out so badly. It was a happy, happy time. I never did have to call on Mr. H. Z. Duke to make up the money I had given to the Lord in tithes.

"Then one day, when the year was about gone and the test was about over, I suddenly realized with shame that I had believed what H. Z. Duke said. He promised to make good anything I lacked because of tithing, and I believed him. But my heavenly Father had made the same promise, and I had not believed Him! I had taken the word of a man when I did not take the promise of God! Now I had proven God's promises and found that He took care of me and my big family on a small salary. I found that $112.50 per month took care of our family better, with God's blessing, than $125 did without being under the blessed covenant which He has made with those who seek first the kingdom of God and who tithe."

That godly country preacher stood there before the congregation weeping. With the deepest emotion he said,

"Now I have tithed for many years. My salary has been increased year after year. We have always had enough. We have never been shamed. The greatest spiritual blessing of my life, aside from my salvation, has been in learning to trust God about daily needs for my home and a big family."

-- Story as told by Dr. John R. Rice.

A mother asked a psychologist, "When shall I start training my child?" "How old is he?" she was asked. "Five." The psychologist said, "Madam, hurry home! You have already lost five years!"

W. B. Knight

Determination

I am only one, but I am one;
I cannot do everything,
But I can do something.
What I can do I ought to do,
And what I ought to do
By God's grace I will do.

—Listen

How sweet, how blessed is the thought
That Thou dost hear Thy people's cries!
And whether Thou dost give, or not,
'Tis love that grants, and love denies.   —Author Unknown.

PRAYER

①

②

③

"Yes, you did, too!"
"I did not!"
Thus the little quarrel started;
Thus by unkind little words
Two fond friends were parted.

"I am sorry."
"So am I."
Thus the little quarrel ended,
Thus by loving little words
Two fond hearts were mended.
—Unknown.

Some parents say, "We will not influence our children in making choices and decisions in the matter of religion!" Why not? TV and radio will! The press will! The movies will! Their neighbors will! The politicians will! We use our influence over flowers, vegetables and cattle. Shall we ignore our children?—Church Herald

He Thundered Against Sin

Billy Sunday, the man who galvanized religion into an active force against social evils, was one of the most colorful characters ever to move across the American scene. A generation of Americans have come and gone since his name was a house-hold word.

Billy Sunday, the baseball evangelist and reformer, never spared himself nor those he wanted to help in the vigor of his attacks on sin. He thundered against evil from the Gay Nineties through the Great Depression. He preached Christ as the only answer to man's needs until his death in 1935.

"I'm against sin," he said. "I'll kick it as long as I've got a foot, and I'll fight it as long as I've got a fist. I'll butt it as long as I've got a head. I'll bite it as long as I've got a tooth. When I'm old and fistless and footless and toothless, I'll gum it till I go home to Glory and it goes home to perdition!"

—Copied

Some Christians seem to think of God as a kind of "spare tire." A spare tire is forgotten for months until suddenly, on the road, we have a flat. Many forget God when things go well with them. When sorrow, sickness and troubles come, then they remember God and want Him to help them. He wants us to call on Him when we are in trouble. He also wants us to remember and serve Him when we are not in trouble.
—W. B. Knight.

A Paying Principle

Phil. 4:1

God honors men who take His Word seriously. Stephen Girard, Philadelphia millionaire, one Saturday bade his clerks come next day and unload a vessel which had just arrived. One young man stepped up to the desk and said, as he turned pale, "Mr. Girard, I cannot work tomorrow." "Very well, sir," said the proprieter, "go to the cashier's desk and he will settle with you."

For three weeks the young man tramped the streets looking for work. One day a bank president asked Mr. Girard to name a suitable person for cashier of the new bank about to be started.

After reflection, Mr. Girard named this young man. "But I thought you discharged him?" "I did," was the answer, "because he would not work on Sunday. The man who will lose his situation from principle is the man to whom you can entrust your money." —The Alliance Witness

Who Can Answer This Question?

Many years ago a Welsh minister, a man of God, beginning his sermon, leaned over the pulpit and said with a solemn air, "Friends, I have a question to ask. I cannot answer it. You cannot answer it. If an angel from Heaven were here, he could not answer it." Every eye was fixed on the speaker. He proceeded, "The question is this: How shall we escape, if we neglect so great salvation?"

—Sunday School Times

Twenty-Third Psalm

(Vest-Pocket Edition)

Beneath me: green pastures;
  Beside me: still waters;
With me: my Shepherd;
  Before me: a table;
Around me: mine enemies;
  After me: goodness and mercy;
Beyond me: the house of the Lord.

NOBODY CARES FOR MY SOUL

Here is an experience related by that famous evangelist, Billy Sunday:

I walked down the street with a man and put to him the invariable question, "Are you a Christian?" He said, "No sir, I am not." Then I used every Scripture and every argument to get him to promise me to give his heart to God, but could not succeed. When about to separate, I said to him, "Are your father and mother alive?" "Both alive," said he. "Is your father a Christian?" "Don't know; he has been a steward in the church for several years." "Is your mother a Christian?" "Don't know; she has been superintendent of the Sunday School of the same church for some time." "Have you a sister?" "Yes, sir." "Is she a Christian?" "Don't know; she has the Primary Department in the Sunday School." "Do your father and mother ever ask the blessing at the table?" "No, sir." "Did your father, mother, or sister ever ask you to be a Christian?" "Mr. Sunday, as long as I can remember, my father or mother or sister never said a word to me about my soul. Do you believe they think I am lost?" I could not answer such an argument.

It is six years this coming October since I heard this. I can hear the words ringing in my ears, "Do you believe they think I am lost?"

Can any one of ours say that we do not care for his soul? *May God save us from the crime of unconcern.*—Billy Sunday.

A Better Likeness Soon

Spurgeon received one day a copy of Andrew Bonar's Commentary on Leviticus. It so blessed him that he returned it, saying: "Dr. Bonar, please place herein your autograph and your photograph." The book was returned to him with the following note from the pen of Dr. Bonar: "Dear Spurgeon, here is the book with my autograph and with my photograph. If you had been willing to wait a short season you could have had a better likeness, for I shall be like Him! I shall see Him as He is."

Avoid Anxiety For Riches

Charles H. Spurgeon

Do not be over-anxious about riches. Get as much of true wisdom and goodness as you can; but be satisfied with a very moderate portion of this world's goods. Riches may prove a curse as well as a blessing.

I was walking through an orchard looking about me, when I saw a low tree laden more heavily with fruit than the rest. On a nearer examination, it appeared that the tree had been dragged to the very earth, and broken by the weight of its treasures. "Oh," I said, gazing on the tree, "here lies one who has been ruined by his riches."

In another part of my walk, I came up with a shepherd who was lamenting the loss of a sheep that lay mangled and dead at his feet. On inquiring about the matter, he told me that a strange dog had attacked the flock, that the rest of the sheep had got away through a hole in the hedge, but that the ram now dead had more wool on his back than the rest, and the thorns of the hedge held him fast till the dog had worried him. "Here is another," said I, "ruined by his riches."

At the close of my ramble, I met a man hobbling along on two wooden legs, leaning on two crutches. "Tell me," said I, "my poor fellow, how you came to lose your legs."

"Why, sir," said he, "in my younger days I was a soldier. With a few comrades, I attacked a party of the enemy, and overcame them, and we began to overload ourselves with spoil. I burdened myself with as much as I could carry. We were pursued. My companions escaped, but I was overtaken and so cruelly wounded, that I only saved my life afterwards by losing my legs. It was a bad affair, sir, but it is too late to repent of it now."

"Ah, friend," thought I, "like the fruit of the tree and the mangled sheep, you may date your downfall to your possessions. It was your riches that ruined you."

A Surety

William Jennings Byran describes securing a few grains of wheat when in Cairo that had slumbered thirty centuries in an Egyptian tomb. Upon thinking of the unbroken chain of life of the grain we sow and harvest today, he wrote, "If this invisible germ of life in the grain of wheat can pass unimpaired through three thousand resurrections, I shall not doubt that my soul has power to clothe itself with a new body suited to its new existence when this earthly frame has crumbled to dust."

A Father's Concern

During the frontier days, the driver of a covered wagon stopped his horses on the street of a young town, and called to a passing man, "Hey, any saloons in this place?"

"Sure, we have four!" boastfully replied the man.

"Giddap," the driver shouted, urging his horses on.

"Stop," called the man.

"I can't stop here," replied the stranger, "I've got four boys in this wagon."

"Why?" again called the man, "What's your business?"

"My business is to raise these boys for God, and I can't do that in a town with four saloons." And he hurried his horses on, soon turning the bend in the road and passing out of sight.

From "The Evangelist"

"De Lawd's Cow"

After many years of preaching the Gospel I sincerely believe that there is hardly any one thing that will soon reveal the character of men and women as the way in which they spend their money. Just tell me what you did with the money that passed through your hands during the past six months and it will not be hard to tell whether you are selfish or unselfish, godly or worldly, generous or grasping. The amount of money you have handled has nothing to do with it. It is the question of your attitude toward it.

Some years ago a couple of stock buyers in the South rode up to the home of an old colored man and noticed a fine milk cow grazing in the yard. One of them said, "Uncle, we would like to buy this cow. Is she yours?" The old Negro replied, "No, sah, boss, dat ain't my cow. Hit's de Lawd's cow. I'm jest a-keepin' her fer Him."

That old man had grasped the great principle of stewardship. We really do not own anything. Whatever we seem to possess is just loaned to us for a little while, for "the earth is the Lord's and the fulness thereof."—*Western Recorder.*

MEDICARE?
—*And we laughed until we hit the pavement!*—

A sample of what might happen under Socialized Medicine is currently making the rounds. It goes something like this:

A man, feeling the need of medical care, went to the Medical Building for that purpose, and upon entering the front door, found himself faced with a battery of doors, each marked with the name of an ailment such as Appendicitis, Heart, Cancer, etc. He felt sure his trouble could be diagnosed as Appendicitis, so he entered the door so marked. Upon entering he found himself faced with two more doors, one marked "Male" and the other "Female". Of course he entered the door marked "Male," and found himself in another corridor where there were two doors, one marked "Protestant" and the other "Catholic."

Since he was a Protestant, he entered the proper door and found himself facing two more doors, one marked "White" and the other "Colored." He entered the door "White" and again was faced with two more doors marked "Taxpayer" and "Non-taxpayer." He still owned equity in his house and wasn't on Government Welfare so he went thru the door marked "Taxpayer" and found himself confronted with still two more doors marked "Single" and "Married."

He had a wife at home, so he entered the proper door and once more there were two doors, one marked "Republican" and the other "Democrat."

He was a Republican, so he entered the proper door and fell nine floors to the alley!

There is a story of an Arab who said at night, "I will loose my camel and trust in God to find it." But a wiser one said, "Tie your camel and trust in God." Prayer and care should go together.

* * *

GIVE US MEN..

"I consider the fortunes of our republic as depending on the extinguishment of the public debt before we engage in any war. If the debt should once more be swelled to a formidable size, its entire discharge will be despaired of, and we shall be committed to a career of debt, corruption and rottenness, closing with revolution.

"We must not let our rulers load us with perpetual debt. We must make our election between economy and liberty, or profusion and servitude. If we run into such debts, as that we must be taxed in our meat and in our drink, in our necessaries and our comforts, in our labors and in our amusements, for our callings and our creed, then we will have no time to think, no means of calling the mismanagers to account; but must merely be glad to obtain subsistence by hiring ourselves to rivet their chains to the necks of our fellow-sufferers."
—Thomas Jefferson

Bob Jones Says . . .

The King James version is, after all, the best translation we have ever had. The very words of the Bible in the original languages were inspired of the Holy Ghost. That is what the Bible claims for itself; and that is what bornagain, Bible-believing Christians believe about the Bible. We are to search the Scriptures as our Lord commanded us; but, remember, there is a curse to those that add to the Word or take away from the Word. The hottest place in Hell will be reserved for these modernistic conspirators who, in a subtle, pious way, are trying to steal the faith of humble Christians in the Word of God. Remember, you do not have to be a scholar. You do not have to be a great authority on languages. You do not have to be a great literary genius. Remember this: Any man who wonders if the Bible is the Word of God has not been born again. All bornagain Christians believe the Word and love the Word.—Bob Jones, Sr.

HIS LAST

Christ's last act was winning a soul.

His last command was to win a soul.

His last prayer was forgiveness to a soul.

One Minute Readings

Nothing Lost

During the summer a clergyman called on a lady who had a very fine collection of roses. She took him out to see them—white roses, red roses, yellow roses, climbing roses, and roses in pots, the gay giant of battles and the modest moss rose—every species he had ever heard of, and a great many he had never heard of, were there in rich profusion. The lady began plucking, right and left. Some bushes with but a single flower she despoiled. The clergyman remonstrated. "You are robbing yourself, dear madam." "Ah, she said, "do you not know that the way to make the rosebush is to pluck its flowers freely? I lose nothing by what I give away." This is a universal law. We never lose anything by what we give away.—From Clerical Library "Anecdotes."

To Any Daddy

There are little eyes upon you, and
they're watching night and day;
There are little ears that quickly
take in every word you say;
There are little hands all eager to
do everything you do.
And a little boy who's dreaming of
the day he'll be just like you.

You're the little fellow's idol, you're
the wisest of the wise;
In his little mind, about you no sus-
picions ever rise.
He believes in you devoutly, holds
that all you say and do,
He will say and do in your way
when he's grown up like you.

This wide-eyed little fellow who believes you're always right.
And his ears are always open and
he watches day and night.
You are setting an example every
day in all you do,
For the little fellow who's waiting
to grow up to be just like you.

—Author unknown

All this modern talk about not believing in Hell is because men have ceased to believe in SIN. Sin always produces Hell. There are ten thousand hells in this world produced by sin. If a man goes to eternity with his character unchanged, he will have Hell in eternity. Jesus most certainly taught that there is a place of future punishment for the wicked. The rich man didn't take one drop of water with him when he went to Hell. But he took his memory. Someone said, "All the Hell I have is in my bosom." The rich man had his bosom in Hell, and that bosom was filled with bitter and tormenting memories. He cried for a drop of water for a parching tongue. He asked Abraham to keep his brothers away from the place of torment. He never said, "Let me get out." This is most significant. The longer men live in sin, the less likely they are to change. Suffering doesn't change people. Suffering has a tendency to harden depraved people. If men die without God, they gather momentum on the down grade of eternal depravity.—Dr. Bob Jones, Sr.

Power of Forgiveness

A young Christian working man told me that he lost a valued tool from his tool kit and recognized it later in the kit of his fellow workman. Being the only Christian at work in the room, he felt it incumbent upon him to show forgiveness. So he went to the thief and said, "I see you have one of my tools, but you can keep it if you need it." Then he went on with his work and put the incident out of his mind. During the next two weeks the thief three times tried to give the value of the tool to its rightful owner—once by offering to give him something else of equal value, again by offering his services between hours, and again by slipping money into his coat pocket. The incident closed with a lasting friendship between the two men because, said the thief, "I couldn't stand being forgiven."

—Henry Van Dyke

"I'm Not Ready Yet"

A man 93 years old in a hospital was asked to receive Christ and become a Christian. "No," he said, "I'm not ready yet." Not ready yet at 93! Next morning his bed was empty. He had died.

"Not ready yet," was his usual answer for many years when asked to receive Christ as Saviour. It had become a habit, then a fixed principle with him. It was all he could say.

Reader, how about you? Have you received Christ? Or do you say, "Not ready yet"?

Read God's answer to that in Second Corinthians 6:2.

He feels perchance that all is well,
And every fear is calmed;
He lives, he dies, he wakes in hell,
Not only doomed but damned.

Oh, where is that mysterious line,
That may by man be crossed,
Beyond which God Himself hath
sworn,
That he who goes is lost?

An answer from the skies repeats,
'Ye who from God depart'
Today, repent, oh hear His voice,
And harden not your heart.

"Fill It Up"

The drinking man steps up to the bar, places his glass on the bar and says to the bartender: "Fill it up!"

Then he drives to the filling station and tells the attendant, "Fill it up!"

Three days later, the cemetery superintendent tells his workmen, after the casket has been placed in the grave, "Fill it up!"

Treasures

By J. Wilbur Chapman

I was standing in Tiffany's great store in New York, and I heard the salesman say to a lady who had asked him about some pearls, "Madam, this pearl is worth $17,000." I was interested at once. I said, "Let me see the pearl that is worth $17,000." The salesman put it on a piece of black cloth and I studied it carefully.

I said, "I suppose Tiffany's stock is very valuable?" And as I looked around that beautiful store, I imagined them bringing all their stock up to my house and saying, "We want you to take care of this tonight." What do you think I would do? I would go as quickly as I could to the telephone and call up the chief of police and say, "I have all Tiffany's stock in my house, and it is too great a responsibility. Will you send some of your trusted officers to help me?" You would do the same, wouldn't you?

But I have a little boy in my home, and for him I am responsible. I have had him for nine years, and some of you may have just another little boy. I turn to this old book and I read this word: *"What shall it profit a man if he shall gain the whole world and lose his own soul? or what shall a man give in exchange for his soul?"* It is as if he had all the diamonds and rubies and pearls in the world, and held them in one hand, and just put a little boy in the other, and the boy would be worth more than all the jewels. If you would tremble because you had $17,000 worth of jewels in the house one night, how would you go up to your Father and your son be not with you?

—**Gospel Herald**

"And five of them were wise, and five of them were foolish." This is what our Lord said about the ten virgins that took their lamps and went out to meet the Bridegroom. All ten virgins believed that the Bridegroom was coming. They were orthodox. They were really fundamentalists. They were looking for the Bridegroom. But five of them did not get into the marriage. They neglected the important thing. *They did not have oil in their lamps!* Orthodoxy is a good thing. It is wonderful to believe the Bible. It is a marvelous thing to be looking for the Lord to come. Yet, it is possible to have a sound creed and actually to look for the return of Jesus at any time and not be ready when He comes.—Dr. Bob Jones, Sr.

Some Day Will Be the Last

If I had died last night I wouldn't have had much to boast of in the day's work done. I am going to try to make other days better than yesterday was.

If YOU had died last night, what kind of day would have been chalked up for or against you? SOME DAY WILL BE THE LAST. It may be a day just around the corner.

Why not make every day that kind of day that you would wish to make your last day? When John Wesley was asked one Sunday what he would do that day if he knew it were his last day, he said, "I would go to the Sunday morning service and preach, just as I had planned; then Sunday afternoon I would fill my speaking engagement, and then visit the sick and the poor; then at night I would preach again, and after the last service of this full day I would go home and cast myself upon my bed, appealing as I do every night for the gracious protective mercy and care of God!" LET US LIVE EVERY DAY AS IF IT WERE THE LAST!

—J. B. Cranfill

Pertinent Points
By Dr. Bob Jones, Jr.

Like it or not, you have to live somewhere forever. So you had better learn how to live.

The men who move this world along right lines believe in an ever-present, real God.

Simplicity is truth's most becoming garb.

The Bible was never intended to teach men science, but the Bible is scientifically correct.

Beware of unreasonable people. Good men are always reasonable.

Beware of the man who "kowtows" to his superiors or who is rude to his inferiors.

Figure on the worst and hope for the best.

When in doubt, play safe.

Make stepping stones out of your stumbling stones.

Don't sacrifice the permanent on the altar of the immediate.

Make chariot wheels out of your difficulties and ride to success.

Jesus never taught men how to make a living. He taught men how to live.

Go as far as you can on the right road.

The right road always leads out at the right place.

The test of your character is what you would do if you knew nobody would ever know.

The measure of your responsibility is the measure of your opportunity.

Christians, Obey the Law!

A student of a Bible institute was travelling on a highway at a terrific rate of speed. Overtaken by a traffic cop, the student was ordered to curb his car. Timely and golden were the words spoken by the officer to the student. On the student's vehicle were printed the words, "Jesus Saves!" Said the officer, "Your wilful violation of the law; your endangering innocent lives, as well as your own, by the illegal and dangerous speed at which you were travelling, is greatly at variance with the words printed on your car, and brings no honor to the One of whom your motto speaks!"

W. B. Knight

Love in the Face and in the Heart

A missionary told how a young Chinese came seeking for baptism, and was asked how he had been saved. He said, "Years ago, in the Boxer uprising, I was one of those who stoned the 'foreign devils.' I threw a stone and hit a missionary, and the blood flowed from a wound down his leg. I was just rejoicing in the success of my stone, when I saw a most remarkable look come over the face of the missionary. It was a look of pity and of love, and I heard him say, 'Father, forgive them, for they know not what they do.' That look," he said, "has haunted me. And when I heard you had come with the same gospel message, I felt I must come and hear it."

Mental Confusion Due to Alcohol Indulgence

Alcohol the Destroyer

Abraham Lincoln's only sister, Sarah, married Aaron Grigsby. Two years later, when she was being attended in childbirth by a midwife, a complication arose which demanded a physician immediately. The nearest doctor who lived two miles away was summoned, but when he arrived he was so drunk that he had to be put to bed. Another doctor was sent for, but before he arrived Sarah and the baby died.

Dr. L. O. Dawson, in his address, "Alcohol in the Laboratory," tells of how when he was a lad his right hand was seriously wounded. The physician who dressed it had had one drink, and allowed a broken finger to slip. For the balance of his life he carried a crooked finger because a doctor had had one drink. Dr. Dawson cites the case of a friend whose doctor let his hand slip by a small fraction of an inch in cutting out a tonsil, and for that one drink the patient gave his life. Dr. Wilfred Grenfell, the famous Labrador physician, said, "I have seen ships lost through collision because the captain had been taking 'a little alcohol.'"

To these examples hundreds like them might be added. Thousands of innocent people have suffered and are suffering from drinking physicians, drinking drivers, or drinking motormen who should have been impelled from high considerations of public duty to keep their minds clear and alert.

Not Ashamed of Christ

I remember hearing a young convert who got up to say something for Christ in the open air. Not being accustomed to speak, he stammered a good deal at first, and when an infidel came right along and shouted out, "Young man, you ought to be ashamed of yourself, standing and talking like that." "Well," the young man replied, "I'm ashamed of myself, but I'M NOT ASHAMED OF CHRIST." That was a good answer.—Moody.

FORGIVENESS

A Scottish physician was noted for his skill and piety. After his death when his books were examined, several accounts had written across them in red ink: "Forgiven . . . too poor to pay."

His wife, who was of a different disposition, said: "These accounts must be paid." She therefore sued for the money.

The judge asked her, "Is this your husband's handwriting in red ink?"

She replied in the affirmative.

"Then," said he, "there's not a tribunal in the land that can obtain the money where he has written, 'Forgiven.'"

So likewise when Jesus writes the word "forgiven" across our account in the ledger of Heaven, we are released from condemnation.

A great many people are afraid of enthusiasm. If a man is enthusiastic they raise the cry, "Zeal without knowledge!" I should rather have zeal without knowledge than knowledge without zeal. I know men as wise as owls without any fire in their souls —and I can't understand how any man can realize his standing before God and not be on fire three hundred and sixty-five days in the year.—D. L. Moody.

What Is Love?

The Bible says, "And now abideth faith, hope, charity (love), these three; but the greatest of these is charity (love)." Love is greater than faith and hope, but love is not the greatest thing in the world. Truth is the greatest thing in the world. The Bible says God is love, but Jesus did not say, "I am the way, the *love*, and the life." He said, "I am the way, the *truth*, and the life." People are being led astray today by modernistic preachers and educators who say, "The trouble is we just do not love each other. We ought to have more love. Love is the greatest thing in the world." But these religious modernistic preachers and educators are not talking about Bible love. They are talking about a sentimental, diluted love. A mother does not love her children like a mother ought to love her children if she does not spank the children when they ought to be spanked. A mother who says, "I love my children too much to punish them," does not really have mother love. It is a watered-down, motherly sentiment. God so loved the world that He sent His Son to die on the Cross to save sinners. God makes it plain in the Bible that nobody, not even a Christian, can do wrong and get away with it.—Bob Jones, Sr.

Original Sin

We heard a colored preacher in Chicago relate a parable to illustrate the heriditary nature of sin and its essential tendency before grace brings about the change. He said a snake and a frog spent the winter together, hibernating in a den that belonged to the frog. When the warm showers of spring began to fall they came back to their normal life and the snake said to the frog, I am going to bite you. Then the frog queried, what harm have I ever done to you, and why are you going to bite me? The snake replied, no harm at all, I have no reason, but it's my nature. I can't help it, I am going to bite you.

Some folks are like the little boy who, when asked by his pastor if he prayed every day, replied, "No, not every day. Some days I don't want anything."

Fundamentalism
vs.
Modernism

The following summary of the belief of "Fundamentalists" and of "Modernists," shows the difference between their position on seven vital questions.

1. The Fundamentalist holds that the Bible is the word of God; the Modernist holds that the Bible contains the word of God.

2. The Fundamentalist holds that Jesus Christ is the Son of God in a sense in which no other is; the Modernist holds that Jesus Christ is a son of God in the sense that all men are.

3. The Fundamentalist holds that the birth of Jesus Christ was supernatural; the Modernist holds that the birth of Jesus Christ was natural.

4. The Fundamentalist holds that the death of Jesus was expiatory; the Modernist holds that the death of Jesus Christ was exemplary.

5. The Fundamentalist holds that man is the product of special creation; the Modernist holds that man is the product of evolution.

6. The Fundamentalist holds that man is a sinner, fallen from original righteousness and apart from God's redeeming grace, hopelessly lost; the Modernist holds that man is the unfortunate victim of environment, but through self-culture can make good.

7. The Fundamentalist holds that man is justified by faith in the atoning Blood of Christ. Result, supernatural regeneration from above. The Modernist holds that man is justified by works in following Christ's example. Result, natural development from within.

Gospel Truths, June, 53

HIS ONE MISTAKE

He wore his rubbers when it rained.

He brushed his teeth TWICE a day . . . with a nationally advertised toothpaste.

The doctors examined him twice a year.

He slept with the windows open.

He stuck to a diet with plenty of fresh vegetables.

He relinquished his tonsils and traded in several worn-out glands.

He golfed — but never more than 18 holes at a time.

He got at least eight hours' sleep every night.

He never smoked, drank or lost his temper.

He did his "daily dozen" daily.

He was all set to live to be a hundred.

The funeral will be held Wednesday. He's survived by eight specialists, three health institutions, two gymnasiums and numerous manufacturers of health foods and antiseptics.

He forgot God, lived as if this world were all, and is now with those who say, **"The harvest is past, the summer is ended, and we are not saved."** (Jeremiah 8:20).

For what shall it profit a man if he shall gain the whole world, and lose his own soul? Or what shall a man give in exchange for his soul? (Mark 8:36, 37).

Subtraction Sometimes Important, Also

When I talk about blessing I not only mean additions, but subtractions, too. A pastor came to one of his fellow pastors and said, "We've had a revival in our church." The other man replied, "That's good. How many were added to your church?" "None were added, but ten were subtracted." That's spiritual prosperity. It may mean subtraction. If some of our churches had the unconverted deacons subtracted, revival would come.

—Moody Monthly

Food for Thought

It is illegal to read the Bible in the public schools of Illinois, but a law requires the STATE to provide a Bible for every convict! Don't worry, kids, if you can't read the Bible in school, you'll be able to when you get to prison!
Baptist Beacon

12 Things to Learn

The value of time—
The need of perseverence—
The pleasure of serving—
The dignity of simplicity—
The true worth of character—
The power of kindness—
The influence of example—
The obligation of duty—
The wisdom of economy—
The virtue of patience—
The nobility of labor—
The teachings of Him who said,
   "Learn of Me."

—Selected.

Christian Friends

Thank you Lord
For Christian friends whose paths you've caused
To meet with mine, and those who've paused
To listen and advise,
Or only listen.

Thank you Lord
For making my path meet with their's
And for their laughter and their tears
That glisten and surmise,
Or only glisten.

Thank you Lord
The most for that One Friend that sticks
So close to me and always picks
My paths and Christian friends
He knows I need.

—Bill Harvey

Recipe for a Happy New Year

Take twelve fine, fullgrown months, see that these are
thoroughly free from all old memories of bitterness, rancor, hate
and jealousy; cleanse them completely from every clinging spite;
pick off all specks of pettiness and littleness; in short, see that
these months are freed from all the past—have them as fresh
and clean as when they first came from the great storehouse
of Time.

Cut these months into thirty or thirty-one equal parts. This
batch will keep for just one year. Do not attempt to make up
the whole batch at one time (so many persons spoil the entire
lot in this way) but prepare one day at a time, as follows:

Into each day put twelve parts of faith, eleven of patience,
ten of courage, nine of work (some people omit this ingredient
and so spoil the flavor of the rest), eight of hope, seven of fidelity, six of liberality, five of kindness, four of rest (leaving this
out is like leaving the oil out of the salad—don't do it), three of
prayer, two of meditation, and one well-selected resolution. If
you have no conscientious scruples, put in about a teaspoonful
of good spirits, a dash of fun, a pinch of folly, a sprinkling of
play, and a heaping cupful of good humor.

Pour into the whole love ad libitum and mix with a vim.
Cook thoroughly in a fervent heat; garnish with a few smiles and
a sprig of joy; then serve with quietness, unselfishness, and cheerfulness, and a Happy New Year will be a certainty.—H.M.S.

BUT WE SEE CHRIST

The world sees horror, desola-
tion
All confusion and frustration,
Naught ahead but condemna-
tion,
But we see Christ.

The world sees riches and am-
bition,
Dissipation, no contrition,
Seldom seeing their condition,
But we see Christ.

The world sees much and still
they're blind;
Carnal eyes and carnal mind
Make them so they seldom find
That they need Christ.

—Bill Harvey.

We thought the eagle was the National bird of America

Not the dove, shrinking from "confrontation" with
anybody and anything. Not some hawk.

The fearless American eagle.

But if the eagle is foolish enough to continue to strip
its much-needed wings to feather the nest of every other bird
in the world, it will soon be easy prey for the red necked
vulture who is interested only in tearing and devouring.

—An American Patriot.

"Will You Meet Me at the Fountain?"

ANCIENT ADVERTISEMENT

Miss Aline Barber of Ft. Mill, S.C. ran across a clipping from an ancient newspaper that told how want ads were worded in 1796:

Wanted for a sober family, a man of light weight, who fears the Lord and can drive a pair of horses. He must oocasionally wait at table, join in household prayer, look after horses and read a chapter in the Bible. He must, God willing, rise at 7 in the morning, and obey his master and mistress in all lawful commands; if he can dress hair, sing psalms and play cribbage, the more agreeable. N. B. He must not be familiar with the maid servants, lest the flesh should rebel against the spirit and he should be induced to walk in the thorny paths of the wicked. Wages 15 guineas a year (about $7 a month).

Many years ago when D. L. Moody was still busy in this country there, was an industrial exposition in Chicago. There was in the exposition ground a fountain which became the rendezvous for folk who arranged to meet each other. One would say to another, "Will you meet me at the fountain?" The answer was, "All right, I will meet you at the fountain."

P. P. Bliss, the gospel song writer, was allured with this meeting place. He wrote the gospel song based on it, lifting the thought from the meeting place in the exposition ground to that higher meeting place, and he wrote this:

Will you meet me at the fountain,
When I reach the glory-land?
Will you meet me at the fountain?
Shall I clasp your friendly hand?
Other friends will give you welcome;
Other loving voices cheer;
There'll be music at the fountain—
Will you, will you meet me there?

Will you meet me at the fountain?
For I'm sure that I shall know
Kindred souls and sweet communion,
More than I have known below;
And the chorus will be sweeter
When it bursts upon your ear,
And my Heaven seem completer,
If your happy voice I hear.

Will you meet me at the fountain?
I shall long to have you near,
When I meet my loving Saviour,
When His welcome words I hear.
He will meet you at the fountain,
His embraces I shall share;
There'll be glory at the fountain—
Will you, will you meet me there?

Her voice comes back to us this afternoon,
"Will you meet me there?" Can we say,
"Yes, I will meet you at the fountain,
At the fountain bright and fair;
Oh, I'll meet you at the fountain;
Yes, I'll meet you, meet you there"?

The natural man cannot judge anything spiritual by how it may look to him. We have to judge what we see by what God says about what we see. An evangelistic campaign that is sponsored by preachers who *believe* in the inspiration of the Bible and all the fundamentals of the faith and by preachers who *do not believe* in the inspiration of the Bible and all the fundamentals of the faith cannot be of God. God makes it plain in His Word that when orthodox, born-again Christians give Christian recognition to people who *do not believe* in the doctrines of Christ, those orthodox, born-again Christians are partakers of the evil deeds of the antichrist. Never mind how good the movement may look. You cannot judge by appearance. You have to judge by the Word of God. The need of this day is revival of faith in the absolute authority of the Bible, which is the Word of God. —Dr. Bob Jones, Sr.

It is not so much the greatness of our troubles, as the littleness of our spirit, which makes us complain.—*J. Taylor.*

Zacchaeus had short legs, but he outran the crowd when Jesus passed through town. Short legs will get you there as fast as long legs if you know how to use them. —*Dr. Bob Jones, Sr.*

When Daniel was faced with a decision,
It didn't take him long to declare;
He would rather sleep with a lion
Than to try to live without prayer.
—C. W. Renwick

Dr. A. C. Dixon of Spurgeon's Tabernacle once wrote, "When we rely on organization, we get what organization can do; when we rely on education, we get what education can do; when we rely on eloquence, we get what eloquence can do; and so on. I am not disposed to undervalue any of these things in their proper place--BUT WHEN WE RELY UPON PRAYER, WE GET WHAT GOD CAN DO!"

Old Friends

There are no friends like old friends,
　And none so good and true;
We greet them when we meet them,
　As roses greet the dew;
No other friends are dearer,
　Though born of kindred mold;
And while we prize the new ones,
　We treasure more the old.

There are no friends like old friends,
　Where'er we dwell or roam,
In lands beyond the ocean,
　Or near the bounds of home;
And when they smile to gladden,
　Or sometimes frown to guide,
We fondly wish those old friends
　Were always by our side.

There are no friends like old friends,
　To help us with the load
That all must bear who journey
　O'er life's uneven road!
And when unconquered sorrows,
　The weary hours invest,
The kindly words of old friends
　Are always found the best.

There are no friends like old friends,
　To calm our frequent fears,
When shadows fall and deepen
　Through life's declining years;
And when our faltering footsteps
　Approach the Great Divide,
We'll long to meet the old friends
　Who wait on the other side.

—David Banks Sickles.

Resolve to edge in a little reading every day. If you gain but 15 minutes a day, it will make itself felt at the end of a year.
--Horace Mann

God Has a Plan for Your Life Too!

Ephesians 2:10.

"The Lord had a job for me,
But I had so much to do
I said, 'You get somebody else
Or wait till I get through.'
I don't know how the Lord came out—
No doubt He got along;
But I felt kind o' sneakin' like!
I knew I'd done God wrong.

"One day I needed the Lord—
Needed Him right away;
But He never answered me at all,
And I could hear Him say,
Down in my accusin' heart,
'Child, I've got too much to do;
You get somebody else,
Or wait till I get through.'

"Now, when the Lord has a job for me,
I never try to shirk;
I drop what I have on hand
And do the Lord's good work,
And my affairs can run along
Or wait till I get through;
For nobody else can do the work
That God's marked out for you."
—Paul Lawrence Dunbar

Be careful for nothing;
Be prayerful for everything;
Be thankful for anything.
—D. L. Moody

There's never a rose in all the world
　But makes some green spray sweeter;
There's never a wind in all the sky
　But makes some bird wing fleeter;
There's never a star but brings to heaven
　Some silver radiance tender;
And never a rosy cloud but helps
　To crown the sunset splendor;
No robin but may thrill some heart,
　His dawn like gladness voicing;
God gives us all some small sweet way
　To set the world rejoicing.
Author Unknown

TOO LATE

I had heard this and read it before, but I ran across the other day this brief but tragic story as told by Dr. R. A. Torrey:

One evening when Mr. Alexander and I were in Brighton, England, one of the workers went from the afternoon meeting to a restaurant for his evening meal. His attention was drawn toward the man who waited upon him, and there came to his heart a strong impression that he should speak to that waiter about his soul, but that seemed to him such an unusual thing to do that he kept putting it off.

When the meal was ended and the bill paid, he stepped out of the restaurant, but had such a feeling that he should speak to that waiter that he decided to wait outside until the waiter came out. In a little while the proprietor came out and asked him why he was waiting. He replied that he was waiting to speak with the man who had waited upon him at the table. The proprietor replied, "You will never speak to that man again. After waiting upon you he went to his room and shot himself." Oh, men and women, there are opportunities open to every one of us tonight that will be gone, and gone forever, before another day dawns. The time is short!

"We have all eternity to celebrate the victories but only a few hours before sunset to win them."—Amy Carmichael.

41

PRAYER FOR RATTLESNAKES:

Once upon a time there was a family of wayward church members who had once been active, but had lost all interest and had fallen away. There were the father and three sons, Jim, John, Sam. The elders had talked to them about their lost condition, the preacher had visited them, and many of the brethren had tried to get them to come back to church—but all this did not seem to do the least bit of good.

One day when the boys were out in the pasture, a large rattlesnake bit John and he became very ill. The physician was called and after an examination, he pronounced John to be in a very critical condition. Said he, "About all you can do now, is pray." The father called the preacher, and told him of John's condition. He asked the preacher to pray for John's recovery and this was his prayer:

"O wise and righteous Father, we thank Thee, for Thou hast in Thy wisdom sent this rattlesnake to bite John, in order to bring him to his senses. He has not been inside the church house for years and it is doubtful that he has in all that time felt the need for prayer. Now we trust that this will prove a valuable lesson to him, and that it will lead to genuine repentance.

"And now, O Father, wilt Thou send another snake to bite Sam, and another to bite Jim, and another BIG ONE to bite the old man. We have all been doing everything we know for years to restore them, but to no avail. It seems, therefore, that all our combined efforts could not do what this snake has done. We thus conclude that the only thing left that will do this family any good is rattlesnakes; so Lord, send us bigger and better rattlesnakes. In the name of Jesus we pray. Amen."

(The Canadian Christian)

For Me

Under an Eastern sky
Amid a rabble cry,
A Man went forth to die
For me!

Thorn-crowned His blessed head,
Blood-stained His every tread,
Cross-laden on He sped,
For me!

Pierced through His hands and feet,
Three hours o'er Him did beat
Fierce rays of noontide heat,
For me!

Thus wert Thou made all mine.
Lord, make me wholly thine,
Give grace and strength divine
To me!

In thought and word and deed,
Thy will to do; oh! lead
My feet e'en though they bleed
To Thee.

—Author Unknown.

George Whitfield, when asked why he preached so often on the text, "Ye must be born again," replied that it was because YE MUST BE BORN AGAIN.

W. B. Knight

Neglected His Advice

Bozo, the noted clown of Ringling Brothers and Barnum and Bailey, spent his later years "performing for the American Cancer Society." He said: "I guess I've made a billion people laugh." His customary close of a show would be "Bye, bye now . . . and be sure to have your doctor check you for cancer." He knew the warning could mean their life, or death. But he fell ill himself and learned at his first checkup that he was hopelessly beyond help—with cancer. His own advice he had neglected.

SIMPLE

One day during the French revolution, a man remarked to Talleyrand, who was Bishop of Autun: "The Christian religion—what is it? It would be easy to start a religion like that."

"Oh, yes," replied Talleyrand. "One would only have to get crucified and rise again the third day."

—Christian Digest

Thy Word Is True

Dwight L. Moody was, at one time, in a southern city preaching about the value of the Word of God in a person's life. Suddenly he was interrupted by the loud voice of a man in the audience.

"Mr. Moody, I do not believe a single word in that collection of old wives' tales you call your Bible!"

"My dear man," replied Mr. Moody, "there is one verse in this Bible that you are forced to believe. 'Whatsoever a man soweth, that shall he also reap.' If a man sows wheat, he does not reap potatoes or peanuts. Take the saloonkeeper, for example. He sows drunkards, and he will reap drunkards."

The man sat down as the audience broke into loud applause. Mr. Moody, of course, did not know the man, but the audience did. He was a notorious, longtime, atheistic saloonkeeper, and all his children, both sons and daughters, were drunkards.—Selected.

"They can conquer who believe they can. He has not learned the lessons of life who does not every day surmount a fear." —Emerson.

42

SAM'S VERSION OF THE GOOD SAMARITAN

A colored man from one of the southern states desired to enter the ministry. He went to a minister to be examined and the following conversation took place:

"Can you read, Sam?"

"Nossah, ah can't read, sah."

"Can you write?"

"Well, no sah, ah can't write, but the ole 'ooman is a good writer."

"Well, do you know your Bible, Sam?"

"O, yassah, ah's purty smaht in de Bible, Sah."

"Tell me, what part of the Bible do you prefer?"

"Well, ah prefers the New Testament, sah."

"And what do you like in the New Testament, Sam?"

"De Book of Mark, sah."

"And what do you like especially about Mark?"

"Ah likes the parables de best sah."

"And which of the parables is your choice?"

"Well sah, de parable of de Good Samaritan is ma special favorite sah, ah likes dat one de best."

"Well, Sam, will you tell me the story of the Good Samaritan?"

"Yassah, I sho will suh." "Once upon a time a man was goin' from Jerusalem to Jericho and he fell among de thorns. De thorns grew up and choked him, an' he went on and didn't hab no money. An' he went to the Queen of Sheba, and she gave him one thousand talents of money and a hundred changes of raiment. An' den he got in a chariot an' drove fuiously. An' when he was driving under a big juniper tree, his har done got caught in de limb of de tree, and he hung dar, an' hung dar many days an' de ravens brought him food to eat an' water to drink, and afterward he was an hungred, an' he ate five thousan' loaves and two small fishes. An' one night while he was ahangin' dar, asleep, his wife Delilah came along an' cut off his har an' he dropped an' fell on stony ground. But he got up an' went on, an' it began to rain an' it rained forty days and forty nights an' he hid hisself in a cave, an' lived on locusts an' wild honey. Den he went on till he met a servant who said, 'Come take supper at mah house,' an' he began to make excuses an' said, 'No, I won't, I married a wife and I cain't go.' An' de servant went out in the highway and in de hedges an' compel him to come in. An' after supper he went on an' came to Jericho an' when he got dar he looked and saw Queen Jesebella sittin' a way up in a high window, an' she laffed at him, an' he said, 'throw her down,' an' they throwed her down, an' he said, 'Throw her down some mo', and so they thro' her down sebenty times seben. An' of the fragments they picked up twelve baskets full, and den dey say, 'Now in de razzerection who alls wife she gwine be?'"

Some people are so constituted that they would rather lose a friend than an argument. Be yourself, simple, honest, and unpretending, and you will enjoy through life the respect and love of friends.—Sherman.

A successful businessman, who faced many problems, has this motto on the wall of his office, "How great a God we have! Our God is so much greater than our greatest need."

Moody's Last Advice

It is reported that Moody's farewell words to his sons as he lay upon his deathbed were. "If God be your partner, make your plans large."

MOODY'S Coat-Tails

By Ivor Powell

One of the loveliest stories I have heard was told by an American minister preaching in Scotland. It concerned the visit of the great evangelist, D. L. Moody, to the church of which he was pastor. He described how the renown of the well-known evangelist had reached every part of the district; how old and young alike flocked to the great auditorium, and many people were won for Christ.

Then one evening a little boy came to the door and endeavoured to enter the church. He was tiny, dirty, and ragged. The steward on duty at the door stopped the lad and told him to go home. He should be in bed! When the boy explained that he desired to hear Mr. Moody the man remained adamant and refused to allow him to enter the church. Frustrated and greatly disappointed, the urchin walked a few yards down the street, and leaning against the building placed his hands to his eyes and wept.

Suddenly a carriage came to the door of the church and Mr. Moody alighted and prepared to enter the building. When he heard the child sobbing, he looked around, to see the boy leaning against the wall. Greatly interested and wondering what had caused the grief, he went along and said, "Son, what is the matter?"

The lad looked up and explained how he had desired to hear Mr. Moody, but the man at the door had refused to allow him inside.

The preacher smiled and answered, "Do you really want to hear Mr. Moody?"

"Yes, sir."

"Well, my boy, I know how you can get in. I know how you can pass the big fellow at the door. But mind, you will need to do all that I tell you. Are you willing?"

"Yes, sir."

The famous preacher took hold of his coat-tails, and pushed these into the hands of the youngster and said, "Sonny, if you hold on to these, I know you will get in. But remember, if you once let go, that big man will stop you again. Will you hold on?"

"Yes, sir."

"All right then; are you ready?"

"Yes, sir."

D. L. Moody entered the building and continued until he reached the platform. Probably he had no need to look back, for instantly he felt the pull of the boy's hands. When he finally reached the pulpit, he turned to say, "Well done. I told you that if you would only hold on, you would get in. Now, my boy, you sit there." He indicated the chair reserved for himself; and there, for the entire service, the boy sat and listened to the great preacher. The minister who told this delightful story to his Scottish audience added, "I know that story is true, for it happened in my church. Yes, I know it is true, because I was the little boy. I heard the great D. L. Moody, but little did I know, when I clung to his coat-tails, that some day I would become the minister of that same church."

When the small child seized Moody's coat-tails and refused to release his hold, no doorkeeper could interfere. No barriers prevailed against him, and it became Moody's task to deal with hindrances. And in like manner when we take hold of Christ, when we determine to follow Him at all costs to any lengths, when we refuse to let Him go, it becomes His delight to undertake for us.

—Ivor Powell, in "Bible Windows"

H. L. Mencken--and His "Apology"

H. L. Mencken, agnostic editor (several years ago) of *The American Mercury*, died an unbeliever. At his funeral, following his request, there was neither song nor sermon. During his life Mencken admitted he might be wrong in his views about God and the immortality of the soul. "But," he explained, "if I am wrong I will square myself when confronted in after life by the apostles with the simple apology: 'Gentlemen, I was wrong.'"

By this time Mencken has found out it isn't as simple as that. The time to repent and admit one is wrong is NOW, before death. *After death it is eternally too late to repent or "square one's self,"* if wrong. Five minutes after death every infidel, every agnostic, every unsaved person, will want to "repent" in the sense of wanting to get out of the place of torment he will find himself in (see Luke 16: 24, and context). Furthermore, Mencken will NOT be confronted "by the apostles," but in due season, at the judgment of the great white throne, he will STAND BEFORE GOD, and he will have no place to hide or retreat to. Brother, I wouldn't trade places with H. L. Mencken for all the gold in the universe. As long as one is alive, even though his record is stained deep with sin or unbelief, Christ will accept him if he comes to HIM. "Him that cometh to me I will in no wise cast out" (John 6:37). But after death the unbeliever has nothing to look forward to but "a certain fearful looking for of judgment and fiery indignation" (Heb.10:26).

—Editorial in *Christian Victory*

Released From Tithing?

Years ago a man knelt with his pastor, and prayed as he committed himself to God to tithe his income. His first week's pay was $10 and the tithe was $1. As he grew older he became more prosperous; his tithe was $7.50 a week, then $10. He moved to another city and his tithe was $100, then $200, then $500! He sent his pastor a wire, "Come to see me." The pastor arrived at the man's beautiful home. They had a good time talking over old times. Finally, the man came to the point. "Do you remember that promise I made years ago to tithe? How can I get released?"

"Why do you want to be released?"

"It's like this," the man replied, "when I made the promise I only had to give a dollar, but now it's $500! I can't afford to give away money like that."

The old pastor looked at his dear friend and said, "I'm afraid we cannot get released from the promise, but there is something we can do. We can kneel and ask God to shrink up your income again so you can afford to give a dollar."

"FINISH THE JOB"

One time a little girl asked Napoleon how many needles full of thread it took to make a shirt. Napoleon replied, "Only one if it is long enough." The reason it is necessary to stop and thread the needle is because the thread is not long enough to finish the job. Very few people have enough thread in their needles to finish an undertaking. On the wall of one of the rooms in the Bob Jones University is this motto, "Finish the job." The men who succeed in this world are men who stay with the proposition until the work is done. A lot of people are failures because they start a job, leave it, and start another one. Nothing is ever finished. That is one of the reasons so many brilliant people with a variety of gifts make a failure of life. It is well to develop all of our gifts; but when we are using one of the gifts, let us finish the job that that gift is supposed to do.

—Dr. Bob Jones, Sr.

Take Time

Be not in such a hurry to "do" that you forget to "be," so anxious to give out that you forget to take in. This is the haste that makes no speed.

Old Nat had a wood pile before him, and he sawed hard to make it smaller. His saw was dull, it needed sharpening, and resetting—it was dreadful work to make it go at all. Said a neighbor, "Nat, why don't you get that saw sharpened? you would do more work and do it easier."

"Now then," said Nat, "don't come bothering here. I've got enough to do without stopping to sharpen the saw."

The man who would do God's work, without taking time for prayer, reading, and study, will find his labor hard, discouraging, and fruitless.

—R. G. Holland, Bulletin.

Blood of Christ

Five persons were studying what were the best means to mortify sin. One said, to meditate on death; the second, to meditate on judgment; the third, to mediate on the joys of heaven; the fourth, to meditate on the torment of hell; the fifth, to meditate on the blood and sufferings of Jesus Christ; and certainly the last is the choicest and strongest motive of all. If ever we would cast off our despairing thoughts, we must dwell and muse much upon, and apply this precious blood to our own souls; so shall sorrow and mourning flee away.

—Brooks.

Recently I heard a radio pastor quote this beautiful poem: I wrote for a copy to share with you.

Tomorrow's Bridge

Tomorrow's bridge as I look ahead
Is a rickety thing to view;
Its piers are crumbled, its rails are down;
Its floor would let me through.
The chasm it spans is dark and deep,
And the waters foam and fret;
I have crossed that bridge a thousand times,
Though I have never reached it yet.

It has crashed beneath to let me through,
Although it is miles away;
But, strange, the bridges that I have crossed
Have all been safe today.
Perhaps I shall find when I reach the one
That lies in the distant blue,
Some hand may have mended its rickety floor,
And its piers may be staunch and new.

And I can pass over, light-hearted, free;
As a bird on the bouyant air;
Forgive me, God, for my fearful heart,
My anxious and foolish care.

Today's Wrong Emphasis

So far as is known, no bird ever tried to build more nests than its neighbor. No fox ever fretted because he had only one hole in the earth in which to live and hide. No squirrel ever died in anxiety lest he should not lay up enough nuts for two winters instead of one. And no dog ever lost sleep over the fact that he did not have enough bones buried in the ground for his declining years. So many people put the emphasis on the wrong things. The Bible says: "But seek ye first the kingdom of God and his righteousness; and all these things shall be added."—*Deland (Mich.) Church Bulletin*

You do not do God a favor by serving Him. He honors you by allowing you to serve Him.
—Victor Nyquist

When God says, "Come," He goes out to meet us. **When He says, "Go," He goes with us!**

Married to a Buzzard

Mother Dove and Father Dove were more than just proud of their little teen-age daughter. She was all they had, and their lives not only were centered around her, but all of their attention and devotion had been applied to her upbringing. They had taught her the value of a good, clean nest! They took her each Sunday morning to the Bible class run by the Right Reverend Hoot Owl. They had taken great pains to see that she was exposed to the finest of culture, and to the most honorable Ringneck sons of their friends.

But one day their little teen-age daughter told mother and father that she was old enough, now, to fly in the woods by herself! "All of my friends are laughing at me, the way I've become a little homebody!" she complained. So she took to flying, first in the neighborhood, then farther out each day, until finally she came across the carcass of a three-day dead rabbit. Above the carcass she saw young Cock Buzzard. "Why do you stoop so low at mealtime as to eat an old dead rabbit?" she cried, filled with horror! "Well, sweet thing," he replied, "I have never had a chance in life like you. My daddy was an old buzzard. My mamma was an old buzzard. In my neighborhood, all I had to run with were buzzards, and I have been pushed back in the corner of culture so long that I find myself doing things like this just from force of habit, and for survival." "But do you have the desire to change?" she asked. With eyes of lust he peered at her and croaked, "Oh, if only I had someone like you to watch over me, and teach me, and encourage me, I know I would change!" And with such words the old buzzard swept little dove off her twig.

Mother and Father Dove were horrified at the news! "But, daughter," cried Father Dove, "you hardly even know the young man!

And besides this—he is a BUZZARD!" "But, Daddy, that's just the thing; he has been treated like a buzzard all his life! He hasn't had a chance to be anything else. He has made efforts, so he told me, to fly with other birds, but they will have nothing to do with him. Whenever he tries to perch on the same limb as other birds, they all flee in horror! Don't you see, Father and Mother, he just needs love! And I love him, I am going to marry him, and take him to my little love nest, and make a new bird out of him!"

The wedding day was set. Of course, Mother and Father Dove were not there! Nor were Cousin Turtledove and Uncle Ringneck Dove. Even the black sheep of the Dove family, Nephew White Wing, refrained from attending. But the wedding was supplied with many guests! All the buzzards were there! And as buzzards do, they had invited their close friends to attend. There was the Raven family, and the Bluejay clan, along with old Amos Magpie. The best man, Billie Butcherbird, adjusted the tie of young groom Buzzard, and the procession began. Two crows seated the relatives present, and two members of the branch water kin sang, "I can't give you anything but love, baby!" as the lovely bride walked down the aisle!

They stood before Judge Bald Eagle, who turned to little Miss Turtle Dove and said, "Do you take this . . . er, ah, buzzard . . . to be your lawful wedded husband?" And the silly little thing cooed, "I do!" "And you, Buzzard; do you take this sweet little dove to be your lawful wedded wife?" and with eyes filled with lust, and with a wing crawling with lice wrapped around his lovely little bride, he croaked, "I do!"

Rice was thrown, and as they flew off for their honeymoon, little Mrs. Buzzard was heard to whisper to her bridesmaid, "I will take him to my little love nest now and you just wait and see the change in a week or two!"

All went well for a few days;

then, one night, Mr. Buzzard failed to come home. Little Dove waited anxiously. Hours turned into a day, and frantically she flew here and there looking for him! She went to their old dating tree, and seeing an old acquaintance she cried, "Have you seen my darling buzzard? Have you seen him? Have you seen him?" was her cry all that day, but each cry received no answer. He was nowhere to be found!

Then in desperation, Little Dove flew out to the old haunt where she had first met Mr. Buzzard, and to her horror, there he was! He and several of his cousins were perched on the carcass of an old dead horse, pulling rotten meat from its bones with their hooked beaks! With magots crawling on his feet, there stood her husband, fighting for his share! "Oh you promised me, darling, that you would never go back to this kind of life! You promised me! Haven't I been a good cook? Haven't I given you the love you lacked? And haven't I pulled you out of the corner and given you a chance?"

But the greedy eyes of the buzzard glanced her way just long enough to say: "Head for home, you silly dove you. I got what I wanted when you married me; now I want what I had besides! Go home to your mother if you want. Go on back to your church and their silly religion. Leave me alone. I'm hungry, and am satisfying myself with the kind of food I was made to eat!" And with the smell of putrefaction on him, he dug his beak into the sorry rotten flesh of the carcass and ate deeply, stopping only long enough to sigh and belch before eating again.

And with weary wing, languished heart, and broken spirit, Little Turtle Dove wept her way back to mother, crying, "You were right . . . you were right, he's just a sorry old buzzard."

Take note, dear reader: YOU JUST CAN'T REFORM AN OLD BUZZARD!

Phil Shuler

When your dog loves you because it is dinnertime, you are not sure of him; but when somebody else tempts him with a bone and he will not leave you, though just now you struck him, then you feel that he is truly attached to you. We may learn from dogs that true affection is not dependent upon what it is just now receiving. —Spurgeon.

Said an English mother to her son: "Charles, your father and I have trained you in righteousness. We have taught you the Word of God. We have lived a godly life before you. If you do not live a godly life, we will stand before God in the day of judgment, and bear witness against you!" That son became one of the world's greatest preachers—Charles H. Spurgeon.

It Does Matter

"It doesn't matter what you believe, as long as you are sincere." With great earnestness he said this to me as I looked into his blue eyes. Here was a man nearly sixty years of age—a good man—who apparently believed that sincerity was all that mattered between him and God.

But let's see if this is true. Mr. Johnson, feeling ill, went to the medicine cabinet and by mistake took the contents of a bottle of poison. An hour afterward he died in great agony. He thought he was taking medicine, but did his sincerity of belief save his life? Surely not.

The Smith family, out for a pleasure ride one Sunday afternoon, sincerely believed that the railroad tracks were clear. But several members of the family were hurled into eternity when the unseen train hit their auto.

Friend, sincerity is a noble virtue. Sincerity may help your friendships. Sincerity may make you a better neighbour. But when it comes to the matter of the salvation of your soul, your sincerity can send you to Hell.

The heathen are in great earnest as they worship images of wood, stone, silver and gold—but they worship false gods and are lost. Mohammedans stop work and drop on their knees wherever they may be and pray to Allah five times daily. Many of them are sincere—but they are lost.

A man's salvation or damnation depends on his belief. If he believes the lies of Satan, he will eternally perish; but if he believes the truth of God, he will be eternally saved. God plainly declares, "He that believeth on the Son hath everlasting life; he that believeth not the Son shall not see life, but the wrath of God abideth on him" (John 3:36).

If you think the pearly gates of Heaven will swing open for you because you are a good moral man or because of the good deeds you have done to merit eternal life, you may be sincere as the day is long, but you will certainly be lost. The Holy Scriptures declare: "For by grace are ye saved through faith; and that not of yourself: it is the gift of God: not of works" (Eph. 2:8, 9).

Yes, it makes a world of difference what you believe! The Holy Scriptures declare that you are utterly helpless to lift yourself toward God, that you have sinned and come short of His glory (Rom. 3:23). But the same Scriptures proclaim the wondrous news that you, as a sinner, can be saved through the Person and work of the Lord Jesus Christ: "For when we were yet without strength, in due time Christ died for the ungodly. . . . For the wages of sin is death but the gift of God is eternal life through Jesus Christ our Lord" (Rom. 5:6; 6:23).

It does matter what you believe. You are invited now to place your faith in the Lord Jesus Christ, the Son of God. "Neither is there salvation in any other; for there is none other name under heaven given among men, whereby we must be saved" (Acts 4:12).

Diaper Service

By Rep. Robert Michel (R.-Ill.)
(Congressional Record)

I take this time to call the attention of the House to a most interesting phase of the poverty program. I understand the Labor Department is going to spend $141,854 of the Manpower Development and Training Administration's funds to train 700 men in the art of diaper service. It may come as a shock to some that the government has uncovered a great shortage of didee service personnel. I do not believe it is the government's responsibility to train personnel for this industry.

But, of course, I realize that the poverty program must cover the waterfront. In this case it is pinning its hopes on a business that is in its infancy, but is generally picking up. Although there is continual danger of its folding at any time and, of course, if the bottom drops out, we will have an awful mess on our hands. There is, of course, the opportunity to clean up a bundle, as they say in the trade.

I bring this matter to the attention of the House solely to help us get to the bottom of this problem—at least in the infant wear division. There may be some who claim that the government is being rash by stepping into the diaper business and I tend to agree.

In conclusion, may I leave with you a thought borrowed from the slogan of the diaper industry—ladies and gentlemen, it's time for a change.

TO ALL PARENTS

"I'll lend you for a little time
   a child of mine," He said,
"For you to love the while she lives
   and mourn for when she's dead.
It may be six or seven years, or
   twenty-two or three,
But will you, till I call her back,
   take care of her for Me?
She'll bring her charms to gladden you,
   and shall her stay be brief,
"You'll have her lovely memories as
   solace for your grief.

"I cannot promise she will stay,
   since all from earth return,
But there are lessons taught down there
   I want this child to learn.
I've looked the wide world over
   in my search for teachers true,
And from the throngs that crowd life's lanes
   I have selected you.
Now will you give her all your love,
   nor think the labor vain,
Nor hate Me when I come to call and
   take her back again?"

I fancied that I heard them say:
   "Dear Lord, Thy will be done!
For all the joy Thy child shall bring,
   the risk of grief we'll run.
We'll shelter her with tenderness,
   and love her while we may,
And for the happiness we've known
   forever grateful stay;
But shall the angels call for her
   much sooner than we've planned,
We'll brave the bitter grief that comes,
   and try to understand."

—Edgar A. Guest

The youngest governor Minnesota ever had—late Governor John A. Johnson, said. "The man who influenced my career more than any other lived in our little home town. He lent me the right books; he taught me what to read and how. Much of what I am I owe to that man—and to those books."

None but God

By Missionary Mel Rutter

We were engaged in combat with the Japanese somewhere on the island of Luzon in the Philippines during World War II. My buddies and I were awaiting orders to go into combat. We read everything that was posted on the bulletin board to keep up with the news of other fronts. I read several news flashes and then my eyes fell upon an article that I could not believe; this was no article for any Army bulletin board. I read it again and the tears began to flow unabated down my cheeks; then, I read it the third time to make sure of what I had read.

The Allied Army (principally British) that had occupied the terrain north of Singapore had almost been driven out. However, there were a few scattered troops that were still being mopped up by the invading Japanese. They used their torture devices when the people would not give the information they desired concerning the whereabouts of the British. In this particular instance, they seized the Chieftain's wife and gave her the usual treatment of driving long splinters of bamboo under her fingernails and toenails. Even though this excruciating pain usually forced them to talk, she refused to tell anything.

Then the crafty Japanese officer noticed that a beautiful bright-eyed little girl seemed to be suffering along with the woman in her torture. He deducted correctly that this must be her daughter, and so devised a plan to torture her. He knew many times this worked when nothing else would.

So they built an intense fire, not like a bon fire for a picnic but just a bed of live coals over which danced white-hot flames of death. They looped a heavy rope and placed it under the armpits of the little girl. Then she was drawn up into the tree on a limb that protruded out and was suspended directly over the livid coals of fire. She was hanging so closely to the flames that the intense heat was not only causing her to perspire freely but causing the very juices of her body to ooze through her pores.

Then the Japanese officer asked the mother where the British had gone. "I will not tell!" was her quick retort. Then the officer drew out his cavalry sabre and very deftly cut a few strands of the rope. "Now where did they go?" he demanded angrily. "I will not tell!" shouted the mother. He cut a few more strands of the rope. This procedure was repeated several times until the rope was dangerously thin. Memories of happy days with her little girl and many plans for her future raced undisturbed through her mind as she quickly decided to talk. She was noticeably shaken as she saw her suffering such excruciating pain and knowing that at any moment she could fall into the torture-pit below and be burned alive before her very eyes. "I will tell you! I will tell you!" she screamed! The pains that she had suffered as they drove the bamboo under her nails had not caused her to talk but that was nothing to compare with the terrific tearing of her mother-heart as she saw her own little

daughter suffering such physical torture.

Up until this time the little girl had not made a single sound, but as she heard her mother scream out, "I will tell you!" she raised her tortured little face toward Heaven and even though it was twisted in suffering, there was a beautiful radiance as she called out, "Mommie, Mommie, don't tell them! Don't tell them! Jesus will take care of me!"

At that very instant a P-40 zoomed over from out of nowhere and sent the Japanese scampering for cover expecting strafing which never came. Strange enough the Japanese never returned to continue their torture and the mother was able to deliver her little daughter from the very jaws of death. Many reasons for the deliverance could be conjured up, but we who know the Lord Jesus as our own personal Saviour know that He was just protecting His little saint who had been faithful even in the face of death. It was NONE BUT GOD!

I was so "choked up" I could not explain to the others why I was crying: so, I turned and walked down toward my tent leaving them to read the article for themselves. I kept thinking, "The same yesterday, today, and forever," the same God who delivered His saints as recorded in His Holy Word. I was thinking also of the ones who had been allowed to die for His Glory—Stephen had looked up and said, "I see Jesus standing at the Father's right hand!" (Then closer home the five who were martyred on the sandy beach of the Curaray River in Ecuador only a few years ago). But these died that others might live! The Holy Spirit again used His bit and auger of love as He drilled deeply into my soul. I could hear His wee small voice saying, "Mel, somewhere back yonder was a real missionary, this time a Britisher, really born again, really called of God, really burdened for souls, and here is one of the products. This little native girl so loved her Saviour that she was willing to die for the British who had brought the Good News of Jesus to her."

Yes, just a little girl, but faithful! Friend, if you know Jesus as your own personal Saviour, how faithful are you? He has only asked that we be faithful. It is not our work, but His; we are not responsible for the results, only to listen to His leadings and do His will. Remember—we who are His blood-bought children are stewards of His grace, love, mercy, and Gospel. First Corinthians 4:2 says, "Moreover it is required in stewards, that a man be found faithful."

To realize the worth of the anchor we need to feel the storm.—Anon.

When Father Prays

When father prays he doesn't use
   The words the preacher does;
There's different things for dif-
   ferent days,
   But mostly it's for us.

When father prays the house is
   still,
   His voice is slow and deep.
We shut our eyes, the clock ticks
   loud,
   So quiet we must keep.

He prays that we may be good
   boys,
   And later on good men;
And then we squirm, and think
   we won't
   Have any quarrels again.

You'd never think, to look at Dad,
   He once had tempers, too.
I guess if father needs to pray,
   We youngsters surely do.

Sometimes the prayer gets very
   long
   And hard to understand,
And then I wiggle up quite close,
   And let him hold my hand.

I can't remember all of it,
   I'm little yet, you see;
But one thing I cannot forget,
   My father prays for me!

—*Author Unknown*

Prayer that is Persistent

There was once a godless seaman who was in a boat fishing with his godless companions when a storm came up which threatened to sink the ship.

His companions begged him to offer a prayer; but he demurred, saying it was years since he had prayed or entered a church. But, finally, upon their insistence, he made this prayer: "O Lord, I have not asked You for anything for fifteen years, and if You deliver us out of this storm and bring us safe to land again, I promise that I will not bother You again for another fifteen years."

Too frequently this is the manner in which we pray. We get in a tight spot, and we call upon God. But once deliverance comes, we cease to plead the promises. Oh, that we might persistently lay hold of God's strength.

—Selected

WASHINGTON'S HUMILITY

A rider on horseback, many years ago, came across a squad of soldiers who were trying to move a heavy piece of timber. A corporal stood by, giving lordly orders to "heave." But the piece of timber was a trifle too heavy for the squad.

"Why don't you help them?" asked the quiet man on the horse, addressing the important corporal.

"Me? Why, I'm a corporal, sir!" Dismounting, the stranger carefully took his place with the soldiers.

"Now, all together, boys— heave!" he said. And the big piece of timber slid into place. The stranger mounted his horse and addressed the corporal.

"The next time you have a piece of timber for your men to handle, corporal, send for the commander-in-chief."

The horseman was George Washington.

Today

One today is worth two tomorrows.—Benjamin Franklin.

Tomorrow life is too late: live today.—Martial.

Be wise today; 'tis madness to defer.—Young.

We know nothing of tomorrow; our business is to be good and happy today.—S. Smith.

Again he limiteth a certain day, saying in David: "To day, after so long a time; as it is said, To day, if ye will hear his voice, harden not your hearts."—Bible.

Tomorrow

Tomorrow do thy worst, for I have lived today.—Dryden.

Boast not thyself of to morrow; for thou knowest not what a day may bring forth.—Bible.

Tomorrow the dreams and flowers will fade.—Moore.

Tomorrow even may bring the final reckoning.—Spurgeon.

Tomorrow comes, and we are where? Then let us live today.— Schiller.

To human hearts what bolder thoughts can rise than man's presumption on tomorrow's dawn? Where is tomorrow?—Young.

Tomorrow!—it is a period nowhere to be found in all the hoary registers of time, unless perchance in the fool's calendar.—Colton.

There is no tomorrow; though before our face the shadow named so stretches, we always fail to o'ertake it, hasten as we may.—Margaret J. Preston.

(From *Western Messenger*)

It is no humility for a man to think less of himself than he ought, though it might rather puzzle him to do that.
—Spurgeon.

HIDDEN MESSAGES THAT MEAN WHAT THEY SAY!

There are no crown-wearers in Heaven that were not cross-bearers here below.
—Spurgeon

Around the dial of a clock in a church in Strasburg, Germany, are these words: "One of these hours the Lord is coming."

Prayer is a serious thing. We may be taken at our words.—D. L. Moody

"The Devil is never too busy to rock the cradle of a sleeping saint."

"When you 'bury the hatchet' don't leave the handle sticking out!"

The wages of sin have never been reduced.

Speak kindly today; when tomorrow comes you will be in better practice.

I like to hear a man preach like he were fighting bumble-bees.—Lincoln

Never put a question mark where God has put a period.

A S. S. teacher is late unless he's a half-hour early.

The cure for crime is not the electric chair but the high chair.
—Edgar Hoover.

The Pig and the Cow

A pig was lamenting his lack of popularity. He complained to the cow that people were always talking about the cow's gentleness and kind eyes, whereas his name was used as an insult.

The pig admitted that the cow gave milk and cream, but maintained that pigs gave more. "Why," the pig complained, "We pigs give bacon and ham and bristles, and people even pickle our feet. I don't see why you cows are esteemed so much more."

The cow thought awhile and said gently, "Maybe it's because we give while we're still living."

Unpalatable

A missionary fell into the hands of cannibals. "Going to eat me, I presume?" asked the missionary. The chief grunted. "Don't do it," he advised, "you won't like me." Thereupon the missionary took out a knife, sliced a piece from the calf of his leg and handed it to him. "Try this and see for yourself." The chief took one bite and choked. The missionary worked on the island for fifty years. He had a cork leg!—Sunday.

A Thanksgiving Offering

The parents of a young man who was killed in World War I gave their church a check for two hundred dollars as a memorial to their loved one. When the presentation was made, another war mother whispered to her husband, "Let us give the same for our boy."

The father said, "Why, what are you talking about? Our boy didn't lose his life."

The mother said, "That's just the point. Let us give it because he didn't."

Every dissipation of youth must be paid for with a draft on old age.—Dr. Bob Jones, Sr.

Never be afraid to trust an unknown future to a known God.

I don't care how loud a brother shouts and how high he jumps just so he walks straight when he comes down.—Bud Robinson

If you would not be forgotten as soon as you are dead, either write things worth reading or do things worth writing.
—Franklin

No angel rolls away the stones
Of cowardice and greed.
It is our strength and ours alone
Can answer for that need.
—Kenneth W. Porter

In the last four thousand years of history, there have been but 268 years entirely free of war.
—Coronet

"Heaven is above all yet; there sits a Judge That no king can corrupt."
—Shakespeare

It has been related that a missionary came to Mr. D. E. Hoste saying: "Pray that I may be nothing." In reply Mr. Hoste said: "Brother, that prayer is answered.

Statistics show that 10,000 people are killed by liquor where only one is killed by a mad dog; yet we shoot the dog and license the liquor. What sense is there to this?
—Bible Crusaders News

Henry Clay Was Not Sleepy

Henry Clay, the great American statesman and orator, once lodged overnight at a humble cabin in his native state of Kentucky. The family was in the habit of holding worship morning and evening, but the father trembled at the thought of doing so in the presence of a guest so distinguished. The children were becoming sleepy, and the wife, by significant gestures, suggested that the time for prayer had come. The man hinted to his guest that perhaps he would like to go to bed. But Mr. Clay with great politeness said that he did not feel at all sleepy, and that, unless it was intrusive, he would be happy to enjoy the company of his host longer. Of course the man could not object. Still the matter of prayer could not be postponed without sending the children to bed contrary to their settled custom.

At last, with considerable trepidation, the father told his guest that he could stay and unite in their devotions or retire at his option. Mr Clay promptly replied that he would remain.

When the wonted exercises, gone through with much fear and trembling, were over, Mr. Clay, with no little feeling, approached the man and said, "My dear sir, never again feel the least hesitation in the discharge of your duty to God on account of the presence of man. I saw your embarrassment, and remained on purpose that you might never feel it again. Remember that every man of sense will respect the individual who is not ashamed to acknowledge his dependence upon his Maker; and he deserves only contempt who can cherish any other feelings than reverence for 'the consecrated hour of man in audience with Deity.' I would rather know that the prayers of a pious man, no matter how humble his position in life, were ascending in my behalf than to have the wildest applause of listening senators." Mr. Clay then retired for the night. The man remarked that it was the best lesson of his life.

"What do you do during the day?" a friend asked an elderly Scotch woman who lived alone. "Well," she said, "I get my hymnbook and sing. Then I get the Bible and let the Lord speak to me. When I get tired of reading and cannot sing anymore, I just sit still and let the Lord love me!"—W. B. Knight

"My Grace Is Sufficient for Thee"

Charles Spurgeon told this story:

"The other evening I was riding home after a heavy day's work. I felt very wearied, and sore distressed, when swiftly, and suddenly as a lightning flash, that text came to me: 'My grace is sufficient for thee.' I reached home and looked it up in the original, and at last it came to me in this way, 'My grace is sufficient for thee,' and I said, 'I should think it is, Lord,' and burst out laughing. I never fully understood what the holy laughter of Abraham was till then. It seemed to make unbelief so absurd. It was as though some little fish, being very thirsty, was troubled about drinking the river dry, and Father Thames said, 'Drink away, little fish; my stream is sufficient for thee.' Or it seemed like a little mouse in the granaries of Egypt, after the seven years of plenty, fearing it might die of famine; and Joseph might say, 'Cheer up, little mouse, my granaries are sufficient for thee.' Again, I imagined a man away up yonder, in a lofty mountain saying to himself, 'I breathe so many cubic feet of air each year, I fear I shall exhaust the oxygen in the atmosphere,' but the earth might say, 'Breathe away, O man, and fill thy lungs ever; my atmosphere is sufficient for thee.'

"Oh, brethren, be great believers! Little faith will bring your souls to heaven, but great faith will bring heaven to your souls."

How He Did It

A Chinaman brought a number of his friends to the mission. When asked how he succeeded in getting so many to come, he said, "I got on my knees and talkee, talkee, talkee. Then I got up and walkee, walkee, walkee." Pray and then work. Prayer without works is vain. Praying without working like working without praying, is dead. Let us all talkee and walkee.

— *Gospel Herald*

CHOICE

Work or starve—Mose and Liza were married but a short time when he came home with a washboard, washtub and a three-foot mirror.

"What's all de truck you brung home?" asked Liza.

Mose replied, "Now yo kin take yo' pick. Yo' can take de tub an' washboard an' go to work, or yo' can take de mirror and watch yo'se'f starve to death."

We are by Christ redeemed;
The cost—His precious blood:
Be nothing by our souls esteemed
Like this great good.

Were the vast world our own
With all its varied store,
And Thou, Lord Jesus, wert unknown,
We still were poor.

The Clearer Vision

When, with bowed head,
And silent-streaming tears,
With mingled hopes and fears,
To earth we yield our dead;
The saints, with clearer sight,
Do cry in glad accord,
"A soul released from prison
Is risen, is risen—
Is risen to the glory of the Lord."
—John Oxenham

"What Think Ye of Christ?"

YOUTH: Too happy to think—time enough!

MANHOOD: Too busy to think—more money first.

MATURITY: Too anxious to think—worry over work!

DECLINING YEARS: Too aged to think—fixed habits.

AS DEATH APPROACHES: Too ill to think—weak and suffering.

DEATH: Too late to think—the spirit has flown.

ETERNITY: Forever to think—God's judgment day.—Prov. 17:1.

A man found an Indian wandering aimlessly in the woods and asked, "Are you lost?" The Indian replied. "No! No! Indian not lost. Wigwam lost!" How like that Indian are many who are too proud to acknowledge their lostness and to pray: "God bo merciful to me a sinner!"—
W. B. Knight

"The Wicked Shall Be Turned Into Hell"

By Bishop J. C. Ryle

Let others hold their peace about Hell if they will: I dare not do so. I see it plainly in Scripture, and I must speak of it. I fear that thousands are on that broad road that leads to it, and I would fain arouse them to a sense of the peril before them.

What would you say of the man who saw his neighbor's house in danger of being burned down, and never raised the cry of "Fire"? Call it bad taste if you like, to speak of Hell. Call it charity to make things pleasant and speak smoothly, and soothe men with a constant lullaby of peace. From such notions of taste and charity may I ever be delivered! My notion of charity is to warn men plainly of their danger. My notion of taste is to declare all the counsel of God. If I never spoke of Hell, I should think I had kept back something that was profitable, and should look on myself as an accomplice of the Devil.

Beware of new and strange doctrines about Hell and the eternity of punishment. Beware of manufacturing a God of your own—a God who is all love, but not holy—a God who has a Heaven for everybody, but a Hell for none—a God who can allow good and bad to be side by side in time, but will make no distinction between good and bad in eternity. Such a God is an idol of your own, as really as Jupiter or the monstrous image of Juggernaut—as true an idol as was ever molded out of brass or clay. The hands of your own fancy and sentimentality have made him. He is not the God of the Bible; and besides the God of the Bible there is no God at all. Your heaven would be no heaven at all. A heaven containing all sorts of characters mixed together indiscriminately would be miserable discord indeed. Alas for the eternity of such a heaven! There would be little difference between it and Hell. Ah reader, there is a Hell! Take heed lest you find it out too late.

Beware of being wise above that which is written. Beware of forming fanciful theories of your own, and then trying to make the Bible square with them. Beware of making selections from your Bible to suit your taste—refusing, like a spoilt child, whatever you think is bitter—seizing, like a spoilt child, whatever you think sweet. What is all this but taking Jehoiakim's penknife and cutting God's Word to pieces? What does it amount to but telling God that you, a poor, short-lived worm, know what is good for you better than He? It will not do; it will not do. You must take the Bible as it is. You must read it all, and believe it all. You must come to the reading of it in the spirit of a little child. Dare not to say, "I believe this verse, for I like it; I receive this, for I can understand it; I refuse that, for I cannot reconcile it with my views." "Nay, but, O man, who art thou that repliest against God?" By what right do you talk in this way? Surely it were better to say, over every chapter in the Word, "Speak, Lord, for thy servant heareth." Ah reader, if men were to do this, they would never try to throw overboard the doctrine of the eternal punishment of the wicked. *"And these shall go away into everlasting punishment; but the righteous into life eternal"* (Matt. 25:46).

The Bible

Born in the East and clothed in oriental form and imagery, the Bible walks the ways of all the world with familiar feet and enters land after land to find its own everywhere. It has learned to speak in hundreds of languages to the hearts of men. It comes into the palace to tell the monarch that he is a servant of the Most High, and into the cottage to assure the peasant that he is a son of God.

Children listen to its stories with wonder and delight, and wise men ponder them as parables of life.

It has a word of peace for the time of peril, a word of comfort for the time of calamity, a word of light for the hour of darkness. Its oracles are repeated in the assembly of the people and its counsels whispered in the ear of the lonely.

The wicked and the proud tremble at its warnings, but to the wounded and the penitent it has a mother's voice. The wilderness and the solitary place have been made glad by it, and the fire on the hearth has lit the reading of its well-worn page.

It has woven itself into our dearest dreams; so that love, friendship, sympathy and devotion, memory and hope, put on the beautiful garments of its treasured speech, breathing of frankincense and myrrh.

No man is poor or desolate who has this treasure for his own. When the landscape darkens and the trembling pilgrim comes to the Valley named in the Shadow, he is not afraid to enter; he takes the rod and the staff of Scripture in his hand; he says to friend and comrade: "Good-bye, we shall meet again," and comforted by that support, he goes toward the lonely pass as one who walks through darkness into light.

—Henry Van Dyke

Compromise

A man starting in the fish business hung out a sign, "Fresh Fish for Sale Today" and invited his friends to the opening. They all congratulated him on his enterprise, but one suggested his sign might be improved. Said he, "Why the 'Today'? Of course it's today, not yesterday or tomorrow." So the fishmonger removed the word. Another said, "Why the 'For Sale'? Everybody knows that, else why the store?" And off came the words. Another complained, "Why the word 'Fresh'? Your integrity guarantees every fish to be fresh." Finally, only 'Fish' remained, but an objector said, "Why the sign? I smelled your fish two blocks away!"

The church that tries to satisfy everybody ends up by pleasing nobody. Put up your sign and stand by it!

—J. H. Dampier

Pastor's Postscript

Fred Somebody, Thomas Everybody, Pete Anybody, and Joe Nobody were neighbors, but they were not like you and me. They were odd people and most difficult to understand. The way they lived was a shame. All four belonged to the same church, but you couldn't have enjoyed worshipping with them. *Everybody* went fishing on Sunday or stayed home to visit with friends. *Anybody* wanted to worship but was afraid *Somebody* wouldn't speak to him so *Nobody* went to church. Really, *Nobody* was the only decent one of the four. *Nobody* did the visitation. *Nobody* worked on the church building. Once they needed a Sunday School teacher. *Everybody* thought *Anybody* would do it! and *Somebody* thought *Everybody* would teach. Guess who did it? That's right . . . *Nobody* . . . It happened that a fifth neighbor (an unbeliever) came to live among them. *Everybody* thought *Somebody* should try to win him; *Anybody* could have at least made an effort. Guess who finally won him to Christ? . . . *Nobody*.

—Copied

God Only

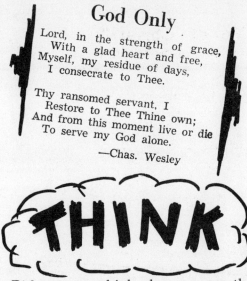

Lord, in the strength of grace,
With a glad heart and free,
Myself, my residue of days,
I consecrate to Thee.

Thy ransomed servant, I
Restore to Thee Thine own;
And from this moment live or die
To serve my God alone.

—Chas. Wesley

THINK

Did you ever think when you see the hearse go by, that sooner or later you and I shall take a ride in that somber hack without a thought of coming back?

Did you ever think when in the quest of gold, a dead man's hand no dollar can hold; that you may strive and skimp and save but you must leave it all this side of the grave? Did you ever think when in the quest of fame, a lofty title, a sounding name, that you owe your life to Him who gave, and that you must answer beyond the grave?

Ah, yes, I have thought of hearse and fame, a lofty title and sounding name and I have thought again of that home over there and the joys for me to share if I but give my life to the Master's cause, observe His precepts and obey His laws, giving my life to Him who lent in peaceful quiet content.

—Ben Smith

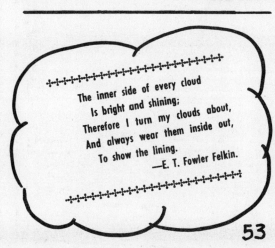

The inner side of every cloud
Is bright and shining;
Therefore I turn my clouds about,
And always wear them inside out,
To show the lining.
—E. T. Fowler Felkin.

Wanted — A Worker

God never goes to the lazy or to the idle when He needs men for His service. When God wants a worker He calls for a worker. When He has a work to be done. He goes to those who are already at work. When God wants a great servant, He calls a busy man. Scripture and history attest this truth.

Moses was busy with his flocks at Horeb.

Gideon was busy threshing wheat by the press.

Saul was searching for his father's lost beasts.

David was busy caring for his father's sheep.

Elisha was busy ploughing with twelve yoke of oxen.

Amos was busy following the flock.

Nehemiah was busy bearing the king's wine cup.

Peter and Andrew were busy casting a net into the sea.

James and John were busy mending their nets.

Matthew was busy collecting customs.

Saul was persecuting the friends of Jesus.

William Carey was busy mending and making shoes.

No Time to Pray

No time to pray!
Oh, who so fraught with earthly care
As not to give to humble prayer
Some part of day?

No time to pray!
What heart so clean, so pure within,
That needeth not some check from sin,
Needs not to pray?

No time to pray!
'Mid each day's danger, what retreat
More needful than the mercy-seat?
Who need not pray?

No time to pray!
Then sure your record falleth short;
Excuse will fail you as resort,
On that last day.

What thought more drear,
Than that our God His face should hide,
And say through all life's swelling tide,
No time to hear!

—Anonymous

From *Inspirational & Devotional Verse* Compiled by Dr. Bob Jones, Jr.

John Bunyan on Prayer

We have run across a few lines on the subject of prayer, written by John Bunyan, the author OF PILGRIM'S PROGRESS, the world's second "best-seller," the Bible being the first, of course. Here is what Bunyan wrote:

"When thou prayest, rather let thy heart be without words, than thy words without thy heart."

"Prayer will make a man cease from sin, or sin will entice a man to cease from prayer."

"Prayer is a shield to the soul, a sacrifice to God, and a scourge for Satan."

Most of us could pray more than we do. Prayer is exercise for the soul and should be as normal for the spiritual man as breathing is for the physical man. Too many of us cease without praying, when we should pray without ceasing. Let us pray fervently—with more heart than words, but with both directed by the Holy Spirit.

THE TWINS

In form and feature, face and limb,
　I grew so like my brother,
That folks got taking me for him,
　And each for one another.
It puzzled all our kith and kin,
　It reached an awful pitch;
For one of us was born a twin,
　Yet not a soul knew which.

One day (to make the matter worse),
　Before our names were fixed,
As we were being washed by nurse
　We got completely mixed;
And thus, you see, by Fate's decree,
　(Or rather nurse's whim),
My brother John got christened ME,
　And I got christened HIM.

This fatal likeness even dogg'd
　My footsteps when at school,
And I was always getting flogg'd,
　For John turned out a fool.
I put this question hopelessly
　To every one I knew--
What WOULD you do, if you were me,
　To prove that you were YOU?

Our close resemblance turned this tide
　Of my domestic life;
For somehow my intended bride
　Became my brother's wife.
In short, year after year the same
　Absurd mistake went on;
And when I died--the neighbors came
　And buried brother John!

　　　　　　　--Henry S. Leigh

"My Album . . . Savage Breasts!"

Robert Moffat, father-in-law of David Livingston, being asked to write in a lady's album, penned the following lines:

"My album is in savage breasts
Where passion reigns, and darkness rests
　Without one ray of light:
To write the name of Jesus there,
To point to worlds both bright and fair,
And see the pagan bow in prayer,
　Is all my soul's delight."
　　　　　　—*Western Recorder*

Sneeringly a young man said to a Christian who had given him a tract, "Tracts everywhere!" "No," answered the Christian, "there are no tracts in hell!"

Madame Guyon, a refined, cultured and exceedingly beautiful woman; yet for Christ's sake, was exposed to the indignities and tortures of the French prisons for ten years—1695-1705. Why? Because she loved the Lord Jesus Christ and was determined to serve Him. While she was in prison she wrote that exquisite poem so filled with thought:

A little bird I am
Shut from the fields of air;
Yet in my cage I sit and sing
To Him who placed me there;
Well pleased a prisoner to be,
Because my God, it pleases Thee.

Naught have I else to do;
I sing the whole day long;
And He whom most I love to please,
Doth listen to my song;
He caught and bound my wandering wing
But still He bends to hear me sing.

My cage confines me round;
Abroad I cannot fly.
But though my wing is closely bound,
My heart's at liberty,
My prison walls cannot control
The flight, the freedom of the soul.

Oh, it is good to soar
These bolts and bars above,
To Him whose purpose I adore,
Whose Providence I love;
And in Thy mighty will to find
The joy, the freedom of the mind.

God has been very merciful to some of us in never letting money come rolling in upon us, for most men are carried off their legs if they meet with a great wave of fortune. Many of us would have been bigger sinners if we had been trusted with larger purses.—Spurgeon.

The ability of God is beyond our prayers, beyond our largest prayers! I have been thinking of some of the petitions that have entered into my supplications innumerable times. What have I asked for? I have asked for a cupful and the ocean remains! I have asked for a sunbeam, and the sun abides! My best asking falls immeasurably short of my Father's giving; it is beyond that we can ask or think. —J. H. Jowett.

No Answer

While contending with the manifold problems of geography and climate in the building of the Panama Canal, Colonel George Washington Goethals had to endure the carping criticism of countless busybodies back home who freely predicted that he would never complete his great task. But the resolute builder pressed steadily forward in his work and said nothing.

"Aren't you going to answer your critics?" a subordinate inquired.

"In time," Goethals replied.

"How?"

The great engineer smiled. "With the canal," he replied.

—Adrian Anderson

Being Busy— Not a Sin

Samuel Johnson paid a high, though unintended, compliment to John Wesley: "His conversation is good, but he is never at leisure. He always has to go at a certain hour. This is very disagreeable to a man who loves to fold his legs and have his talk out as I do." John Wesley's legs were "unfolded" most of his ninety years. He had felt his Master's passion for souls, and sought to save the lost.

—From Christian Word

Alcohol—They Said It

Shakespeare: "Alcohol is a poison men take into the mouth to steal away the brain."

Gladstone: Strong drink is "more destructive than war, pestilence and famine."

Sir Wilfred Lawson: "The devil in solution."

Abraham Lincoln: "A cancer in human society, eating out its vitals and threatening its destruction."

Robert Hall: "Distilled damnation."

Lord Chesterfield: "An artist in human slaughter."

Ruskin: "The most criminal and artistic method of assassination ever invented by the bravos of any age or nation."

General Pershing: "Drunkenness has killed more men than all of history's wars."

General Robert E. Lee: "My experience thru life has convinced me that abstinence from spiritous liquors is the best safeguard to morals and health."

President Taft: "He who drinks is deliberately disqualifying himself for administration."

Five Ways to Get Rid of Your Pastor

1. Sit up front, smile, and say "Amen" every time he says something good. He will preach himself to death.

2. Pat him on the back and tell him what good work he is doing in the church and community. He will work himself to death.

3. Increase your offering to the church. He will suffer from shock.

4. Tell him you've decided to join the visitation group and help win souls for the Lord. He will probably suffer a heart attack.

5. Get the whole church to band together and pray for him. He will get so efficient that some other church will hear about him and give him a call. That will take him off your hands.

> God judges what we give by what we keep.
> --George Muller

RECIPE
(For Getting to Sunday School on Time)

Set that clock,
Iron that frock
Saturday night.
   Shine those boots,
   Press those suits
   Saturday night.
      Sew that button,
      Roast that mutton
      Saturday night.
         Lesson read,
         Early to bed
         Saturday night.
—Selected.

HOW SIR WALTER SCOTT WORKED

Sir Walter Scott put in fifteen hours a day at his desk, rising at four o'clock in the morning. He averaged a book every two months, and turned out the "Waverly Novels" at the rate of one a month. Fritz Kreisler, despite his native genius, finds it necessary to devote eight to ten hours a day to practise. One of the Wesleys preached three sermons a day for fifty-four years, traveled 290,000 miles by horseback and carriage, wrote more than eighty different works on many subjects and edited a fifty volume library.

—Gospel Herald

Not After the Pattern

Some time ago a Salvation Army captain preached in Hyde Park (London) when a man in the crowd interrupted him. "We haven't anything agin' Jesus of Nazareth," said the interrupter, "but we have something agin' you Christians because you ain't up to sample."

THE CHRISTIAN HOME

The importance of the home cannot easily be overstated. It is the great world-fountain of health or disease, of medicine or poison. It is God's best workshop or the devil's best forge. It is a supreme factor in the salvation or ruination of our race. It is a determining factor in the solution of many problems.

As is the home, so will be the church, the state, and the nation. By weakening the pillars of the home in the "interest" of the state, ancient Greece sealed its own doom. Because of corruption in the families, the boasted civilization of Rome could not endure. And today the threads of destiny of our own nation are being silently woven within the narrow confines of our family circles. Upon the walls of every institution which fails to include in its reckoning the home, no matter how glowing its prospects may seem, no matter how sumptuous and hilarious its feasting may be there is traced by secret hand the writing: "Thou hast been weighed in the balance and found wanting."

In the home where the Gospel of Jesus Christ lives and reigns there will be a consciousness of the immeasurable privilege of true parenthood. A greater and holier work can scarcely be imagined than to build a home, to correctly rear a family, to root and ground one's own in the truth, and to send them out as living epistles to glorify their God and serve their fellowmen. A neighbor once asked a mother, "Do you do any literary work?"

"Yes," she replied, "I am writing two books."

"What are their titles?"

"John and Mary," she answered. "My business is to write upon the hearts and minds of my children the lessons they will never forget."

GENERAL Policy

It is a good story, and it illustrates the point:

A centipede with arthritis sought the advice of a wise old owl.

"Centipede," the owl said, "you got a hundred legs, all swollen up with arthritis. Now if I was you, I'd change myself into a stork. With only two legs, you'll cut your pain ninety-eight per cent, and if you use your wings you can stay off your legs."

The centipede was elated. "I accept your suggestions without hesitation, Owl," he said. "Now, just tell me specifically, how do I go about making this change?"

"Oh," said the owl, "I wouldn't know about the details. I'm in general policy."

A backslidden radio preacher was once asked about certain details of worldly dress, make-up, cosmetics, etc. His "wise-old-owl" reply was, "Whatsoever you do, do all to the glory of God." His answer was not unscriptural, but it was only "general policy." He was cleverly careless "about details."

There is a woeful lack of "details" in modern fundamental preaching. Why give only "general policy"? Don't plead ignorance "about details." When it comes to doctrine, you say, "The Bible says." When you come to duty and detail, do not shun the cross. Be specific. Why not say, "The Bible says." You know it says plenty.

Consider the glorious *doctrines* of Romans 1 to 8. Next note the practical *duties* and *details* of Romans 12. Do not say there are no specific commandments in the New Testament. There are some "forty distinct commandments" in Romans 12. Preachers of "General Policy" only are usually Pussyfooters. First, preach good Doctrine, then be just as faithful with Duty—yes, and Detail.

From *Prairie Overcomer.*

DYING WORDS

"I would give worlds, if I had them, if the 'Age of Reason' had never been published. O Lord, help me! Christ, help me! Stay with me! It is Hell to be left alone.— Tom Paine

WHAT IS A SQUARE?

Everybody knows a few squares. I know one. He's that strong, polite, God-fearing young fellow who freely admits that he prays, weeps for joy, plays with little kids, kisses his mother, goes to Dad for advice, thinks old folks are nice, and blushes. He wears jeans he can bend in, puts savings in the bank, cuts his hair, likes school, can't imitate all the television comics, avoids dirty discussions about sex, goes to worship, drinks milk, drives 30 miles an hour in a thirty-mile-per-hour speed zone, is in bed by eleven, doesn't smoke, and expects purity in girls.

As a result of his odd and outlandish behavior, he suffers the loss of gang companionship; but he gains the gratitude and devotion of his parents, school honors, family respect, unjaded imagination and spiritual security. I know him; he is a strange fellow, but I like him.

--Reprinted from Tennessee Future Farmer Magazine

In the morning when thou findest thyself unwilling to rise, consider with thyself presently, if it is to go about a man's work that I am stirred up. Or was I made for this, to lay me down, and make much of myself in a warm bed.—Marcus Aurelius.

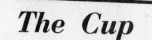

The Cup

Another cup, dear Lord? And must
I drink this too?
Of late so much I've had
Of bitter brew!

"Trust Me, dear child; would I
Put to your lip
Or bid you drink a cup from which
I did not sip?

Come, taste, and you will find
My balm can make
Like honey any draught that I
Ask you to take!"
—Martha Snell Nicholson

Don't worry about originality, brethren; Christ never claimed it. He says: 'The words that I speak are not mine, but his that sent me.' The Holy Spirit did not claim it, for it is written, 'He shall not speak of himself, but whatsoever he shall hear, that shall he speak.' In fact, the only original thinker and speaker in the Bible is he of whom it is written, 'When he speaketh a lie, he speaketh of his own.'
—Spurgeon.

One word of God is like a piece of gold, and the Christian is the goldbeater, and can hammer that promise out of whole weeks.
—Spurgeon

Hypocritical Hymn-singing

1. We sing *"Sweet Hour of Prayer"* and are content with 5-10 minutes a day.
2. We sing *"Onward Christian Soldiers"* and wait to be drafted into His service.
3. We sing *"O for a Thousand Tongues to Sing"* and don't use the one we have.
4. We Sing *"There Shall Be Showers of Blessing"* but do not come when it rains.
5. We sing *"Blest Be the Tie That Binds"* and let the least little offense sever it.
6. We sing *"Serve the Lord With Gladness"* and gripe about all we have to do.
7. We sing *"I Love to Tell the Story"* and never mention it at all.
8. We sing *"We're Marching to Zion"* but fail to march to worship or church school.
9. We sing *"Cast Thy Burden on the Lord"* and worry ourselves into a nervous breakdown.
10. We sing *"The Whole Wide World for Jesus"* and never invite our next-door neighbor.
11. We sing *"O Day of Rest and Gladness"* and wear ourselves out traveling, cutting grass or playing golf on Sunday.
12. We sing *"Throw Out the Lifeline"* and content ourselves with throwing out a fishing line.

I found this poem in a book by Dr. W. B. Riley. It is so good, I wish to share it with you.

The Curse of Empty Hands

At dawn the call was heard,
And busy reapers stirred
Along the highway leading to the wheat.
"Wilt reap with us?" they said.
I smiled and shook my head.
"Disturb me not," said I, "my dreams are sweet."

I sat with folded hands
And saw across the lands
The waiting harvest shining on the hills;
I heard the reapers sing
Their song of harvesting,
And thought to go, but dreamed and waited still.

The day at last was done,
And homeward, one by one,
The reapers went, well laden as they passed.
Theirs was no misspent day,
Not long hours dreamed away.
In sloth that turns to sting the soul at last.

A reaper lingered near
"What," cried he, "idle here!
Where are the sheaves your hands have bound to-day?"
"Alas," I made reply,
"I let the day pass by
Until too late to work. I dreamed the hours away."

"O foolish one!" he said,
And sadly shook his head,
"The dreaming soul is in the way of death.
The harvest soon is o'er,
Rouse up and dream no more!
Act, for the summer fadeth like a breath.

"What if the Master came
To-night and called your name,
Asking how many sheaves your hands had made?
If at the Lord's command
You showed your empty hands,
Condemned, your dreaming soul would stand dismayed."

Filled with strange terror then,
Lest chance come not again,
I sought the wheat-fields while the others slept.
"Perhaps ere break of day
The Lord will come this way,"
A voice kept saying, till with fear I wept.

Through all the long, still night,
Among the wheat-fields white,
I reaped and bound the sheaves of yellow grain.
I dared not pause to rest,
Such fear possessed my breast;
So for my dreams I paid the price in pain.

But when the morning broke
And rested reapers woke
My heart leaped up as sunrise kissed the lands;
For came he soon or late,
The Lord of the estate
Would find me bearing not the curse of empty hands.

HELL

HELL! the prison house of despair,
Here are some things that won't
  be there:
No flowers will bloom on the
  banks of Hell,
No beauties of nature we love so
  well;
No comforts of home, music and
  song,
No friendship of joy will be found
  in that throng;
No children to brighten the long,
  weary night;
No love nor peace, nor one ray
  of light;
No blood-washed soul with face
  beaming bright,
No loving smile in that region of
  night;
No mercy, no pity, pardon nor
  grace,
No water; O God, what a terrible
  place!
The pangs of the lost no human
  can tell,
Not one moment's peace—there is
  no rest in HELL.

HELL! the prison house of despair,
Here are some things that will be
  there:
Fire and brimstone are there, we
  know,
For God in His Word hath told us
  so;
Memory, remorse, suffering and
  pain,
Weeping and wailing, but all in
  vain;
Blasphemers, swearers, haters of
  God,
Christ-rejectors while here on
  earth trod;
Murderers, gamblers, drunkards
  and liars,
Will have their part in the lake
  of fire;
The filthy, the vile, the cruel and
  mean,
What a horrible mob in Hell will
  be seen!
Yes, more than humans on earth
  can tell,
Are torments and woes of Eternal
  HELL!
                              —Catherine Dangell

So live that you would not mind giving the family parrot to the village gossip.—Irish Digest.

To know the will of God is the greatest knowledge, to find the will of God is the greatest discovery, and to do the will of God is the greatest achievement.
—George W. Truett.

The church is not a gallery for the exhibition of eminent Christians but a school for the education of imperfect ones.
--Henry Ward Beecher

The Bible

Born in the East and clothed in oriental form and imagery, the Bible walks the ways of all the world with familiar feet and enters land after land to find Its own everywhere. It has learned to speak in hundreds of languages to the hearts of men. It comes into the palace to tell the monarch that he is a servant of the Most High, and into the cottage to assure the peasant that he is a son of God.

Children listen to its stories with wonder and delight, and wise men ponder them as parables of life.

It has a word of peace for the time of peril, a word of comfort for the time of calamity, a word of light for the hour of darkness. Its oracles are repeated in the assembly of the people and its counsels whispered in the ear of the lonely. The wicked and the proud tremble at its warnings, but to the wounded and the penitent it has a mother's voice. The wilderness and the solitary place have been made glad by it, and the fire on the hearth has lit the reading of its well-worn page.

It has woven itself into our dearest dreams; so that love, friendship, sympathy and devotion, memory and hope, put on the beautiful garments of its treasured speech, breathing of frankincense and myrrh.

No man is poor or desolate who has this treasure for his own. When the landscape darkens and. the trembling pilgrim comes to the Valley named in the Shadow, he is not afraid to enter; he takes the rod and the staff of Scripture in his hand; he says to friend and comrade: "Good-bye, we shall meet again," and comforted by that support, he goes toward the lonely pass as one who walks through darkness into light.

—Henry Van Dyke

Wait on the Lord

The late Dr. J. H. Jowett said that he was once in a most pitiful perplexity, and consulted Dr. Berry, of Wolverhampton.

"What would you do if you were in my place?" he entreated.

"I don't know, Jowett, I am not there, and you are not there yet. When do you have to act?"

"On Friday," Dr. Jowett replied.

"Then," answered Berry, "you will find your way perfectly clear on Friday. The Lord will not fail you."

And surely enough, on Friday all was plain. Give God time, and even when the knife flashes in the air the ram will be seen caught in the thicket. Give God time, and even when Pharaoh's host is on Israel's heels, a path through the waters will be suddenly open. Give God time, and when the bed of the brook is dry, Elijah shall hear the guiding voice.—*F. W. Boreham*

The Difference!

There is a vast difference between a person with a vision and a visionary person. The person with a vision talks little but does much. The person who is visionary talks much but does nothing.
—*Selected.*

John Wesley Said

I am content with whatever entertainment I meet with. That must be the spirit with all who take journeys with me. If a dinner ill dressed, a hard bed, a poor room, a shower of rain, or a dirty road will put them out of humor, it lays a burden upon me greater than all the rest put together. By the grace of God I never fret; I repine at nothing; I am discontented with nothing. And to have persons at my ear fretting and murmuring at everything is like tearing the flesh off my bones.—Selected

John Wanamaker's Bible

When he had become one of the country's greatest merchants, John Wanamaker once said, "In my lifetime, I have made many purchases. I have bought things which have cost me thousands of dollars. But the greatest purchase I ever made was when I was a boy twelve years old.

Then I bought a Bible for two dollars and fifty cents. That was my greatest purchase, for that Bible made me what I am today."

MY SUBSTITUTE

By Sir James Simpson, M.D.
(Discoverer of Chloroform)

When I was a boy at school I saw a sight I can never forget— a man tied to a cart and dragged before the people's eyes through the streets of my native town, his back torn and bleeding from the lash. It was a shameful punishment. For many offenses? No; for one offense. Did any of the townsmen offer to divide the lashes with him? No; he who committed the offense bore the penalty all alone. It was a penalty of a changing human law, for it was the last instance of its infliction.

When I was a student at the university, I saw another sight I can never forget—a man brought out to die. His arms were pinioned, his face was already pale as death —thousands of eager eyes were on him as he came from the jail in sight. Did any man ask to die in his room? Did any friend come and loose the rope and say, "Put it around my neck, I die instead"? No; he underwent the sentence of the law. For many offenses? No, for one offense. He had stolen a money parcel from a stagecoach. He broke the law at one point and died for it. It was the penalty of a changing human law in this case also; it was the last instance of capital punishment being inflicted for that offense.

I saw another sight I shall never forget—myself a sinner, standing on the brink of ruin, condemned to eternal punishment in the lake of fire. For one sin? No, for many, many sins committed. I looked again, and behold, Jesus Christ became my Substitute. He bore in His own body on the tree all the punishment for my sin. He died on the cross that I might live in the glory. He suffered the JUST for the unjust that HE might bring me to God. He redeemed me from the curse of the law. I sinned and was condemned to eternal punishment; He bore the punishment and I am free. The law of God required a perfect righteousness which I never had. Again I look unto HIM and I found that Christ is the end of the law for righteousness to every one that believeth. The law required spotless purity and I was defiled with sin. Again I looked unto HIM who loved us and washed us from our sins in HIS own blood. I was a child of Satan, a child of wrath, but as many as received HIM to them gave HE power to become the sons of God, even to them that believe on His name. And I found in HIM not only my Substitute, but the full supply of every need of my life.

I long to tell you of this Saviour for there is none other Name under Heaven given among men whereby we may be saved.

Don't Let This Happen to You

There was a man who lived by the side of the road and sold hot dogs.

He was hard of hearing so he had no radio.

He had trouble with his eyes so he read no newspapers.

But he sold good hot dogs.

He put up signs on the highway telling how good they were.

He stood on the side of the road and cried, "Buy a hot dog, Mister?"

And people bought his hot dogs.

He increased his meat and bun orders.

He bought a bigger stove to take care of his trade.

He finally got his son home from college to help out.

But then something happened.

His son said, "Father, haven't you been listening to the radio?

"Haven't you been reading the newspaper?

"There's a big recession on.

"The European situation is terrible.

"The Domestic situation is worse."

Whereupon the father thought, "Well, my son's been to college, he reads the papers and he listens to the radio, and he ought to know."

So the father cut down his meat and bun orders, took down his signs, and no longer bothered to stand out on the highway to sell his hot dogs.

His sales fell overnight.

"You're right, son," the father said to the boy.

"We certainly are in the middle of a big recession."

↓

Forgiving Your Enemies

In a local home for the aged in Grand Rapids, two Christian men had been quarreling for many years. One was finally upon what he believed to be his deathbed, so he called the other and said, "John, I forgive you for what you have said and done against me over the years, and I want you to do the same for me." The other with tears said that he would. For a moment a faraway look came into the eyes of the man lying in the bed, and then he said with some spirit, "But John, IF I GET BETTER, THIS doesn't count!"

Friendship

I'd like to be the sort of friend that you have been to me,
I'd like to be the help that you've been always glad to be:
I'd like to mean as much to you each minute of the day
As you have meant, old friend of mine, to me along the way.
I'd like to do big things and the splendid things for you,
To brush the gray from out your skies and leave them only blue;
I'd like to say the kind of things that I so oft have heard
And feel that I could rouse your soul the way that mine you've stirred.
I'd like to give you back the joy that you have given me,
Yet that were wishing you a need I hope will never be:
I'd like to make you feel as rich as I, who travel on
Undaunted in the darkest hours with you to lean upon.
I'm wishing at this New Year time that I could but repay
A portion of the gladness that you've strewn along the way.
And could I have one wish this year, this only would it be:
I'd like to be the sort of friend that you have been to me.

—*Detroit Free Press*

One of the stories told by that beloved Texas pastor, the late Dr. George W. Truett, was that of a young lady brought before the church for discipline because of a violation of the church covenant. It was suggested that she be dropped from the roll of the church. As the debate developed the pastor said, "Let us also call the church treasurer and have him read the record of the giving of every member, and let us vote to drop everyone who has violated God's law against covetousness." That bombshell cleared the air of accusers, as did the reminder of Jesus: "He that is without sin among you, let him first cast a stone at her" (John 8:7).

Conscience is not a safe guide, because very often conscience won't tell you have done wrong until after you have done it, but the Bible will tell you what is wrong before you have done it.—D. L. Moody.

Credo

Not what, but Whom I do believe!
  That, in my darkest hour of need,
  Hath comfort that no mortal creed
  To mortal man may give.
Not what, but Whom!
  For Christ is more than all the creeds,
  And His full life of gentle deeds
  Shall all the creeds outlive.
Not what, but Whom!
  Who walks beside me in the gloom?
  Who shares the burden wearisome?
  Who all the dim way doth illume.
  And bids me look beyond the tomb
  The larger life to live?
Not what I do believe, but Whom!
Not what, but Whom!

—John Oxenham

When arguing with a fool always make sure that he is not similarly engaged.

"George Washington Never—"

By Clay P. Morgan

He never wrote on a typewriter either, for typewriters were unknown until about 1840.

He never rode a bicycle. Bicycles were not introduced into the United States until 1819, and the early ones were very crude affairs as compared with modern bicycles.

He never rode on a steamboat or a railway train; a street car or an elevator; an electric trolley, or a ferris wheel. The first steamboat was invented by Robert Fulton in 1807, and the first steamboat crossed the Atlantic in May 1819. The first railway in the United States on which a steam locomotive was utilized was laid in Pennsylvania, from Carbondale to Honesdale, a distance of 16 miles, in 1829. The first regular horse street car line in the world was opened on Fourth avenue in New York City in 1832. The first electric trolley was put into operation only about forty years ago. The first passenger elevator used in this country was installed in 1850. The ferris wheel was invented by a man named Ferris, and was first used at the World's Fair in Chicago, in 1893.

No Matches

George Washington never lighted a fire with a match, for matches were unknown until 1827, when John Walker, an English druggist, discovered the method for making them. He never saw a stove of any description, for stoves were not invented until a number of years after his death. In his day the great fireplaces served for both heating and cooking. He never saw a gas, kerosene, or electric light. Gas was first used for lighting in 1816, kerosene in or about 1860, and the electric light globe was invented by Thomas A. Edison in 1879.

He never wore long trousers, or sox, or a store-bought suit of clothes. He never wore a tuxedo, or a full dress suit, such as are worn now, and he never wore an opera hat, or a wrist watch. He never used any kind of tooth paste, shaving cream, or safety razors. He never ate lunch in a drug store. He never heard of a cafeteria, a "round table cafe," a delicatessen, nor a "self-serve" grocery. He never drank any pasteurized milk, and never heard of proteins, carbohydrates, calories, and vitamins. He never heard of the G.O.P., Tammany Hall, Uncle Sam, bolshevism, communism, facism, or technocracy.

He never saw a modern game of baseball, basketball or football, and never tossed a medicine ball or played a game of golf in order to "keep fit."

He never talked over a telephone, for the telephone was not invented until 1876. He never sent nor received a telegram or a cablegram. The telegraph was not perfected until 1844, and the first Atlantic cable was not completed until 1866.

No Bath Tubs

He was never guilty of "singing in the bath tub," for there were no bath tubs until about the middle of the last century, and no shower baths until much later.

He never saw a "movie," for there were no such things until more than a hundred years after his death. He never saw an automobile, or an airplane, and never "listened in" on a radio. He never danced to "jazz," for it had not yet emerged from the African jungles.

He never sang "The Star Spangled Banner," "America," "Home Sweet Home," "Silent Night! Holy Night!" "Onward Christian Soldiers," or many of the other songs we like so well, because none of these were written until many years after his death.

Although he was President of the United States for eight years he never lived in the White House and never lived in Washington, District of Columbia. During his first year in office the seat of the Federal Government was in New York city, then from 1790 to 1800 it was in Philadelphia, and in July, 1800, it was moved to the new National Capital at Washington, District of Columbia.

George Washington was born Feb. 22, 1732, and died Dec. 14, 1799. Although he never had many of the things we of today seem to think are so necessary to our happiness and welfare, yet he was not only the first President of the United States, but he was also a great and good man. And he probably got as much real pleasure out of life as we do, perhaps more than many of us get, for after all, "a man's life consisteth not in the abundance of the things which he possesseth."

—From Ohio Independent Baptist

This summer Dr. Robert Sumner gave us a brief devotional in our morning devotions here at the office. He related to us a blessed incident. When I asked him to "re-tell" it to me so I could pass it on to you, he said I could find it in *How I Know God Answers Prayer*, by Rosalind Goforth. In that little volume she writes of this remarkable answer to prayer.

The most precious recollections of early childhood are associated with stories told us by our mother, many of which illustrated the power of prayer.

One that made a specially deep impression upon me was about our grandfather, who as a little boy went to visit cousins in the south of England, their home being situated close to a dense forest. One day the children, lured by the beautiful wild flowers, became hopelessly lost in the woods. After trying in vain to find a way out, the eldest, a young girl, called the frightened, crying little ones around her and said: "When mother died she told us to always tell Jesus if we were in any trouble. Let us kneel down, and ask Him to take us home."

They knelt, and as she prayed one of the little ones opened his eyes, to find a bird so close to his hand that he reached out for it. The bird hopped away, but kept so close to the child as to lead him on. Soon all were joining in the chase after the bird, which flew or hopped in front or just above, and sometimes on the ground almost within reach. Then suddenly it flew into the air and away. The children looked up to find themselves on the edge of the woods and in sight of home.

God uses a bird to answer prayer. Isn't that remarkable?

THE TIME TO DECIDE

A student came to a Scottish professor, asking him how long he might safely put off decision for Christ. "Until the day before your death," was the strange reply. "But I cannot tell when I shall die," said the youth. "True," replied the professor "then **decide now**."

A Coffin
for the Living

A beautiful, modern, up-to-date casket made for a man who was still alive—and did not dream he was going to need it!

By Evangelist Bill Rice, Contributing Editor

I met Johnny Cox during a three-week revival campaign with the First Baptist Church of Gas City, Indiana. He was not only a fine, clean-cut young man of pleasing personality but a fine Christian. He was the youngest man on the Board of Deacons and Kenneth Beilby, the pastor, often expressed his regret that he did not have a dozen more just like Johnny Cox.

This young man was not only a fine consecrated Christian but an up-and-coming young businessman. He was an undertaker and the owner of a successful funeral home.

Because of the babies Mrs. Cox did not get to attend all of the revival services. But Johnny was there for every single service of the revival — day and evening services, prayer meetings, visitation—everything.

Going for Dinner

A number of times Johnny came by the home where I was staying to visit with me. He was just full of Bible questions and he always wanted me to pray for him. Several times when the pastor had other engagements Johnny went with me to visit someone we were trying to win to Christ or trying to get into the services.

I will never forget Johnny. Now, during these many years I have conducted dozens of revival campaigns and I certainly do not remember all of the wonderful people I have met and have worked with. Since I have worked with so many pastors, I do not even remember all of them. But I will always remember Johnny Cox because of what happened the day I went to eat dinner with him.

As a rule I do not linger long after a meal. My mother taught me that it was not polite to "eat and run" but I always do it just the same. I am busy and simply do not have time to spend three or four hours a day eating a noon meal! As a rule when I am invited to a home for dinner I make it clear that I will not be able to stay very long after the meal.

So, after eating dinner with Johnny Cox and his wife and children I read a portion of the Word of God, discussed it, had prayer and was ready to go. But Johnny urged me to stay for "just

a few minutes" and look at his establishment. He had the latest equipment and was justly proud of his business. Although I really was busy and needed to get back to my room I just didn't have the heart to refuse his eager invitation. So I agreed to look around the place before leaving.

Ten minutes later I was sorry I hadn't rushed on off like I intended. And I was also sorry I had eaten any dinner!

Look—No Pockets!

First he led me to a room in the basement. He wanted to show me, he said, how they did embalming.

O.K., I thought, so he wants to show me an embalming table and a few shiny new stainless steel instruments.

That's what I thought. But when I walked through the door — I realized I had another thought coming. Oh, there was an embalming table, all right—and the body of a man lying on it that I had not been prepared for!

The body was covered with a sheet and Johnny pulled the sheet down to the fellow's waist. The fellow had one eye closed and one eye partly open—and I would have sworn that he was staring straight at me!

The piggly wigglies were running up and down my back like a window shade.

Only faster!

Johnny casually began to explain how they made an incision under one arm and under one leg and pumped the frigid fluid into the body forcing the blood out.

As I stood there in an uneasy stupor the young undertaker was earnestly discussing the advantages of his embalming technique. He was obviously trying to make a good impression on me. In this he failed miserably.

The only thing I wanted to hear him say was, "Let's get out of here!"

But he did say one thing that I have never forgotten. He showed me a closet full of clothing, took out a man's suit on a hanger and said, "Look. This suit has no pockets. After all, a dead man doesn't need pockets."

That's right—a dead man doesn't need pockets. Corny as it may sound it is still true that,

"You can't take it with you." When old man John D. Rockefeller died someone asked, "How much did he leave," and his pastor wisely replied, "He left it all."

It is as foolish as it is wicked to neglect Jesus Christ for money or anything else. No matter how much money you may have, you won't need pockets in your burial suit.

You can't take it with you!

The Largest Selection of Caskets

We left the embalming room and I said, "Thanks, Johnny, for everything. I really must be going. As you know these are busy days for me and I have a great deal to do before the evening's service."

But he wanted me to stay a bit longer. "Look, Bill," he said, "we have the largest selection of caskets this side of Chicago and you simply must see them before you go. It will just take a few minutes and I honestly believe it will be well worth your time."

Very reluctantly I allowed myself to be led to a large L-shaped room crowded with caskets.

Johnny Cox said, "I have already shown you that a dead man doesn't need any pockets in his clothes because he must leave everything behind when he dies. Now there's another sermon for you in these caskets. The Bible says that 'it is appointed unto men once to die, but after this the judgment,' and these caskets prove it."

He then went on to point out that some caskets were expensive metal ones, others very inexpensive cloth-covered ones. Some were very small for babies, others a bit larger for children, still others larger for adults. Here was mute testimony that people of every age whether rich or poor die.

The Unusual Casket

Again I thanked Johnny for "everything" and started to leave. But again he urged me to stay just "one more minute." He had a casket he simply must show me. This casket, he said, had modern improvements that even he had never seen before.

I know very little about caskets but this one did appear to be well constructed and it was certainly beautifully made of imported rosewood. I am not sure what "rosewood" is but the grain was beautiful and it was polished to a high gloss.

This was not only a beautiful casket, Johnny told me, but it had the very latest scientific improvements.

"I'll bet this is something you have never seen before," he said as he picked up a small crank—about the size and shape of the one a car window is rolled up and down with—and inserted it in the side of the casket. He rapidly turned the little handle, explaining that this made the casket airtight. This was something new to me. And there was another refinement I had not seen previously.

"Look at this," he said, pointing to a small button on the side just below the lid. He punched the button and the top half of the coffin lid slowly began to open! The thing was counter-balanced someway and the little button released a catch that allowed the lid to open slowly and silently.

"No more of this grabbing the lid and pushing it open," Johnny said. "This is the modern, scientific way to do it quietly and with dignity."

He then raised the lower half of the lid until the entire casket was open.

"Look at that," Johnny exulted. He pointed to the beautiful material with which the entire casket was lined on the inside. It was not only beautiful and luxurious but would, I was assured, last for years and years.

"And just feel the mattress in the bottom of this casket," he went on. "It's as fine as any Beauty-rest."

Then, as I hesitated, he put the flat of his hand on the mattress and pumped vigorously as he repeated, "C'mon, feel this mattress."

Gingerly I put my hand inside and felt the mattress with one finger.

"Why," he enthused, "a fellow could rest in this just as comfortably as in a nice hotel. Just get in and lie down for a minute—you'll be surprised!"

That did it! If there is anything I never expect to try on for size it is a coffin.

"This thing isn't for me so why should I try it out?" I remarked as I headed for the door.

"If this casket is not made for you, who do you think it is made for?" Johnny asked as he fell in step.

"That's easy to answer—it was made for a dead man."

"You're wrong," he replied. "That casket was made for a living man!"

I paused by the door. "You mean you bury them alive around here?" I said sarcastically.

"Not at all," Johnny replied. "We do not bury them until they die. But dead people are already buried. This casket was made for a living man . . . who is going to die right away!"

"What's more," he continued, "some man will probably be buried in that casket within the next few days. More than likely it will be some man who does not even dream he is going to die right away. It may even be some man who has been to hear you preach in this revival campaign."

What he said was obviously the truth . . . and yet I had never thought of it before in all my life. Caskets are made for living men! Dead men are already buried but casket makers continue to turn out coffins because those who are now alive will die. And it seems that death does come unexpectedly so many, many times. Doubtless there are multiplied thousands of people who are dead today who thought they would still be alive years and years from now.

I was a very thoughtful evangelist as I drove to my room. And that night in my message I told of the modern up-to-date casket that emphasized an ancient truth—"It is appointed unto men once to die."

In my message I warned that some man in that very service might be the man who would be buried in that very casket.

It turned out that I was right!

That Casket Was Made For—

My next revival was in the First Baptist Church of Allegan, Michigan. From there I went to Orestes, Indiana, just eighteen miles from Gas City. On the opening night in Orestes Brother Beilby and a delegation of ninety came from Gas City to be in the services.

After dismissal that night Ken Beilby and I got together for a visit. About the first thing Ken said to me was, "I suppose you heard about the great loss our church has suffered since you closed the meeting two weeks ago."

His face was so grave and his behaviour so sober that I felt he had experienced a real tragedy and I wondered if the church had burned.

"We have lost," he said, "the youngest and one of the very finest deacons we have ever had —Johnny Cox!"

"You mean," I said, "Johnny Cox sold out his business and moved away from Gas City?"

"No," Ken replied, "I mean Johnny Cox died and we buried him just last Tuesday."

I could hardly believe it. The very first thing I thought of was the coffin he had shown me with such pride.

That coffin—the one that was made for a living man!

"Ken," I said with some excitement, "did you preach the funeral?"

"I took part in the service," he modestly replied.

"What kind of a coffin was he buried in?" I quickly asked.

"What kind of a coffin?" Ken asked in surprise.

"Yes, what kind of a coffin was Johnny buried in? Was it made of highly polished wood?"

"Yes it was," he said.

"Was there a little crank on the side that was turned to make the casket airtight?"

"Well," Ken said, "there was a little crank that was turned for some reason or other. I never saw one like it before but. . . ."

"And was there," I interrupted, "a button that looked like a doorbell that caused the top half of the lid to open slowly by itself?"

"Yes there was," Ken said in surprise. "But how in the world did you know. . . .?"

I told Brother Beilby the story and we sat in startled silence. Johnny Cox had shown me a casket. A casket that, he said, was made for some man who was then alive but who would die soon. Someone who probably did not even dream that he was going to die. Someone, perhaps, who had even been to hear me preach in the revival campaign.

And Johnny Cox himself had been buried in that very casket ten days later!

Where Is Your Casket?

Good Neighbor, whether you are young or old, sickly or in excellent health, rich or poor, saved or lost—you have an appointment with death. Only an utter fool will refuse to face this obvious truth. The Bible says, **"It is appointed unto men once to die, but after this the judgment"** (Heb. 9:27).

I do not know the date of your appointment with death. I do not know the date of my appointment with death. But I do know that either of us may die before these words are even printed. That is why the Bible warns us, **"Boast not thyself of tomorrow; for thou knowest not what a day may bring forth"** (Prov. 27:1).

A COFFIN (CONTINUED)

And we are reminded in I Peter 1:24, "For all flesh is as grass, and all glory of man as the flower of grass. The grass withereth, and the flower thereof falleth away."

Hebrews 2:3 asks, "How shall we escape, if we neglect so great salvation. . . .?"

That is why we are admonished in II Corinthians 6:2, "Now is the day of salvation. . . ."

I wonder if my coffin has already been constructed. I wonder where the casket is that you are going to be buried in. Perhaps the wood is still in a lumber yard. Or perhaps the casket you will be buried in is partly completed in a factory right this minute. Or—who knows—the casket you are going to be buried in may actually be in your home town right this minute waiting for you at the undertaking parlor.

But where your casket is at this moment is not nearly as important as where **you** will be when your body is in that casket! With all the sincerity of my heart I urge that you turn to Jesus Christ right this minute and trust Him to save you and forgive you of your sins. Do it and then won't you please write to let me know?

(As published in THE BRANDING IRON, the small but rich and charming monthly paper of the Bill Rice Ranch, Franklin Road, Murfreesboro, Tennessee. You may have a year's subscription for $1.00.)

The Little White Assassin

He is a small fellow—this little white assassin. But like the even smaller microbes, he multiplies by the billions. He carries no gun or knife. He has no need for these crude weapons. This little white assassin is A REFINED KILLER, dealing only in poison, arson and asphyxiation. He has a way of charming his victim, so that they stupidly enjoy the processes of their assassination.

He is a great entertainer. Just about every night in America, he gathers millions of his victims and would-be victims together and entertains them with some of the top television talent of the land. He is greedy, but not stingy, for he spends about 150 million dollars a year to entertain, coax and lull his current crop of victims and to recruit new ones.

How successful is he in his recruiting program?

He signs up 4,500 new teen-agers every day! These all become potential victims marked for death by poison, arson or slow strangulation. Yet, he makes them like it. Every year an army of 1,642,500 young volunteers for slow, torturous assassination, all lulled to a hypnotic sleep by soft music, sultry-voiced women and an array of athletic young men, or men who "think for themselves," or just plain people in general who "know how to have fun."

Once he gets his victims in their hypnotic trance, he goes to work. He multiplies into an army of 490 billion other little white assassins like himself. These billions are short-lived. They all die in a year, EACH BURNING HIMSELF OUT doing his part to destroy American lives.

They set fires to beds, homes, and hotels, and hundreds of people die as a result.

An average of 103 Americans die of lung cancer every day, part of the germ warfare of this little white assassin.

Millions die of slow strangulation, as the 490 billion little assassins burn their way into vital organs.

Heart trouble, high blood pressure, paralytic strokes are frequently caused by LWA.

Children are particularly hard hit. The incidence of premature births is two and a half times higher among mothers who are victims of LWA than among those who aren't.

Babies born alive to his victims are ounces lighter than those allowed to develop normally before birth.

Even science has not yet discovered all the ways by which the little white assassin kills his victims. But more than 37,000 die EVERY YEAR of lung cancer alone. Hundreds of thousands more die of other diseases induced or made fatal by him.

One million children now in our public schools are already marked for death by lung cancer. This is only part of the deadly work of the little white assassin.

His name is CIGARETTE.—*The Defender.*

Quittin' Meetings

I read this story recently that is to the point: Sam Jones used to have "Quittin' Meetings" during his revivals. He gave the people opportunity to confess their sins and to repent. Many quit swearing, drinking, smoking, gossiping. . . . He asked one woman what she planned to quit and she replied, "I ain't been doing nothing and I am goin' to quit that too."—*R. W. Pelton, Louisville, Ky.* Kokomo South (Ind.) Church Bulletin

A boy was dressing to go out for the evening. He asked his mother, "Mother, is this shirt dirty?" Without so much as looking, she replied: "Yes, it's dirty; put on a clean one." When he had dressed, he entered his mother's room and asked how she knew the shirt was not clean when she had not even looked at it. "If it had been clean," she replied, "you would have known it and not asked me. Remember, Son, if it's doubtful, it's dirty."

—Selected.

The measure of a man's real character is what he would do if he knew he would never be found out.

—Macaulay.

THE ONE THING WORSE THAN A QUITTER IS THE MAN WHO IS AFRAID TO BEGIN.—SELECTED.

Eagle-Free

An eaglet in its downy nest surveyed the scene below
And asked with animated zest, "Oh, Mother, I would know...
Will I someday begin to fly as high and far as you?"
The answer came, "Of course you'll fly, for that's what eagles do."

"Highborn you are and high you'll stay, and higher, still you'll go
And never know an earth-bound day, nor crawling to and fro.
Now dashing down, now soaring high... now floating on the air...
Now flying where you will to fly... now free to do and dare;

"Your eyes will view a vast domain and nothing will you fear...
Lions will admit your reign when your great wings appear.
Be angry in your sov'reignty... be fierce and claim your own.
Fight bravely... independently... fight bravely... fight alone!

"Your spreading wings, your angry eyes, your talons, curving beak,
Are symbols, all, where freedom cries and independence speaks,
With strength to flay the largest foe that threatens little ones...
With raging cry to let them know that you'll protect your sons.

"I'll take the down from out the nest and let the thorns protrude;
I'll let the thorns disturb your rest and halt your nesting mood.
Then soon you'll climb upon the edge and stretch your pinions out;
You'll totter on the eerie ledge and ponder space... and doubt.

"Then, with a wing I'll knock you off to flounder, flap and fly...
And, with a swoop, I'll pick you up and never mind your cry.
I'll put you on the perch again, then knock you off the nest
To see if you will stand the strain and stand the acid test.

"I'll give you opportunity to prove that you can fly
And then a final chance to see if you will fly or die.
I'd rather rugged, jagged rocks would claim you as their own,
Than bear the taunts and jeers and mocks that say you've never flown.

"But, fly you must, and fly you will, and conquer gravity,
And know the zephyr's golden thrill and fly for all to see;
My eagle-son, this word I give: Keep looking to the sky!
For, though an eagle flies to live... an eagle lives to fly!"

Bill Harvey, 1961

65

WHEN JESUS WAS BORN

By Olive Weaver Ridenour

Mary

Joseph is sleeping, and the Babe
Is quiet now. The morning light
Tells me another day has come.
Can it be true that just last night
His holy birth took place—
The dream is now reality?
Jesus, the Son of God, is born!
My Son . . . God's Son . . . how can it be?

So good a man is Joseph!
He could have brought me
And the Child to public shame,
Had he not believed God's messenger
Appearing in a dream. Since then
He has been quoting prophecies,
Things that the ancient Scriptures say.

The trip from Nazareth was hard,
But we were glad to get away
From knowing looks and wagging tongues
That followed us for many a day.
And we both knew the prophecy
That when God sent His Son to men,
The great Messiah, long foretold,
Was to be born in Bethlehem.

The shepherds said an angel spoke
And told them of a Saviour's birth;
A heavenly chorus sang God's praise,
"Glory to God! And peace on earth!"
How wonderful, to have His birth
Announced by angels in the night!
I do not comprehend it quite.

The Babe stirs in His sleep. Meanwhile
I keep recalling prophet's words,
And pondering, will this come true?
"His kingdom . . . there shall be no end . . .
A Saviour . . . every tongue shall own
Him Lord . . . He shall be great, and reign
And God shall give Him David's throne!"

Joseph is sleeping, and the Babe
Is quiet now. The dawning light
Tells me another day has come.

Joseph

Today the sons of Abraham
Are slaves beneath the Roman yoke—
Romans who scorn our prophecies
Of which the ancient fathers spoke.
Strange that by Caesar's own decree,
Just at this sacred time, we came
To David's city, Bethlehem,
To register, for tax, our names.

When we arrived in Bethlehem,
Each house was crowded to the door.
Mary was tired . . . her time was near;
Where could we go? She must have rest
And shelter—and at once! We knew
No one. Strangers we were, in need.
This stable, then, would have to do.

Strange! But I love that little mite
As though He were, in truth, my own.
I shudder when I call to mind,
But for a dream, I had not known
The wonder of His coming as
Fulfillment of the prophecy—
"A virgin shall bring forth a Son . . ."
And God chose her—Mary—to be
The one! I was so hurt, so grieved,
Until that night the angel said,
"Fear not to take Mary, thy wife."

But then my doubts and fears all fled,
And I recalled old prophecies,
That God would send His Son to earth
"Born of a virgin"—and this town
Of Bethlehem would see His birth.

Strange . . . that by Caesar's own decree,
Just at this sacred time, we came
To David's city Bethlehem.

A Shepherd

There never was another night
So glorious. The radiance
Has vanished now from mortal sight;
The music of the skies has ceased;
But to my dying day, I know
That song will linger in my heart;
That hymn will never pass away!

If I, alone, had heard the song
And seen the light, I might have thought
It nothing but a wondrous dream.
But this great miracle was seen
By all us shepherds in the fields,
And each one heard the angel say:

"Fear not! Behold in Bethlehem
The Saviour . . . Christ . . . is born today!"
We made our way (to prove the sign)
With haste to Bethlehem, to see
Jesus, the newborn Babe divine,
And wrapped in swaddling clothes, He lay
There in a manger! Mary's face
Was radiant! A holy air
Of mystery was in the place!

All day the curious have come
To ask us if the tale were true
About the Babe of Bethlehem,
About the heavenly chorus, too.
We have retold it many times.

So many disbelieve! They say
If this Babe were indeed God's Son,
He would not lie there on the hay,
But in a bed with silken sheets.
No swaddling clothes would God's Son wear—
As child of humble peasant folk—
But richest clothes and raiment fair.

Yet our ears heard the heavenly choir,
And we have been to Bethlehem.
We humble shepherds are the first
Of all men living to behold
The one true God in human form,
The Saviour for so long foretold.

There never was another night
So glorious. To my dying day
That song will linger in my heart.

The Inn Keeper

The inn was crowded . . . each room filled
Last night, before this Joseph came
In search of lodging for the night,
His wife half faint with weariness.
She must have rest, and shelter, too,
For she would be a mother soon.
I had no choice! All I could do
Was offer them the stable.
It was not much—as they could see—
But it was shelter. There these two
Would have at least some privacy.

Sometime between the midnight hour
And dawn, some humble shepherds came,
Inquiring of a newborn Child—
A Babe, they said, of wondrous fame.
They told the strangest story of
A great light shining in the sky,
And angels telling of the One
Who in a manger-bed did lie
This very night. At first I thought
They might have too much red wine;
But talking further I soon learned
Their eyes had seen a marvelous sign
Up in the heavens. Yes, and heard
An angel telling of the birth
Of Christ, the Saviour, and a choir
Of angels singing, "Peace on earth!"

The shepherds did not linger long.
But since the moment that they left,
The curious have made a path
To this same door. I'm quite bereft
Of my right senses—answering
Their questions. Some have gone to see
The newborn Child. And some believe
He is the Christ of prophecy!

The inn was crowded—each room filled
Last night, when this man Joseph came
In search of lodging for the night.

THERE'S A MESSAGE THERE!

(CAN YOU FIND THEM?)

Some people fail to recognize o p p o r- t u n i t y because it so often c o m e s to them in overalls and l o o k s like work.

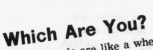

Which Are You?

A lot of people are like a wheel-barrow—not good unless pushed.

Some are like canoes—they have to be paddled.

Some are like kites—If you don't keep them on a string they fly away.

Some are like footballs — you can't tell which way they bounce next.

Some are like baloons—full of wind and ready to blow up.

Some are like trailers — they have to be pulled.

Some are like a good watch—open face, pure gold, quietly busy and full of good works.

Tithing

A. A. Hyde, a millionaire manufacturer, said he began tithing when he was one hun-dred thousand dollars in debt. Many men have said they con-sidered it dishonest to give God a tenth of their incomes while they were in debt. Mr. Hyde said he agreed with the thought until one day it flashed upon him that God was his first creditor.Then he began paying God first, and all the other credi-tors were eventually paid in full. If a man owes you money, it would be wise business policy on your part to encourage him to pay his debt to God first.

—Sunday School Times

A London paper offered a prize for the best definition of money. This was the winning answer:

Money is an instrument that can buy you everything but happiness and pay your fare to every place but Heaven.

GRUMBLE CORNER

"Fine day," said a man to a farmer.

"Bad for the potatoes," was the discontented reply.

Next day, being wet, the man said, "Fine weather for potatoes."

"Yes, but bad for the corn," said the farmer.

Many, like him, stay at Grumble Corner.

—Selected.

SHHHHHHHHHHHH!!!!!

If all we have said this past year, and with never a word left out, were printed in clear black and white, 'twould make queer reading, no doubt.

And then, just suppose, ere our eyes would close, we must read the whole record through; then wouldn't we sigh, and would not we try a great deal less talking to do?

And I more than half think that many a kink would be smoother in life's tangled thread, if one-half that we say along life's way, were left forever unsaid.

—Selected.

The Lord's Loss

Little Johnny was given two dimes one Saturday evening. "One of the dimes," said his father, "is for Sunday school tomorrow, and the other is for an ice cream cone for yourself."

As Johnny ran to the confection-ery to get his ice cream cone, he stumbled and one of the dimes rolled into the sewer drain. "Oh," said Johnny, "there goes the Lord's dime."

Why do families use money they haven't earned to buy things they don't need to impress people they don't like!

During last summer's heat-wave, a church in the Midwest put this on its bulletin board: "You think it's hot here?"—Reville

---

The names of Sunday school teachers are written on God's honor roll although few peo-ple in this world ever hear of teachers. Usually the pupils are the ones who are known and remembered as is D. L. Moody. Who was the Sunday school teacher who talked with him about Christ in the back room of his uncle's shoe store? It was Edward Kim-ball.

An Exalted Position

When Andrew Jackson was president of these United States, a certain man asked to be appointed to a responsible post. Mr. Jackson asked him about his present occupation. He replied that he was a min-ister of the Gospel. "Well, sir," said the President, "you will have to come down from that exalted position in order to ac-cept the highest office I could give you in this government."

Power Over Death

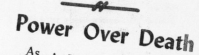

As a young man, D. L. Moody was called upon sud-denly to preach a funeral sermon. He hunted all through the four Gospels trying to find one of Christ's funeral sermons, but search-ed in vain. He found that Christ broke up every funer-al He ever attended. Death could not exist where He was. When the dead heard His voice they sprang to life. Jesus said, I am the resurrection, and the life.

A man may have too much money or too much honor, but he cannot have too much grace.—Spurgeon.

The following is one of Dr. Walter L. Wilson's favorite illustrations.

A ten-year-old boy whose father was a preacher had a deep desire to follow in his father's footsteps. He thought he should begin early in life to train for this noble work of preaching the Gospel. He cast about in his mind as to how he could best train for the various phases of the Christian ministry.

This boy had a black cat which died one night, and was found dead on the back porch in the morning. The lad thought that perhaps this would be just the opportunity to begin practicing to be a preacher. He knew that preachers preached funeral sermons, and here was an opportunity.

He obtained a shoe box and tenderly placed the corpse in this box. The cat had died with its head to one side, and the young fellow could not turn it so it would face up, as he had seen in the coffins at funerals. He therefore cut a hole in the lid of the box and caused the tail to protrude so that visiting friends could see some part of the cat. He dug a grave in the backyard under the peach tree, obtained some string with which to lower the casket, and invited the neighbor children to attend the service.

The sermon was given on the the front porch, the funeral procession proceeded to the backyard, and the cat was gently interred in the grave. When the boys filled the grave, the cat's tail was left unburied. Every two or three days the young preacher pulled up the cat, using the tail for a handle, in order to investigate its condition. After a few such times, the tail would hold no longer and the body remained buried.

Now, said Dr. Wilson, many troubled hearts do this with their sins. They confess them, they put them under the blood, but they continue to drag them up, pull them out, spread them before the Lord, weep over them afresh, and forget that God has blotted them out, to remember them no more.

How foolish we are to bring back those ugly things which God Himself put under the blood when we first confessed. Let us leave them buried, and do as our Lord has done—remember them no more.

Those who wait to repent until the eleventh hour often die at ten thirty.

O what a happy soul am I
  Although I cannot see,
I am resolved that in this world
  Contented I will be;
How many blessings I enjoy
  That other people don't,
To weep and sigh because I'm blind,
  I cannot and I won't.
—Written by Fanny Crosby
at the age of eight.

In the Name of Jesus

During the Civil War a young soldier passing over a battlefield came across a friend who was shot and rapidly nearing the end of life. He straightened out the shattered limbs, washed the blood from his comrade's face, and asked if there was something more that he might do. "Yes," replied the dying soldier, "if you have a piece of paper, I will dictate a note to my father, and I think I can sign it. My father is a prominent judge in the North, and if you take him this message, he will help you." The note read: Dear father, I am dying on the battlefield; one of my friends is helping me. If he ever comes to you, be kind to him for Charlie's sake." Then with rapidly stiffening fingers he signed his name.

After the war the young soldier in ragged uniform sought out the judge. The servants would not admit him, for he looked like a tramp. Finally the judge came out and read the note. He was convinced it was a beggar's appeal. But as he studied the signature, he saw it was indeed his own son's. He embraced the soldier, led him into his home, and said with tears coursing down his cheeks: "You can have anything that my money can buy and everything that my influence can secure." What wrought such a change in the attitude of the judge? It was Charlie's name signed to the note.

Jesus said, "Whatsoever ye shall ask the Father in my name, he will give it."

How a Famous Hymn Was Written

As Tennyson's nurse was sitting one day at his bedside, sharing to a degree the general anxiety about the patient, she said to him suddenly:

"You have written a great many poems, sir, but I have never heard anybody say that there is a hymn among them all. I wish, sir, you would write a hymn while you are living on your sickbed. It might help and comfort many a poor sufferer."

The next morning, when the nurse had taken her quiet place at the bedside, the poet handed her a scrap of paper, saying, "Here is the hymn you wished me to write."

She took it from his hands with expressions of gratified thanks. It proved to be "Crossing the Bar," the poem that was sung in Westminster Abbey at Tennyson's funeral, and which has touched so many hearts.—Evening Mail.

CROSSING THE BAR

Sunset and evening star
  And one clear call for me!
And may there be no moaning of
    the bar,
  When I put out to sea.

But such a tide as moving seems
    asleep,
  Too full for sound or foam,
When that which drew from out
    the boundless deep
  Turns again home.

Twilight and evening bell,
  And after that the dark!
And may there be no sadness of
    farewell,
  When I embark.

For tho' from out our bourne of
    Time and Place
  The flood may bear me far,
I hope to see my Pilot face to face
  When I have crossed the bar.
—Alfred Tennyson

The Best For Christ

By Rev. T. DeWitt Talmage

As He sat at meat there came a woman having an alabaster box of ointment of spikenard very precious—Mark 14:3.

That woman could have gotten a vase that would not have cost so much as those made of alabaster. She might have brought perfume that would have cost only fifty pence; this cost three hundred. As far as I can understand, her whole fortune was in it. She might have been more economical; but no—she gets the very best box, and puts in it the very best perfume, and pours it all out on the head of her Redeemer.

My brothers and sisters in Christ, the trouble is that we bring to Jesus too cheap a box. If we have one of alabaster and one of earthenware, we keep the first for ourselves, and we give the latter to Christ.

We owe Jesus the best of our time, the best of our talents, the best of everything. Is there an hour in the day when we are wider awake than any other, more capable of thought and feeling, let us bring that to Christ. We are apt to take a few moments in the morning when we are getting awake, or a few moments at night when we are getting asleep, to Jesus. If there be an hour in the day when we are most appreciative of God's goodness, and Christ's pardon, and heaven's joy, oh, that is the alabaster box to bring to Jesus. We owe Christ the very best years of our life. When the sight is the clearest, when the hearing is the acutest, when the arm is the strongest, when the nerves are the steadiest, when the imagination is the brightest, let us come to Jesus, and not wait until our joints are stiffened with rheumatism, and the glow is gone out of our temperament, and we arise in the morning as weary as when we laid down at night.

Never go out to meet trouble. If you will just sit still, nine times out of ten someone will intercept it before it reaches you.

—Calvin Coolidge

The Switching

A Story for Children

One day Peter felt very mean in school. He wouldn't put his gym shoes away. He wouldn't finish his number work. He kept on talking when the children were supposed to be quiet.

The teacher sent him to the principal and the principal called his mother. "We are sending Peter home," he said. "He cannot stay in school if he doesn't follow the rules and obey his teacher."

Peter felt very cross and unhappy as he went home. He could hardly believe that the principal had actually sent him away from school. He didn't like it when his teacher was cross with him. He knew the boys and girls would tease him about being sent home.

Sure enough, his mother had a big switch when he came in the door. But she didn't look angry. She looked sad. She asked Peter to sit down on the couch.

"Why are people disobedient and bad?" she asked him.

"I don't know," answered Peter. "Because they feel like it I guess."

"But what makes them feel like it?" Since Peter couldn't answer, Mother answered her own question. "They feel like being bad because they are thinking only of themselves and want their own selfish way. But God says that when we try to get our own selfish way, we aren't the only ones who get hurt."

"Who else gets hurt?" Peter wanted to know.

"The Lord Jesus Himself never did anything wrong. But He died on the Cross to take the punishment that you deserve for your selfishness," his mother explained. "And when you are bad, I am hurt, too."

"What do you mean?" asked Peter. "You never get spanked! I'm the only one who gets spanked!"

"Because I love you, Peter, I am hurt inside," answered his mother. "You hurt me each day with your disobedience and badness. But to help you to understand, I am going to let you hurt me in a different way. Here is the switch. Today you may give me a spanking." At last he took the switch and hit her just a little bit.

"No, hit harder!" commanded his mother. "Hit me as though I had really been selfish and disobedient!"

"No, no!" cried Peter.

"Yes," said his mother.

At last Peter hit his mother across the legs with the switch. He saw tears come into her eyes. Then he threw the switch on the floor and began to cry. "I don't want to hurt you, Mother. I love you!"

His mother put her arms around him. "But you do hurt me, Peter. Every day, by your selfishness and sinfulness, you hurt me far more than any whipping could ever do. The Lord Jesus loves you, too, and because He does, your disobedience hurts Him in the same way."

Peter had never understood that before. "I'm sorry, Mother. I want to tell Jesus I'm sorry, too."

Then Peter prayed and asked Jesus to forgive him and to take away his selfishness and disobedience. Somehow, when he had finished praying, he felt better than he ever had before. Somehow, he didn't even want to be mean anymore.

Mother took Peter back to school in the car.

"I'm ready to obey my teacher now," Peter told the principal. Then the principal let him go back to his room. There, Peter asked his teacher to forgive him. She smiled and seemed happy, then. The children didn't tease him either. They were glad that he was going to try to be different.

And from that time on, Peter was different because he kept asking the Lord Jesus to help him.

—*Primary Days*

To sin by silence, when they should protest, makes cowards of men.
--Abraham Lincoln.

There is no time lost in waiting if you are waiting on the Lord.

Is It Good Night, or Good-By?

A True Incident

A devoted Christian businessman was struck by an automobile and seriously injured. He was hurried to a hospital, where he was informed he had only about two hours to live. But he had implicit faith in the goodness of God and in future life. To him death was only a gateway leading to a better world. He called his family, and gave each member a parting message.

Addressing his wife, he said: "You have been the greatest woman in the world to me. Through sunshine and shadow we have walked together. You have been my inspiration in everything I have undertaken, especially in our service for God. Many times I have seen the glory of God shining in your face. I love you far more than on the day you became my bride. Good night, dear; I'll see you in the morning."

Turning to one of his daughters, he said, "Mary, you are our first-born. What a joy you have been to your father! How glad I am that you have followed in the footsteps of your mother. In face and spirit you have always reminded me of her. I see in you the sweet, beautiful young woman who left her home to be the builder and keeper of mine. What a Christian you are, Mary! Never forget how your father loved you. Good night, Mary, good night."

He then turned to his oldest son: "Will, your coming into our home has been an unmixed blessing. You were a manly boy; you have become an exemplary man. You love the God of your father. How proud I am of such a son! You will continue to grow in every Christian grace and blessing. Good night, Will, good night."

Charlie was next. But Charlie had fallen under evil influences and had grievously disappointed his father and mother. The dying man passed over him, and spoke to the youngest child instead.

"Gracie," he said, "your coming was like the breaking of a new day in our home. You have long been a song of gladness, a ray of light. You have filled our hearts with music. When you surrendered your life to Christ, your father's cup of happiness was full to overflowing. Good night, little girl, good night."

Then the dying man called Charlie to his side, and there were blinding tears in his eyes as he said: "Good-by, Charlie. What a promising boy you were, Charlie. Your father and mother believed you would develop into a noble man We gave you all the opportunities we gave to the other children. If there has been any difference, you yourself must admit that the difference was all in your favor. But you have disappointed us. You have followed the broad, downward road. You have not heeded the warning of God's Word. You have not listened to the call of the Saviour. But I have always loved you, and love you still, Charlie. God only knows how much I love you. Good-by, Charlie, good-by, good-by."

Charlie seized his father's hand and between sobs he cried out, "Father, why have you said good night to the others and good-by to me?"

"For the simple reason that I will meet the other members of the family in the morning," he answered. "But the same promises of God's Word which assure us of a reunion deny me the hope of seeing you over there. Good-by, Charlie, good-by."

Charlie fell on his knees by his father's bed, and cried out in agony of soul, praying God to forgive his sins and to give him hope of meeting his father again.

"Do you mean it, Charlie? Are you in earnest?" the father asked.

"God knows I am," said the heartbroken young man.

"Then God will hear you and save you, Charlie. Now I can say good night to you, instead of good-by. Good night, Charlie, good night. I am grateful to God that it is not good-by. Good night, my boy." And he was gone.

Charlie is now a preacher of the gospel. He prepared to meet his loved ones in heaven—and his Saviour—while he still had time. Have you?

—*The Pentecostal Evangel*

His New Brother

Say, I've got a little brother,
Never teased to have him, nother,
  But he's here;
They just went ahead and bought him,
And last week the doctor brought him;
  Wa'nt that queer?

When I heard the news from Molly,
Why! I thought at first 'twas jolly,
  'Cause, you see:
I s'posed I could go and get him,
An' then Mamma 'course she would let him
  Play with me.

But when I had once looked at him,
"Why," I says, "my sakes! is that him?
  Just that mite?"
They said, "Yes," and "ain't he cunnin?"
  He's a sight.

He's so small, it's just amazin',
And you'd think that he was blazin',
  He's so red.
And his nose is like a berry,
And he's bald as Uncle Jerry
  On the head.

Why, he isn't worth a dollar;
All he does is cry and holler
  More and more;
Won't sit up, you can't arrange him;
I don't see why Pa don't change him
  At the store.

Now we've got to dress and feed him,
And we really didn't need him
  More'n a frog;
Why'd they buy a baby brother
When they know I'd good deal ruther
  Have a dog?

Author Unknown

Compensation

I never knew a night so black
Light failed to follow in its tracks;
I never knew a storm so gray
It failed to have its clearing day;
I never knew such bleak despair
That there was not a rift somewhere;
I never knew an hour so drear
Love could not fill it full of cheer.

—Edwin H. Stuart

No matter what a man's past may have been, his future is spotless.

I believe that if there is one thing which pierces the Saviour's heart with unutterable grief, it is not the world's iniquity but the church's indifference.—F. B. Meyer.

Deathbed repentance is burning the candle of life in the service of the devil, and then b l o w i n g the smoke into the face of God.—Billy Sunday

Followin' Father Home

Years ago, when I
    Was jest a little lad,
An' after school hours used to work
    Around the farm with dad,
I used to be so wearied out
    When eventide was come,
That I got kinder anxious-like
    About the journey home;
But dad, he used to lead the way,
An' once in a while turn 'round and say,
    So cheerin' like, so tender, "Come!
Come on, my son, you're nearly home!"
    That allers used to help me some;
An' so I followed father home.

I'm old an' gray and feeble now,
    An' trembly at the knee,
But life seems jest the same today
    As then it seemed to me.
For while I'm still so wearied out
    When eventide is come,
An' still git kinder anxious-like
    About the journey home,
But still my Father leads the way,
An' once in a while I hear Him say,
    So cheerin' like, so tender, "Come!
Come on my son, you're nearly home!"
    An' same as then, that helps me some,
And so I'm following Father home.

—*Author Unknown*

71

Two Little Pairs of BOOTS

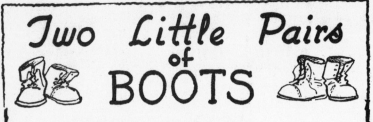

Two little pairs of boots to-night,
 Before the fire are drying,
Two little pairs of tired feet
 In a trundle bed are lying;
The tracks they left upon the floor
 Make me feel much like sighing.

Those little boots with copper toes!
 They run the lifelong day,
And oftentimes I almost wish
 That they were miles away,
So tired am I to hear so oft
 Their heavy tramp at play.

They walked about the new-ploughed ground,
 Where mud in plenty lies;
They rolled it up in marbles round,
 And baked it into pies,
And then at night upon the floor,
 In every shape it dries.

To-day I was disposed to scold,
 But when I see to-night,
These little boots before the fire,
 With copper toes so bright,
I think how sad my heart would be
 To put them out of sight.

For in a trunk up-stairs I've laid
 Two socks of white and blue;
If called to put those boots away,
 O God, what should I do?
I mourn that there are not to-night
 Three pairs, instead of two.

I mourn because I thought how nice
 My neighbor 'cross the way
Could keep her carpets all the year
 From getting worn and gray;
Yet well I know she'd smile to own
 Some little boots to-day.

We mothers weary get and worn,
 Over our load of care;
But how we speak of little ones,
 Let each of us beware;
For what would our fireside be at night
 If no little boots were there?
        —Selected From *Home Duties* by R. T. Cross

When a Fly Acted as a Missionary

God sometimes uses strange messengers to do His work. An infidel wished to see the effects of the preaching of the great Whitefield. He had heard so much about his marvelous work and the number converted under his preaching that he was curious.

The services were held in the open air, so the infidel decided to climb a tree, where he could witness what was going on. He wanted to see but he was determined that he would not listen to one word that the preacher said. So when he had climbed a tree close to the speaker, he plugged both ears with his fingers.

By and by, a persistent fly landed on his nose, annoying him greatly as it walked over his face. He stood the annoyance as long as he could, then his hand left one ear in order to brush the annoying fly. The open ear heard the preacher saying, "He that hath ears to hear, let him hear." This was a remarkable utterance, just when he was doing his best to close his ears!

Stranger still, he heard the preacher say, "They stopped their ears, that they should not hear"—just what he had been doing! And listen, "It is come to pass, that as he cried, and they would not hear; so they cried, and I would not hear, saith the Lord of hosts."

The message so impressed the infidel that he turned to the Lord and pleaded for forgiveness, thereby escaping the doom of those who would not listen.

Truly God's hand is not shortened that He cannot save, when He can make use of such an insignificant little messenger as a fly to bring about the conversion of an infidel.—Esther Dalziel Hooey in **Christian Life Missionary**.

Keep your words sweet — you may have to eat them.

A woman told Billy Sunday that she had a bad temper, but it was over in a minute. "So is a shotgun, but it blows everything to pieces," was his reply.—Selected.

So much to do; so little done!
Ah! yesternight I saw the sun
Sink beamless down the vaulted gray—
The ghastly ghost of yesterday.

So little done; so much to do!
Each morning breaks on conflicts new;
But eager, brave, I'll join the fray,
And fight the battle of today.

So much to do; so little done!
But when it's o'er—the victory won—
O then, my soul, this strife and sorrow
Will end in that great, glad tomorrow.

—James Roberts Gilmore.

Nagging

Nagging has sent many a man to destruction and driven some women to despair. You can nag in any language that human lips have spoken. You can nag when your lips are tight shut by lifting the eyebrows, tossing the head, or sneering a sneer. It is not confined to sex. It is due to disposition. The one who nags injures himself and is cruel in the extreme to the one attacked. A good, old-fashioned quarrel is preferable. If the continual dropping of water wears away a stone, it is no less true that constant nagging will ruin the best disposition.

If you have a complaint, make it, but don't nag. If you have been injured, say so, and don't nag. If you have a request to make, make it, but stop nagging. Most people nag when they are tired; some, when they are ill or neglected; others, when they themselves are not right; and some, because of downright, old-fashioned meanness. Nagging is a sin against yourself, your household, your husband, your wife, your friends. Why not list it with other sins? That is where it belongs. No Christian can be guilty of it and be a true follower of Jesus.—Selected.

—*Gospel Herald*

"Nails Gone—Scars Remain!"

During my early childhood I had a fiery temper which often caused me to say or do unkind things.

One day, after an argument had sent one of my playmates home in tears, my father told me that for each thoughtless, mean thing I did he would drive a nail into our gatepost. Each time I did a kindness or a good deed, one nail would be withdrawn.

Months passed. Each time I entered our gate, I was reminded of the reasons for those ever-increasing nails, until, finally, getting them out became a challenge.

At last the wished-for day arrived—only one more nail! As my father withdrew it I danced around proudly exclaiming, "See, Daddy, the nails are all gone."

Father gazed intently at the post as he thoughtfully replied, "Yes, the nails are gone—but the scars remain."

—Hazel Farris,
Lexington, Kentucky

His Yoke Is Easy

The world deceives me; it offers peace and joy and rest.
But ever leaves me with hungry heart and second best,
I came to Jesus, and there I found it all I'd missed!

My soul was thirsty; I hewed me broken cisterns vain;
My heart was fainting; but all I found was failures' pain
Till I met Jesus, who watered me with Heaven's rain.

For songs in nighttime, for joy in pain and help in need,
My Saviour hears me, forgives my sins and guides my deeds;
I love to serve Him, and so I follow where He leads.

My life was empty of all that's good and true and clean;
Until I met Him, no peace my wicked heart had seen;
But all earth's tempests stirr'd up its sea of mire unclean.

A slave to Jesus, oh gladly would I ever be;
His labor joyful, reproach for Him is sweet to me;
Ten thousand blessings repay all pain I'll ever see.

His yoke is easy, His burden light;
His way is happy and always bright.
In this world's midnight, He is my light.
His yoke is easy, His burden light.

John R. Rice

Anxiety for Conversion of Children

There was in my ancestral line an incident so strangely impressive that it seems more like romance than reality. It has sometimes been so inaccurately put forth that I now give you the true incident.

My grandfather and grandmother, living at Somerville, New Jersey, went to Baskingridge to witness a revival under the ministry of the Rev. Dr. Finley. They came home so impressed with what they had seen that *they resolved on the salvation of their children.* The young people of the house were to go off for an evening party, and my grandmother said, "Now, when you are all ready for the party come to my room, for I have something very important to tell you." All ready for departure, they came to her room, and she said to them, "Now, I want you to remember, while you are away this evening, that I am all the time in this room praying for your salvation, and I shall not cease praying until you get back." The young people went to the party, but amid the loudest hilarities of the night they could not forget that their mother was praying for them.

The evening passed, and the night passed. The next day my grandparents heard an outcry in an adjoining room, and they went in and found their daughter imploring the salvation of the Gospel. The daughter told them that her brothers were at the barn and at the wagon-house under powerful conviction for sin. They went to the barn. They found my uncle Jehiah, who afterwards became a minister of the Gospel, crying to God for mercy. They went to the wagon-house. They found their son David, who afterwards became my father, imploring God's pardon and mercy. Before a great while the whole family were saved; and David went and told the story to a young woman to whom he was affianced, who, as a result of the story, became a Christian, and from her own lips—my mother—I have received the incidents. The story of that converted household ran through all the neighborhood, from family to family, until the whole region was whelmed with religious awakening, and at the next communion in the village church at Somerville over two hundred souls stood up to profess the faith of the Gospel.—Talmage.

No Enemies?

He has no enemies, you say?
  My friend, your boast is poor:
He who hath mingled in the fray
  Of duty, that the brave endure,
Must have made foes. If he has none
  Small is the work that he has done.
He has hit no traitor on the hip;
  He has cast no cup from tempted lip;
He has never turned the wrong to right,
  He has been a coward in the fight.

—Anon.

In the Shelter of the Fold

Learn a parable from the sheep! The following item was clipped from the *Canadian Baptist* magazine.

"What's keeping the shepherd?" asked one of the ninety and nine. "Doesn't he know his place is here with us?"

"Oh, he's out scouring the country again, looking for young Balaam, no doubt."

"Balaam still as wild as ever?" queried a third. "Probably has crashed over a precipice by now. I've insisted for a long time that his name should be taken off the roster of this fold."

"He certainly hasn't meant much to us," said the second speaker. "I think it's time the shepherd realized who pays his salary. It's our wool that goes to market."

"You're right," the first speaker agreed. "Since we granted him a travel allowance the shepherd's been burning up the back roads, doing things for individuals who don't contribute an ounce of wool to his upkeep."

"I feel we're being neglected," bleated the other. "Look at tonight, for instance. Five minutes before the time for our mid-week meeting, and the shepherd nowhere in sight. Looks as though we'll have to cancel it for this week."

"Now, now, you three," interposed an older member of the flock. "We are not so helpless as all that. We can carry on; and it wouldn't be the first time."

"That's just the trouble," grumbled one of the trio. "It's getting altogether too frequent. I know we can manage, but we pay the shepherd a full-time salary and he owes his full time to us."

"I strongly support that," said another, "and I propose that we call the fold to order and get a motion on the books to the effect, *Flock Attention.*"

"Not much response," deplored the third. "What's all that hubbub at the door? The shepherd, you say? Bringing Balaam with him? Two of Balaam's companions as well?"

"What a demonstration" exclaimed the first. "This is no time to present my motion. Just forget about it. After all, you have to give the shepherd credit; he's built up this fold to a self-sustaining level, and I suppose it will make things more comfortable for the rest of us, to have three more contributing from their fleeces to the flock."

Ann Landers Answers

DEAR ANN LANDERS:

"A year ago our two-year-old son, Earl, had difficulty breathing so we took him to a doctor. We learned Earl is allergic to cigarette smoke. My husband said we both had to quit smoking right then and there. He hasn't touched a cigarette since. I went back to smoking that same night.

"I don't smoke when little Earl is in the room and it's awfully hard on me. My husband doesn't know I smoke so I make excuses to go to the basement or out in the garage whenever I want a cigarette. Sneaking around is making me nervous.

"Do you think it would be wrong if we let a nice couple adopt little Earl—a nice couple who don't smoke? Then I could smoke in the open and my husband could take it up again, too.

"The only problem is that my husband is crazy about the boy. I love him, too, but I am more the practical type. What do you think, Ann? Mrs. E. R. M."

DEAR MRS. _____:

"I think a lot of people who read this letter are going to say I made it up. It's utterly fantastic that a mother would put cigarettes ahead of her own child.

"Don't present your wild idea to your husband. I wouldn't blame him if he decided to keep little Earl and unload YOU."

How would you have answered this almost inhuman "lady"—to use the term loosely? Probably she will not die too soon of cancer! Pity the poor child who will be raised under such a roof!

HE DID--HE CAN--HE WILL

The God that stopped the sun on high,
And sent the manna from the sky,
Laid flat the walls of Jericho,
And put to flight old Israel's foe.
Why can't He answer prayer today,
And drive each stormy cloud away?
Who turned the water into wine,
And healed a helpless cripple's spine—
Commanded tempests, "Peace be still."
And hungry multitudes did fill,
His power is just the same today.
So why not labor, watch and pray?
He conquered in the Lion's den,
Brought Lazarus back to life again.
He heard Elijah's cry for rain,
And freed the sufferers from pain.
If He could do those wonders then,
Let's prove our mighty God again.
Why can't the God Who raised the dead,
Gave little David Goliath's head—
Cast out the demons with a word,
Yet sees the fall of one wee bird—
Do signs and miracles today,
In that same good old-fashioned way?
HE CAN. He's just the same today.

—Martin Luther

There is a tradition that Jonathan Edwards, third president of Princeton and America's greatest thinker, had a daughter with an ungovernable temper. But, as is so often the case, this infirmity was not known to the outside world. A worthy young man fell in love with this daughter and sought her hand in marriage. "You can't have her," was the abrupt answer of Jonathan Edwards. "But I love her," the young man replied. "You can't have her," said Edwards. "But she loves me," replied the young man. Again Edwards said, "You can't have her." "Why?" said the young man. "Because she is not worthy of you." "But," he asked, "she is a Christian, is she not?" "Yes, she is a Christian, but the grace of God can live with some people with whom no one else could ever live."

Two Drinks

On the last day of Lincoln's life, the great emancipator said: "We have cleared up a colossal job. Slavery is abolished. After reconstruction the next great question will be the overthrow and suppression of the legalized liquor traffic."

That evening, Mr. Booth stopped in a saloon, filled himself with liquor to nerve himself for his planned tragedy. That night Lincoln's bodyguard left the theater for a drink of liquor at the same saloon. While he was away Booth shot Lincoln. Those two drinks were the most costly drinks in American history. Liquor is the greatest enemy of mankind.

70 Years

If one lives to be 70 years of age and is the average person he spends:

23 years sleeping
19 years working
9 years playing
6 years traveling
6 years eating
4 years sick
2 years dressing himself
1 year in the house of the Lord.

—Selected

God's Christmas Gift

The festive spirit fills the air,
And people's hearts are gay,
There're trees and lights and lots of toys
'Twill soon be Christmas day;
So much is said of Santa Claus
And of the gifts he gives,
So little said of God's dear Son
Whose own birthday it is.

Wild merriment is on every hand,
They drink and dance and curse,
They must forget what Christmas is,
Why Jesus came to earth;
If He should speak at Christmastime,
I'm sure that He would say,
"I'd rather you My birth not keep
Than do it in this way."

E'en as it was one bygone night
In far off Bethlehem,
When Jesus in a manger lay,
No room within the inn;
Today He's shut outside men's hearts,
Hearts filled with sin and wrong,
They care not that with nail pierced hand
He's knocked there oh so long.

They give their presents to their friends,
Receive gifts from each one,
Neglecting God's great Christmas gift—
He gave His only Son
To die upon the awful cross
And pay our debt of sin,
To open wide the gates of Heaven
And let us enter in.

The gift's still waiting at the tree,
So few His Word believe,
Though offered freely to all men,
They will not Christ receive;
The tree is just a cross of wood,
Unsightly to behold,
But oh, the gift the dear Lord gives
Is better far than gold.

There are no lights to light His tree,
No decorations fine,
No pretty tinsel, balls, and bells
That glitter, gleam, and shine;
And yet there're stains of His own blood
To ransom our whole race,
There's light to guide the wanderer home
That shines from His dear face.

Why should His gift rejected be?
How God must grieve today!
When He has paid so great a price,
Should Christ be turned away?
Oh! open now your heart's door wide,
Receive God's gift of love,
His joy and peace and grace He'll give,
Eternal life above.

Russell Stellwagon

Evangelical Alliance missionary
in Japan who sent this for THE
SWORD OF THE LORD, 1955.

Catching Men

I SOMETIMES HEAR OF PERSONS GETTING VERY ANGRY AFTER A GOSPEL SERMON, AND I SAY TO MYSELF, "I AM NOT SORRY FOR IT." SOMETIMES WHEN WE ARE FISHING THE FISH GETS THE HOOK INTO HIS MOUTH, HE PULLS HARD AT THE LINE; IF HE WERE DEAD, HE WOULD NOT; BUT HE IS A LIVE FISH, WORTH THE GETTING; AND THOUGH HE RUNS AWAY FOR AWHILE, WITH THE HOOK IN HIS JAWS, HE CANNOT ESCAPE. HIS VERY WRIGGLING AND HIS ANGER SHOW THAT HE HAS GOT THE HOOK AND THE HOOK HAS GOT HIM. HAVE THE LANDING-NET READY; WE SHALL LAND HIM BY AND BY. GIVE HIM MORE LINE; LET HIM SPEND HIS STRENGTH, AND THEN WE WILL LAND HIM, AND HE SHALL BELONG TO CHRIST FOREVER.—CHARLES SPURGEON.

Teaching Righteousness Early:

I tell you, my friends, the reason we don't reclaim all our children from worldliness is because we begin too late. Parents wait until their children lie before they teach them the value of truth. They wait until their children swear before they teach them the importance of righteous conversation. They wait until their children are all wrapped up in this world before they tell them of a better world. Too late with your prayers. Too late with your discipline. Too late with your benediction. You put all care upon your children between 12 and 18. Why do you not put the chief care between 4 and 9? It is too late to repair a vessel when it has got out of the dry-dock!—Talmage.

I Must Die

I must die.
Not waiting 'til my hair is white,
Or falling in a battle fight,
Or sleeping on a final night,
But daily.

Self must die.
All that self ever hoped to be;
Self dies hard, not easily.
In its place my Lord must see
A corpse.

I must die.
Clay I was and clay I'll be;
Let my Potter fashion me,
Then I'll be whatever He
Would wish.
—Bill Harvey.

I have seen the Christian man in the depths of poverty, when he lived from hand to mouth, and scarcely knew where he should find the next meal, still with his mind unruffled, calm and quiet. If he had been as rich as an Indian prince, yet could he not have had less care. If he had been told that his bread should always come to his door, and the stream which ran hard by should never dry; if he had been quite sure that ravens would bring him bread and meat in the morning, and again in the evening—he would not have been one wit more calm. There is his neighbor on the other side of the street not half so poor, but wearied from morning till night, working his fingers to the bone, bringing himself to the grave with anxiety.—Spurgeon.

Dying Happy

Mr. Rowland Hill used merrily to say when he got old that he hoped that they had not forgotten him. That is how he came to look at death; and he would go to some old woman if he could and say, "Now, dear sister, if you go before I go, mind that you give my love to John Bunyan and the other Johns. Tell them that Rowley is stopping behind a little while, but he is coming on as fast as he can."

Oh! it is a sweet thing gradually to melt away and have the tenement gradually taken down, yet not to feel any trouble about it, but to know that you are in the great Father's hands, and you shall wake up where old age and infirmities will all have passed away, and where, in everlasting youth, you shall behold the face of Him you love.—Charles Spurgeon.

What A Contrast

Byron wrote before he died:
"*My days are in the yellow leaf;
The flowers and fruits of love are gone;
The worm, the canker, and the grief
Are mine alone!*"

Paul wrote just before he died: "I have fought a good fight, I have finished my course, I have kept the faith: henceforth there is laid up for me a crown of righteousness."
— *Moody Monthly*

The Table Liquor Spreads

The story is told of a poor woman who went to a saloon in search of her husband. She found him there, and setting a covered dish, which she had brought with her, upon the table, she said, "Thinking that you are too busy to come home to dinner, I have brought you yours," and departed. With a laugh the man invited his friends to dine with him; but on removing the cover from the dish he found only a slip of paper, on which was written, "I hope you will enjoy your meal. It is the same as your family have at home."

—*Gospel Herald*

Big Men

George Washington shocked General Lafayette one morning by merely being what the father of our country described as a gentleman. It seems George Washington and Lafayette were talking together when a slave passed. The old colored man paused, tipped his hat, and said, "Good mo'nin', Gen'l Washin'ton."

Immediately George Washington removed his hat, bowed and wished the man a pleasant day.

After a moment of shocked silence General Lafayette exclaimed, "Why did you bow to a slave?"

The great man smiled and replied, "I would not allow him to be a better gentleman than I."

Soul Winning

Even if I were utterly selfish, and had no care for anything but my own happiness, I would choose if I might, under God, to be a soul winner, for never did I know perfect overflowing, unalterable happiness of the purest and most enabling order till I first heard of one who had sought and found the Saviour through my means. No young mother ever rejoiced over her first-born child, no warrior was ever so exultant over a hard won victory.

—C. H. Spurgeon.

"QUOTABLE QUOTES"

Seventy-five per cent of the victory depends on preparation.
—Dr. C. E. Matthews

⚒

I don't like these cold, precise, perfect people who, in order not to speak wrong, never speak at all, and in order not to do wrong, never do anything.—Beecher.

⚒

It is a mistake to suppose that men succeed through success; they much more often succeed through failures.—Samuel Smiles

⚒

The best way to show that a stick is crooked is not to argue about it or to spend time denouncing it, but to lay a straight stick alongside it.—D. L. Moody

⚒

No man ever repented on his deathbed of being a Christian.—Hannah Moore

⚒

The aim, if reached or not, makes great the life,
Try to be Shakespeare—leave the rest to fate.
Robert Browning

⚒

One child said to another, "If one of us would get off this tricycle I could ride it much better."—Dr. Henrietta C. Mears

---

On his dining room wall Augustine had written these words, "He who speaks evil of an absent man or woman is not welcome at this table."

—

There is no time in life when books do not influence a man.—Walter Besant.

—

Faith is not believing that God **can**, but that God **will**!

—

When you have nothing left but God, then for the first time you become aware that God is enough.—Maude Royden

—

It's a good safe rule to sojourn in every place as if you meant to spend your life there, never omitting an opportunity of doing a kindness, speaking a true word or making a friend.—Ruskin

—

Galeazius, a man of great wealth, who suffered martyrdom at St. Angelo, in Italy, when warmly entreated by his friends to recant, and to save his life, replied: "Death is much sweeter to me with the testimony of truth, than life with its least denial."

—

COURAGE is what it takes to stand up and speak; it is also what it takes, on occasion, to sit down and listen.—Selected.

—

Christ died for sin; the believer dies to sin; the unbeliever dies in sin.
—D. L. Moody

Long prayers injure prayer meetings. Fancy a man praying for twenty minutes, and then asking God to forgive his shortcomings.—Spurgeon

⚒

It is mine to obey His commands; it is not mine to direct His counsels. I am His servant, not His solicitor. I call upon Him, and He will deliver me.—C. H. Spurgeon.

⚒

God always gives His best to those who leave the choice with Him.

—Jim Elliot

⚒

You cannot repent too soon, because you know not how soon it may be too late.

⚒

Three short prayers:
"Lord, save me" (Peter)
"Lord, help me" (Syrophenician woman)
"Lord, remember me" (dying thief)

⚒

Robert Murray M'Cheyne used to pray, "O God, make me as holy as a pardoned sinner can be made!"

⚒

I would sooner be a cat on hot bricks or a toad under a harrow than let my own children be my masters.—Spurgeon.

7 Men Went Singing Into Heaven

"One of the strangest experiences in my life is connected with war," says Nordenberg, an eminent engineer in Finland.

"I offered my services to the Government and was appointed an officer in General Mannerheim's army. It was a terrible time. We besieged the town. It had been taken by the Red Army and we re-took it. A number of Red prisoners were under my guard. Seven of them were to be shot at dawn on Monday. I shall never forget the preceding Sunday. The seven doomed men were kept in the basement of the town hall. In the passage my men stood at attention with their rifles.

"The atmosphere was filled with hatred. My soldiers were drunk with victory and taunted their prisoners, who swore as much as they could and beat the walls with their bleeding fists. Others called for their wives and children who were far away. At dawn they were all to die.

"We had the victory, that was true enough; but the value of this seemed to diminish as the night advanced. I began to wonder whether there did not rest a curse on arms whichever side used them.

"Then something happened: one of the men doomed to death began to sing! 'He is mad!' was everybody's first thought. But I had noticed this man, Koskinen, had not raved and cursed like the others. Quietly he had sat on his bench, a picture of utter despair. Nobody said anything to him—each was carrying his burden in his own way and Koskinen sang, rather waveringly at first, then his voice grew stronger and filled out, and became natural and free. All the prisoners turned and looked at the singer who now seemed to be in his element.

Safe in the arms of Jesus,
Safe on His gentle breast,
There by His love o'ershadowed,
Sweetly my soul shall rest.
Hark, 'tis the voice of angels,
Born in a song to me
Over the fields of glory,
Over the jasper sea.

"Over and over again Koskinen sang that verse and when he finished everyone was quiet for a few minutes until a wild-looking individual broke out with 'Where did you get that, you fool? Are you trying to make us religious?'

"Koskinen looked at his comrades and his eyes filled with tears. Then he asked quietly: 'Comrades, will you listen to me for a minute? You asked me where I got that song: it was from The Salvation Army, I heard it there three weeks ago. At first I also laughed at this song but it got me. It is cowardly to hide your beliefs: the God my mother believed in has now become my God also. I cannot tell you how it happened, but I know that it has happened. I lay awake last night and suddenly I felt that I had to find the Savior and to hide in Him. Then I prayed—like the thief on the cross—that Christ would forgive me and cleanse my sinful soul, and make me ready to stand before Him whom I should meet soon.

" 'It was a strange night,' continued Koskinen. 'There were times when everything seemed to shine around me. Verses from the Bible and from the Song Book came to my mind. They brought a message of the crucified Savior and the blood that cleanses from sin and of the Home He has prepared for us. I thanked Him, accepted it, and since then this verse has been sounding inside me. It was God's answer to my prayer. I could no longer keep it to myself! Within a few hours I shall be with the Lord, saved by His grace.'

"Koskinen's face shone as by an inward light. His comrades sat there quietly. He himself stood there transfixed. My soldiers were listening to what this Red revolutionary had to say.

" 'You are right, Koskinen,' said one of his comrades at last. 'If only I knew that there is mercy for me, too! But these hands of mine have shed blood and I have reviled God and trampled on all that is holy. Now I realize that there is a Hell and that it is the proper place for me.'

"He sank to the ground with despair depicted on his face. 'Pray for me, Koskinen,' he groaned, 'tomorrow I shall die and my soul will be in the hands of the Devil!'

"And there these two Red soldiers went down on their knees and prayed for each other. It was no long prayer, but it opened Heaven for both, and we who listened to it forgot our hatred. It melted in the light from Heaven, for here two men who were soon to die sought reconciliation with God. A door leading into the invisible stood ajar and we were entranced by the sight.

"Let me tell you shortly that by the time it was four o'clock all Koskinen's comrades had followed his example and began to pray. The change in the atmosphere was indescribable. Some of them sat on the floor, others talked of spiritual things.

"The night had almost gone and day was dawning. No one had had a moment's sleep. 'Sing the song once more for us, Koskinen,' said one of them. And you should have heard them sing! Not only that song but verses and choruses long forgotten came forth from their memories as buds in the sunshine. The soldiers on guard united their voices with them.

"The town clock struck six. How I wished I could have begged for grace for these men, but I knew that this was impossible.

"Between two rows of soldiers they marched out to execution. One of them asked to be allowed once more to sing Koskinen's song. Permission was granted. Then they asked to die with uncovered faces—and with hands raised to Heaven they sang with might and main:

Safe in the arms of Jesus,
Safe on His gentle breast.

When the last lines had died out the lieutenant gave the word 'Fire!' and the seven Red soldiers had fought their last fight. We inclined our heads in silent prayer.

"What had happened in the hearts of the others I do not know; but so far as I was concerned I was a new man from that hour. I had met Christ in one of His lowliest and youngest disciples and I had seen enough to realize that I too, could be His. 'The Lord looketh from heaven; he beholdeth all the sons of men' " (Psalm 33:13).

Jesus said: "I am the resurrection and the life: he that believeth in me, though he were to die, yet shall he live" (John 11:25, R.V.).

—(Translated for "All the World" by Major Clara Becker.)—*The War Cry.* Reprinted here from *Sword Book of Treasures.*

Half-Wit Jack and the Agnostic

By Dr. T. J. McCrossan

A Philadelphia friend told us this story. He said an agonstic lawyer lived for years in the next block to him on the same street. He was naturally a very kindly man and had a host of friends; but, because of this fact his evil influence (religiously) was all the greater.

One morning, while the agnostic and this friend were waiting for the same car, a truck drove up and unloaded a great tent on the corner lot opposite, and other men began immediately to put the tent up. Being curious to know what the tent was for, the lawyer went over to inquire, and found that an evangelist was beginning meetings there that evening. That evening the tent meeting began, and soon a great crowd was attending, for the evangelist was a real man of God.

About the fourth morning after the meetings started, the lawyer heard that a little fellow about fourteen years old, known throughout the whole community as Half Wit Jack, had been saved the night before. That same morning our friend was waiting for the car, when he saw the lawyer come out of his gate and walk toward the corner. Suddenly little Half Wit Jack came around that corner walking toward the lawyer. The lawyer stopped him and said something. Little Jack replied, and then walked rapidly away. When the agnostic reached the corner to take his car, he just nodded to our friend and all other acquaintances, and then walked off by himself. When they boarded the car, he went away up front and sat by himself. He tried to make his friends believe he was reading his paper, but our friend, who was watching him keenly, could see that he was not reading. Next morning the lawyer was just as queer and unfriendly. Again he went to the front of the car, and had nothing to say to anyone. The result was that all that knew him were asking one another: What is wrong with Lawyer A?

After this strange conduct of lawyer A. had lasted about three days, that night our friend and his wife went to the tent meeting; and, to their great surprise, they saw lawyer A. there. The evangelist preached a splendid gospel sermon, and then urged all the unsaved who desired to accept Christ as the Saviour, to come to the altar. The first man to go was lawyer A., the agnostic. Some one told the evangelist who he was, and he went down and spoke with him; and, in a few minutes, they both arose and walked to the platform. The evangelist then said: Lawyer A., whom you all know has accepted Christ as his Saviour, and he desires now to tell you neighbors what led him to do so.

The lawyer then stood up and said: Neighbors, you all know that for many years I have been a conscientious agnostic, and that I have talked against the Bible because it taught that there was a Heaven after death for the good, and a Hell for the wicked. Well, three days ago I heard that little Half Wit Jack had got religion here the night before; and, as I was walking to take the car the next morning, I saw Jack coming toward me. I stopped him and said: Jack, they tell me you got religion last night. Yes, Mr. A., I did. Well, Jack, haven't I often told you that there isn't any Heaven and there isn't any Hell? Yes, Mr. A., you have: but last night God was talking to me, and I began to think for myself. I reasoned like this: Suppose there isn't any Heaven, and suppose there isn't any Hell, then, Mr. A., I will be just as well off as you are when I die. But if there is a Heaven, and if there is a Hell, then I will have two chances to your one of going to Heaven, and you will surely go to Hell; and, Mr. A., I am no fool: and he walked rapidly away.

The lawyer then told the audience how God had used those words of Half Wit Jack to make him think, as never before. All day long, except when busy with clients, the Holy Ghost would repeat to him little Jack's words: "Suppose there isn't any Heaven, and suppose there isn't any Hell, then, Mr. A., I will be just as well off as you, when I die. But if there is a Heaven, and if there is a Hell, then I will have two chances to your one of going to Heaven, and you will surely go to Hell; and, Mr. A., I am no fool." Then at night, he said, God would wake him up, and again and again—like a voice speaking to him from within—he would hear little Jack's words: "Suppose there isn't any Heaven, and suppose there isn't any Hell, then, Mr. A., I will be just as well off as you when I die. But if there is a Heaven, and if there is a Hell, then I will have two chances to your one of going to Heaven, and you will surely go to Hell; and, Mr. A., I am no fool." The result was, friends, he added, that I saw myself as a poor lost sinner who needed a Saviour; so I came here tonight, and God has saved me for time and eternity.

(From *The Bible: Its Hell and Its Ages*).

Reveille--Not Taps

A soldier said, "When I die do not sound taps over my grave, but reveille-- the morning call, the summons to rise."

"It Kicks Me"

A missionary in India tells of a Brahman priest who listened to the preaching of the Gospel. He was given a Telugu Testament on condition that he would read it. He did so—then, meeting the missionary, he said in Telugu: "I wish you to take the Book back. As I read it, it kicks me, and makes me feel very unhappy."—King's Business

The Resurrection Is Sure

A Hungarian countess, a professed unbeliever, commanded that her body be interred in a stone casket in a mausoleum that was to be built about it. A plate was placed on the front of the mausoleum giving her name and some particulars of her death, and then the words, "Not to be opened for eternity." She would defy God to raise her from the dead!

But while they were building that mausoleum and before sealing the body in that tomb, an acorn dropped into the tomb, and today there is an oak tree rising out of the center of it. It is broken asunder and the casket is exposed. It was opened by an acorn under the hand of Almighty God.

You cannot thwart God; you cannot hinder God's omnipotent working. Pilate said, "Make it as sure as you can," and they did everything that human ingenuity could suggest to keep the body of Jesus in that grave in Judea. All their effort was overthrown. He who had yielded up Himself to death, took His life back again by commandment from God. He was raised from the dead by the glory of the Father.
—H. A. Ironside.

On Tithing

I wonder why the Lord did ask,
    For tithes, from you and me;
When all the treasures of the earth,
    Are His—eternally?

And why should He depend on us,
    To fill His house with meat;
When we have so very little,
    And His storehouse is replete?

But He said to bring our little,
    And He would add His much;
Then all the heavenly windows,
    Would be opened at His touch.

And blessings running over—
    Even more than has been told—
Will be ours; but there's no promise
    If His portion we withhold.

Are we afraid to prove Him?
    Is our faith and love so small,
That we tightly grasp our little,
    When He freely gave His all?

—Roselyn C. Steere

Is the Plural of Ox "Oxes"?

Never laugh at a person's efforts to speak or write English correctly. Of the four major languages, it is the most difficult to learn: Here's why:

We'll begin with the box, the plural of which is boxes; but the plural of ox is oxen, not oxes.

One fowl is a goose, and two are called geese; but the plural of mouse is never meese.

You may find a lone mouse, or a whole nest of mice; but the plural of house is houses, not hice.

If the plural of man is men, why shouldn't the plural of pan be pen?

If I speak of a foot and you show me two feet, or give you a boot, would a pair be called beet?

If one is a tooth and a whole set are teeth, why shouldn't the plural of booth be beeth?

Then, the masculine pronouns are he, his, and him; but imagine the feminine as she, shis, and shim!"

A PRAYER for STEADFASTNESS . . .
Lord, keep us steadfast in Thy Word;
Curb those who fain by craft or sword
Would wrest the Kingdom from Thy Son
And set at nought all He hath done.
Lord Jesus Christ, Thy power make known,
For Thou art Lord of lords alone.
Defend Thy Christendom, that we
May evermore sing praise of Thee.
O Comforter, of priceless worth,
Send peace and unity on earth;
Support us in our final strife,
And lead us out of death to life.
           Martin Luther, 1541.

LITTLE BLOSSOM

"Oh, dear, I'm so tired and lonesome!
  I wonder why mamma doesn't come;
She said to shut my pretty blue eyes
  And when I waked up she'd be home.
She said she'd go to see grandma—.
  She lives over the river so bright—
I guess my mamma's fallen in there
  And p'raps she won't tum tonight.

"I dess I'se 'fraid to stay up here
  Without any fire or light.
But God's lighted the lamps in Heaven,
  I see them all twinkling and bright.
I'd better go down and meet papa;
  I know he has stopped at the store;
It's a great pretty store full of bottles,
  I wish he would go there no more.

"Sometimes he's so sick when he comes home
  He stumbles and falls up the stair;
And once when he came in the parlor
  He kicked at my poor little chair.
And mamma was all pale and frightened,
  And hugged me close up to her breast,
And called me her poor little Blossom,
  And I dess I'se forgotted the rest.

"But I 'member he striked at my mamma—
  His face was so red and so wild;
Yes, I 'member he striked at poor mamma,
  And hurted his poor little child.
But I love him, I dess I'll go find him;
  P'rhaps he will come with me home;
And then it won't be dark and lonesome
  Waiting for mamma to come."

Out in the night went the baby,
  The dear little Blossom so fair.
With eyes as blue as the clear sky
  And a halo of golden brown hair.
Out in the night went the baby,
  Her little heart beating with fright,
Till the tired feet reached the gin palace,
  All radiant with music and light.

The little hand pushed the door open.
  Tho' her touch was as light as a breath,
And the little feet entered the portal
  That leads but to ruin and death.
Away down the long floor she pattered,
  The pretty blue eyes opened wide,
When she spied in a corner her papa,
  And the tiny feet paused at his side.

"O papa!" she cried as she reached him,
  And her voice rippled out sweet and clear.
"I thought if I come I would find you
  And now I am glad I am here.
The lights are so pretty, dear papa,
  And I think the music's so sweet,
But I dess it's most supper time, papa,
  For Blossom wants something to eat."

A moment the red eyes gazed wildly
  Down in the face sweet and fair.
And then as the demon possessed him
  He grasped at the back of a chair.
A moment, a second, 'twas over,
  The work of the fiend was complete,
And the poor little innocent Blossom
  Lay broken and crushed at his feet.

Then swift as the lights came his reason,
  And showed him the deed he had done;
With a groan that a demon might pity
  He knelt by the quivering one,
He pressed the slight form to his bossom,
  He lifted the fair golden head;
A moment the baby lips trembled,
  Then dear little Blossom was dead.

The law in its majesty seized him
  And exacted just penalty, death—
For only a fiend or a madman
  Would deprive a baby of breath.
But the man who had sold him the poison
  That made such a demon of Hell—
Why, he must not be less respected,
  Because he is licensed to sell.
                              —Sel.

Shamgar had an ox goad,
David had a sling,
Samson had a jawbone,
Rahab had a string,
Mary had some ointment,
Aaron had a rod,
Dorcas had a needle,
All were used for God.
—Harvest Mission

The world's most disappointed people are those who get what's coming to them.

* * *

It's a shame that nature did not provide everyone with two additional senses—horse and common.

* * *

The reason why people miss church when it rains is the reason why we have church.

Not a Sacrifice but a Joy

A rich businessman and a prominent attorney were traveling around the world. They saw many impressive sights, but agreed that something they saw in Korea was most impressive of all.

One morning as they walked along a country road in Korea, they saw a boy pulling a plow which was steered by an old man. It amused the attorney so much that he insisted on taking a picture of the scene with his little pocket camera. Later he showed the picture to a missionary in the next village, remarking about the peculiar spectacle.

"Yes," said the missionary, "it seems a very strange way to plow a field, but I happen to know the boy and old man well. They are very poor. However, when the little church was built here in the village, they wanted to contribute something. They had no money. They had no grain to spare and winter was coming on, so they sold their ox and gave the money to the church building fund, and now, minus the valuable animal, they have to pull the plow themselves."

The men looked at each other for a moment, then the attorney said, "But what a stupendous sacrifice! Why did you allow it?"

"They did not feel that way about it. They regarded it as a great joy that they had an ox to give to the Lord's work."

America is finer than its headlines

You can get deathly sick at heart, reading any issue of any newspaper—mob violence if the mob doesn't happen to like something; rape, stabbings, murders; cowards screaming that they won't fight for their country; courts pampering criminals; teen-age animals.

As a nation, as a community, we should be desperately ashamed. But let's not lose sight of some of the things we can still be proud of, too:—

Church and Sunday School attendance is at an all-time high.

Nurses' aides and Red Cross workers doing menial work, with no pay—when they could be having a good time.

The finest fighting men in the world, proud to wear their U.S. uniforms, proud to represent us well, around the globe.

Individuals and business contributing more to charity and education than ever before and more per capita than any other nation dreams of.

Millions of mothers doing the unglamorous job of running a home economically and raising their children to be decent citizens.

Millions of men working long hours at not very interesting jobs but doing them the best they know how, and cutting down on lunches, perhaps, to save money to pay Junior's way to college—and not demonstrating for "rights" or something "free."

And these same Americans hoping their politicians will wake up to the fact these are the true Americans who want what's best for their country, not what will get the most votes come November.

Yes, the screaming headlines are sickening, but the silence which is Amrica going about its business quietly—that's pretty wonderful.—By a Patriot.

Total Bill: $0.00

Albert E. Bailey tells the story about two bills. Harry's bill to his mother, and Mother's bill to Harry. The first bill itemized the various jobs Harry had done about the house, and ended: "Total that Mother owes Harry: $3.00." The bill was promptly paid.

But the next morning Harry found a statement from his mother, and this is what it said:

Food for Harry,
  10 years _____$0.00
For clothing and home,
  10 years _____$0.00
For toys, skates and
  bicycle _____$0.00
For dishwashing, cooking and ironing, 10
  years _____$0.00
For nursing Harry during pneumonia _____$0.00
Total Harry owes
  Mother _____$0.00

"What hast thou done for ME?"

I GAVE My life for thee,
  My precious blood I shed,
That thou might'st ransomed be,
  And quickened from the dead;
I gave My life for thee,
What hast thou given for ME?

My Father's house of light,
  My glory-circled throne,
I left for earthly night,
  For wand'rings sad and lone;
I left it all for thee,
Hast thou left aught for ME?

I suffered much for thee,
  More than thy heart can know,
Of bitterest agony,
  To rescue thee from woe;
I've borne it all for thee,
What hast thou borne for ME?

And I have brought to thee,
  Down from My home above,
Salvation full and free,
  My pardon and My love;
Great gifts I brought to thee,
What hast thou done for ME?
—FRANCES R. HAVERGAL.

What Have You Suffered?

We do not know who it was who had this dream, quoted in the Presbyterian Survey. But the unknown dreamer could be any one of us, could it not?

I saw in a dream that I was in the Celestial City—though when and how I got there I could not tell. I was one of a great multitude which no man could number, from all countries and peoples and times and ages. Somehow I found that the saint who stood next to me had been in Heaven more than 1,860 years.

"Who are you?" I said to him. (We both spoke the same language of heavenly Canaan, so that I understood him and he me.)

"I," said he, "was a Roman Christian; I lived in the days of the Apostle Paul, I was one of those who died in Nero's persecutions. I was covered with pitch and fastened to a stake and set on fire to light up Nero's gardens."

"How awful!" I exclaimed.

"No," he said, "I was glad to do something for Jesus. He died on the cross for me."

The man on the other side then spoke: "I have been in Heaven only a few hundred years. I came from an island in the South Seas — Erromanga. John Williams, a missionary, came and told me about Jesus, and I too learned to love Him. My fellow-countrymen killed the missionary, and they caught and bound me. I was beaten until I fainted and they thought I was dead, but I revived. Then next day they knocked me on the head, cooked and ate me."

"How terrible!" I said.

"No," he answered, "I was glad to die as a Christian. You see the missionaries had told me that Jesus was scourged and crowned with thorns for me."

Then they both turned to me and said, "What did you suffer for Him? Or did you sell what you had for the money which sent men like John Williams to tell the heathen about Jesus?"

And I was speechless. And while they both were looking at me with sorrowful eyes, I awoke, and it was a dream! But I lay on my soft bed awake for hours, thinking of the money I had wasted on my own pleasures; or my extra clothing, and costly car, and many luxuries; and I realized that I did not know what the words of Jesus meant: "If any man will come after Me, let him deny himself, and take up his cross, and follow Me."

Service for God Lasts

$1 spent for lunches lasts five hours.

$1 spent for gas lasts for a few miles.

$1 spent for a finger wave lasts for a few days.

$1 spent for stockings lasts for a few weeks.

$1 spent for a hat lasts for a season or two.

$1 spent for a home lasts for generations . . .

But $1 spent for Christian service will last for eternity!

WHAT'S YOUR IMPRESSION OF A CHRISTIAN WHO . . . .

Doesn't read his Bible,

Doesn't tithe his income,

Doesn't witness to others,

Doesn't say grace at meals,

Doesn't attend Sunday School,

Doesn't attend prayer meeting,

Doesn't invite his friends to church,

Doesn't attend Sunday evening services,

Doesn't have private and family devotions,

Doesn't regularly observe the Lord's Supper,

Doesn't wish to follow the Lord in Baptism,

DOESN'T DO ANYTHING??????

"Believe a Lie and Be Damned"

A person may have the wrong kind of life while retaining the right kind of creed, but no man can have the right kind of life with the wrong kind of creed. "It makes no difference what men believe just so they live right," some people say. The people who say that are wrong. What a man believes not only regulates his conscience but also affects his conduct. The Bible teaches that it is possible to believe a lie and be damned. The man who does not believe in the virgin birth of Jesus Christ does not believe the Bible. The Bible teaches that Jesus Christ was God manifest in the flesh. "For in Him dwelleth all the fulness of the Godhead bodily." The incarnation of Jesus Christ is the fundamental truth of Christianity. According to the Word of God, every spirit that denies that Jesus Christ was God manifest in the flesh is the spirit of the Antichrist, which is the spirit of the devil.—Dr. Bob Jones, Sr.

An Atheist Answered

Once an atheist asked a Christian lady if she believed the Bible was true. "Yes," said the lady. "Then," said the atheist, "tell me how a whale swallowed Jonah as a whale's stomach is no bigger than a man's head."

"I don't know," said the lady; "but when I get to Heaven I will ask him." "What if Jonah is not there," said the atheist. "Then you ask him," said the lady.

It Hurts Me

He who holds a grudge injures himself more than the one against whom he cherishes the spirit of spite. Hatred and malice, like anger and worry, are injurious to the body, since they poison the blood. More serious is the injury which they bring to personality. A bad spirit paralyzes the powers which could help to refine our natures and make for finer character. And this spirit of ill will has a strange way of increasing, for "a grudge is the only thing that does not get better when it is nursed."

—The Watchman-Examiner

The House by the Side of the Road

Sam Foss liked to walk. But he had wandered a bit too far today in the blazing sun, lost in his thoughts; and now suddenly he realized how hot and tired he was. The big tree at the side of the road looked tempting, and he stopped for a moment to rest in its shade.

There was a little sign on the tree, and he read it with surprise and pleasure: *"There is a good spring inside the fence. Come and drink if you are thirsty."*

Foss climbed over the fence, found the spring, and gratefully drank his fill of the cool water. Then he noticed a bench near the spring, and tacked to the bench was another sign. He went over to it and read: *"Sit down and rest awhile if you are tired."*

Now thoroughly delighted, he went to a barrel of apples nearby—and saw that here, too, was a sign! *"If you like apples, just help yourself,"* he read. He accepted the invitation, picked out a plump red one, and looked up to discover an elderly man watching him with interest.

"Hello, there!" Foss called. "Is this your place?"

"Yes," the old man answered. "I'm glad you stopped by." And he explained the reason for the signs. The water was going to waste; the bench was gathering dust in the attic; the apples were more than they could use. He and his wife thought it would be neighborly to offer tired, thirsty passers-by a place to rest and refresh themselves. So they had brought down the bench and put up the signs—and made themselves a host of fine new friends!

"You must like people," Foss said.

"Of course," the old man answered simply. "Don't you?"

All the way home Sam Foss kept thinking of the line from Homer's ILIAD: *"He was a friend of man, and lived in a house by the side of the road."* How perfectly that described the kindly old man he had just met, living in his house by the side of the road, eagerly sharing his water and the comfort of his shady grounds, befriending every stranger who passed by!

The lines of a poem began to shape up in his mind. It would be a poem about friendship, simple and sincere as the old man himself. He would call it THE HOUSE BY THE SIDE OF THE ROAD. . . .

There are hermit souls that live withdrawn
In the place of their self-content;
There are souls like stars, that dwell apart,
In a fellowless firmament;
There are pioneer souls that blaze their paths
Where highways never ran—
But let me live by the side of the road
And be a friend to man.

Let me live in a house by the side of the road,
Where the race of men go by—
The men who are good and the men who are bad,
As good and as bad as I.
I would not sit in the scorner's seat,
Or hurl the cynic's ban—
Let me live in a house by the side of the road
And be a friend to man.

I see from my house by the side of the road,
By the side of the highway of life,
The men who press with the ardor of hope,
The men who are faint with the strife.
But I turn not away from their smiles nor their tears,
Both parts of an infinite plan—
Let me live in a house by the side of the road
And be a friend to man.

I know there are brook-gladdened meadows ahead,
And mountains of wearisome height;
That the road passes on through the long afternoon
And stretches away to the night.
But still I rejoice when the travelers rejoice,
And weep with the strangers that moan,
Nor live in my house by the side of the road
Like a man who dwells alone.

Let me live in my house by the side of the road,
Where the race of men go by—
They are good, they are bad, they are weak, they are strong,
Wise, foolish—so am I;
Then why should I sit in the scorner's seat,
Or hurl the cynic's ban?
Let me live in my house by the side of the road
And be a friend to man.

The Friends

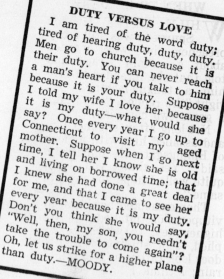

I called him John; he called me Jim;
Nigh fifty years that I knowed him
An' he knowed me; an' he was square
An' honest all that time an' fair.
I'd pass him mornin's goin' down
Th' road or drivin' into town,
An' we'd look up th' same old way,
An' wave a hand an' smile, an' say:
    "'Day, John!"
    "'Day, Jim!"

I guess you don't real often see
Such kind of friends as him an' me;
Not much on talkin' big; but, say,
Th' kinds of friends that stick an' stay.
Come rich, come poor, come rain, come
    shine,
Whatever he had was mine,
An' mine was his; an' we both knowed
It when we'd holler on th' road:
    "How, John!"
    "How, Jim!"

An' when I got hailed out one year
He dropped in on me with that queer
Big smile, upon his way to town,
An' laid two hundred dollars down
An' says: "No int'rest, understand:
Or no note!" An' he took my hand
An' squeezed it; an' he drew away
'Cause there wa'n't nothin' more to say:
    "S'long, John!"
    "S'long, Jim!"

An' when John's boy came courtin' Sue,
John smiled, an'—well, I smiled some, too,
As though things was a-comin' out
As if we'd fixed 'em, just about.
An' when Sue blushed an' told me—why,
I set an' chuckled on th' sly;
An' so did John—put out his hand—
No words but these, y' understand:
    "Shake, John!"
    "Shake, Jim!"

An' when Sue's mother died, John come
An' set with me; an' he was dumb
As fur as speech might be concerned;
But in them eyes of his there burned
A light of love an' sympathy
An' friendship you don't often see.
He took my hand in his that day
An' said—what else was there to say?—
    "H'lo, John!"
    "H'lo, Jim!"

Somehow, th' world ain't quite th' same
Today! Tho' trees is all aflame
With autumn, but there's somethin' gone—
Went out of life, I guess, with John.
He nodded that ol' grizzled head
Upon th' piller of his bed,
An' lifted up that helpin' hand
An' whispered: "Some time! — Under-
    stand?"
    "'Bye, John!"
    "'Bye, Jim!"

        —James W. Foley

DUTY VERSUS LOVE

I am tired of the word duty; tired of hearing duty, duty, duty. Men go to church because it is their duty. You can never reach a man's heart if you talk to him because it is your duty. Suppose I told my wife I love her because it is my duty—what would she say? Once every year I go up to Connecticut to visit my aged mother. Suppose when I go next time, I tell her I know she is old and living on borrowed time; that I knew she had done a great deal for me, and that I came to see her every year because it is my duty. Don't you think she would say, "Well, then, my son, you needn't take the trouble to come again"? Oh, let us strike for a higher plane than duty.—MOODY.

"Extinguishing" the Bible

An old colored preacher of the South was asked by a Northerner why it was that colored ministers preached so much about Hell. "Well, sah," he replied, "I don't knows just why dat am, but I done suppose dat de reason am caus we culled folks haven't got learnin' enough to splanify de tex and extinguish de Bible like you white folks am." We must admit there is more truth than poetry in his statement.

    —Sunday School Times

Profit and Loss

I counted dollars while God counted crosses.
I counted gains while He counted losses!
I counted my worth by the things gained
    in store.
But He sized me up by the scars that I
    bore.
I coveted honors and sought for degrees;
He wept as He counted the hours on my
    knees.
And I never knew 'til one day at a grave,
How vain are these things that we spend
    life to save!

The greatest security against sin is to be shocked at its presence.—Carlyle.

86

WHEN TO BE DEAF

WHILE Charles Haddon Spurgeon was still a boy preacher, he was warned about a certain virago and told that she intended to give him a tongue-lashing. "All right," he replied, "but that's a game two can play."

Not long after, she met him and assailed him with a flood of Billingsgate. He smiled and said: "Yes, thank you, I am quite well; I hope you are the same."

Then came another burst of vituperation, pitched in a yet higher key, to which he replied, still smiling, "Yes, it does look rather as if it might rain; I think I had better be going on."

"Bless the man!" she exclaimed, "he's as deaf as a post. What's the use of storming at him?"

And so her railings ceased, and were never again attempted. Under provocation we do well to hold our peace.

—*The Sunday School Times*

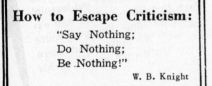

How to Escape Criticism:

"Say Nothing;
Do Nothing;
Be Nothing!"

W. B. Knight

DON'TS FOR DAUGHTERS

Don't forget that you can greatly lighten mothers' burden by your sympathy and help.

Don't allow yourself to say words to your parents that will be thorns in your pillow afterwards.

Don't despise your mother because she is not so smart or so well educated as you are.

Don't forget that your younger brothers and sisters are consciously or unconsciously, copying your conduct.

Don't let this fact escape you, that many have been made great, and many more have been made good, by their sisters.

Don't forget that it is **character and not beauty of face**, that forms woman's true attraction.

Don't spend more time in adorning your person than in beautifying your mind; and in adding to the wealth of your soul.

Don't imagine that a pretty face will atone for an empty head.

Don't forget that untidiness of dress is unpardonable in a young woman.

Don't encourage that thought that it is better to be clever than to be good.

Don't forget that to be able to see to the welfare of a home is a finer accomplishment than to be able to play a piano, or to paint a picture.

Don't have secret correspondence with any one, or clandestine meetings of which you would be ashamed to tell your mother.

Don't encourage the attention of any young man who **speaks lightly of home** or of sacred things.—Selected.

Sir Winston Churchill on the Bible

"We reject with scorn all those learned and labored myths that Moses was but a lengendary figure upon whom the priesthood and the people hung their essential social, moral, and religious ordinances. We believe that the most scientific view, the most up-to-date and rationalistic conception will find its fullest satisfaction in taking the Bible story literally and in identifying one of the greatest human beings with the most decisive leap forward ever discernable in the human history. We remain unmoved by the tomes of Professors Gradgrind and Dr. Dryasdust. We may be sure that all things happened just as they are set out according to Holy Writ. We may believe that they happened to people not so very different from ourselves, and that the impressions those people received were faithfully recorded and have been transmitted across the centuries with far more accuracy than many of the telegraphed accounts we read of goings on of today. In the words of a forgotten work of Mr. Gladstone, we rest with assurance upon 'The Impregnable Rock of Holy Scripture.'

"Let the men of science and learning expand their knowledge and probe with their researches every detail of the records which have been preserved to us from these dim ages. All they will do is to fortify the grand simplicity and essential accuracy of the recorded truths which have lighted so far the pilgrimage of man."

HINDRANCES IN THE PULPIT

Wesley once said, "There are some men who preach so well when in the pulpit, that it is a shame they should ever come out of it; and when they are out of it, they live so illy that it is a shame they should ever enter it."

We have heard of many people who trusted God too little, but have you ever heard of anyone who trusted Him too much?—J. Hudson Taylor

OLD SCARECROW AND THE COWS

CALF-A-TERIA NEWS

Cows of Distinction Choose Old Scarecrow

**By Robert W. Moon
in Tem-Press**

Just suppose there were one hundred fifty million cows in America. Let's suppose there is an industry doing a great business selling a certain kind of hay. This hay, called Old Scarecrow, while made entirely from locoweed, is alluringly described as a blend of old straw aged in the cornfield. As a result, cows by the millions turn from their sober diet of alfalfa and begin chewing Old Scarecrow.

Now let's suppose that this stuff makes the cows do silly things such as running into barbed wire fences, jumping off bridges or running into automobiles—so much so that five hundred thousand are killed or injured every year. Suppose milk production is cut down because the users of Old Scarecrow lose fifty million "cow-days" a year.

Suppose the life expectancy of the cows who chew it regularly is reduced by an average of 12%. Suppose that it makes four million cows so sick that much of the time they are useless and suppose that for every one that is cured, the industry makes ten more Old Scarecrow addicts.

Suppose that caring for the victims of Old Scarecrow requires 80% of the farmer's time.

And now, just suppose that in spite of all this, the merchants of this fatal fodder are allowed to advertise the stuff in every pasture, so that on almost every fence there appear large pictures of contented "Cows of Distinction" munching away on Old Scarecrow. And suppose that the manufacturers of Old Scarecrow are making a tremendous profit out of all this trouble and tragedy they cause the farmer.

How would you expect the farmers to take all of this? Would you expect them to take it sitting down? Or would you expect them to stand up and say to the producers of Old Scarecrow, "That ain't hay," and then put forth an effort to protect their cows by banning the advertising and promotion of Old Scarecrow from the range?

And now just suppose that you cared as much about your children and your fellowmen as you would expect the farmer to care about his cows! What do you suppose you would do about drinking?

Who Is Responsible?
By Mrs. Henry Peabody

At a very beautiful tea, where I felt less at home than at a missionary meeting, I was approached by a charming woman who greeted me cordially and said, "I have been so interested in your prohibition work." I said, with some surprise, "You do not look like a reformer." She was the picture of a leader in social life. "Oh," she said, "I have been the wife of an army officer. I have seen what this thing does to young men."

Then she said, "I was converted to prohibition as a girl, here in the South. I came in one day from the plantation to the county seat. In front of the little store I saw a family in an old wagon with a mule team. The woman wore a sunbonnet, had no shoes, and four little children sat on the wagon floor. They were all radiantly happy. I wondered why, and going into the store for my errand found they had driven in to get money for their tobacco crop, which the man and wife together had cultivated. It was their only income during the year. The man took them into the store and said to the owner, 'You give her what she wants. I'll be back with the money.'

"So the woman chose, and I waited to see their happiness. They wanted everything, shoes and sheets, sugar and flour, all the things to eat and to wear that they had done without. The kind storekeeper gave the children some candy and I left them, to go back again later.

"I was delayed, and when I returned the picture had changed. There was tragedy in the woman's voice, but no tears. The children, feeling the changed atmosphere, were crying, and as I came in the woman said, pointing to the row of bundles ready for her to take home, 'I think you had better put them back; he hasn't come.'

"I could not leave, and waited for the end. Later the old team came up with a drunken man on the seat. He stumbled out, cursing, screaming, and fell across the doorsteps of the store, helpless, beastly.

"Again the woman said, helplessly, 'Put them back.' Every cent was gone and she lifted the man, with the help of the storekeeper, and carried him to the wagon, and herself drove home. I never recovered from the shock and the horror of that drama of life. It made me a prohibitionist."

"This," says Mrs. Peabody, "is the picture we are beginning to forget."

—Woman's Missionary Friend

The Walk

A holiday's w'en Fathers play
   Wif little Boys.
He sees why don't my motor go,
An' shows me how to catch an' fro'
   An' mends my toys.

But w'en we take th' long, long
   walk
   His stick goes, too,
'Cause it mus' wave an' point right
   out
What Fathers—they mus' talk
   about
   An' 'splain to you.

W'en it's "all tired out" it hangs
   Right on his arm,
But Little Boys sit down to rest
Right on a stone—'cause that is
   best:
   Close by a farm.

Now, 'twon't be long before we'll
   meet
   Ole trolley car.
My little hand can make it stop,
'N' 'en we'll climb up, me an' my
   Pop
   Now, 'twon't seem far,

'Cause he takes hold my little hand
   An' we bof run.
It's big an' warm—a Father's hand.
Ain't tired now; I feel just grand.
   We have such fun!

"You like to hold my little hand
   Better 'n Old Stick?"
W'en he says, "Um-m" that way to
   me
'N' 'en I mus' hear it more, you
   see,
   An' ask him over quick.

—Marie Louise Tompkins

Cancelling Unkind Words

Some of the older boys and girls doubtless have studied cancellation in school. But there is another kind of cancellation that can be used by the youth of all ages. For example, two boys were speaking of another boy.

"He is slow in games," said one.

"Yes," replied the other, "but he always plays fair."

"He is so stupid at school!" said the first boy.

"But he always studies hard," answered the second.

Thus you see every unkind word spoken by the first boy was cancelled by a kind word from the second. Suppose the next time you hear an unkind word you try to cancel it by putting a kind one in its place.

—Gospel Herald

Someone has given this definition of a baby: "A baby is a small member of the animal kingdom that makes love stronger, days shorter, nights longer, the bank roll smaller, the home happier, clothes shabbier, the past forgotten, and the future worth living for."

WELL ADJUSTED

Bud Robinson, the well-known Holiness preacher, was taken by friends to New York and shown around the city. That night in his prayers he said, "Lord, I thank You for letting me see all the sights of New York. And I thank You most of all that I didn't see a thing that I wanted!" Blessed is the man who can sit loose to the charms of this old world, independent of them because he doesn't want them.

MY FRIEND

I could sail the waters of all the world
   Bitter and wild and blue,
And never I'd find a friend to love
   Like the friend I've found in you.

I could walk down all the roads of the
   world
   And knock on the doors forever,
And never I'd find a friend like you,
   Never, never, never!

—J. P. McEvoy

When we stand before the judgment seat of Christ, He is not going to look for medals, but for scars. Who of us can say with Paul: "I bear in my body the marks of the Lord Jesus" (Gal. 6:17).
—W. B. Knight

Said Jack Dempsey to a manufacturer of cigarettes who sought his endorsement of his brand of cigarettes: "You could not get me to sign that for ten times what you offer. I do not smoke cigarettes and never did. Do you think I am going to ask the thousands of boys who have read about me to take up cigarette smoking?"

Some people think a 30-minute sermon is too long, so they substitute a 300-column Sunday paper.

When Calvin was banished from ungrateful Geneva, he said, "Most assuredly if I had merely served man, this would have been a poor recompense; but it is my happiness that I have served Him who never fails to reward His servants to the full extent of His promise."—Spurgeon.

Temptation rarely comes in working hours. It is in their leisure time that men are made or marred. — W. T. Taylor

The cross is the last argument of God.—Spurgeon

The promises of the Bible are very large; you can lie down and stretch out on them and you can't kick the footboard, scratch the headboard, or touch the railing on either side.—Bud Robinson.

Certainties in Life

John Newton, on being asked his opinion on some subject, replied, "When I was young I was sure of many things; there are only two things of which I am sure now: one is, that I am a miserable sinner; and the other, that Jesus Christ is an all-sufficient Saviour."

The Bible a Comfort in Death

After the battle before Richmond had been over several days, a man was found dead with his hand on the open Bible. The summer insects had taken the flesh from the hand, and there was nothing but the skeleton left; but the skeleton fingers lay on the open page, and on this passage—"Yea, though I walk through the valley of the shadow of death, I will fear no evil: for thou art with me; thy rod and thy staff they comfort me." Well, the time will come when all the fine novels we have on our bedroom shelf will not interest us, and all the good histories and all the exquisite essays will do us no good. There will be one Book, perhaps its cover worn out and its leaf yellow with age, under whose flesh we shall behold the opening gates of heaven.—*Talmage.*

The Judge and His God

Does God ever sit on the Judge's bench? He does if the judge really seeks Him, thinks Federal Judge Harold R. Medina, who presided over the trial of the eleven top-ranking U. S. communists. Last week the *Living Church* quoted from a speech by Episcopalian Medina on the subject, "The Judge and His God":

"There is much in the Bible about judges, but I do not know of any judge who has discussed the impact of religion upon his profession . . . Fortunately for me, I was taught to pray from so early a time that I cannot remember going to bed at night without saying my prayers . . . I do not see why a judge should be ashamed that he prays for divine guidance and for strength to do his duty . . .

"There came a time . . . when I did the most sincere and the most fervent praying that I have ever done in my life. I suddenly found myself in the midst of the trial of the communists. It took me a long time to realize what they were trying to do to me. But as I got weaker and weaker, and found the burden difficult to bear, I sought strength from the one source that never fails.

"Let me be specific. There came a time when one of the defendants on the stand refused to answer a question, pleading a supposed constitutional privilege which obviously had no application. I gave him time to consult with his counsel. I held the matter in abeyance overnight, and on the next day . . . I sentenced the man to prison for 30 days, unless he should sooner purge himself of contempt by answering the question. Pandemonium broke loose. The other ten defendants and their lawyers, and many of the spectators, rose to their feet; there was a great shouting and hullabaloo, and several of the defendants started toward the bench.

"In all that excitement, I felt just as calm as I do now . . . I did not raise my voice . . . I singled out several of those men, identified the language they were using, got it on the record, and sentenced each of them to imprisonment for the balance of the trial.

"I tell you . . that I never had the will and the self-control to do these things. If ever a man felt the presence of someone beside him, strengthening his will and giving him aid and comfort, I certainly did on that day . . .

"After all is said and done, it is not we who pull the strings; we are not the masters, but the servants of our Master's will; and it is well that we should know it to be so."

—Time Magazine.

"YES, DEAR, BUT REMEMBER, I HAVE HAD TO LISTEN TO YOU FIVE TIMES TODAY!

It was at the close of a Lord's Day, and Dr. Harry A. Ironside had been busy in the King's business. Five times had he spoken. On the way home--how human it all was--a simple question of Mrs. Ironside was turned aside with irritation. The Holy Spirit quickly convicted this man of God. Contritely, he asked his wife's forgiveness with, "Forgive me. I am quite tired. Remember, I have preached five times today." And then came the answer: "Yes, dear, I know; but remember, I have had to listen to you five times today!"

--Moody Monthly

My RESOLUTIONS

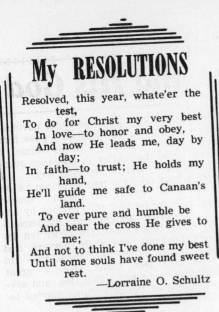

Resolved, this year, whate'er the
test,
To do for Christ my very best
In love—to honor and obey,
And now He leads me, day by
day;
In faith—to trust; He holds my
hand,
He'll guide me safe to Canaan's
land.
To ever pure and humble be
And bear the cross He gives to
me;
And not to think I've done my best
Until some souls have found sweet
rest.

—Lorraine O. Schultz

I Promise . . .

**Resolutions penned by William Booth,
founder of The Salvation Army, in December 1849, and found—faded and worn
—after his death.**

*THAT I will rise every morn-
ing sufficiently early (say twenty
minutes before seven o'clock) to
wash, dress and have a few minutes, not less than five, in private
prayer.*

*THAT I will as much as possi-
ble avoid all that babbling and
idle talking in which I have lately
so sinfully indulged.*

*THAT I will endeavor in my
conduct and deportment before the
world and my fellow servants especially to conduct myself as a
humble, meek and zealous follower
of the bleeding Lamb, and by serious conversation and warning endeavor to lead them to think of
their immortal souls.*

*THAT I will read no less than
four chapters in God's Word every
day.*

*THAT I will strive to live
closer to God, and to seek after
holiness of heart and leave providential events with God.*

*THAT I will read this over
every day or at least twice a week.*

*God help me, enable me to
cultivate a spirit of self denial and
to yield myself a prisoner of love
to the Redeemer of the world.
Amen and Amen.*

—*War Cry*

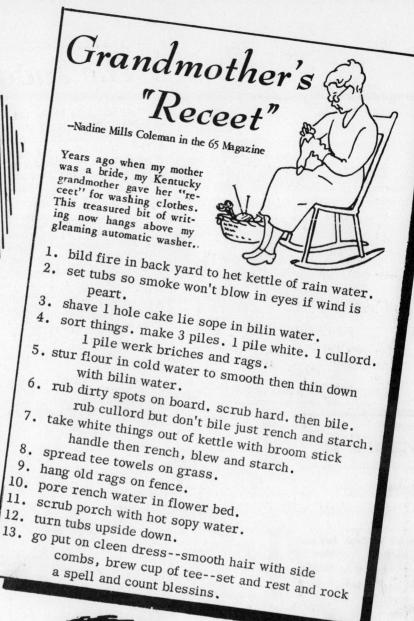

Grandmother's "Receet"

--Nadine Mills Coleman in the 65 Magazine

Years ago when my mother
was a bride, my Kentucky
grandmother gave her "re-
ceet" for washing clothes.
This treasured bit of writing now hangs above my
gleaming automatic washer..

1. bild fire in back yard to het kettle of rain water.
2. set tubs so smoke won't blow in eyes if wind is peart.
3. shave 1 hole cake lie sope in bilin water.
4. sort things. make 3 piles. 1 pile white. 1 cullord.
   1 pile werk briches and rags.
5. stur flour in cold water to smooth then thin down
   with bilin water.
6. rub dirty spots on board. scrub hard. then bile.
   rub cullord but don't bile just rench and starch.
7. take white things out of kettle with broom stick
   handle then rench, blew and starch.
8. spread tee towels on grass.
9. hang old rags on fence.
10. pore rench water in flower bed.
11. scrub porch with hot sopy water.
12. turn tubs upside down.
13. go put on cleen dress--smooth hair with side
    combs, brew cup of tee--set and rest and rock
    a spell and count blessins.

Mothers Make Preachers

When young Matthew Simpson
tremblingly broke the news to his
widowed mother that he felt called
to preach, which would necessitate
his leaving the home, she exclaimed with tears of joy: "Oh, my son,
I have prayed for this hour every
day since you were born. At that
time, we dedicated you to the
Christian ministry."
Campbell Morgan says: "My
dedication to the preaching of the
Word was maternal. Mother never
told it to the baby or the boy, but
waited. When but eight years old
I preached to my little sister and
to her dolls arrayed in orderly
form before me. My sermons were
Bible stories which I had first
heard from my mother."
—*The Voice*

No Song?

Hushed now the song the redbird sang
Ere he lay cold and dead;
His bright eye, dimmed; his feathers, crushed
Though still a gaudy red.
Pinioned in death, he cannot soar
And sing in cloudless sky.
Our voices, too, will soundless be
When our time comes to die?

So sad the redbird's sudden death!
So beautiful was he!
But, sadder still, his golden song
Is silenced; not so we
Who know the resurrected Christ,
For our song we shall sing
In highest Heaven's glorious realm
To praise the Saviour-King!

—Miss Willie Brumitt
Editorial Office of
Sword of the Lord

Just Suppose . . .

Just suppose the Lord would begin tomorrow to make people as sick as they claim to be on Sunday.

Just suppose the Lord should take away the child whom the parents use as an excuse for staying away from church.

Just suppose the Lord should make people as poor as they claim to be when asked to help finance His program.

Just suppose the Lord should have everyone stoned to death for covetousness as was Achan.

Just suppose the Lord should let some parents look into the future and see what their example and lax control did for their children.

Just suppose—and then, by the help of the Lord go forth and live and serve as if eternity was soon coming.

IT IS!! I come quickly says the Lord.

—Selected.

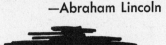

"To sin by silence when they should protest makes cowards out of men."

—Abraham Lincoln

"Give Them Their Letters at Once"

When Henry Ward Beecher was yet a young man in the ministry, he was faced with the demand of a prominent member of his church to put the soft pedal on the slavery question. He was told if he did not keep quiet he would lose six of his most prominent families. He answered, "Give me their names now, please, that I may give them their letters at once!"

He rightly judged that such families who tried to hog-tie the true testimony of the preacher were better out of the church than in.

How to Read the Bible

That great prayer warrior, George Mueller, tells us how to read the Word of God.

"1. **Read the Scriptures regularly through.** Read, alternately, portions from the Old and New Testaments. Begin at the beginning of each. Mark where you leave off, and begin there next time. When you have finished each Testament, begin it again.

"2. **Read with prayer.** You cannot by your own wisdom understand the Word of God. In all your reading of the Scriptures, seek carefully the help of the Holy Spirit. Ask for Jesus' sake that He will enlighten you.

"3. **Read with meditation.** Ponder over what you read. The truth is thus applied to your heart. You see new and deeper meanings. It is better to think over a little than merely to read a great deal.

"4. **Read with reference to yourself.** Never read only with a view to instructing others, but for your own teaching. Receive blessings yourself first, and you will communicate it to others. Always ask yourself, 'How does this affect me?'

"5. **Read with faith.** Not as statements which you may believe or not but as the revealed word of God. Receive every word as true, with simple, childlike trust. Rest upon the promises. Read them as made for you.

"6. **Read in order to carry into practice.** We must accept His Word as being the revelation of His will. In it He tells us what to be and what to do. He expects us to be 'obedient children'."

We can pray, believe, and receive, or we can pray, doubt, and do without.

Satan—An Angel of Light

Some years ago, a radio announcer presented one of America's well-known liberal ministers for a broadcast. The announcer wanted to give the minister a good build-up. He said, "Today I have the pleasure of presenting to you America's outstanding prince of the power of the air," meaning of course, that the minister was a prince among the radio clergy. He obviously did not know that the words he used referred to Satan (cf. Eph. 2:2).—Told by W. Woodward Henry

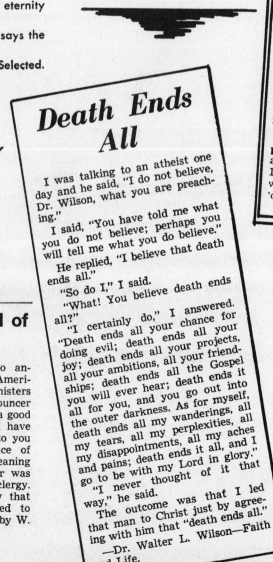

Death Ends All

I was talking to an atheist one day and he said, "I do not believe, Dr. Wilson, what you are preaching."

I said, "You have told me what you do not believe; perhaps you will tell me what you do believe."

He replied, "I believe that death ends all."

"So do I," I said.

"What! You believe death ends all?"

"I certainly do," I answered. "Death ends all your chance for doing evil; death ends all your joy; death ends all your projects, all your ambitions, all your friendships; death ends all the Gospel you will ever hear; death ends it all for you, and you go out into the outer darkness. As for myself, death ends all my wanderings, all my tears, all my perplexities, all my disappointments, all my aches and pains; death ends it all, and I go to be with my Lord in glory."

"I never thought of it that way," he said.

The outcome was that I led that man to Christ just by agreeing with him that "death ends all."

—Dr. Walter L. Wilson—Faith and Life.

Trials

"No physician ever weighed out medicine to his patients with half so much care and exactness as God weighs out to us every trial. Not one grain too much does He ever permit to be put in the scale."

—Henry Ward Beecher

There are no depths of cruelty and criminality in the history of the human race to which people have not descended when under the influence of liquor.—Dr. Robert G. Lee.

The Bible Test

An exchange tells of a Mohammedan trader in India, who once asked a European whether he could not secure a Bible for him. "What for?" he asked in surprise, "You would not be able to read it."

"True," replied the Mohammedan. "What I want is a European Bible."

When the European asked, "What for?" he answered:

"Well, when a ship brings a trader who is unknown to me who wishes to trade with me, I put the Bible in his way and watch him. If I see that he opens it and reads it, I know that I can trust him. But if he throws it aside with a sneer, or even a curse, I will have nothing to do with him, because I know that I cannot trust him."
—*Christ Life and Word of the Cross*

The Essential Thing

Soul-saving was Paul's essential work. Other things are important; this thing is absolutely necessary. It is important that men be fed; that women and children be clothed; that free education be provided; that the sanitary condition of homes be studied and improved. It is important that sociological reforms be effected; *but the indispensable thing is that the soul be saved.*

When life is over and we come into the presence of God, one may be a Gladstone for intellect, another a Spurgeon for eloquence, a third a Rockefeller for wealth, a fourth a Stanley for explorations, a fifth a Newton for mathematics, a sixth a Bacon for philosophy, a seventh a Milton for poetry, an eighth a Beethoven for harmony, a ninth a Michelangelo for art, a tenth a Wesley for organization; but if he has neglected the Master's commission, he will stand a pitiable pauper in spirit, whilst the humblest soul-winner will be honoured with a crown set with stars destined to shine forever and ever, because he did the essential thing.

Dr. W. B. Riley.

"Lady—Are You Rich?"

They huddled inside the storm door—two children in ragged outgrown coats.

"Any old papers, Lady?"

I was busy. I wanted to say no—until I looked down at their feet. Thin little sandals sopped with sleet. "Come in and I'll make you a cup of hot cocoa." There was no conversation. Their soggy sandals left marks upon the hearthstone.

Cocoa and toast with jam to fortify against the chill outside. I went back to the kitchen and started again on my household budget. . . .

The silence in the front room struck through to me. I looked in. The girl held her empty cup in her hands, looking at it. The boy asked in a flat voice: "Lady, . . . are YOU rich?"

"Am I rich? Mercy no!" I looked at my shabby slipcovers.

The girl put her cup back in its saucer—carefully. "Your cups match your saucers." Her voice was old with a hunger that was not of the stomach.

They left then, holding their bundles of papers against the wind. They hadn't said thank you. They didn't need to. They had done more than that. Plain blue pottery cups and saucers. "But they matched." I tested the potatoes and stirred the gravy. Potatoes and brown gravy . . . a roof over our heads, my man with a steady job . . . "these things matched, too."

I moved the chairs back from the fire and tidied the living room. The muddy prints of small sandals were still wet upon my hearth. I let them be. I want them in case I ever again forget "how very rich I really am."

—Marion Doolan, Your Life.

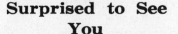

Surprised to See You

"How's your wife?" a fellow asked his old friend whom he hadn't seen in some years.

"She's in Heaven," replied the friend.

"Oh, I'm sorry," the fellow answered. Then realizing that was not the best phrase to use; he said, "I mean, I'm glad . . . well, what I really mean is, I'm surprised."

THE SECRET OF FEARLESSNESS

Of all the memorials in Westminster Abbey there is not one that gives a nobler thought than that inscribed on the monument to Lord Lawrence — simply his name, with the date of his death, and these words: "He feared man so little, because he feared God so much."

Effect of Applause

Once, when a great fire broke out at midnight, and people thought that all the inmates had been taken out, way up there in the fifth story was seen a little child crying for help. Up went a ladder, and soon a fireman was seen ascending to the spot. As he neared the second story the flames burst in fury from the windows, and the multitude almost despaired of the rescue of the child. The brave man faltered, and a comrade at the bottom cried out, "Cheer," and cheer upon cheer arose from the crowd. Up the ladder he went and saved the child because they cheered him. If you cannot go into the heat of the battle yourself, if you cannot go into the harvest field and work day after day, you can cheer those that are working for the Master.

—Moody.

Her Thanksgiving Day Sermon

Eben E. Rexford

Now Dan'el, this is Thanksgivin'—a day when the good Lord meant
We should all sit down and think over the blessin's He has sent,
And give Him the credit that's due Him for the good things He bestows;
But you've got into the habit, as ev'ry one 'round you knows,
Of finding fault with most things, while you overlook the good,
An' you don't thank the Giver for them, as ev'ry Christian should.

Now, Dan'el, I'm goin' to be honest, an' tell you plain an' square.
What I think about your grumblin'—you don't use the good Lord fair;
You fret 'cause the corn was a failure; you worried about the grass,
But never a word, my husban', about the dear little lass
That the Lord in His merciful kindness gin back when we thought she must die;
What's all the corn in the country, an' ev'rything else, say I,
To the child that the Lord has spared us? So, if you are bound to complain,
Act honest an' give Him the credit fcr our blessin's as well as our pain.

You know just as well as I do that the sun don't always shine,
But all of our worry an' frettin' won't clear your sky or mine.
It's a good deal better, my husban', to take things as they be,
When we can't make 'em any different, as sensible folks agree.
If a thing can't be helped don't worry, but make the best of it, dear,
An' think about all life's good things till the cloudy sky gets clear.
It's foolish an' wicked—yes, wicked! I say it out plain an' square—
To look at the dark side always. 'Taint using the good Lord fair.

What if the corn was a failure? We'd a good big crop o' wheat,
An', with that an' the meat an' potatoes, we're sure of enough to eat.
You don't expect ev'rything, do you? Things might ha' been worse, my dear,
Think how we'd feel, my husban', if our little girl weren't here.
Be honest, and give the Lord, dear, the credit He ought to get.
Jest reckon up all our blessin's an' you'll find we're deep in His debt;
You'll see you ain't actin' right, Dan'el, to dwell on the dark side; so
Give Him the credit that's due Him, an' you'll have a Thanksgivin',
I know. —The S. S. Banner.

Good Marksmanship

During the pastorate of Henry Ward Beecher in Indianapolis he preached a series of sermons upon drunkenness and gambling, incidentally scoring the men of the community who profited by these sins. During the ensuing week he was accosted on the street by a would-be assailant, pistol in hand, who demanded a retraction of some utterance of the preceding Sunday.

"Take it back, right here!" he demanded with an oath, or "I will shoot you on the spot!"

"Shoot away!" was the preacher's response as he walked calmly away, hurling over his shoulder this parting remark:

"I don't believe you can hit the mark as well as I did!"
—Gospel Herald.

"Lost, yesterday, somewhere between sunrise and sunset, two golden hours set with sixty diamond minutes. No reward is offered, for they are gone forever."—(Horace Mann, American Educator.)

Great Thought Nuggets

One who never turned his back,
But marched breast forward,
Never doubted clouds would break,
Never dreamed, though right were worsted, wrong would triumph,
Held we fall to rise, are baffled to fight better,
Sleep to wake.
—Robert Browning

The Promises of God

No promise is of private interpretation. Whatever God has said to any one saint He has said to all. When He opens a well for one it is that all may drink. When He openeth a granary door to give out food, there may be some one starving man who is the occasion of its being opened, but all hungry saints may come and feed, too.—Spurgeon.

No Boundaries

Love that knew no boundaries,
Love that spurned the cost;
Love that pierced the darkness
Seeking for the lost;
Love that wrought redemption
There on Calvary;
Praise His Name forever,
His love included me!
—E. F. Reibetanz

"That Is Impossible"

Here is a story that we all would do well to lay to heart. It has been told before, but will bear repetition.

A farmer's wife had spread a slanderous story about her pastor through the village, and soon the whole countryside had heard it. Some time later the woman became sick and confessed the story was untrue. After her recovery she came to the pastor and craved his pardon. The old pastor said, "Of course I will gladly pardon you if you will comply with a wish of mine." "Gladly," replied the woman. "Go home, kill a black hen, pluck the feathers, and put them in a basket and bring them here."

In half an hour she was back. "Now," said the pastor, "go through the village and at each street corner scatter a few of these feathers, the remaining ones take to the top of the bell tower and scatter them to the winds, then return." She did so. "Now go through the village and gather the feathers again, and see that not one is missing."

The woman looked at the pastor in astonishment and said, "Why, that is impossible! The wind has scattered them over the fields everywhere!"

"And so," said he, "while I forgive you gladly, do not forget that you can never undo the damage your untrue words have done."

If any little word of mine
    May make a life the brighter,
If any little song of mine
    May make a heart the lighter,
God help me speak the little word,
    And take my bit of singing
And drop it in some lonely vale,
    To set the echoes ringing!
                              —Anon.

WHEN YOUR EYE OF FAITH IS
    DIM,
STILL HOLD ON JESUS, SINK OR
    SWIM;
STILL AT HIS FOOTSTOOL BOW
    THE KNEE,
AND ISRAEL'S GOD THY PEACE
    SHALL BE.
                              —SELECTED.

A teen-age tough was picked up by the police in an eastern city. The officer sought
for the ruffian's mother. They
found her at a woman's club
lecturing to the group on the
subject, "How to Bring Up
Children!"—W. B. Knight

Now

If you have hard work to do,
        Do it now.
Today the skies are clear and blue,
Tomorrow clouds may come in view,
Yesterday is not for you;
        Do it now.

If you have a song to sing,
        Sing it now.
Let the notes of gladness ring
Clear as song of bird in Spring,
Let every day some music bring;
        Sing it now.

If you have kind words to say,
        Say them now.
Tomorrow may not come your way.
Do a kindness while you may,
Loved ones will not always stay;
        Say them now.

If you have a smile to show,
        Show it now.
Make hearts happy, roses grow,
Let the friends around you know
The love you have before they go;
        Show it now.

                              Anon.

A PREACHER'S SON

My son of six came in one day---
He'd heard one of the neighbors say,
"I know he's a preacher's son,
But they tell more lies than anyone".
His little heart is sore and hurt
When he overhears some person blurt
"Oh, he's a preacher's son".

My son is just like other boys.
He has his troubles and his joys.
And, after all is said and done,
He'll grow up just like anyone.
So why should he feel sudden shame
When he hears a thoughtless soul exclaim.
"So, he's a preacher's son"?

Now our boy is being raised
Right in a home where God is praised,
And it seems to me a preacher's son
Would have more chance than anyone
To make his dad and mother proud
That with this boy they were endowed,
"This little preacher's son".

I could name you many a lad
Who has erred and "gone bad".
I could name them one by one
And there'd scarcely be a preacher's son.
And if you'd count I think you'd see
That above the average would be
"The slandered preacher's son".

Though he's just a little boy
He's his mother's pride and joy;
And for something he has done,
For some glory he has won,
I expect to hear someday,
In great surprise, somebody say,
"Why, he's a preacher's son"! - SELECTED

The Christian Home

In the family of Andrew Murray,
of South Africa, eleven children grew
to adult life. Five of the sons became ministers and four of the daughters became ministers' wives. The
next generation had a still more striking record in that ten grandsons became ministers and thirteen became
missionaries. The secret of this unusual contribution to the Christian
ministry was the Christian home.
                         --John R. Mott

The Drinking House Over the Way

The room was so cold and cheerless and bare,
    With its rickety table and one broken chair,
With its curtainless window with hardly a pane
    To keep out the snow, the wind and the rain.
A cradle stood empty, pushed up to the wall,
    And somehow that seemed the saddest of all.

In the rusty old stove the fire
        was dead.
    There was snow on the floor at
        the foot of the bed
And there, all alone, a pale wo-
        man was lying,
    You need not look twice to see
        she was dying,
Dying of want, of hunger and
        cold.
    Shall I tell you her story—the
        story she told:

"No, Ma'am, I'm no better; my
        cough is so bad;
    It's wearing me out, tho, and
        that makes me glad,
For it's wearisome living when
        one's all alone,
    And Heaven, they tell me, is
        just like a home.
Yes, Ma'am, I've a husband, he's
        somewhere about,
    I hoped he'd come in 'fore the
        fire went out;
But I guess he has gone where
        he's likely to stay,
    I mean to the DRINKING
        HOUSE over the way.

"There alone a pale woman was dying"

It was not always so, and I hope you won't think
    Too hard of him, lady, it's only the drink.
I know he's kind hearted, for, oh! how he cried
    For our poor little baby the morning he died.
You see he took sudden, and grew very bad,
    And we had no doctor—my poor little lad—
For his father had gone, never meaning to stay
    I am sure, to the DRINKING HOUSE over the way.

And when he came back, 'twas far in the night,
    And I was so tired and sick with fright,
Of staying so long with my baby alone,
    And it cutting my heart with its pitiful moan.
He was cross with the drink; poor fellow, I know
    It was that, not his baby that bothered him
        so;
But he swore at the child, as panting it lay,
    And went back to the DRINKING HOUSE
        over the way.

I heard the gate slam, and my heart seemed to
        freeze
    Like ice in my bosom, and there on my knees
By the side of the cradle all shivering I
        stayed,

"He touched the cold little hand"

I wanted my mother. I cried and I prayed.
The clock, it struck two, ere my baby was still,
    And my thoughts went back to my home on the hill,
Where my happy girlhood had spent its short day,
    Far, far from the DRINKING HOUSE over the way.

Could I be a girl, I, the heart-broken wife,
    There watching alone while the dear little life
Was going so fast that I had to bend low
    To hear if it breathed, 'twas so faint and so slow.
Yes, it was easy, his dying, he just grew more white
    And his eyes opened wider to look for the light.
As his father came in 'twas just break of day—
    Came in from the DRINKING HOUSE over the way.

Yes, ma'am he was sober, at least mostly I think,
    He often stayed that way to wear off the drink.
And I know he was sorry for what he had done,
    For he set a great store by our first little one.
And straight did he come to the cradle-bed, where
    Our baby lay dead, so pretty and fair.
I wondered that I could have wished him to stay
    When there was a DRINKING HOUSE over the way.

He stood quiet a while, did no
        understand,
    You see, till he touched th
        cold little hand.
Oh! then came the tears, and h
        shook like a leaf,
    And he said 'twas the drinkin
        that made all the grief.
The neighbors were kind and th
        minister came,
    And he talked of my seeing m
        baby again,
And of the bright angels—I wo
        dered if they
    Could see in the DRINKIN
        HOUSE over the way.

And I thought when my bab
        was put in the ground.
    And the men with their spad
        were shaping the mound,
If somebody only would help m
        to save
    My husband who stood by th
        side of the grave.
If only it were not so handy t
        drink—
    The men that make law
        ma'am, sure didn't think

Of hearts they would break, of the souls they would slay,
    When they licensed the DRINKING HOUSE over the way.

I've been sick since, and it cannot be long,
    Be pitiful, lady, to him when I'm gone.
He wants to do right, but you never can think
    How weak a man grows when he's fond of drink.
And it's tempting him here and its tempting him there—
    Four places I've counted in this very square,
Where a man can get whiskey by night and by day,
    Not to mention the DRINKING HOUSE over the way.

There's a verse in the Bible the minister read,
    No drunkard shall enter the kingdom, it sa
And he is my husband, and I love him so,
    And where I am going I want him to go.
Our baby and I will both want him there—
    Don't you think the dear Saviour will answ
        our prayer?
And please, when I'm gone, ask someone to pr
    For him at the DRINKING HOUSE over t
        way.

*(From tract put out by Pilgrim Tracts Inc., Rane
man, N. C.)*

One Minute Readings

School Inspector

A school inspector, to get an idea of the standard of teaching, entered a classroom while the lesson was in progress and decided to ask the children some questions.

Calling on one small boy he asked, "Who broke down the walls of Jericho?" The boy answered, "Not me, sir." The inspector turned to the teacher and asked, "Is this the usual standard in this class?" The teacher replied, "The boy is usually quite honest so I believe him."

Leaving the room in disgust the inspector sought out the headmaster and explained what had transpired.

The headmaster said, "I've known both the teacher and boy concerned for several years and I'm sure that neither of them would do a thing like that."

By this time the inspector was furious and reported the incident to the director of education.

The director said, "I feel, you know, we are making a mountain out of a molehill in this case. I suggest we pay the bill and write the sum off."

Frustration

My teacher says that I'm the best
  And smartest boy in school;
I'm never careless like the rest;
  I never break a rule.
If visitors should come to call,
  She has me speak a piece,
Or tell what makes an apple fall
  Or binds the Coast of Greece.
You might expect that since my brain
  Holds such an awful lot,
I'd be extremely proud and vain;
  But, oh — oh not.
For Willie Brown's a cleverer lad
  Than I can hope to be;
Why I'd give anything I had
  To be as smart as he.
He can't recite, "Hark, Hark the Lark,"
  He's not the teacher's pet;
He never gets a perfect mark
  In 'rithmatic—and yet
Could I be he, I'd waste no tears
  On foolish things like sums;
For Willie Brown can wag his ears
  And dislocate his thumbs.

WHERE WILL YOU SPEND ETERNITY?

"Eternity! — where?" it floats in the air:
Amid clamor, or silence, it ever is there,
The question so solemn: "Eternity!—where?"

"Eternity!—where? oh, Eternity!—where?"
With redeemed ones in glory, or fiends in despair?
With one or the other: "Eternity —where?"

"Eternity!—where?" is well worth a care;
Oh, shall we, oh, can we e'en venture to dare,
Oh naught till we settle: "Eternity!—where?"

"Eternity!—where? oh, Eternity! —where?"
Friend, sleep not, nor take in this world any share,
Till you answer the question: "Eternity!—where?"

—Anon

How Much I Owe

When this passing world is done,
When has sunk yon glowing sun,
When we stand with Christ in glory,
Looking o'er life's finished story,
Then, Lord, shall I fully know—
Not till then—how much I owe.

When I stand before the throne,
Dressed in beauty not my own,
When I see Thee as Thou art,
Love Thee with unsinning heart,
Then, Lord, shall I fully know—
Not till then—how much I owe.

When the praise of heaven I hear,
Loud as thunder to the ear,
Loud as many water's noise,
Sweet as harp's melodious voice,
Then, Lord, shall I fully know—
Not till then—how much I owe.

Even on earth, as through a glass
Darkly, let Thy glory pass,
Make forgiveness feel so sweet,
Make Thy Spirit's help to meet.
Even on earth, Lord, make me know
Something of how much I owe.

—Robert Murray McCheyne.

My days are days of small affairs of trifling worries and little cares.

A lunch to pack, a bed to make, a room to sweep, a pie to bake, a hurt to kiss.

A tear to dry, a head to brush, a bow to tie, a face to wash, or rent to mend.

A meal to plan, a fuss to end, a hungry husband to be fed, a sleepy child to be put to bed,

I, who hoped some day to gain success, perhaps a bit of fame,

Must give my life to small affairs

Of trifling worries, little cares.

But should tomorrow bring a change, my little house will grow still and strange,

Should all the cares I know today, be swept quite suddenly away.

Where now a hundred duties press, would be but an ache of loneliness.

No child's gay ribbon to be tied, no wayward little feet to guide,

To heaven then would rise my prayers. "Oh GOD, give me back my little cares."

—Author unknown

"Churches Doesn't Die Dat Way"

A devout colored preacher whose heart was aglow with missionary zeal, gave notice to his congregation that in the evening an offering would be taken for missions, and asked for liberal gifts. A selfish, well-to-do man in the congregation said to him before the service: "Yer gwine to kill this church if yer goes on saying 'give.' No church can stan' it. Yer gwine ter kill it."

After the sermon the colored minister said to the people: "Brodder Jones tol' me I's gwine ter kill dis church if'n I kep' astin yer to give, but, my breddern, churches doesn't die dat way. If'n anybody knows of a church which died 'cause its been givin' too much to de Lord, I'se be very much 'bliged ef my brodder will tell me whar dat church is, for I'se gwine to visit it, and I'se'll climb on de walls ov dat church, under de light of de moon and cry, 'Blessed are de daid dat die in de Lawd.'"

A Good Thanksgiving

Said old gentleman Gay on a Thanksgiving Day:
"If you want a good time, then give something away."
So he sent a fat turkey to shoemaker Price,
And the shoemaker said: "What a big bird! How nice!
With such a good dinner before me I ought
To give Widow Lee the small chicken I bought."
"This fine chicken, oh, see!" said the sweet Widow Lee,
"And the kindness that sent it—how precious to me!
I'll give washwoman Biddy my big pumpkin pie."
"And, oh, sure," Biddy said, "'tis the queen o' all pies!
Just to look at its yellow face gladdens my eyes!
Now it's my turn, I think, and a sweet ginger cake
For the motherless Finnigan children I'll bake."
Cried the Finnigan children, Rose, Denny and Hugh:
"It smells sweet of spice, and we'll carry a slice
To little lame Jake, who has nothing that's nice."
"Oh, I thank you and thank you!" said little lame Jake;
"What a bootiful, bootiful, bootiful cake!
And oh, such a big slice! I'll save all the crumbs,
And give them to each little sparrow that comes."
And the sparrows, they twittered, as if they would say,
Like old gentleman Gay: "On a Thanksgiving Day,
If you want a good time, then give something away."
—Selected.

Spurgeon Speaks

I never like people to tell me secrets, for I cannot keep them.

— * —

Why, the very spelling of the Devil's name shows what he is—Devil, evil, vile, ill, hell!

— * —

Men who conquer go in for attack.

— * —

Never have a meeting you cannot invite Christ to.

— * —

Everybody was against Jeremiah, yet they would not go to Egypt without him.

— * —

Education without religion is like the solar system without the sun.

The story is told about two boys who were playing together. They had been reading about the animal sacrifices in the Old Testament. In their little game they built a small altar of stones and placed some wood upon it. When the altar was finished, one boy turned to the other and said, "Now we must find a sacrifice."

The other little boy looked at his toys. His eyes fell on a wooden camel. One of the legs was broken off. Picking it up, he said, "Here, let's sacrifice this! It's no good anyhow."

How many times we Christians are just like the little boy with the camel—give God something not worth anything.

The Preacher's Black Book

A noted preacher had a shrewd way of handling critics in his congregation. He had in his desk a special black book labeled "Complaints of Members Against One Another." When one of his people called to tell him about the faults of another, he would say, "Well, here is my complaint book. I will write down what you say, and you can sign it. Then when I have time I will take up the matter officially concerning this brother." The sight of the open book and the ready pen had its effect. "Oh, no, I couldn't sign anything like that!" they would say. The result of it all was that in forty years this preacher opened his black book a thousand times but never got anyone to write a line in it.

Just a Minute

The dictionary is the only place where success comes before work.
—Selected

cepted Christ but, having found Him good, are making Him known to others. And every member is a leper.—Moody Monthly.

A Church of Tithers!

Do you know a church composed entirely of tithers? An account of it would be worth while if you do. Dr. Hugh McKean of Chiengmai, Siam, tells of one in that country. There are 400 members, and every member tithes. They receive 40 stangs (less than twenty cents) and their rice each week. Of this, each gives weekly one-tenth. Because of this they have more for Christian work than any other church in Siam. They pay their own pastor, and have sent two missionary families to spread the Gospel in a community cut off from the outside world. They are entirely responsible for this work and are very earnest about it. They are intensely interested in all forms of Christian work, especially work for unfortunates of every kind, and their gifts for this kind of work are large. They not only have ac-

There is nothing so swift of wing, so strong of grasp, so loud of call as prayer.

THANKSGIVING FOR TRIALS

Because we cannot see just what God is saving us from, we venture our foolish reproaches, if we could see this, we would often kneel down and thank God for certain trials as the richest of His mercies.
—Selected

LITTLE HATTIE'S CHAIR

The day that little Hattie died
  The house seemed strange and queer;
The furniture looked different,
  And everything was drear;
We children all would huddle close
  Upon the steps and try
To think of Heaven where she was,
  And then we all would cry.

Then Bobbie sneaked off by himself,
  And we hunted everywhere
Till Father found him in the yard
  In little Hattie's chair;
He was hid behind the lilac bush
  Where she would often play,
And his face was streaked with tears
  And he called, "Oh, keep away."

But Father kissed him on the head
  And lifted chair and all
And carried him into the house
  And on up through the hall;
Until he reached the attic door,
  And we kept following, too,
Because we wondered what it was
  That he was going to do.

He got a hammer and a nail
  And drove it 'way up high,
And said, "Now, children, you may kiss
  The little chair good-bye;
But you must never take it down
  And never sit on it"--
And there stood Mother, watching us--
  And we all cried a bit.

One Saturday when Bobbie was
  A-tracking to its lair,
A wild beast of the forest,
  He climbed the attic stair--
Quite softly in his stocking feet
  And peeped in through the door,
And there by little Hattie's chair
  Knelt Mother on the floor.

"O Jesus, spare the others--
  And make them pure and good,
Help me to train them carefully
  As a Christian mother should";
Then Bobbie tiptoed down the stairs
  And told us what he'd heard,
And we looked at one another
  But didn't speak a word.

That evening after Father came,
  And we got the songbooks out,
And took our turn in reading
  A Bible verse about;
He said he'd heard that we had been
  So very good all day,
But no one told him 'twas because
  Bobbie heard Mother pray.

Grace W. Haight

> Don't get the wrong idea
> of God. When you pervert
> Christianity, God Almighty
> gets mad.—Dr. Bob Jones, Sr.

Too Many Generals!

Two boys were playing war. They were dressed like real soldiers. Their father asked them, "What are you doing, boys?"

"Oh, we are playing war!"

"But," said the father, "I don't hear any firing of guns, nor do I see any clashing with the enemy!"

"Oh, but we are generals, Dad!" proudly answered the boys.

In the Lord's army, are there not too many "generals" who are ensconced in "the seats of the mighty," in places of ease and safety? Are there not altogether too few slogging foot soldiers who battle the enemy and storm the forts of entrenched wrong and "spiritual wickedness in high places"?

—Selected

Just Less Ashamed

The great Canadian physician, Sir William Osler, was lecturing one day on alcohol. "Is it true," asked a student, "that alcohol makes people able to do things better?" "No," replied Sir William, "it just makes them less ashamed of doing them badly." —From Moody Monthly.

99

THE Strange CASE OF GEORGE WILSON

In 1829 two men—Wilson and Porter—were convicted of robbing the United States mails, and sentenced to death by hanging. Three weeks before the time set for Wilson's execution, he was pardoned by President Andrew Jackson.

Strangely enough, Wilson refused the pardon. The case went to the Supreme Court (United States vs. George Wilson, 7 Peters' Report, p. 150) and the court finally handed down its decision: "A pardon is a deed, to the validity of which delivery is essential, and delivery is not complete without acceptance. It may then be rejected by the person to whom it is tendered; and if it is rejected, we have discovered no power in this court to force it upon him."

Most people would agree that Wilson was a fool for refusing to accept a pardon. Yet these same people daily reject the pardon which God has provided for them.

Because God is just, He must punish our sins. But because God is merciful, He Himself suffered the awful penalty when Jesus Christ, His Son, suffered all the wrath of God against our sins as He died on the cross of Calvary. "For God so loved the world, that he gave his only begotten Son, that whosoever believeth in him should not perish, but have everlasting life."

Your pardon has been signed by God Himself. Now all you need to do is accept it by telling God in prayer that you wish to be counted among those for whom Christ died. Unless you accept the pardon, you remain condemned.

Wilson's was a strange case. But then, Wilson was a fool.

Beatitudes for the Married

Blessed are the husband and wife who continue to be affectionate, considerate and loving after the wedding bells have ceased ringing.

Blessed are the husband and wife who are polite and courteous to one another as they are to their friends.

Blessed are they who have a sense of humor, for this attribute will be a handy shock absorber.

Blessed are the married couples who abstain from alcoholic beverages.

Blessed are they who love their mates more than any other person in the world, and who joyfully fulfill their marriage vow of a lifetime of fidelity and mutual helpfulness to one another.

Blessed are they who remember to thank God for their food before they partake of it, and who set aside some time each day for reading the Bible and prayer.

Blessed are they who attain parenthood; for children are a heritage of the Lord.

Blessed are those mates who never speak loudly to one another and who make their home a place "where seldom is heard a discouraging word."

Blessed are the husband and wife who faithfully attend the worship service of the church together for the advancement of Christ's kingdom.

Blessed are the husband and wife who humbly dedicate their lives and their home to Christ and practice the teachings of Christ in the home by being unselfish, loyal and loving.

BLANCHARD ON INGRATITUDE

Wrote Dr. Charles A. Blanchard:

I read years ago of a mother who had raised six boys to manhood and her work done, had lain down to die. The boys came home to see their mother and her oldest son, a great, powerful man, knelt by her and, wiping the death-dew from her forehead, said to her: "Mother, you have always been a good mother to us boys." The tired woman closed her eyes and great tears pushed out under the lids and ran down her wasted cheeks. Then she opened her eyes, looked searchingly into the face of her firstborn and said to him:

"My boy, I prayed more that I might be a good mother to you six boys than for anything else. I was afraid that I should fail in some way to be all that I ought to you, and I never knew whether you boys thought I had failed or not until now. Not one of you ever told me I was a good mother until today."

Was it not an unspeakable tragedy that the dear mother should bear the six sons, should nurse them through the sicknesses of babyhood, s h o u l d make their clothes and wash them and iron them, should prepare their meals a thousand times a year until they were g r o w n to manhood, should see them, one by one, move out into the world, all the while wondering in her heart if they thought she had been a success as a mother, and not one of the six ever say, "You have been a good mother," until she was ready to die? They were good boys, good men, but they did n o t express their thanksgivings.

Communism is the religion of failures

DON'T think the danger of communism in this country is past. Men and women who are failures will always try to tear you down to their level, and communism promises them the chance. They label themselves; here's who they are:

—politicians who promote government ownership of the means of production — the neverfailing opening wedge of the communist state.

—those who urge us not to "antagonize" Russia and her satellites, supporters and friends, but to "get along with" them (which means giving in to them).

—the greedy who say "the state" should educate and feed them, guarantee them security without obligation.

The price of these noble-sounding ideas is loss of liberty bit by bit. And that is how communism always enters. America rewards with self-respect those who work. Communism rewards with petty power the failures who destroy. Watch for them.

Christ's Last Will and Testament:

He left His purse to Judas; His body to Joseph of Arimathea; His mother to John; His clothes to the soldiers; His peace to His disciples; His supper to His followers; Himself as an example and as a servant; His Gospel to the world; His presence always with God's children!

—Selected

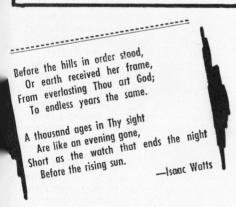

Before the hills in order stood,
Or earth received her frame,
From everlasting Thou art God;
To endless years the same.

A thousand ages in Thy sight
Are like an evening gone,
Short as the watch that ends the night
Before the rising sun.

—Isaac Watts

"Be willing to die for your convictions but not your preferences. (God give us wisdom to know the difference.)"—Jack Hyles.

What Meaneth The Cross?

What does it mean this wood
So stained with blood;
This tree without a root
That bears such fruit;

This tree without a leaf
So leaved with grief?
What does its height proclaim
Whose height is shame;

Its piteous arms outspread
Where death lies dead;
And in the midst a heart
Cleft wide apart?

Though blind, I cannot miss
The meaning this;
My sin's stupendous price—
His sacrifice!

—Author Unknown

The Art of Self-Defense

"Do you think it wrong for me to learn the art of self-defense?" asked a young man of his pastor.

"Certainly not," answered the minister. "I learned it in youth myself, and I have found it of great value during my life."

"Indeed, sir! Did you learn the old English system or Sullivan's system?"

"Neither. I learned Solomon's system."

"Solomon's system?"

"Yes; you will find it laid down in the first verse of the 15th chapter of Proverbs, 'A soft answer turneth away wrath.' It is the best system of self-defense of which I know."

—Western Recorder

Hudson Taylor's Last Half-Crown

By Phyllis Thompson

It was past ten o'clock on a dark night, and the raggedly dressed man accompanying him was a complete stranger. Nineteen-year-old Hudson Taylor fingered his one remaining half a crown to make sure it was still in his pocket, and looked around him rather apprehensively. He had been along these poor, narrow streets before, and even in broad daylight they were not inviting. Now, with street lamps flickering feebly at the corners of dark alleys, and suspicious looking people slinking into doorways, the neighborhood looked anything but safe and respectable. It was certainly not the sort of place one would choose to walk in with ragged strangers after dark. But, after all, if he was going to China he must no doubt get used to this sort of thing, so he went on.

"Why didn't you ask a priest to come and pray with your wife?" he asked his companion, rather glad to hear the familiar sound of his own voice! The man had come to him with the story that his wife was dying. "Will you come and pray for her soul?" he had requested, and Hudson Taylor had readily agreed. Now, however, he was beginning to wonder. The man was evidently a Roman Catholic. If his wife were indeed dying, why had he not obtained the services of a priest, of whom there seemed always an adequate supply in this Irish quarter of Hull? Why come to a Protestant?

The man explained. He had been to the priest. The priest, however, had demanded one shilling and sixpence down before rendering his services. And as he and his family were starving already, and had no money left at all, a fee of one and sixpence for a prayer was quite out of the question.

Starving! Hudson fingered his one remaining half a crown uneasily. It was all he had; apart from two bowls of porridge in his lodging he had neither food nor money. He could scarcely be expected to part with that one remaining coin. He felt unreasonably annoyed with the man, and reprimanded him severely for having allowed things to get to such a

pass. Why had he not gone to the Poor Law officer, and asked for help? A dying wife and a starving family, and doing nothing about it, indeed!

"I went," replied the man dismally. "He told me to come back tomorrow morning at eleven. But my wife, she be dying. She'll be gone before morning, I'm fearing . . . ."

Hudson's heart was touched. His own position had seemed precarious enough, but how much worse was the lot of his companion. If only his half a crown were in two shilling pieces and a sixpence, he thought to himself, how gladly he would have given him one of the shillings!

The man turned suddenly out of the street, into a dark courtyard. Hudson had been here before, and he remembered the last occasion very distinctly. He had been buffeted and pommelled by the indignant slum-dwellers who had torn up the tracts he gave them, and bade him begone. If ever he shewed his face here again, let him beware! The priest with his crucifix and prayers to Holy Mary was welcome enough, but not a young English Protestant preacher, begorrah! Hudson had departed with what dignity he could muster, little thinking he would ever be invited to return. And as he felt his way gingerly up a rickety flight of stairs in one of the tenement houses, he sincerely hoped that his presence would not become widely known in the area! He was quite relieved when they reached the top of the stairs and he heard his companion open a door. They had reached their destination.

What a sight met his eyes! The dim light from a cheap, guttering candle revealed bare boards, curtainless window, and a room almost devoid of furniture. On the floor in a corner lying on a straw mattress was a thin, exhausted woman, and beside her a new-born baby, not yet two days old. Standing around, or lying on the floor, were four or five other people—children in ill-fitting clothes, without shoes or stockings, who looked towards their father and the

stranger he had brought with him, with large, listless, hungry eyes.

Hudson stood silently in the room, acutely conscious of his half a crown. Oh, if only it were in two separate shillings and a sixpence, he thought. Certainly he would immediately produce one of the shillings *and* the sixpence, and give to these poor people. But it was no use wishing. He pulled himself together, remembered that he was a preacher and intended being a missionary, and decided he must tell these people about God.

"You know, things are very bad for you just now," he faltered. "But you mustn't be cast down. We have a Father in Heaven Who loves us and cares for us, and if we trust Him . . ."

The words seemed to stick in his throat. "Hypocrite!" something inside him seemed to say. "Telling these people about a kind and loving Father in Heaven— *and not prepared to trust Him yourself,* without your half a crown!"

Hudson gave up trying to preach. The family looked at him in silence, as he stood there before them in his long-tailed coat and wide wing collar, wearing real leather shoes and with a top hat! What if his clothes were getting threadbare, and his shoes needed mending? Compared with them he appeared wealthy beyond their dreams. How were they to know he had only half a crown left in the world? Hudson felt very depressed indeed. Oh, if only that half a crown were a florin and a sixpence, he would give them the florin, he really would, and keep only the sixpence for himself? But it wasn't a florin and a sixpence . . . .

He turned to the man, and said: "You asked me to come and pray with your wife. Let us pray now." It would be easy to pray, he thought, as he knelt on the bare floor. But it wasn't. No sooner had he commenced "Our Father Who art in Heaven," than that accusing voice within said again, " . . . that half a crown in your pocket." He pressed through his prayer, feeling more and more miserable, and then rose to his feet.

And as he did so, the man said to him in desperation: "You can see what a terrible state we're in, sir. For God's sake, help us!"

Poor Hudson! There was nothing for it now. He remembered suddenly something he had read often enough in the Sermon on the Mount. "Give to him that asketh of thee . . . ." Give . . . .

Slowly he put his hand in his pocket. The half a crown, all of it, would have to go.

"You may think I'm well off," he said to the man as he handed him the coin. "But as a matter of fact, that's all the money I've got in the world." Surprisingly, he began to feel quite cheerful. "But what I've been telling you is true, you know. God really is a Father, and we can trust Him. *I* can trust Him. . . ." And he realized he could. He found himself speaking with great assurance and confidence about trusting God, now that the half a crown was out of his pocket and in the man's! He was amazed at the difference it made to his feelings. He was positively buoyant now. He and the family parted from each other, with mutual expressions of good will, he made his way down the rickety stairs and out into the courtyard, walking home with his head in the air, coat tails flapping jauntily, singing at the top of his voice, without a care or a penny in the world! And when he reached the small bed-sitting room in Drainside where he was lodging, and prepared to eat his last but one bowl of porridge, he felt as happy as a king.

An interesting thought occurred to him as he sat there. He remembered that he had read somewhere that "he that giveth to the poor lendeth to the Lord." It put that half a crown in quite a different light to feel that, having given it to some poor people, he had merely lent it to God. The idea of lending God half a crown might seem rather startling, but as it was in the Bible he knew it was all right. So when he knelt to say his prayers before going to bed, he mentioned the matter of the loan, requesting that it might be replaced soon, otherwise he would have no dinner the next day!

The following morning he arose as usual, and looked at his last bowl of porridge. A hard day's work lay before him, and while one good bowl of porridge was enough to start on, it was scarcely enough to continue on. When would God repay that loan?

He sat down and commenced eating. The postman's rat-tat-tat was heard on the front door, but he paid little attention, since he rarely received letters on Monday mornings. But within a few seconds the landlady appeared at his door.

"Here's a little package for you, Mr. Taylor," she said cheerfully, holding it towards him in her apron, for her hands were wet.

"Oh—thank you!" replied Hudson, rather surprised. He took it from her, and looked at it. It was addressed to him all right but he certainly did not recognize the writing. The postmark was blurred, so that did not help him, either. He decided to open it. Slitting open the envelope, he drew out a sheet of paper. Inside was a pair of kid gloves.

"Whoever is sending me kid gloves?" he thought, mystified, as he opened them out. And then something fell out. It was a very small object, and it gleamed. He stooped to pick it up—it was a golden half-sovereign.

He stared at it in amazement; looked through the paper wrapping for a letter; scanned the handwriting and the postmark for a clew as to who had sent it. All in vain. He never discovered where it came from. And at that moment he did not really care. As far as he was concerned, it had come straight from Heaven! It dawned on him that not merely had his half a crown been returned, but three more besides. Suddenly he laughed aloud.

"That's good interest!" he exclaimed jubilantly. "Ha! Ha! Half a crown invested in God's bank for twelve hours brings me ten shillings! This is the bank for me!"

(From the book, GOD'S VENTURER—HUDSON TAYLOR, published by China Inland Mission Book Dept. 237 W. School Lane, Philadelphia 44, Pennsylvania. Used by permission.)

What Repentance Is

Old John Knight—a saintly old man he was—was sitting back in the church one night listening to George Smith preach, and George was preaching of repentance and he was agoing it, and he was speaking of evangelical repentance and legal repentance, splitting hairs a mile long and quartering them, showing which was legal repentance and which was evangelical repentance. Old Uncle John Knight sat back there listening to old Uncle George until he was tired, and Old Uncle John stood up and said: "George, won't you stop a minute and let me tell them what repentance is?" And George said, "Yes, Uncle John. I always like to hear you talk." And Uncle John started up the aisle this way, and he said, "I am going to hell; I am going to hell; I am going to hell;" and when he got up about the end of the aisle, he started right back, and he said, "I am going to heaven; I am going to heaven; I am going to heaven." "Now," said he, "George, tell 'em to turn around; that means repentance; that means conversion; and don't stand there splitting hairs on evangelical and legal repentance."

—Sam Jones

Better Than a One-way Ticket

A Christian woman was once talking to a servant of Christ about the assurance of her safety in the Saviour and said, "I have taken a single ticket to Glory, and do not intend to come back." Whereupon the man of God replied: "You are going to miss a lot. I have taken a return ticket, for I am not only going to meet Christ in Glory, but I am coming back with him in power and great glory to the earth."

—Sunday School Times

"When I get to Heaven, I shall see three wonders there—the first wonder will be to see many people there whom I did not expect to see; the second wonder will be to miss many people whom I did expect to see; and the third and greatest wonder of all will be to find myself there."—John Newton

The Preciousness of a Brother's Prayer

By the late Dr. W. B. Riley

"Ye also helping together by prayer for us."—II Corinthians 1:11.

The prayer to which the Apostle here refers, was concerning a collection which had been taken, doubtless for the Apostle's support. It is called "the gift bestowed upon us by the means of many persons," and for that Paul desired that "thanks may be given by many on our behalf."

There are some of us who count the great prayer fraternity, who hold us constantly before God's throne, as our fortune. We believe that intercessory prayer is a power; and while we do not attempt to explain it, we bear witness to this fact of experience, namely that when our burdens have been heaviest, our danger most imminent, when the Adversary seemed most determined against us, we have discovered that somehow the Spirit of God, anticipating all of that, had stirred many people to pray; and more than once we have been compelled to assign victory to intercessory prayers.

Some years since I was passing through a great trial and I believed at that time that it was the greatest of my life. In the very midst of it when I was utterly unfitted for any duty, I had to keep an engagement of long standing in Chicago.

On reaching that city, I found an old-time friend eager for me to come out to Morgan Park and dine at his home. In answer to his urgent invitation, I went. His wife and mother were marvelously godly women—women who walked in the Spirit. At the dinner table, imagine my amazement to have

the wife say to me, "Dr. Riley, two nights ago mother and I were led to spend the whole night in prayer for you. We did not know why, but we found it impossible to do else." The speech astonished me immeasurably, but it also lent me hope in an hour that was otherwise dark, for I knew prayers so prompted by the Spirit would prevail.

Years before that, while yet pastor in Chicago, and owing to the financial stringency that began in '93, affecting profoundly my little church, I had faced exceedingly perilous problems; and to secure time to pray them through, I had gone to Southern Illinois for a day or two of outing.

A man came to me in a hunting field, and handed me a postal card. It was written by the wife of my senior deacon, a great and godly woman. The postal card read, "I know your burden this week, and I want you to know that day and night I am interceding."

It was like a sunburst from behind the blackest cloud; but better yet is another thought, namely, that the brother of all brothers, even our Elder Brother Christ, does not forget us. You remember how that night when He was about to leave the upper room and go to the Garden for His agony and betrayal, Jesus first prayed for His disciples, committing them to the keeping power of God, and pleading that they might be sanctified in the truth, made one in the faith, effective in service, and received at last into Glory. To be sure, in their weakness they slept when He needed them; but even that failure did not keep them from the Father's blessing, for Christ had prayed for them.

We sometimes forget that Christ is the same yesterday, today and forever. The Christ of Peter is your Christ and my Christ; and that even as He said to Peter, "Simon, Simon, behold, Satan hath desired to have you, that he may sift you as wheat: But I have prayed for thee, that thy faith fail not" (Luke 22:31,32), so He speaks to us and pleads in our behalf, that we, when we recover, might strengthen our brethren. Yea, that we in response might, like Peter, be ready to say, "Lord, I am ready to go with Thee, both into prison, and to death" (Luke 22:33).

Courageous Men Needed

There is a story to the effect that a certain society in South Africa once wrote to David Livingstone: "Have you found a good road to where you are? If so, we want to know how to send other men to join you."

Livingstone replied, "If you have men who will come only if they know there is a good road, I don't want them. I want men strong and courageous, who will come if there is no road at all." What a crying need there is for such men in the work of Christ today!—Christian Business Men's League Bulletin

---

I Ain't Mad No More

Let's play horse—'at's what le's do!
I ain't mad no more wif you;

Wasn't it a long time, though,
'At you wouldn't speak t' me
An' I wouldn't speak t' you?
It was mostly half-past two
When you wanted what I had
An' I sassed you back so bad,
An' it's now most half-past
free!

I ain't mad no more wif you—
Le's play horse—at's what le's
do!

—Strickland Gilliland

Is It Right?

Is it right to build churches to save men, and at the same time license shops that destroy men?

Is it right to license a man to sell that which will make a man drunk, and then punish the man for being drunk?

Is it right to license a man to make paupers, and then to tax sober men to take care of them?

Is it right to license a saloon to teach vice and then to tax people for schools to teach virtue?

Is it right to derive a revenue out of a traffic which no decent man defends?

Is it right to teach your boy to be honest, and then vote to license a place where he may be taught to gamble?

Is it right to preach justice and charity, and then vote to license a thing which robs the widows and orphans of their bread?

—Selected.

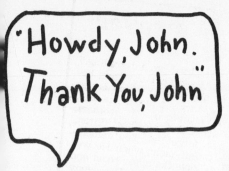

"Howdy, John. Thank You, John"

A beautiful story is told of Dr. Broadus, the American scholar, seminary president and homiletics professor. In his younger days, in the town in which he lived, he was converted to Christ. He had been attending some meetings, and next day he went to one of his schoolmates, Sandy Jones, a red-haired, awkward chap, and said to him: "I wish you would be a Christian; won't you?" And Sandy said: "Well, I don't know. Perhaps I will."

And sure enough, after a while, one night in the little church, Sandy Jones accepted Christ. Straightway, he stalked across that little meeting house, held out his hand and said, "I thank you, John, I thank you, I thank you, John."

Dr. Broadus went forth from that little town, and became a great scholar, a great exegete and theological president. Every summer when he went home to that little town (and he hardly missed a season), this awkard, red-haired old farmer, in his plain clothes, with red sand in his boots, would come up, stick out his great bony hand, and say, "Howdy, John. Thank you, John; thank you, John; thank you, John. I never forget, John."

And they say that when Dr. Broadus lay dying, his family about him, he said: "I rather think the sound sweetest to my ears in Heaven, next to the welcome of Him, whom having not seen I have loved and tried to serve, will be the welcome of Sandy Jones, as he will thrust out his great hand, and say, 'Howdy John; thank you, John; thank you, John; thank you, John.'"

When we die,
Our loved ones cry,
Our close friends sigh.
But to die,
Is not "good-by,"
We do but fly
"Thru the sky,"
To Heaven high—
The "Sweet by-and-by."

Wang, The Tiger
By Pearl Palmer

Wang was the son of a wealthy Chinese farmer. His father gave him interesting home and farm duties, provided him with all the food and clothing he needed, and taught him the sayings of Confucius; but Wang was selfish and wild. At night he would slip out of his house to join a group of hoodlums in town.

His father tried to keep him out of trouble. He bolted the gates, but Wang climbed over the walls. He tied him with ropes, but Wang broke the ropes and escaped. The father pleaded with him, but Wang just laughed in his face.

Wang finally ran away to stay, and the father heard of him only through rumor: "Wang is leader of the bandit tribe! Wang helped to sack a nearby village! Wang, Wang, the Tiger!" Everyone was afraid of him.

For a long time no news was heard of Wang. Then to the surprise of his home community, notice was given of his death and the time of his funeral. Great crowds assembled at the family burial ground. The funeral procession came with loud laments of hired mourners. The casket was placed ready for burial. Before the earth was lifted, Wang's father stepped forward and opened the casket. Wang himself stepped forth.

The awestruck villagers listened while Wang spoke:

"You have heard of the life I was living among the bandits. The more homes I could destroy the smarter I thought I was. I was Wang the Tiger!

"One day I met a man who was not afraid of me. I threatened to destroy his home, but he said his God was able to deliver him. I was curious about this new God, and he told me that he was a Christian. As he spoke I had such a hunger in my soul for the peace that he had! When I despaired at the thought of ever controlling myself, he said that Christ, the Son of God, could change me.

"Oh, the wonder that came to my soul! What walls and chains had failed to do, Christ was able to do. Wang, the Tiger, is truly dead. This is a new man in Christ you see before you."

Wang went back to his father's home. He took his place on the farm. Through his leadership, many found Christ, and a church grew up in the village.

The Christlife Magazine

The Unknown Teacher

I sing of the unknown teacher. Great generals win campaigns, but it is the unknown soldier who wins the war. It is the unknown teacher who delivers and guides the young. She lives in obscurity and contends with hardship. For her no trumpets blare, no chariots wait, no golden decorations are decreed. She keeps the watch along the borders of darkness and makes the attack on the trenches of ignorance and folly. She awakens sleeping spirits. She quickens the indolent, the unstable. She communicates her own joy in learning and shares with boys and girls the very best treasures of her mind. She lights many candles which, in later years will shine back to cheer her. This is her reward.

—Henry Van Dyke

Two Epitaphs

In Warwickshire, England, near an ivy-grown church, may be found a stone on which is the following inscription:

"Here lies a miser who lived for himself
And cared for nothing but gathering pelf,
Now where he is or how he fares,
Nobody knows and nobody cares."

The other epitaph is in St. Paul's Cathedral, London. It is a simple and plain monument. Beneath a figure are these words:

"Sacred to the memory of Charles George Gordon,
who at all times and everywhere gave his strength to the weak, his substance to the poor, his sympathy to the suffering, his heart to God."

—Teacher's Lesson Quarterly.

THOUGHTS WORTH REPEATING...

Temptation is the tempter looking through the keyhole into the room where you are living; sin is your drawing back the bolt and making it possible for him to enter.
—J. Wilbur Chapman

J. Edgar Hoover says, "Most juvenile crime has its inception in the dance hall, either public or private."

BIGNESS IN GOD'S SIGHT IS MEASURED IN TERMS OF QUALITY. NOT QUANTITY.—BOB JONES, JR.

Death is not a period but a comma in the story of life.
—Dr. Amos J. Traver

God writes with a pen that never blots, speaks with a tongue that never slips, and acts with a hand that never fails.

"Count that day lost whose low descending sun, Views from thy hand no worthy action done."—Selected.

Our temper is one of the few things that improves the longer we keep it.—W. B. Knight

---

"YOU CAN'T TAKE your money with you—but you can send it on ahead."

The beginning of anxiety is the end of faith. The beginning of true faith is the end of anxiety.—George Muller

---

Don't despise small things; remember a little lantern can do what a great sun can never do—it can shine in the night.

The monument I want after I am dead is a monument with two legs going around the world—a saved sinner telling about the salvation of Jesus Christ.—D. L. Moody.

Tender-handed stroke a nettle,
And it stings you for your pains;
Grasp it like a man of mettle,
And it soft as silk remains.
Aaron Hill, (1685-1750)

They are never alone who are accompanied by noble thoughts.—Sydney.

Find your niche, and fill it. If it be ever so little, if it is only to be hewer of wood or drawer of water, do something in this great battle for God and truth.—Spurgeon.

Jonathan Edwards, when a boy, wrote in his journal, "Resolved to live with all my might while I do live."

Ere a child has reached to seven
Teach him all the way to Heaven;
Better still the work will thrive
If he learns before he's five.
—C. H. Spurgeon.

Ponce de Leon searched the Everglades of Florida, looking for the Fountain of Youth. He never found it. Jesus Christ has never yet and never will, fail that soul in search of the Fountain of Life.

Prayer is not the overcrowding of God's reluctance; it is the taking hold of God's willingness.—Phillips Brooks.

"My talent is to speak my mind," said a woman to John Wesley. To which Wesley answered, "I am sure, sister, that God wouldn't object if you buried THAT talent."

Men are born with two eyes, but with one tongue, that they may see twice as much as they say.—Cotton.

No sermon is ever quite a success which leaves men satisfied with themselves.

106

What Is a Minority?

What is a minority? The chosen heroes of this earth have been in the minority. There is not a social, political, or religious privilege that you enjoy today that was not bought for you by the blood and tears and patient sufferings of the minority. It is the minority that have vindicated humanity in every struggle. It is the minority that have come out as iconoclasts to beat down the Dagons their fathers have worshiped — the old abuses of society. It is the minority that have stood in the van of every moral conflict, and achieved all that is noble in the history of the world. You will find that each generation has been always busy in gathering up the scattered ashes of the martyred heroes of the past, to deposit them in the golden urn of a nation's history.

Minority! If a man stands up for the right, though the right be on the scaffold, while the wrong sits in the seat of government; if he stands for the right, though he eat with the right and truth a wretched crust; if he walk with obloquy and scorn in the by-lanes and streets, while falsehood and wrong ruffle it in silken attire—let him remember that wherever the right and truth are, there are always "troops of beautiful tall angels" gathering around him, and God Himself stands within the dim future and keeps watch over His own! If a man stands for the right and the truth, though every man's finger be pointed at him, though every woman's lip be curled at him in scorn, he stands in a majority, for God and good angels are with him, and greater are they that are for him than all they that be against him!

—John B. Gough

For who that leans on His right arm
Was ever yet forsaken?
What righteous cause can suffer harm
If He, its part has taken?
Though wild and loud
And dark the cloud,
Behind its folds
His hands upholds
The calm sky of tomorrow.
—Martin Luther

Suppose

Suppose it were your birthday
And all your friends would come
And gather round your fireplace
There in your happy home.

They come with smiles and gladness,
And bring their presents, too.
But when they start to share them,
There's not a one for you.

They give them to each other,
A grand and costly lot.
But for the quest of honor,
They somehow just forgot.

You say such things don't happen,
Nor should it ever be;
It seems too crude and cruel,
For folks like you and me.

But friend, have you considered
Just this is what men do?
Not, of course, to humans,
But of our Lord, 'tis true.

We celebrate His birthday
With all our pomp and style;
But give to one another
And grieve Him all the while.

'Tis Christ we claim to honor
At this glad Christmastime;
Don't spend on friends the dollars
And give Him just a dime.

To give to one another
Indeed is very nice;
But best of all to Jesus,
For Him let's sacrifice.

His cause too long has suffered
By thoughtless, selfish men.
Let's bring to Christ the firstfruits,
And give our best to Him.

—Fred D. Jarvis

Love of Bible

The Psalms were the favorite book of Hooker, of Horne, and of Luther, who regarded them as the choicest trees in the garden of the Lord. The epistles of Paul were seldom out of the hands of Chrysostom, the golden-mouthed orator of the early church. The martyr Ridley tells us incidentally, in his farewell to his friends, that he had learned nearly the whole of them in the course of his solitary walks at Oxford. Boyle could quote in the original Greek any passage of the New Testament that might happen to be named. On Daniel and Revelation Sir Isaac Newton spent some of the ripest hours of his life. Locke devoted twelve years to the study of the epistles and of the whole Bible, which he has carefully analyzed. It is a proof of the esteem in which Leighton held the whole book, that his French Bible, preserved in the library of Dunblane, is filled with manuscript extracts from ancient commentators; while in an English copy he was accustomed to use there is hardly a line unmarked by his pencil.—H. L. Hastings.

A Priest Accepted the Gift

One Sunday morning, a Roman Catholic priest appeared before a congregation of a thousand persons in an Illinois town and said, "My people, I resign my priesthood," though he had been there thirty years. At their earnest request he gave his reasons why he did so: "Last night I spent every hour praising God. All sleep had left me. After reading the New Testament I saw that salvation is in Jesus Christ, and is the gift of God's eternal love. Penance is not in it. Purgatory is not in it. Absolution is not in it. On my knees in my room I accepted the Gift, and I love the Giver, and I walked the room most of the night saying to myself: "I accept the Gift, and I love the Giver'." And thus for an hour and a half Father Chiniquy expounded to the people the grace of God. At the close of the sermon he asked how many of them would join with him in accepting the Gift and loving the Giver. Every man, woman, and child, except about forty, responded. And that is a Presbyterian church today.—Dr. A. C. Dixon

His First Bible

A little boy's first Bible
  Is the greatest thrill he's known.
There's a sweet, unique excite-
    ment
  In a Bible all his own!

And yet my heart is smitten
  As this touching sight I see—
Has his reverence for that Bible
  Depended much on me?

As I see him with his Bible,
  I bow my head and pray—
May he always love that Bible
  The way he does today.

Then I hear a voice within me
  Speak in solemn w o r d s and
    true;
How he cherishes that Bible
  Will depend a lot on you.

I love my Bible better
  Since I've seen the beaming joy
This wonderful possession
  Has afforded to my boy.

May I seek to give mine daily
  A devotion he can see,
For the love he bears his Bible
  Will depend a lot on me.

—*United Presbyterian*

Surely Good

The tobacco company sent packages of cigarettes to some high school boys with this explanation: "We are sending you a package of our cigarettes. We hope you will use them to your satisfaction and want more."

One of the boys used the cigarettes, and wrote the tobacco concern: "I received the package of cigarettes, and put them in a quart of water. With it I sprayed our bug-infested rose bushes. Every bug died! The cigarettes are surely a good poison. I want more to use next spring if any bugs survive!"

—Christian Advocate

No Time for God

No time for God? . . .
What fools we are, to clutter up
Our lives with common things,
And leave outside heart's gate
The Lord of Life, and Life itself—
Our God!

No time for God? . . .
As soon to say no time
To eat, or sleep, or love, or die.
Take time for God,
Or you shall dwarf your soul;
And when the angel, Death,
Comes knocking at your door,
A poor, misshapen thing you'll be
To step into eternity!

Some day you'll lay aside
This mortal self, and make your way
To worlds unknown;
And when you meet Him face to face
Will He—should He—
Have time for you?

—*Selected*

Bolt That Door!

Each sin has its door of entrance.
Keep--that--door--closed!
Bolt it tight!
Just outside, the wild beast crouches
In the night.
Pin the bolt with a prayer,
God will fix it there.

--John Oxenham

Talk not of wasted affection,
  affection never was wasted;
If it enrich not the heart of
  Another, its waters, returning
Back to their springs, like the
  rain, shall fill them full of
  refreshment.

--Longfellow

ADVISORY MEMBERS. An American Negro, who was so singularly lazy as to be quite a problem, got converted in a revival. His associates in the church were extremely anxious to know whether he would now bestir himself and go to work. The Negro attended a meeting and offered a prayer, in which occurred the petition, "Use me, Lord, use me—in an advisory capacity."

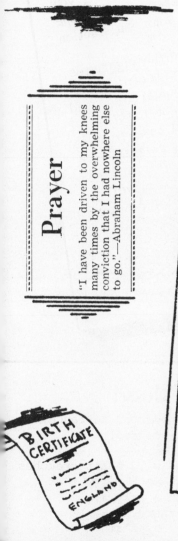

Prayer

"I have been driven to my knees many times by the overwhelming conviction that I had nowhere else to go."—Abraham Lincoln

Forget Success

FORGET about success. Three words and our advice to young men and women might end in this season of graduations, when their ambitions first begin to knock against realities.

Diplomas in hand, they seek to climb the pyramid of success from which they can win the admiring glances of others. Money and power too often afford the prestige which they seek. The world measures wrong as it measures success—and hence our contention: Forget about success.

Charles Schwab as president of the world's largest independent steel company was a financial success—but he died broke after living on borrowed money the last five years of his life. Richard Whitney went from the presidency of the New York Stock Exchange to Sing Sing. Many a tycoon in Wall Street has closed the doors to his office suite—and committed suicide.

Warren G. Harding rose to the presidency of the United States. That was in the day before corruption in high places was permissible. His administration is remembered as one of disgrace because political cronies, such as Albert Fall, went to prison.

Stalin and Mao were men of power and their slaves acclaimed them a success. But, remember Hitler and Mussolini had their day before God and decent men tired of their evil.

The dictionary says success is "a favorable or prosperous course or termination of anything attempted." But too often the world applauds those who attempted the unworthy and achieved. They had success.

Jesus knew the definition of success. He gave it two thousand years ago but the world refuses to understand. "Whosoever will be great among you, let him be your minister." The words are emphatic. But, knowing of man's ignorance he repeated: "And whosoever will be chief among you, let him be your servant."

The world may yet learn. Parades and monuments may yet honor those who cared not for success, but achieved it through humble service.

Success and reputation too often are confused. Reputation may just as easily be the very opposite.

Jesus had the one and only measurement of success in this world. Believing that and following Him, we have success during this life's span in the life to follow.

Forget about man-measured success. Follow the course charted two thousand years ago—the only course to true happiness and real success.

—*The Christian Index*

Birth Does Not Make the Christian

In the inquiry-room a person came in, and I said, "Are you a Christian?" "Why," says she, "of course I am." "Well," I said, "how long have you been one?" "Oh, sir, I was born one!" "Oh, indeed! Then I am very glad to take you by the hand; I congratulate you; you are the first woman I ever met who was born a Christian. You are more fortunate than others; they are born children of Adam." She hesitated a little, and then tried to make out that because she was born in England she was a Christian.—Moody.

I will decide as the colonists of Connecticut did; they said they would be guided by the laws of God until they had time to make better.—**Spurgeon**

A fellow told me one time, "Brother Jack, if you'll trim your message you'll go all the way to the top." I said, "I've fished some, and I know one thing: When fish are alive, they stay at the bottom; when they are dead, they come to the top. I'll stay alive."—Jack Hyles.

109

THE LAMBS AND THE OLD SHEEP

A pastor once tabulated 253 believers to determine what age group is most receptive to the Gospel. Results:

Under 20 years	138 were saved
Between 20 and 30	85 were saved
Between 30 and 40	22 were saved
Between 40 and 50	4 were saved
Between 50 and 60	3 were saved
Between 60 and 70	1 was saved

—Eternity

When Two Fell Out

Dr. M. D. Hoge, of Richmond, Va., told of two Christian men who fell out. One heard that the other was talking about him, and he went to him.

"Will you be kind enough to tell me my faults to my face, that I may profit by your Christian candour, and try to get rid of them?"

"Yes, sir," replied the other. "I will do it."

They went aside and the former said, "Before you commence telling what you think wrong in me, will you please bow down with me, and let us pray over it, that my eyes may be opened to see my faults as you will tell them? You lead in prayer."

It was done, and when the prayer was over, the man who had sought the interview said, "Now proceed with what you have to complain of in me."

But the other replied, "After praying over it, it looks so little that it is not worth talking about. The truth is I feel now that in going around talking against you, I have been serving the Devil, and I have need that you pray for me and forgive me the wrong I have done you."

—Selected

Here is the original epitaph of Benjamin Franklin:

The body of B. Franklin
Printer
Like the cover of an old book
Its contents torn out
And stript of its lettering and gilding
Lies here food for worms.
But the work shall not be wholly lost
For it will, as he believes, appear once more
In a new and more perfect edition
Corrected and amended
By the Author.

A Praying Farmer

An honest farmer was asked to dine with a gentleman. The farmer, according to his custom, gave thanks to God. Whereupon his host jeered him, "That is old-fashioned; it is not customary nowadays for well-educated people to pray at the table." The farmer stated that it was customary with him but not with some members of his household. "Oh, then," said the gentleman, "they are sensible and enlightened. Who are they?" "They are my pigs," answered the farmer.

There may be a wrong way to do the right thing, but never a right way to do a wrong thing.	*Christianity helps us to face the music, even when we don't like the tune.—Phillips Brooks*
Watch out for temptation—the more you see of it the better it looks!—Anon.	*Our children are the only earthly possessions we can take with us to glory.*

6-13-43

It Can Happen Again

A BOY gave his lunch to Jesus and 5,000 men, besides women and children, were fed.

A SLAVE GIRL spoke to her mistress about God—and her master, healed of his leprosy, became a devout believer.

ANDREW told Peter about Jesus and three years later Peter preached a sermon that won 3,000 souls for the Kingdom.

AN AGED MONK counseled Martin Luther to trust God's forgiveness of his sins—and Luther, finding peace with God, became the pioneer of Protestantism.

A SUNDAY SCHOOL TEACHER visited Dwight Moody in the shoeshop where he worked, and spoke to him about Christ, and Moody became a world-renowned evangelist leading thousands to Christ.

HUDSON TAYLOR SAID "YES" UNRESERVEDLY TO GOD—and more than 1,200 missionaries have gone forth to China under the banner of the China Inland Mission which he founded.

A LITTLE GROUP OF STUDENTS met by a haystack to pray for the lands where the Gospel was unknown—and the great movement of American foreign missions was launched.

IT CAN HAPPEN AGAIN! Will it happen to you? "Ye shall be my witnesses" (Acts 1:8).
—Selected.

Ten thousand times ten thousand
In sparkling raiment bright,
The armies of the ransomed saints.
Throng up the steeps of light:
'Tis finished, all is finished,
Their fight with death and sin:
Fling open wide the golden gates
And let the victors in!

Oh, then what raptured greetings
On Canaan's happy shore,
What knitting severed friendships
up
Where partings are no more!
Then eyes with joy shall sparkle,
That brimmed with tears of late;
Orphans no longer fatherless,
Nor widows desolate!
—Henry Alford

The Pessimist's Creed

What's the use of sunshine?
Only blinds your eyes.
What's the use of knowledge?
Only makes you wise.
What's the use of smiling?
Wrinkles up your face.
What's the use of flowers?
Clutters up the place.
What's the use of eating?
Nothing—only taste.
What's the use of hustling?
Haste is only waste.
What's the use of music?
Just a lot of noise.
What's the use of loving?
Only for the joys.
What's the use of singing?
Only makes you glad.
What's the use of goodness
When the whole world's bad?
What's the use of health?
You might as well be sick.
What's the use of doing
Anything but kick?

—Selected

"I want to be willing to make enemies because of my position but not because of my disposition." —Jack Hyles

---

Learn to say "no"! It will be of more use to you than to be able to read Latin.—C. H. Spurgeon.

Die when I may, I want it said of me by those who knew me best, that I always plucked a thistle and planted a flower where I thought a flower would grow.
—Abraham Lincoln

Dr. J. Wilbur Chapman, in his *Revival Sermons,* under the heading "Where Is the Difference?" tells us this pathetic story:

"A friend of mine was one day preaching a sermon to a great congregation, when a well-known woman turned to her husband, one of the most distinguished men in the community, and said, as the minister pleaded with them to lift their hands and accept Jesus Christ,

"'My dear, could you not lift your hand now?' And he made no response.

"She whispered to him again, Would it not be a good thing to lift your hand now?' Still no response. As they walked out of the church, she said to him, with a note of pathos in her voice, 'I had hoped that this would be the night of your decision.' But he never answered.

"When they came into their home and were seated together, he said, 'My dear, you asked me to lift my hand, and I made no response. I do not mean to be rude to you, but you are a Christian, and I am not. I do not want to be unkind, but tell me wherein our lives differ. You play cards, and I also play cards. You go to the dance, and I go to the dance. You visit the theatre, and I also visit the theatre. For the life of me I can see no difference in our living. Now, you will not misunderstand me, and God knows I would not be cruel to you, but where is the difference in our living?'"

It pays us Christians to live like Christians, doesn't it?

"False Doctoring"

A Sunday school teacher asked her class, "What is false doctrine?" One of her pupils, the son of a physician, had this answer: "False doctorin' is when a doctor gives sick people the wrong stuff." How true! False doctrine is "false doctoring" indeed; false prophets give the wrong "stuff" to sin-sick people.

THE CHRISTMAS BABY

"Tha'rt welcome, little bonny brid,
But shouldn't ha' come just when tha' did:
Teimes are bad."

—*English Ballad.*

HOOT! ye little rascal! ye come in on me this way,
Coaxin' yerself among us this blusterin' winter's day
Knowin' that we already have three of ye, an' seven,
An' tryin' to make yerself out a Christmas present o' Heaven?

Ten of ye have we now, Sir for this world to abuse;
An' Bobbie he has no waistcoat, an' Nellie she has no shoes,
An' Sammie he has no shirt, Sir (I tell it to his shame),
An' the one that was just before ye we ain't had time to name!

An' all o' the banks are smashin', an' on us poor folk fall;
An' Boss he whittles the wages when work's to be had at all;
An' Tom he has cut his foot bad, an' lies in a woful plight,
An' all of us wonders at mornin' as what we shall eat at night;

An' but for your father an' Sandy a findin' somewhat to do,
An' but for the preacher's good-wife, who often helps us through,
An' but for your poor dear mother a-doin' twice her part,
Ye'd 'a' seen us all in Heaven afore ye was ready to start!

An' now ye have come, ye rascal! so healthly an' fat an' sound.
A-weighin', I'll wager a dollar, the full of a dozen pound!
With your mother's eyes a flashin', yer father's flesh an' build,
An' a good big mouth an' stomach all ready for to be filled!

No, no! don't cry, my baby! hush up, my pretty one!
Don't get my chaff in yer eye, boy—I only was just in fun.
Ye'll like us when ye know us, although we're cur'us folks;
But we don't get much victual, an' half our livin' is jokes!

Why, boy, did ye take me in earnest? come, sit upon my knee;
I'll tell ye a secret, youngster, I'll name ye after me.
Ye shall have all yer brothers an' sisters with ye to play,
An' ye shall have yer carriage, an' ride out every day!

Why, boy, do ye think ye'll suffer? I'm gettin' a trifle old,
But it'll be many years yet before I lose my hold;
An' if I should fall on the road, boy, still, them's yer brothers, the
An' not a rogue of 'em ever would see ye harmed a hair!

Say! when ye come from Heaven, my little namesake dear
Did ye see, 'mongst the little girls there, a face like this one here
That was yer little sister—she died a year ago,
An' all of us cried like babies when they laid her under the snow

Hang it! if all the rich men I ever see or knew
Came here with all their traps, boy, an' offered 'em for you,
I'd show 'em to the door, Sir, so quick they'd think it odd,
Before I'd sell to another my Christmas gift from God!

By Will Carleton

Saints in Wrong Places

A Discouraged Worker. Elijah under the juniper tree. 1 Kings 19:4.

A Backsliding Believer. Abraham in Egypt. Gen. 12:10.

A Disobedient Servant. Jonah in the sea-monster. Jonah 2.

A Lazy Saint. David on the house-top. 2 Sam. 11:2.

A Silenced Witness. Lot in Sodom. Gen. 14:12.

A Miserable Disciple. Peter before the fire. Luke 22:55.

A young man who had just received his degree from college rushed out and said, "Here I am, world; I have my A.B."

The world replied: "Sit down, son, and I'll teach you the rest of the alphabet."

Do not attempt to go sneaking to Heaven along some back lane; come into the King's highway; take up your cross and follow Him. I would persuade you to an open confession.—Spurgeon

---

A small boy observed his mother put a penny on the offering plate at the morning service. On the way home from church, she freely criticized the poor sermon they had heard. "But, Mother," said the boy, "what could you expect for a penny?"

One Minute Readings

Jesus Sits by the Treasury

The late Dr. W. B. Riley records how one memorable Sunday Dr. John A. Broadus, when his ushers were about to take the offering, left his pulpit and walked down to where one usher was beginning his collection and went along with him and looked at every penny, nickel, dime, quarter and dollar that went into the basket. You may well imagine that some of the people were angry. Some were confused. Others were shamefaced. Others were filled with amazement. All were evidently surprised.

When the collection was over, Dr. Broadus went back to his pulpit to speak from his morning's text. He said to his congregation: "My people, if you take it to heart that I have seen your offerings this day and know just what sacrifices you have made and what sacrifices you have not made, remember that the Son of God, your Saviour, goes about the aisles with every usher and sees with His sleepless eye every cent put into the collection by His people."

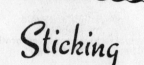

Sticking

"There was a little postage stamp
No bigger than your thumb,
But still it stuck right on the job
Until its work was done.
They licked it and they pounded it
'Til it would make you sick.
But the more it took a lickin'
Why the tighter it would stick.

So friend, let's be like the postage stamp
In playing life's rough game,
And just keep on a-sticking
Though we hide our heads in shame,
For the stamp stuck to the letter
'Til it saw it safely through.
There's no one could do better,
Let's keep sticking and be true."

—The Samaritan.

I Reared a Criminal

In the August 1960, issue of the *Ladies' Home Journal* is an article entitled, "I Reared a Criminal." It is the true story of a heartbroken mother.

We quote:

We loved him, but—his father was too busy to be with him when he was young.

I couldn't bring myself to punish him for misbehaviour.

We sided against his teachers when they complained about his work (and conduct) in school.

As he grew up he would hardly discuss the time of day with us.

He was expelled from school.

We gave him money so he wouldn't steal again.

I wept when the police called and I had to turn my boy over to them. . . . As I watched them search him my life seemed to end.

—Allegheny Conference Messenger

It is the right and the privilege of the genuine child of God to possess the assurance of Christ's perfect love and perpetual protection. Old Latimer used to say that when he had this steadfast trust in his Master he could face a lion; when he lost it, he was ready to run into a mouse hole. Why should a redeemed follower of Christ ever worry himself sick with wretched doubts and insulting fears? If I have put my everlasting all in Christ's hands, He is responsible for the trust—as long as I leave it with Him. If I check my trunk to Philadelphia, it belongs to the baggage master until I get there. Surely I ought to have as strong a faith that my immortal blood-bought soul is forever safe in the keeping of the omnipotent Son of God. His Spirit beareth witness with my spirit; and I am persuaded that neither death nor life, principalities nor powers, things present nor things to come, shall be able to separate me from the love of God which is in Christ Jesus our Lord!

—Dr. Theodore L. Cuyler.

We Love Him Since He Loved Us

After Mother had finished a task, she said to her little girl, "You may come now, dear." The girl said, "I am so glad, for I wanted to love you so much." "But I thought you were happy with your dolly," said the mother. "Yes, Mother, I was, but I soon get tired of loving her, for she cannot love me back."

There is profound wisdom in the answer of the wee philosopher. God could have stopped His creative work with in inanimate creation; but no: He wanted to be loved back! And so He made man and then He revealed to man His sacrificial love, on the cross; and sinful men who see that love trust God and love Him back. So God will have in Heaven, not mere "dolls," machines; but He will have redeemed men who will love and serve Him for all He has done for them!

"We love him, because he first loved us" (I John 4:19).

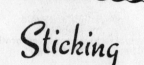

An Old Question

An old question: Can I be a Christian without joining the church or attending worship?

Answer: Yes, it is possible. It is something like being:

A student who will not go to school;
A soldier who will not join the army;
A citizen who does not pay taxes or vote;
A salesman with no customers;
An explorer with no base camp;
A seaman in a ship without a crew;
A businessman on a deserted island;
An author without readers;
A football player without a team;
A politician who is a hermit;
A scientist who does not share his findings;
A bee without a hive.

—Flaming Torch

The Last Leaf

I saw him once before,
As he passed by the door,
And again
The pavement stones resound,
As he totters o'er the ground
With his cane.

They say that in his prime,
E're the pruning-knife of Time
Cut him down,
Not a better man was found
By the Crier on his round
Through the town.

But now he walks the streets
And he looks at all he meets
So forlorn;
And he shakes his feeble head,
That it seems as if he said,
"They are gone."

The mossy marbles rest
On the lips that he has prest
In their bloom,
And the names he loved to hear
Have been carved for many a year
On the tomb.

And if I would live to be
The last leaf upon the tree
In the spring,
Let them smile, as I do now,
At the old forsaken bough
Where I cling.

—Oliver Wendell Holmes

A Slumbering Church

A father took his little child out into the field one Sunday, and he lay down under a beautiful shady tree, it being a hot day. The little child ran about gathering wild flowers and little blades of grass, and coming to his father and saying: "Pretty! pretty!" At last the father fell asleep, and while he was sleeping the child wandered away. When he awoke, his first thought was "Where is my child?" He looked all around, but he could not see him. He shouted at the top of his voice, and all he heard was the echo of his own voice. Running to a little hill he looked around and shouted again, but all he heard was the echo of his own voice. No response! Then going to a precipice at some distance, looked down, and there upon the rocks and briers, he saw the mangled form of his loved child. He rushed to the spot, and took up the lifeless corpse, and hugged it to his bosom, and accused himself of being the murderer of his own child. WHILE HE WAS SLEEPING HIS CHILD HAD WANDERED OVER THE PRECIPICE. I thought as I heard that, what a picture of the church of God! How many fathers and mothers, how many Christian men are sleeping now while their children wander over the terrible precipice a thousand times worse than that precipice, right into the bottomless pit of hell. Father, where is your boy tonight?—Moody.

Preparing for Death

A mother explained to her little daughter, who could not comprehend her father's death, that God had sent for him, and that by-and-by He would send for them all—how soon they could not tell. "Well, then, mother," said the child, "if God is going to send for us soon, and we don't know just when, hadn't we better begin to pack up and get ready to go?"—Biblical Museum.

How To Be Great

Do not try to do a great thing; you may waste all your life waiting for the opportunity which may never come. But since little things are always claiming your attention, do them as they come, from a great motive, for the glory of God, to win His smile of approval, and do good to men. It is harder to plod in obscurity, acting thus, than to stand on the high places of the field, within the view of all, and do deeds of valor at which rival armies stand still to gaze. But no such act goes without the swift recognition and the ultimate recompense of Christ.

To fulfill faithfully the duties of your station; to use to the uttermost the gifts of your ministry; to bear the chafing unthankful and evil; to be content to be martyrs who bore the pillory and stake; to find the one noble trait in people who try to molest you; to put the kindest construction on unkind acts and words; to love with the love of God even the unthankful and evil; to be content to be a fountain in the midst of a wild valley of stones, nourishing a few lichens and wild flowers, or now and again a thirsty sheep; and to do this always, and not for the praise of man, but for the sake of God—this makes a great life.—F. B. Meyer.

I must have God!
  I couldn't walk this thorny way
With stone beneath and cloud above,
  Or meet the struggle of each day
Without His love.

I must have God!
  I couldn't stand the hours at night
Or troubled day with all its length,
  Or overlook what others say
Without His strength.

I must have God!
  I couldn't share the grief of those
Who need my help along life's way,
  Or comfort one in need of peace
Unless I pray.

—Author Unknown

Be good, get good, and do good. Do all the good you can; to all the people you can; in all the ways you can; as often as you can; and as long as you can.—Spurgeon.

★ How?

"How can a God of love send a man to Hell?" asked a fellow traveller of John Seddon in a train.

"I will ask you another question by way of reply," said he. "How can a God of righteousness take a sinner to Heaven?"

—Selected

In New York City stands a bronze statue of Nathan Hale. His arms and feet are tied, his shirt collar open, his handsome face looks upward. Hale died saying, "I regret that I have but one life to give for my country." God must have no less devotion.

"A Success" and He Doesn't Drink

Van Cliburn, the 23-year old Texan, winner of Moscow's International Tschaikowsky Piano Competition is, according to Time magazine, deeply religious and a *conscientious teetotaler*. He is a twice-over tither; i.e., he gives 20% of his net earnings to the Baptist church. During Evangelist Billy Graham's Manhattan crusade last year, Van sang in the Madison Square Garden choir alongside Ethel Waters. He once skipped a $500 concert date so that he could play for a church banquet in Paramus, N. J. Buffalo Philharmonic Conductor Josef Krips recalls the time that Van came into his dressing room before a performance and said, "Maestro, let us pray." Krips, a Roman Catholic dropped to his knees with the pianist. Said Van: "God give us his grace and power to make good music together."

All of which, young people, would indicate that it is not necessary to follow the crowd who say "everybody's doing it," to be a success!—National Voice.

Were You There, Charlie?

Two men — Joe and Charlie — were arguing about Genesis 1:1. Joe said he believed the record of creation just as it was written. Charlie was an infidel, and went to great length in giving his own theory of how the world began and then developed from a primordial cell through reptiles, monkeys, and up to man.

When he was all through, Joe looked at him and said, *"Were you there, Charlie?"* It was a good question.

"Of course I was not there," said Charlie. Joe had the answer. He said, "Well, God was there. He was the only One there and I'll take the word of the 'eye witness' rather than the guesses of those who go only by 'they say.'"

"Were you there, Charlie?" What presumption for the creature to question the word of the Creator. —M. R. DeHaan.

Not Coming Home

An' raise a child er two
We'll build a home together—
Boy, that's what I'm looking to."
Yup, seems like yesterday
That lad with boyish grin
Lay all bloody, stilled forever—
He's not coming home again.
Over there within a valley
There're crosses, row on row,
An' little flags a flutterin'
Now thu drums beat sad an' slow.
All the things that boy wanted
Are yours an' mine today,
An' he gave them up forever—
Don't ferget that lad today.

—R. W. Cooper

I kin see him now—
A lad with a boyish grin,
Browned and lightly-bearded,
With "peach-fuzz" on his chin.
An' his fox-hole conversation
Belied the weight of war,
As his eyes began to twinkle,
In spite of din and roar.
"When this here war is over,
Then I'm a-goin' home,
An' I'm never gonna wander
Back across this briny foam.
Gonna settle in the rocker—
Mebbe rock a time er two,
An' when I've rested somewhat,
I'll find a job tuh do.
An' I'll buy un automobile
An' I ain't a-goin' ta walk
Any farther than I hafta—
Mebbe now an' then uh block,
Then mebbe I'll marry Judy

Dr. Walter Wilson and a missionary friend were praying for a car which was greatly needed for the missionary's work in Africa. The missionary prayed, "O God, You know how badly I need a car for my work. Do, Lord, send me a car. Any kind of an old, ramshackle car will do!" Dr. Wilson interrupted. "Stop praying that way, brother! God is not in the junk business!"— W. B. Knight

Do Not Delay

On Sunday night, October 8, 1871, D. L. Moody preached to a large crowd in Chicago on the text, "What shall I do then with Jesus which is called the Christ?" At the conclusion of the message he told the people to go home and think for a week. Then they were to return and decide what to do with Christ.

Sankey began to sing:

Today the Saviour calls; for refuge fly;
The storm of justice falls, and death is nigh.

The hymn was never finished. The rush and roar of fire engines broke in. Before sunrise Chicago lay in ashes. Moody resolved never again to tell people to decide later what to do with Christ.

Monkey Business

In North Africa the natives have a very easy way to capture monkeys. A gourd, with a hole just sufficiently large so that a monkey can thrust his hand into it, is filled with nuts and fastened firmly to a branch of a tree at sunset. During the night a monkey will discover the scent of food, and its source, and will put his hand into the gourd and grasp a handful of nuts. But the hole is too small for the monkey to withdraw his clenched fist, and he has not sense enough to let go of his bounty so that he may escape. Thus he pulls and pulls without success, and when morning comes he is quickly and easily taken.

Multitudes of human beings—in no way related to the monkey, by the way—have little more sense than he. "For what shall it profit a man, if he shall gain the whole world, and lose his own soul?" the Saviour asked (Mark 8:36).

—The Pilgrim

Take care that the face which looks out from your mirror in the morning is a pleasant face. You may not see it again all day, but others will.—Selected.

Search me, O God, and know my heart today;
Try me, O Saviour, know my thoughts, I pray:
See if there be some wicked way in me:
Cleanse me from ev'ry sin, and set me free.
—E. Orr.

A SEARCHING TEST

A man testified in one of Mr. Moody's meetings: "I have been for five years on the Mount of Transfiguration."

"How many souls did you lead to Christ last year?" was the sharp question that came from Mr. Moody in an instant.

"Well, I don't know," was the astonished reply.

"Have you led any?" persisted Mr. Moody.

"I don't know that I have," answered the man.

"Well," said Mr. Moody, "we don't want that kind of mountaintop experience. When a man gets so high that he can't reach down to save poor sinners, there is something wrong." How different from Paul (I Corinthians 9:18-22).

Why She Rejoiced

Though we may have little of this world's goods we have much for which to praise God. A woman was dying in the poorhouse. The doctor bent over her and heard her whisper, "Praise the Lord." "Why, auntie," he said, "how can you praise God when you are dying in a poorhouse?" "Oh, doctor," she replied, "it's wonderful to go from the poorhouse to a mansion in the skies!"—*The Christian*.

The *stops* of a good man are ordered by the Lord as well as his *steps*.—George Mueller

How to Destroy an Enemy

A Quaker had a quarrelsome, disagreeable neighbor whose cow often got into the Quaker's well-cultivated garden. One morning the Quaker drove the cow to his neighbor's home. Said he, "Neighbor, I have driven thy cow home once more. If I find her in my garden again—." Before the Quaker could finish the sentence, the neighbor said angrily, "Suppose you do? What will you do?" "Why," said the Quaker softly, "I'll drive her home to you again!" The cow didn't give the Quaker any more trouble.— W. B. Knight

The Boy Who Was Not "With" Her

In an afternoon service in a New England city, a woman rose in the crowded church and passed out of the building. The verse, "For how shall I go up to my father, and the lad be not with me?" had just been quoted, and it went like an arrow into her soul, for she had one boy. He was at high school, and she realized that she had never invited him to be a Christian. She went to his school, waited for him to come out, and said to him, "My son, I've just listened to a text of Scripture that has stirred me through and through. It was this: 'How shall I go up to my father, and the lad be not with me?' I am a Christian, and I have never asked you to be one. I could not wait until you reached home." And he did come, for what boy would not come under such circumstances?

—J. Wilbur Chapman

The Death of John Huss

When John Huss, the Bohemian martyr, was brought out to be burnt, they put on his head a triple crown of paper, with painted devils on it. On seeing it, he said, "My Lord, Jesus Christ, for my sake, wore a crown of thorns; why should not I then, for His sake, wear this light crown, be it ever so ignominious? Truly I will do it, and that willingly." When it was set upon his head, the bishops said, "Now, we commend thy soul to the Devil." "But I," said Huss, lifting his eyes to Heaven, "do commit my spirit into Thy hands, O Lord Jesus Christ; to Thee I commend my spirit, which Thou hast redeemed." When the fagots were piled to Huss' neck, the Duke of Bavaria was officious enough to desire him to adjure. "No," said Huss, "I never preached any doctrine of an evil tendency; and what I taught with my lips I now seal with my blood."

Procrastination has never landed one soul in Heaven, but it has doomed many to an eternal Hell.—Anon.

117

FEDERAL AID

"Federal aid is giving yourself a transfusion by drawing b l o o d from your right arm, and returning it to your left—and spilling some on the way across." (Modern Medicine).

When a man has not a good reason for doing a thing, he has one good reason for letting it alone.
—Sir Walter Scott

LORD, LAY SOME SOUL

Lord, lay some soul upon my heart,
And love that soul through me,
And may I ever do my part
To win that soul to Thee.

When the lights in the auditorium went out suddenly, a Chinese man in the audience said, "Now, if all of us will raise our hands, maybe the lights will go back on."

They all raised their hands, and the lights went back on. Then he explained how it happened, saying, "It all goes to prove the old Chinese proverb, 'Many hands make light work.'"

Delinquency

Once there was a little boy. When he was three weeks old his parents turned him over to a baby-sitter. When he was two, they dressed him up like a cowboy and gave him a gun. When he was three everybody said, "How cute," as he went about lisping a beer commercial jingle. When he was six, his father occasionally dropped him off at Sunday school on his way to the golf course. When he was eight they bought him a BB gun and taught him to shoot sparrows. **He learned to shoot windshields by himself.** When he was ten he spent his after-school time squatting at a drugstore newsstand reading comic books. His mother wasn't home and his father was busy. When he was thirteen, he told his parents other boys stayed out as late as they wanted to—so they said he could too. It was easier that way. When he was fourteen they gave him a deadly two-ton machine, wrangled a license for him to drive it, and told him to be careful. When he was fifteen, the police called his home one night and said, "We have your boy. He's in trouble." "In trouble?" screamed the father. "It can't be **my** boy!" But it was!

MORAL: As the twig is bent, **it is apt to snap back in your face!**

—Henry G. Bosch

Dear Teacher

Please find attached to this note one five-year-old boy, much cleaner and quieter than usual and with new haircut and dungarees. With him go the prayers of his mother and father.

He's good at creating airplanes and chaos, very adept at tying knots and attracting stray dogs. He especially likes peanut butter, horses, TV westerns, empty boxes and his shirttail out.

He is allergic to baths, bedtime, taking out trash and coming the first time he's called.

He needs to be taught and spanked, loved and spanked, and reminded to blow his nose and come straight home from school.

After having him in your class and on your nerves, you may not be the same, but I believe you'll be glad to know him because, while he strews books, toys and clothes, he has a special way of scattering happiness!

Written, I'm afraid, with prejudice.

His mother.
—Mildred B. Duncan
in Guideposts

Tears Shed for a City

It is said that after the death of Robert Murray McCheyne, the great Scottish preacher, a young man came into the church previously pastored by this great man of God. He remarked to the caretaker that he would like to preach like McCheyne preached. The caretaker invited him to the study of McCheyne, and after seating him in the great chair that stood before the desk, he said, "Young man, put your elbows on the desk." He complied. "Now, put your face in your hands, and weep over the Word of God as McCheyne wept, and you might preach as he preached."

Then up to the high pulpit he took the young man. As he stood in the place where McCheyne preached with such inflamed passion, he said, "Put your face in your hands, young man, and weep over this congregation as I have seen McCheyne weep, and perhaps you will preach as he preached."

↓

"This country didn't stop producing men like Lincoln; we just stopped ELECTING men like him."

Whatever I have tried to do in life, I have tried with all my heart to do well; whatever I have devoted myself to, I have devoted myself to completely; in great aims and in small, I have always been thoroughly in earnest.—Dickens.

When? Soon. (An Easy Answer)

A business consultant of Louisville, Kentucky, has learned that brevity pays off. He was negotiating a sizable deal with a New York firm, but his repeated inquiries went unanswered.

In desperation, he sent off this note: "Dear Sirs: When?"

In the next mail came this reply: "Dear Sir: Soon."

But "soon" is not soon enough when eternal verities are under consideration. It must be "today," or "now." We are warned against even a day's delay.

"Boast not thyself of to morrow; for thou knowest not what a day may bring forth" (Prov. 27:1). "To day if ye will hear his voice, harden not your hearts" (Heb. 3:15).

The wise man said: "Remember now thy Creator in the days of thy youth, while the evil days come not, nor the years draw nigh, when thou shalt say, I have no pleasure in them" (Eccl. 12:1).

The Apostle Paul said: "Behold, now is the accepted time; behold, now is the day of salvation" (II Cor. 6:2).—Tom Olson in NOW.

What Is Evangelism?

It is the sob of God.

It is the anguished cry of Jesus as He weeps over a doomed city.

It is the cry of Paul, "I could wish that myself were accursed from Christ for my brethren, my kinsmen according to the flesh."

Evangelism is the heart-wringing plea of Moses, "Oh, this people have sinned . . . yet now, if Thou wilt forgive their sin . . . ; If not blot me, I pray Thee, out of the book which Thou has written."

It is the cry of John Knox, "Give me Scotland or I die."

It is the declaration of John Wesley, "The world is my parish."

It is the prayer of Billy Sunday, "Make me a giant for God."

It is the sob of a parent in the night, weeping over a prodigal child.

It is the secret of a great church.

It is the secret of a great preacher and of a great Christian. —William T. Hall

Controversy May Be a Duty!

Controversy in religion is a hateful thing. It is hard enough to fight the devil, the world, and the flesh, without private differences in our own camp. But there is one thing which is even worse than controversy, and that is false doctrine tolerated, allowed and permitted without protest or molestation.

It was controversy that won the battle of the Protestant Reformation. If the views that some men hold were correct, it is plain we never ought to have had any Reformation at all! For the sake of peace, we ought to have gone on worshipping the Virgin, and bowing down to images and relics to this very day!

Away with such trifling. There are times when controversy is not only a duty but a benefit. Give me the mighty thunderstorm rather than the pestilential malaria. The one walks in darkness and poisons us in silence, and we are never safe. The other frightens and alarms for a little season. But it is soon over and it clears the air. It is a plain scriptural duty to "contend earnestly for the faith once delivered to the saints" (Jude 3).

—Bishop J. C. Ryle.

How to Save

The story is told of a man who contributed the money to build a church. Later on he lost all his property. "If you had the money you put into that church," some one said to him, "you could start again." But the good man wisely replied: "That is the only money I have saved. If I had not given it to the Lord it would have gone with the rest. Now it will always be mine." —Moody Monthly.

Time

I have only just a minute, only sixty seconds in it, forced upon me —can't refuse it, didn't seek it, didn't choose it, but it's up to me to use it. I must suffer if I lose it, give account if I abuse it. Just a tiny little minute—but eternity is in it!—Copied.

Father, looking over his son's report card: "One thing is in your favor. With these grades you couldn't possibly be cheating."

Character Not for Sale

A local committee of a certain community called on an old Scot, a leading merchant, and threatened to boycott his store if he did not withdraw his support from a certain moral issue. His reply came back, "I want you to know, gentlemen, that my goods are on sale but not my character."

When a dove begins to associate with crows, its feathers remain white but its heart grows black.

—German Proverb

LITTLE PIECES OF MINDS

The religions of the world say "do and live." The religion of the Bible says, "live and do."—Dr. Bob Jones, Sr.

I never saw a useful Christian who was not a student of the Bible.
—Dwight L. Moody

I believe the promises of God enough to venture an eternity on them.
—G. Campbell Morgan

If you know these two things—yourself a sinner and Christ a Saviour—you are scholar enough to go to Heaven.—Spurgeon.

If you cannot do great things, you can at least do small things in a great way!
—Author unknown.

I had rather be in the heart of Africa in the will of God than on the throne of England out of the will of God.—David Livingstone.

A pastor once said, "Do away with the Sunday schools for 15 years and the church will be cut half in its membership."—A. S. London

God will not look you over for medals, degrees or diplomas, but for scars.

The Christian who is careless in Bible reading is careless in Christian living.

—Max Reich

If the blind put their hand in God's, they find their way more surely than those who see but have not faith or purpose.
—Helen Keller.

Sincere repentance is continual. Believers repent until their dying day.—Spurgeon.

"A wise old owl sat in an oak;
The more he saw the less he spoke;
The less he spoke the more he heard;
Let's try to imitate that bird."

God pity those who cannot say
"Not mine, but Thine"; who only pray,
"Let this cup PASS," and cannot see
The purpose in Gethsemane.
—Ella W. Wilcox

Repeal is costly to every American. The U.S. is producing alcoholics at the rate of more than 1200 a day—over 50 an hour.
—Dr. Andrew C. Ivy.

If you have so much business to attend to that you have no time to pray, depend on it that you have more business on hand than God ever intended you should have.—D. L. Moody.

Clean your fingers before you point at my spots.—Benjamin Franklin

It is no disgrace to fail. It is a disgrace to do less than your best to keep from failing.
Dr. Bob Jones, Sr.

It is a great deal easier to do that which God gives us to do, no matter how hard it is, than to face the responsibilities of not doing it.
—Dr. J. R. Miller.

The pessimist says, "If I don't try, I can't fail." The optimist says, "If I don't try, I can't win."

An old lady said she just had two teeth and she thanked God that they met.

When obstacles and trials seem
Like prison walls to me,
I do the little I can do
And leave the rest to Thee.
—Frederick W. Faber

"'It is finished'"—PROVIS-ION enough;
'It is written' — PROOF enough!"

A Christian should not be a question mark for God, but an exclamation point!
—Vance Havner

Take care of your life and the Lord will take care of your death.
—George Whitefield.

Hating Sin

There is only one thing to do with sin—hate it. Hate it in your own life. Hate it in the lives of others. The following selected illustration should encourage us:

"When the Emperor of Constantinople arrested Chrysostom, and thought of trying to make him recant, the great preacher slowly shook his head. The Emperor said to his attendants, Put him in prison.' 'No,' said one of them 'he will be glad to go, for he delights in the presence of his God in quiet.' 'Well, then let us execute him,' said the emperor. 'He will be glad to die,' said the attendant, 'for he wants to go to Heaven—I heard him say so the other day. There is only one thing that can give Chrysostom pain, and that is, to make him sin; he said he was afraid of nothing but sin. If you can make him sin, you will make him unhappy.'" Oh, that God would make us like Chrysostom! —Selected.

Where is HAPPINESS?

NOT IN MONEY... Jay Gould, the American millionaire, had an enormous fortune. When dying, he said, "I suppose I am the most miserable man on earth."

NOT IN PLEASURE . . . Lord Byron lived a life of pleasure and ease. He wrote: "The worm, the canker and grief are mine alone."

NOT IN MILITARY GLORY ... Alexander the Great conquered the known world in his day. Then he wept, "There are no more worlds to conquer."

NOT IN POLITICAL POWER . . . William Tweed became the brilliant boss of Tammany Hall and ruled New York City. He said: "My life has been a failure in everything."

NOT IN UNBELIEF . . . Voltaire was an infidel of the most pronounced type. He wrote: "I wish I had never been born."

NOT IN POSITION AND FAME . . . Lord Beaconsfield enjoyed more than his share of both. He wrote: "Youth is a mistake; manhood a struggle; old age a regret."

WHERE IS HAPPINESS?

The answer is simple: In Christ alone. HE said: "Your heart shall rejoice, and your joy no man taketh from you."

"Whoso trusteth in the Lord, happy is he." (Prov. 16:2)

Think You're Busy Today?

Grandmother on a winter's day, milked the cows, slopped the hogs, saddled the mule and got the children off to school (no bus), did a washing, mopped the floor, cooked a pan of home grown fruit, pressed Dad's Sunday suit, swept the parlor, made the beds, baked a dozen loaves of bread, cleaned the lamps and put in oil, stewed some apples she thought might spoil, churned the butter, baked a cake, then exclaimed, "For Goodness Sakes the calves have gotten out of the pen" and went and chased them in again. The fence fixed, she gathered the eggs, closed the stable, went back to the house, set the table, cooked supper, which was delicious and afterwards washed up all the dishes, fed the cat, mended a basket of socks, sprinkled the clothes, and then opened the organ and began to play, "When You Come to the End of a Perfect Day."

True Riches

A tax assessor came one day to a poor minister of the Gospel to determine the amount of taxes he would have to pay. "What do you possess?" he questioned.

"Oh, I am very wealthy," replied the minister.

"List your possessions, please," the assessor instructed.

The man of God replied: "First, I have everlasting life—John 3:16. Second, I have a mansion in Heaven—John 14:2. Thirdly, I have peace that passeth understanding —Philippians 4:7. Fourth, I have joy unspeakable—I Peter 1:8. Fifth, I have divine love that never faileth—I Corinthians 13:8. Sixth, I have a faithful, pious wife —Proverbs 31:10. Seventh, I have healthy, happy, obedient children —Exodus 20:12. Eighth, I have true, loyal friends—Proverbs 18: 24. Ninth, I have songs in the night—Psalm 42:8. Tenth, I have a crown of life awaiting—James 1:12."

The tax collector closed his book and said, "Truly, you are a very rich man, but your property is not subject to taxation!"—H. G. B.

How to Read Your Bible More Effectively

Read your Bible—not as a newspaper, but as a letter from home.

If a cluster of heavenly fruit hangs within reach, gather it.

If a promise lies upon the page as a blank cheque, cash it.

If a prayer is recorded, appropriate it and launch it as a feathered arrow from the bow of your desire.

If a truth is revealed in all its intrinsic splendor, entreat that its brilliance may ever irradiate the hemisphere of your life like a star.

Entwine the climbing creepers of holy desire round the lattice work of Scripture. So shall you come to say with the Psalmist, "O how love I thy law! it is my meditation all the day" (Ps. 119: 97).

—F. B. Meyer.

Have You Heard...

SPEAK TELLINGLY

"Were half the breath oft vainly spent,
To heaven in supplication sent;
Our cheerful song would oftener be,
'Hear what the Lord has done for me!'"
—William Cowper

Attitude Important

Perhaps you heard about the Yankee shoe salesman who went to Africa and wired his manufacturer, "I want to come home. Nobody wears shoes in this part of Africa." So they brought him home and sent another salesman who shipped back order after order. He wrote the home office, "Everybody here needs shoes!"

Christians should always look for the "best side." And there always is one.

If we work upon marble,
It will perish;
If we work upon brass,
Time will efface it;
If we rear temples,
They will crumble into dust;
But, if we work upon immortal souls,
If we imbue them with principles,
With the just fear of God
And the love of fellow man,
We engrave on those tablets
Something which will brighten all eternity.

—Daniel Webster

Original inscription on tombstone:

Remember, friend, when passing by,
As you are now, so once was I;
As I am now, soon you will be,
Prepare for death and follow me.

Added comment to inscription:

To follow you I'm not content
Until I know which way you went.

To be seventy years young is sometimes far more cheerful and hopeful than to be forty years old.
—O. W. Holmes

After a great snowstorm, a little fellow began to shovel a path through a large snowbank before his grandmother's door. He had nothing but a small shovel with which to work. "How do you expect to get through that big drift?" asked a man passing by. "By keeping at it," said the boy cheerfully. What a lesson!—Selected.

"I Can Do What I'm Told"

A little boy entered a shop, in the window of which was a card, "Boy Wanted." Thinking he was too weak for the work, the gentleman said, "Well, my lad, what can you do?" The boy replied, "I can do what I'm told, sir." This so pleased the shopkeeper that he said, "You'll do, my boy."

Have you ever led a soul to Christ?

You can make more friends in two months by becoming interested in more people than you can in two years by trying to get other people interested in you.
—Dale Carnegie.

A liberal minister, with great show of learning, exerted himself in explaining away certain passages of the Bible, saying with finality that God didn't mean what the passages obviously said. An aged saint asked him at the close of his lecture, "If God didn't mean what He said, why didn't He say what He meant?" The unbeliever had no answer to that— W. B. Knight

---

Doing nothing is about the most tiresome work in the world because you cannot stop and rest.

Beautiful Feet...

Hardly a generation has passed since the founder of the China Inland Mission, Hudson Taylor, has gone to Heaven. He was a man with great vision, and in the early days when China was still murdering people who came in as foreigners—especially foreigners who wanted to inject any new ideas about God or religion—Hudson Taylor went to China and spent his life there. But he didn't go by plane, as many of us have done. There were no planes. In fact there weren't even many roads.

It is said Hudson Taylor walked so much that his feet were calloused. There were huge, thick callouses on his feet that made it painful for him to walk in the latter years of his life. Bones gave way a bit. Still he kept walking until the day of his death because there was so much to be done. . . .

So Hudson Taylor, through all the years of his life, walked to get to these people—to reach new areas with the news that Jesus loves sinners.

As he grew older, his wife became too feeble to go with him on his long journeys. Far back in the interior of China where Hudson Taylor died, she'd wait in the village, eager for the twilight when her husband would come home. He would come finally, his frail body absolutely at the breaking point and worn out—beaten down with the sun, thirsty, tired. And those feet would be aching, aching, aching from the walk. He'd come in and put aside his garments, and his wife would come with a wash basin. Looking up into that noble face, and seeing there all the love of Jesus for the lost and for these Chinese, she'd weep a little at the price she saw it cost her husband to keep on going. Then she would put a wash basin, just an ordinary old tin wash basin on the floor, and she'd fill it with warm water. Then, old as she was and unable to walk out through the villages as he did, she'd get on her knees with a little towel and a little bit of soap, and then she would wash those gnarled and calloused and knobby old feet and with her aching hands would massage them.

Time and time again he would tell her where he'd been for Jesus that day. He would talk about the demon-possessed person he'd prayed for; or the woman with a great cancer as an open sore on her leg that he pointed to Jesus; or the little village where he had gone where there were fifty or sixty per cent of the people blind or going blind with trachoma, and where he had talked about Jesus who came to restore sight to the blind.

He would tell this story, and she would just massage his feet and wash them. Finally, when she had done the best she could to ease the burning pain in those joints worn out for Jesus, time and time again she would just look up and say, "Hudson, it's been a busy day, and you are so tired; and I just want you to know that like your face that shines for Jesus, these feet too, are beautiful. They are not only beautiful to me, but to your Lord; for He said 'How beautiful upon the mountains are the feet of them that bring good tidings, that publish peace, that bring good tidings of good, and bring salvation.' "

The Bible says, "Look, these glamourized portions of life aren't the whole thing." The Bible is saying, "You've got ignored, despised gifts and talents." Maybe you're just ringed in by what seems the most ordinary, commonplace things among men. All you've got to use or work with or give to God are feet. And the Bible is saying, "There are things to be done that make the humblest and most despised beautiful."

And God is wanting you to give Him the despised, the humdrum things in your life—like feet—and let Him make them beautiful.

—Author Unknown

Robert E. Lee wrote a recommendation for a man who had bitterly criticized him. "How can you give that man a reference?" he was asked, "Don't you know he has been your severest critic?" Lee replied, "I was asked to give my opinion of him, not his opinion of me." Troublesome times offer us opportunities to show what we are. When the critics are hottest, our faith is being tested; and what we are will show in how we worship God.—Stainback.

I would rather fail in the cause that some day will triumph than triumph in a cause that some day will fail.—Woodrow Wilson.

Billy Sunday's Estimate of the Bible

One of the most beautiful and truthful tributes to the Bible ever written is that by Billy Sunday, voiced by him in his preachings.

"Twenty-nine years ago, with the Holy Spirit as my Guide, I entered at the portico of Genesis, walked down the corridor of the Old Testament art-galleries, where pictures of Noah, Abraham, Moses, Joseph, Isaac, Jacob and Daniel hang on the wall. I passed into the music room of the Psalms where the Spirit sweeps the keyboard of nature until it seems that every reed and pipe in God's great organ responds to the harp of David, the sweet singer of Israel.

"I entered the chamber of Ecclesiastes, where the voice of the preacher is heard, and into the conservatory of Sharon and the lily of the valley where sweet spices filled and perfumed my life.

"I entered the business office of Proverbs and on into the observatory of the Prophets where I saw telescopes of various sizes pointing to far off events, concentrating on the bright and morning Star which was to rise above the moonlit hills of Judea for our salvation and redemption.

"I entered the audience room of the King of kings, catching a vision written by Matthew, Mark, Luke and John. Thence into the correspondence room with Paul, Peter, James and John writing their Epistles.

"I stepped into the throne room of Revelation where tower the glittering peaks, where sits the King of kings upon His throne of glory with the healing of the nations in His hand, and I cried out:

" 'All hail the power of Jesus' name!
Let angels prostrate fall;
Bring forth the royal diadem,
And crown Him Lord of all.' "

Spurgeon's Letter to an Unsaved Boy

Would you like to read a letter that that great prince of preachers, Charles H. Spurgeon, wrote to an unsaved boy? This is recorded in Spurgeon's autobiography, by his wife, in Volume 1:

"Knowing, in some humble measure, at least, the value of religion, let me also bring it before your attention. If you give yourself time to think, you will soon remember that you must die; and if you meditate one more moment, you will recollect that you have a soul, and that soul will never die, but will live for ever; and if you die in your present state, it must live in endless torment.

"You are an accountable being; God, who made you, demands perfect obedience. But you must own that you have sinned; say not, 'I am not a great sinner,' for one sin only would be sufficient to sink your soul for ever in the pit of perdition. The sentence of death stands against you, and mercy alone stays its execution. Seeing now that you are in such danger, how do you think to escape? Surely you will not be content to die as you are, for you will one day find it no light matter to endure the hot displeasure of an angry God. Do you imagine that, if you live better for the future, God will forgive your past offences? That is a mistake; see if you can find it in the Bible.

"Perhaps you intend to think about religion after you have enjoyed sin a little longer; or possibly you think that you are too young to die. But who knows whether that future time will be afforded, and who said that you can turn to Christ just when you please? Your heart is deceitful above all things, and your natural depravity so great that you will not turn to God. Trust not, then, to resolutions made in your own strength, they are but wind; nor to yourself, who are but a broken reed; nor to your own heart, or you are a fool. There is no way of salvation but Christ; you cannot save yourself, having no power even to think one good thought; neither can your parents' love and prayers save you; none but Jesus can, He is the Saviour of the helpless, and I tell you that He died for all such as feel their vileness, and come to Him for cleansing.

"You do not deserve salvation; well, there is not a jot of merit on the sinner's part mentioned in the covenant. You have nothing; you are nothing; but Christ is all, and He must be everything to you, or you will never be saved. None reach Heaven but by free-grace, and through free-grace alone. Even a faint desire after any good thing came from God, from whom you must get more, for He giveth liberally, and no poor sinner, begging at His door, was ever yet sent empty away.

"Look at the blessedness of real religion, no one is truly happy but a child of God. The believer is safe, for God has promised to preserve him; and if once you have the pearl of great price, it cannot be taken from you. The way to Heaven is faith, 'looking unto Jesus;' this faith is the gift of God, and none but those who have it know its value. Oh, may you possess it!—is the earnest prayer of—
Yours faithfully,
Charles H. Spurgeon

"Anywhere provided it be forward."-- David Livingstone.

The Big Engineer

Thomas Edison said: "No one can study chemistry and see the wonderful way in which certain elements combine with the nicety of the most delicate machine ever invented, and not come to the inevitable conclusion that there is a Big Engineer who is running this universe."

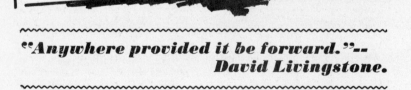

If you want to be poor— hoard
If you want to be rich— give
If you want to be wealthy —scatter
If you want to be a pauper —grasp

A good thing about telling the truth is that you don't have to remember what you say.

Somebody laughed at a Boy Scout for going to church. Jesus went. Theodore Roosevelt, Wilson, Coolidge, Hoover went. Runner De Mar even taught a Sunday School class in a Baptist church! Edgar Guest gives reasons galore for his going, so does Roger Babson. So do all great, good and true souls. A good scout is trustworthy, loyal, helpful, friendly, courteous, kind, obedient, cheerful, thrifty, brave, clean and REVERENT.

"Soul-Winning Sophie"

"Aunt Sophie," a converted washerwoman who was really a soul winner, was accused of talking about Christ to a wooden Indian in front of a cigar store. Some people laughed at Sophie for doing this. She replied, "Some people say they saw me talking to a wooden Indian about Christ. I may have done it; my eyesight is not good. But talking to a wooden Indian about Christ is not as bad as being a wooden Christian and never talking to anybody about Jesus."

"I did not like the way you conducted this evangelistic service," a very formal minister said to an evangelist after a revival service in which a number of people were saved. "How do you do it?" the evangelist inquired. "I do not do it at all," the formal minister answered. "Well, I like the way I do it better than the way you do not do it," the evangelist said.

Tobacco...
A Parable

(The Miami Herald)

Then shall the kingdom of Satan be likened to a grain of tobacco seed, which, being cast into the ground, small, though exceedingly grew, and became a great plant; and spread its leaves rank and broad, so that huge and vile worms formed a habitation thereon. And it came to pass, in the course of time, the sons of men looked upon it, and thought it beautiful to look upon, and much to be desired to make lads look big and manly.

So they put forth their hands and did chew thereof. And some it made sick and others vomit most filthily. And it further came to pass that those who chewed it became weak and unmanly and said, "We are enslaved, and cannot cease from chewing it."

And the mouths of those that were enslaved became foul, and they were seized with a violent spitting; and they did spit, even in ladies' parlors and in the house of the Lord of Hosts. And the saints of the Most High were plagued thereby. And in the course of time it came to pass that others snuffed it; and they were taken suddenly with fits, and they did sneeze insomuch that their eyes filled with tears, and they did look exceedingly silly. And yet others cunningly wrought the leaves into rolls, and did suck vehemently at the other end thereof, and did look very grave and calf-like; and the smoke of their torment ascended up forever and ever.

And the cultivation thereof became a great and mighty business on the earth; and the merchantmen waxed rich by the commerce thereof. And it came to pass that the saints of the Most High defiled themselves therewith; even the poor, who could not buy shoes nor books nor bread for their little ones, spent their money for it. And the Lord was greatly displeased therewith and said, "Wherefore this waste, and why do these little ones lack bread and shoes and books? Turn now your fields into corn and wheat, and put this evil far from you; and be separate, and defile not yourselves any more; and I will bless you and cause my face to shine upon you."

But with one accord they all exclaimed, "We cannot cease from chewing, and sniffing, and puffing."

Comfort in Crisis

Everybody has heard of George Muller and his world-famous orphanage at Bristol, England. When he began his work for orphans in 1836 he resolved to depend solely upon God for help. From then to the end of 1959 his institution received in free-will gifts more than three million pounds sterling— about $9 million—solely in answer to prayer and without anyone's being asked for a donation. Think of praying for $9 million! But God sent it and more than 17,000 orphans have been blessed thereby.

Muller's faith became almost proverbial, and inspired countless others to put their trust in God. All his needs, great and small, he spread out before the Lord, with absolute assurance that they would be supplied.

On one occasion when he was crossing the Atlantic his ship ran into a fog. Approaching the captain he said, "I have come to tell you that I must be in Quebec on Saturday afternoon."

"Impossible," said the captain.

"Very well," replied Muller, "if your ship cannot take me, God will find some other means. I have never broken an engagement in fifty-seven years."

"I would willingly help you if I could," said the captain, "but there's nothing anyone can do."

"Let us go to the chartroom and pray," said Muller.

"Do you know how dense the fog is?" asked the captain.

"No," was Muller's answer. "My eye is not on the density of the fog but on the living God who controls every circumstance of my life."

Together they went to the chartroom and Muller prayed: "O Lord, if it is consistent with Thy will, please remove the fog in five minutes. You know the engagement You made for me in Quebec on Saturday. I believe it is Your will."

When he had finished, the captain was about to pray, but Muller touched him on the shoulder and told him not to do so. "First," he said, "you do not believe He will; and second, I believe He has, so there is no need for you to pray about it."

The captain looked amazed and Muller continued: "Captain, I have known my Lord for fifty-seven years, and there has never been a single day that I have failed to gain an audience with Him. Get up and open the door. You will find the fog gone."

The captain opened the door. The fog had disappeared!

Let's Go Soul Winning

WITH JACK HYLES

Some of the cutest and funniest experiences that ever happen, happen to soul winners; and some of the most clever statements ever made are made by those getting converted or just recently converted.

Just the other day I heard a soul winner say that he had explained the plan of salvation to a man in his eighties. The old man immediately looked at the soul winner and said, "Well, when can we get with it?"

A soul-winning friend of mine was leading a sinner to Christ. As the soul winner prayed, he said, "Dear Lord, I think this sinner is sincere," whereupon the sinner said, "Lord, don't *think* nothin' about it. I *know* he's sincere!"

One time I was leading a mechanic to the Lord, and his prayer was, "Lord, I am coming for a general overhauling."

A young fellow came down the aisle in our church recently with hands tucked in his pockets and asked, "Where is the 'gettin'-saved place'?"

A lady came down the aisle in First Baptist Church about five years ago wearing a fur coat. She grabbed me on each side of my face, squeezed my cheeks with her hands, and said, "Guess what, Preacher! I am about to get saved!"

Many years ago when I was a kid preacher a young lady came down the aisle to receive Christ. I wanted to know if she were coming by letter, by statement, or by transfer, so I asked, "Young lady, how are you coming?" With much emotion and many tears, she replied, "Pretty good. How are you getting along?"

An alcoholic got saved in our church in Texas. He asked me what a new Christian should do. I said that a new Christian ought to start giving a tenth to the Lord, whereupon he replied, "I don't know much about this tenth business, but I got two fifths in the car I will give up."

A lady who was won to Christ in a previous pastorate was told to come forward when the others came forward. Hence, she walked the aisle with the ushers and stood at the altar as if to help them take the offering.

These are just a few of the many humorous statements and experiences that come to one who obeys the commission of our Lord to go into all the world.

Ankle Deep

Rev. T. DeWitt Talmage, D. D.

"Launch out into the deep"— Luke 5:4.

There is no book in the world that demands so much of our attention as the Bible. Yet nine-tenths of Christian men get no more than ankle deep. They think it is a good sign not to venture too far. They never ask *how* or *why;* and if they see some Christians becoming inquisitive about the deep things of God, they say: "Be careful; you had better not go out so far from shore."

My answer is: The farther you go from shore the better, if you have the right kind of ship. If you have mere worldly philosophy for the hulk, and pride for a sail, and self-conceit for the helm, the first squall will destroy you. But if you take the Bible for your craft, the farther you go the better; and, after you have gone ten thousand furlongs, Christ will still command: *"Launch out into the deep."*

Ask some question, as "Who is God?," and go on for ten years asking it. Ask it at the gate of every parable; amidst the excitement of every miracle; by the solitariness of every patriarchal threshing-floor; amidst the white faces of Sennacherib's slain turned up into the moonlight; amidst the flying chariots of the Golden City.

Ask *Who Jesus Is,* and keep on asking it of every Bible lily, of every raven, of every star, of every crazed brain cured, of every blind man come to sunlight, of every coin in a fish's mouth, of every loaf that got to be five loaves, of every wrathful sea pacified, of every pulseless arm stretched forth in gratulation; ask it of His mother, of Augustus, of Herod, of the Syrophoenician woman, of the damsel that woke up from the death-sleep; of Joseph, who had Him buried; of the angel, posted as sentinel at His tomb; of the dumb earth that shook and groaned and thundered when He died.

What Money Cannot Do

Money, no doubt, is a power; but a power of well defined and narrow limits. It will purchase plenty, but not peace; it will furnish your table with luxuries, but not you with an appetite to enjoy them. It will surround your sick bed with physicians, but not restore health to a sickly frame; it will encompass you with flatterers, but never procure you one true friend; it will bribe for you into silence the tongues of accusing men, but not an accusing conscience; it will pay some debt, but not the largest one of all, your debt to the law of God; it will relieve many fears, but not those of guilt—the terrors that crown the brows of Death. He stands as grim and terrible by the dying bed of wealth as by the pallet of the poorest beggar whom pitiless riches has thrust from her door.

—Guthrie.

We have the biggest sellout these days that America has ever known. We have men who do not believe in the blood of Christ sponsoring evangelistic campaigns, sitting in the "Amen" corners! Instead of calling on them for prayer, Paul asked God to curse them.—Dr. Bob Jones, Sr.

A CORRECT MENTAL ATTITUDE

Dr. R. G. Lee said, "Look on visitation as a business, not an incidental matter; as work, not play; as time well spent, not wasted; as a privilege, not a boresom duty."

God is looking, not for the man of ability but for the man of faith; the man who refuses to doubt; the man who believes that God is sufficient. He is looking for the man who believes not only God can, but is fully persuaded that God will. —D. R. Shepson.

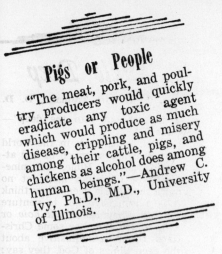

Pigs or People

"The meat, pork, and poultry producers would quickly eradicate any toxic agent which would produce as much disease, crippling and misery among their cattle, pigs, and chickens as alcohol does among human beings."—Andrew C. Ivy, Ph.D., M.D., University of Illinois.

If Socrates would enter the room we should rise and do him honor. But if Jesus Christ came into the room we should fall down on our knees and worship Him. —Napoleon

In the Nick of Time

I am never tired of pointing out that the Greek phrase translated, "In the time of need," is a colloquialism, of which the "nick of time" is the exact equivalent: "That we may have grace to help in the 'nick of time.'" Grace just when and where I need it. You are attacked by temptation, and at the moment of assault, you look to Him, and the grace is there to help in "the nick of time." No postponement of your petition until the evening hour of prayer; but there, man there in the city street, with the flaming temptation in front of you, turn to Christ with a cry for help, and the grace will be there in "the nick of time."

—G. Campbell Morgan

little explained. A little endured. A little forgiven—the quarrel is cured.

Early Impressions on Children

I stood in a house in one of the Long Island Villages, not long ago, and I saw a beautiful tree, and I said to the owner: "That is a very fine tree; but what a curious crook there is in it." "Yes," said he; "I planted that tree, and when it was a year old, I went to New York, and worked as a mechanic for a year or two, and when I came back I found they had allowed something to stand against the tree and *so it has always had that crook.*" And so I thought it was with the influence upon children. If you allow anything to stand in the way of moral influence against a child on this side or that side, to the latest day of its life on earth and through all eternity it will show the pressure. No wonder Lord Byron was bad. Do you know his mother said to him, when she saw him one day limping across the floor with his unsound foot: "Get out of my way, you lame brat!" What chance for a boy like that!—Talmage.

Joining The Church

An old sea-captain was riding in the cars towards Philadelphia, and a young man sat down beside him. He said, "Young man, where are you going?" "I am going to Philadelphia to live," replied the young man. "Have you letters of introduction?" asked the old captain. "Yes," said the young man, and he pulled some of them out. "Well," said the old sea-captain, "haven't you a church certificate?" "Oh yes," replied the young man, "I didn't suppose you would want to look at that." "Yes," said the sea-captain, "I want to see that. As soon as you get to Philadelphia, present that to some Christian church. I am an old sailor, and I have been up and down in the world, and it's my rule, as soon as I get into port, *to fasten my ship fore and aft to the wharf,* although it may cost a little wharfage, rather than have my ship out in the stream, floating hither and thither with the tide." —Talmage.

John Wesley traveled two hundred and fifty thousand miles a day for forty years; preached forty thousand sermons; produced four hundred books; knew ten languages. At eighty-three he was annoyed that he could not write more than fifteen hours a day without hurting his eyes, and at eighty-six he was ashamed he could not preach more than twice a day. He complained in his diary that there was an increasing tendency to lie in bed until 5:30 in the morning.

The Arkansas Baptist

Why Doubt God's Word?

It is strange we trust each other,
And only doubt our Lord.
We take the word of mortals,
And yet distrust His word;
But oh, what light and glory
Would shine o'er all our days,
If we always would remember
God means just what He says.

A. B. Simpson

Tale-bearing emits a threefold poison; for it injures the teller, the hearer and the person concerning whom the tale is told.

—Spurgeon

The two kinds of people on earth I mean
Are the people who lift and the people who lean.
—Ella W. Wilcox

BOY NUMBER 92

By Dorothy C. Haskin

Jim stood by the window, looking out so he would not be expected to play with the other boys. He felt too miserable to play. Life had been tough enough when his father died and he and his mother lived alone.

But now, she was gone. The man at the church said she had gone to be with Jesus. Then, this day, Aug. 8, 1839, the man had brought Jim to this orphanage in Bristol, Eng.

A boy came up to him and said, "I'm Davey. You'll like it here."

Jim didn't answer. He wasn't sure he would ever like it.

"Look, that's him," Davey whispered.

"Who?" Jim asked, staring out at the man who was coming out of a house across the street. He was an ordinary looking man, except he had such a pleasant expression.

"Why, Mr. Muller who prays for us orphans! He says he himself doesn't take care of us; he just prays for us every day, and God does the work."

"That's a lot of praying," Jim answered. He had not done much praying though he knew his mother had.

"Mr. Muller has to pray if we are to eat."

Jim's eyes grew big. He had hoped that at the orphanage he wouldn't miss any meals. He had missed a lot of them since his mother had been sick, and missing meals gave him an awful gone feeling. "Doesn't he have any other way to get food?"

"No, he doesn't have any money at all, but God sends what we need."

That didn't sound too dependable to Jim. He glanced at the bunch of boys and figured it would take a lot of food to feed them. "Are there many of us?"

"I heard that you are boy number 92."

That was a lot and maybe God had only enough food for 91 boys! He was 92 and if there wasn't enough food, he'd be the one who didn't get any!

Jim shook his head. It was all new to him. All he had ever heard was you worked and got money and bought food. It was bad enough losing his mother without having been brought to a place like this, where the only way to get food was to pray for it.

A loud gong struck. Davey said, "Come on, that's supper."

Good! Jim thought. Now he'd see if there was enough food. Shortly Jim sat down at one end of a long table and glanced down. There was a spoon, plate and mug for each boy, but no food! He swallowed a big lump.

At the end of the table stood George Muller. He smiled kindly and said, "Boys, as you know we have a Father who is Father of the fatherless. Some of you have been with me several years. Have you ever gone to bed hungry?"

"No," answered the boys. "And we know that Jesus Christ is the same yesterday and today and forever. As He provided for us in the past He will provide for us today. We do not, as yet, have our evening meal. But I have gathered that we might say Grace, thanking our Father, for we know He will provide."

The boys bowed their heads and George Muller prayed.

There was a long, shrill ring of the doorbell. Jim looked up. Mr. Muller said, "Wait, boys, this is our answer." He disappeared into the hall.

"Do you think it is?" Jim whispered.

"Sure." Davey nodded.

Jim grit his teeth as he waited.

In a few minutes George Muller came back into the room. Smiling he said, "That was a man with some money for us. It will take a little while to get the food but soon it will be on the table. Boys, always trust God. In the years I have run this orphanage no meal ever has been more than a half hour late, and it won't be tonight."

Jim sighed. He felt fine. It was wonderful to know that he, too, could have a heavenly Father to take care of him! —Power.

"Gone With The Wind"

By Cam Thompson

Picture a madman hurling twenty dollar bills into the Atlantic, or an idiot sowing diamonds in a swamp, and you have a good view of how we are dispensing the golden vials of TIME which God places in our hands at each sunrise.

The average life of a fundamental Christian is 75 years' duration. He spends six months in worship, six years in eating, nine years in amusement, seven and a half years in dressing, six years in traveling, nineteen years in working, and twenty-three years asleep!

We hear our friends say, "I wish I had time to read my Bible and pray and witness." You have it. Each morning twenty-four hours are presented to you. You have time to read three chapters or five chapters, systematically, a day. You will never make an inch of spiritual progress unless you do. Yours are the desert and the snakes and the sand and the wandering and the murmuring, if you substitute sermons or isolated verses, or devotional books or radio programs. "The words that I speak unto you—they are SPIRIT, they are LIFE" (John 6:63). You have time to pray—to sit at the feet of Christ Jesus—one or two hours each day.

Dr. Walter Wilson decided to keep a minute record of how he passed each minute of the day. He was appalled—and you will be appalled—at the hideous waste of time. We are all experts on how the government wastes money. But at the Judgment Seat of Christ, we shall give an account of OURSELVES, and what we did with the days that shall never be repeated, never be replaced, forever and ever. "This I say, brethren, the time is short . . ." (I Cor. 7:29). "Little children, it is the last time . . ." (I John 2:18).

—From *Christian Victory*

The sermon is the house; the illustrations are the windows that let in the light.—Spurgeon.

"Mind Your Own Business!"

One of God's soul-winning servants became greatly burdened for the salvation of an unsaved girl. She resented his efforts to cause her to see her lostness and need of the Saviour. She told her mother of her displeasure. Said the mother angrily, "The next time he speaks to you about being saved, tell him to mind his own business!"

"But mother," protested the girl, "he talks like this IS his business!" It IS the business of every born-again believer to do their dead-level best to bring the lost, perishing ones to Jesus!

I went out to find a
friend,
But could not find
one there;
I went out to be a
friend,
And friends were
everywhere!

Don't Blame My Hands

Thomas K. Beecher despised deceit in any form. Finding that a clock in his church was habitually too fast or too slow, he hung a placard on the wall above it, reading in large letters: "Don't blame my hands—the trouble lies deeper."

That is where the trouble lies with us when our hands do wrong, or our feet, or our lips, or our thoughts. The trouble lies so deep that only God's miracle power can deal with it. Sin goes deep; but Christ goes deeper and changes the heart and the will.—Selected.

Better is a handful with quietness, than two handsful with labor and striving after winds.—Eccles. 4:6.

Someone has said, "Moses was the child of a slave and the son of a king. He was born in a hut and lived in a palace. He inherited poverty and enjoyed wealth. He led armies and was the keeper of flocks. He was a mighty soldier and the meekest of men. He was educated in the court but dwelt in the desert. He had the wisdom of Egypt and the faith of a child. He was backward in speech, but he talked with God. No man assisted at his funeral; yet God buried him. His lips are silent, but his voice yet speaks."

What It Takes to be a Friend

A cowboy explained his idea of Christian living: "Now I'm working for Jim here. If I'd sit around, telling what a good fellow Jim is, and singing songs for him, and getting up in the night to serenade him, I'd be doing just what a lot of Christians do; but I wouldn't suit Jim, and I'd get fired mighty quick. But when I buckle on my chaps and hustle among the hills, and see that Jim's herd is all right and not suffering from lack of water or feed or getting off range and branded by cattle thieves then I'm proving my love and serving Jim as he wants to be sered."

—Courage and Confidence from the Bible.

After Work

Lord, when Thou seest that my
work is done,
Let me not linger on,
With failing powers,
Adown the weary hours—
A workless worker in a world of
work.
But, with a word,
Just bid me home.
And I will come
Right gladly—
Yea, right gladly
Will I come.

—John Oxenham.

Be slow in choosing a friend, slower in changing.
—Benjamin Franklin

Spurgeon penned these words to one who had given him a gift: "I do not know how I can better have it than by being allowed to give it away. What I have is best enjoyed by myself personally when I can use it in some way or other for the advantage of the work of God. . . ."

And it was this same Spurgeon who said, "Poor men should give that they may not be always poor. Rich men should give that they may not become poor."

Jim Elliot, martyr: "He is no fool who gives what he cannot keep, to gain what he cannot lose."

I SHOULD BE AFRAID TO GO FORWARD IF I DID NOT BELIEVE THAT THERE LAY AT THE FOUNDATION OF ALL OUR THOUGHT THIS UNIMPEACHABLE WORD OF GOD. IF WE CANNOT DERIVE OUR STRENGTH THENCE, THERE IS NO SOURCE FROM WHICH WE CAN DERIVE IT. HAVING NOW ABOVE FOURTEEN YEARS TRIED THIS WAY, I CAN MOST FULLY, IN THE FEAR OF GOD, COMMEND IT.

—SPOKEN BY WOODROW WILSON

Resigned and Re-Signed

Dr. Thomas T. Villiers says, "I once heard John Robertson speak. He told us that a year before he had felt he must leave the ministry. He said, 'I struggled all night in prayer with God about the matter, and about the time the eastern light began to stream in the windows, I said, "O God, here is my commission; I resign." But God, in His infinite mercy, said to me, "My son, you need not resign your commission. I will re-sign your commission." And ever since then I have been preaching under a re-signed commission.'"

—Wonderful Word

The Story of Two Brothers

There were two boys in the Taylor family. The older said he must make a name for his family, and so turned his face toward Parliament and fame. The younger decided to give his life to the service of Christ and so turned his face toward China and duty. Hudson Taylor, the missionary, died, beloved and known on every continent. "But when I looked in the Encyclopedia to see what the other son had done, I found these words, 'The brother of Hudson Taylor.'"

—Gospel Herald

Woman's Trust

"Good wife, what are you singing for? You know we've lost the hay,
And what we'll do with horse and cow is more than I can say;
While like as not, with storm and rain, we'll lose both corn and wheat."
She looked up with a pleasant face, and answered low and sweet:
"There is a Heart, there is a Hand, we feel, we can not see;
We've always been provided for, and we shall always be!"

He turned around with sullen gloom. She said: "Love, be at rest;
You cut the grass, worked soon and late, you did your very best.
That was your work; you've naught to do with either wind and rain,
And do not doubt but you will reap rich fields of golden grain."

"That's like a woman's reasoning—we must because we must."
She softly said: "I reason not; I only work and trust;
The harvest may redeem the hay; keep heart what'er betide;
When one door's shut I've always found another open wide."

He kissed the calm and trustful face; gone was his restless pain;
She heard him, with a cheerful step, go whistling down the lane,
And went about her household cares full of glad content,
Singing to time her busy hands, as to and fro she went.

Days come and go—'twas New Year's day, and the great fire burned so
clear.
The farmer said: "Dear wife, it's been a good and happy year;
The fruit was gain—the surplus corn has bought the hay, you know."
She lifted then a smiling face and said: "I told you so;
For there's a Heart, and there's a Hand, we feel, but cannot see;
We've always been provided for, and we shall always be!"
—Pioneer

What of Yesterday?

What of Yesterday?
It is to sift.
A part will need to stay
With you to lift.
Keep sifting, separating
Good from bad.
Keep sifting, not berating
Times you had.
That part you will repent,
Perhaps forgive
And then forget. 'Twas sent
To learn to live
And better love today;
So sift again.
Those things you had to say
That cause you pain
When you remember now
Just sift them too
And they will teach you how
To speak anew,
But softly now today.
There are so many ways
To sift and clean away
Our Yesterdays.

—Bill Harvey

He Never Gave

The old German shoemaker had just sent his boy with a basket of garden stuff to a poor widow. He worked hard at his trade and cultivated his little garden patch, yet nothing was more common in his life than some such deed as this.

"How can you afford to give so much away?" I asked him.

"I give nothing away," he said. "I lend it to the Lord, and He repays me many times. I am ashamed that people think I am generous when I am paid so much. A long time ago, when I was very poor, I saw someone in want, and I wondered if I could give, but I could not see how. I did give, and the Lord helped me. I have had more work, my garden grows well, and never since have I stopped to think twice when I have heard of some needy one. No, if I gave away all, the Lord would not let me starve. It is like money in the bank, only this time the bank never breaks, and the interest comes back every day."

—Selected

Oh, Those Shining Faces!

Oh, those shining faces,
When we enter Gloryland!
Waiting at the portals,
We will find our loved ones stand.
Ev'ry sorrow ended,
Tears all dried, care ever past.
Oh, what praise and gladness,
When we see our Lord at last!

Roses never fade there,
Winter brings the saints no cold.
We will all be young then,
Never tired, distressed, nor old.
Sinful self all conquered,
Hateful sin and weakness gone.
Oh, we'll praise our Saviour,
When we join redemption's song!

See the converts coming
From the North, South, East and West!
See rewards for souls won,
Reapers' joy and Heaven's rest.
There'll be pay for heartache;
Those who suffered with Him, reign.
Hope becomes possession;
Faith is sight and loss is gain!

Gates of pearl all gleaming;
Jasper walls and streets of gold!
Trees of life all blooming
By the river, we are told.
Then our mansions' beauty
And the song of angels grand,
Face to face with Jesus—
Oh, delightful Gloryland!

But to see Jesus! Jesus who saved me.
Just to see Jesus is Heaven at last!
—John R. Rice

*Tell Him about your heartache
And tell Him your loneliness too,
Tell Him your baffled purpose
When you scarce know what to do.
Then leaving all your weakness
With the One divinely strong,
Forget that you bear the burden
And carry away the song.*

Anon.

Titanic Incident

It was reported that eleven millionaires went down on the *Titanic*. Major A. H. Peuchen left $300,000.00 in money, jewelry, and securities in a box in his cabin. "The money seemed a mockery at that time," he later said. "I picked up three oranges instead."

A lad who heard his father pray for missions, and especially for the needs of missionaries, that they might be supplied, and that their institutions might be amply sustained, said to him, "Father, I wish I had your money." "Why, my son, what would you do with it?" asked the father. "I would answer your prayers," was the reply.
—Selected

Holman Hunt displayed his masterpiece, CHRIST THE LIGHT OF THE WORLD. The picture shows Christ holding a lantern outside a closed door; He is knocking at the door. A critic told Mr. Hunt that he had made an error in the painting because there was no door latch. Mr. Hunt replied, "That is to depict the door to the human heart. It can only be opened by the occupant from the inside." Christ stands ready to enter and to redeem any who let Him in. (See Revelation 3:20).

Here is another illustration from Scripture. God said, 'Noah, there is going to be a flood.' What did Noah do? He built the ark. God told him just how to build it, so long and so wide. After many years the flood came. What did Noah do? He did the easiest thing in the world. Noah got saved out of the flood without any trouble at all. He just walked into the ark and sat down. He didn't even have to shut the door. God shut the door. Not even spray from the waves could get in. Noah just walked into the ark and sat down, and God shut the door!

Most of you would have tried to swim through the flood. But, brother, listen: God provided Jesus Christ, the Ark of Safety, and you can walk into the Ark and sit down. I can imagine Noah sitting there saying, "All right, Ham, go feed the elephants." I can imagine him teaching a parrot to talk, or talking to his wife and having a good time. "But, Noah, aren't you afraid of this flood?" "No, the flood is none of my business. I just got in the ark and the Lord shut the door. This flood doesn't worry me at all. That is the Lord's business."

Isn't it wonderful to get in the Ark, to quit working and rest! Are you in the Ark? Have you quit trying to swim through the wrath of God? Have you given up trying to make it by your own valor, or strength, or wisdom, or goodness? Have you come into the Ark? Thank God, I am in the Ark resting! **--Dr. John R. Rice.**

Mother's Work

Nobody knows of the work it makes,
  To keep the home together;
Nobody knows of the steps it takes,
  Nobody knows—but Mother.

Nobody listens to childish woes,
  Which kisses only heal;
Nobody pained by naughty blows,
  Nobody—only Mother.

Nobody knows of sleepless care
  Bestowed on baby brother;
Nobody knows of the tender prayer,
  Nobody—only Mother.

Nobody knows of the lessons taught
  Of loving one another;
Nobody knows of patience sought,
  Nobody—only Mother.

Nobody knows of anxious fears
  Lest darlings may not weather
The storm of life in after years,
  Nobody knows—but Mother.

Nobody kneels at the throne above
  To thank the Heavenly Father
For the sweetest gift—a Mother's love.
  Nobody can—but Mother.
—Selected

There is an old story which tells of an Italian duke who went on board a galley ship. As he passed the crew of slaves he asked several of them what their offenses were. Every one laid the blame to someone else, saying his brother was to blame or the judge was bribed. One sturdy young fellow said: "My lord, I am justly in here. I wanted money and I stole it. No one is to blame but myself." The duke on hearing this seized him by the shoulder, saying, "You rogue! What are you doing here among so many honest men? Get you out of their company!" The young fellow was then set at liberty, while the rest were left to tug at the oars.
—Spurgeon.

Upon the threshold of another year
    We stand again.
We know not what of gladness and good cheer,
    Of grief or pain
May visit us while journeying to its close.
    In this we rest,
God dealeth out in wisdom what He knows
    For us is best.
—*Thomas Wearing*

Don't Judge by Size!

The wonderful things in nature are the smallest.

A flea leaps 200 times its length. A man would have to jump 1,200 feet to equal this proportionately.

The housefly takes 440 steps to travel three inches, and does it in a half second—corresponding to a man running 20 miles in a minute.

An ant lifts a load many, many times its own weight—a man would have to lift a diesel locomotive and carry it on his back to compare with that of the ant.

Turnip seeds, under good conditions, increase their weight 15 times a minute, and in rich soil turnip seeds may increase their weight 15,000 times a day.

There is no force more powerful than a growing squash. A squash 18 days old has been harnessed in such a way that in its growing process it lifted 50 pounds on lever—19 days later it lifted 5,000 pounds.

"Bless the LORD, O my soul, O LORD my God, thou art very great . . . O LORD, how manifold are thy works! In wisdom hast thou made them all: the earth is full of thy riches."—Ps. 104:1, 24.

If I Had A Son

If I had a son, I'd feel that it would be my fault if he didn't grow up to be a fine, honest man —a good citizen in every sense of the word.

If I had a son I'd swear to do one thing; I'd teach him the truth. I'd never let him catch me in a lie, because I wouldn't tell him any lies. I wouldn't skimp the truth either, and in return I'd insist that he tell the truth.

I'd try to be absolutely fair with my son, and to the extent of my capacity, I'd try to be understanding. Boys will get into trouble now and then. They can't help it. So, if my boy made an honest mistake, I wouldn't punish him unless he lied about it.

As a matter of course, I'd have my son go to church. What's more I'd go with him. Apart from religious instruction, churchgoing is a means by which the young man would meet persons of character.

But above everything else, I'd try to understand my son. For I fully realize that if I didn't, I'd be a failure as a dad.—J. Edgar Hoover.

THOUGHTS
WORTH THINKING ABOUT !!!

GOD COULD HAVE KEPT DANIEL OUT OF THE LION'S DEN . . . HE COULD HAVE KEPT PAUL AND SILAS OUT OF JAIL . . . HE COULD HAVE KEPT THE THREE HEBREW CHILDREN OUT OF THE FIERY FURNACE . . . BUT GOD HAS NEVER PROMISED TO KEEP US OUT OF HARD PLACES . . . BUT WHAT HE HAS PROMISED IS TO GO WITH US THROUGH EVERY HARD PLACE, AND TO BRING US THROUGH VICTORIOUSLY!

Misinformation

"Bishop," said the westerner, "I do not refuse to accept the story of the ark; I can accept the ark's great size, its odd shape and the vast number of animals it contained; but when I am asked to believe that the children of Israel carried this unwieldy thing in the wilderness for forty years, I must confess that my faith breaks down."
—George A. Huntley

Dr. Bob Jones, Sr., says: "It is all right for the preacher to comfort the distressed, but it is also the preacher's duty to distress the comfortable."

The Negro Boy's Surprise

At a slave market in one of the Southern states, a smart, active colored boy was put up for sale. A kind master who pitied his condition, wishing him not to have a cruel owner, went up to him, and said, "If I buy you, will you be honest?" The boy, with a baffled expression, replied, "I will be honest whether you buy me or not."
—Sunday School Times

No, no, it is not dying
To go unto our God;
This gloomy earth forsaking,
Our journey homeward taking,
Along the starry road.

No, no, it is not dying
Heaven's citizen to be;
A crown immortal wearing,
And rest unbroken sharing,
From care and conflict free.
—Henry Bosch

The work is solemn—therefore don't trifle;
The task is difficult—therefore don't relax;
The opportunity is brief—therefore don't delay;
The path is narrow—therefore don't wander;
The prize is glorious—therefore don't faint.
—D. M. Panton

Sir William Osler, the famed physician, was examining a patient who was a heavy drinker.

"You'll have to cut out alcohol," ordered Osler.

"But, doctor," protested the other, "I've heard it said that alcohol makes people do things better."

"Nonsense," said Osler, "it only makes them less ashamed of doing them poorly."—Listen.

"Many are called, few are chosen." Many are cold, and a few are frozen.

"If you dread growing old, think of the many who never have that privilege."

—M. R. DeHaan

When our earthly day is closing,
And the night grows still and deep,
Let us, in Thine arms reposing,
Feel Thy power to save and keep.
Blessed Jesus,
Give Thine own beloved sleep.

—Selected

Zinzendorf testified that he owed much of his religious fervor to the casual sight of a picture of the crucifixion with the simple inscription at the bottom: "All this for thee; how much for me?"

—Selected.

I do not ask my cross to understand,
My way to see;
Better in the darkness just to feel Thy hand
And follow Thee.

—Adelaide Proctor.

A CHRISTIAN MINISTER ONCE SAID, "I WAS NEVER OF ANY USE UNTIL I FOUND OUT THAT GOD DID NOT INTEND ME TO BE A GREAT MAN."

—SELECTED.

You may need to fight with all your might, but keep sweet. You ought to love everybody, but you don't have to trust everybody. God didn't tell you to do that.

—Dr. Bob Jones, Sr.

Ol' Jonah

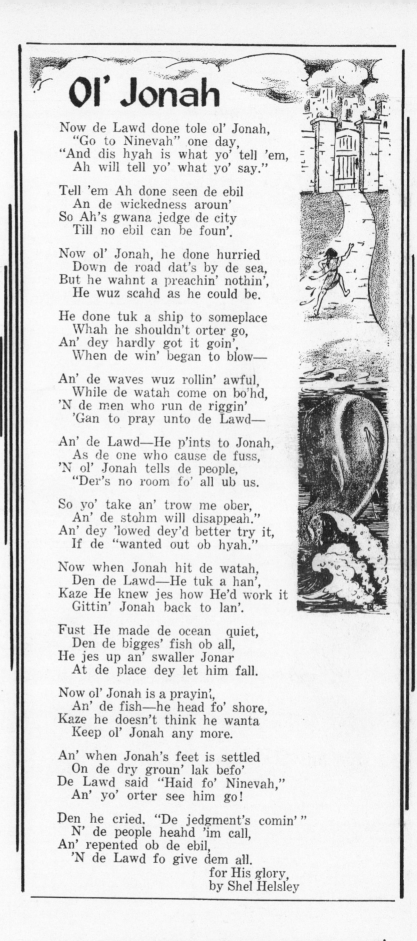

Now de Lawd done tole ol' Jonah,
  "Go to Ninevah" one day,
"And dis hyah is what yo' tell 'em,
  Ah will tell yo' what yo' say."

Tell 'em Ah done seen de ebil
  An de wickedness aroun'
So Ah's gwana jedge de city
  Till no ebil can be foun'.

Now ol' Jonah, he done hurried
  Down de road dat's by de sea,
But he wahnt a preachin' nothin',
  He wuz scahd as he could be.

He done tuk a ship to someplace
  Whah he shouldn't orter go,
An' dey hardly got it goin',
  When de win' began to blow—

An' de waves wuz rollin' awful,
  While de watah come on bo'hd,
'N de men who run de riggin'
  'Gan to pray unto de Lawd—

An' de Lawd—He p'ints to Jonah,
  As de one who cause de fuss,
'N ol' Jonah tells de people,
  "Der's no room fo' all ub us.

So yo' take an' trow me ober,
  An' de stohm will disappeah."
An' dey 'lowed dey'd better try it,
  If de "wanted out ob hyah."

Now when Jonah hit de watah,
  Den de Lawd—He tuk a han',
Kaze He knew jes how He'd work it
  Gittin' Jonah back to lan'.

Fust He made de ocean quiet,
  Den de bigges' fish ob all,
He jes up an' swaller Jonar
  At de place dey let him fall.

Now ol' Jonah is a prayin',
  An' de fish—he head fo' shore,
Kaze he doesn't think he wanta
  Keep ol' Jonah any more.

An' when Jonah's feet is settled
  On de dry groun' lak befo'
De Lawd said "Haid fo' Ninevah,"
  An' yo' orter see him go!

Den he cried. "De jedgment's comin'"
  'N' de people heahd 'im call,
An' repented ob de ebil,
  'N de Lawd fo give dem all.
        for His glory,
        by Shel Helsley

If Jesus Christ be God, and He died for me, then no sacrifice can be too great for me to make for Him.—C. T. Studd.

Peter's Song

He said He was praying for me,
Jesus of Galilee.
He could see up ahead
My sorrow and dread
And the heartaches I could not see
When He said He was praying for me.
Then they came to take Him
And I would gladly have died then;
What made me forsake Him?
What made me seek another place to hide then?

He said He was praying for me,
Jesus of Galilee.
Though I turned and fled
He did what He said
With a love I could not see
When He said He was praying for me.

He waited for me on the shore,
Jesus of Galilee.
In my sorrow and shame
He called me by name
And He seemed to love me the more
When He waited for me on the shore.
Though I had denied Him
And said I did not know Him,
There's none else beside Him
And I know somehow He really loves me.

He waited for me on the snore,
Jesus of Galilee.
From sorrow and shame
My love became
What it never had been before,
When He waited for me on the shore.

He waited for me by the fire,
Jesus of Galilee.
I was cold and afraid
But the fire that He made
Was more than I could desire
When He waited for me by the fire.
And I could remember
A fire I had been near,
And each glowing ember
Reminded me of all my doubt and fear.

He waited for me by the fire,
Jesus of Galilee.
The food that He fed,
The words that He said,
My poor heart did inspire,
When He waited for me by the fire.
—Bill Harvey

Sanctified Troublemaking

By Dr. Robert Shuler

Jesus said: "Think not that I am come to send peace on earth: I came not to send peace, but a sword" (Matt. 10:34).

The prophets were troublemakers. Moses made trouble in Egypt. David made trouble for Saul. Nathan made trouble for David when he said, "Thou art the man." Christ Himself was accused of making trouble.

The Church of today must be a troublemaker when it comes to the liquor business, to gambling, to impurity in social life, and to the almost numberless evils of our day.

The Church that is approved of God must be a troublemaker when it comes to worldliness and conformity to the cheapening and often morally depleting trends of our times.

The Church should make serious trouble for television, because of its immoral advertising. The Church of God should make trouble for social drinking and the injurious use of tobacco. The Church has a tremendous task of troublemaking in these days of abounding wickedness.

WAR ON WICKEDNESS

If some doubting reader should ask me where to begin our troublemaking as disciples of Jesus, I would answer that we should follow the example He set. We should make trouble for the scribes and Pharisees and hypocrites. We should make trouble for the blind guides and the wolves in sheep's clothing.

Indeed, the Church need not go outside itself to discover enough work to keep it busy throughout the present generation in sanctified troublemaking. There is enough atheism and infidelity and skepticism in our schoolrooms and even in our pulpits to keep any man of God occupied for a lifetime.

Luther made trouble for a corrupt, formal, apostate church. Wesley followed by making trouble for a church that had fallen prey to the world, the flesh, and the devil.

Evangelists like Moody, Sam Jones, Billy Sunday, and the young evangelists of our day made trouble and are making trouble for a Church that has lost its passion for souls and is content to serve tables and increase in goods!

SUCCESS, WHAT IS IT?

It is being able to carry money without spending it;
Being able to bear an injustice without retaliating;
Being able to do ones duty even when one is not watched;
Being able to keep on the job until it is finished;
Being able to accept criticism without letting it whip you.
—Selected

Just Five Minutes

Five minutes spent in the companionship of Christ every morning, Aye, two minutes, if it is face to face and heart to heart—will change the whole day, will make every thought and feeling different, will enable you to do things for His sake that you would not have done for your own sake or for another's sake.

—Henry Drummond.

DID YOU KNOW...

Jesus on Trial

In all, Jesus appears to have had seven distinct trials: the first before Annas; the second and third before Caiaphas; the fourth before Pilate; the fifth before Herod Antipas; and the sixth and seventh before Pilate. Never was there a man in this world, before or since, tried so often in so short a time, and yet, after all of His trials, condemned with so little pretense of justice. —F. D. Kershner

Prayer Track

In a certain West African village the native Christians had no privacy for prayer in their huts. So each Christian made off to the bush, behind his hut, for seasons of prayer. After a while there was a worn track from the hut to the place of prayer. Then if it ever happened that the track became overgrown from want of use, another Christian villager would admonish his neighbor, "Brother, there is something wrong with your prayer track."—Power.

Once when introducing Thomas A. Edison at a dinner, the toastmaster mentioned his many inventions, dwelling at length on the talking machine. The aged inventor then rose to his feet, smiled and said gently to his audience: "I thank the gentleman for his kind remarks, but I must insist upon a correction. God invented the talking machine. I only invented the first one that can be shut off."

It is not at all necessary for you to see any help in sight, nor is it really necessary for God to have any relief on hand. He does not need anything to begin on. In the beginning God created the heaven and the earth. What did He make them out of? Nothing, absolutely nothing! Trust Him and He will see you through.—Keswick Calendar

Any Excuse

One man says, "I do not go to church on Sundays because I was never taught to go when I was young, so I did not form the habit."

Another man says, "I do not go to church on Sundays because I was forced to go when I was young and it grew distasteful to me." One excuse is as good as another when you do not want to do a thing.

—*Religious Cyclopedia of Anecdotes*

I am often asked by doctors, "Aren't you sometimes sorry you left the practice of medicine and the healing of men's bodies—left a noble profession to become a despised preacher?" My answer is always *no!* All the patients I used to treat died sooner or later, but the people who take the medicine I now offer them (the Gospel) never die. The cure is permanent, and gives *eternal life*. The Gospel is God's panacea!

—Dr. M. R. DeHaan.

Alcohol is poison. It injures the brain cells, abnormally accelerates the heartbeat, helps destroy the blood vessels, and causes at least temporary loss of thinking faculties.

The first drink may bring laughter; later it will bring groans.

The expert examining the records of forty-two insurance companies concluded that the habitual drinker shortens his life by ten to twelve years.

"You can get along with a wooden leg, but you can't get along with a wooden head."

—Dr. Mayo

Lost or strayed (I hope not stolen) a few hundred of the Lord's sheep. Not seen for several weeks. Please return tomorrow morning—Sunday—to the green pastures of St. Mary's Church where a table will be prepared and the cup will be running over! No questions will be asked.—Put in Lost and Found section of a local paper by the Rev. Joseph Witkofski, rector of St. Mary's Episcopal Church, who reported, "Fine Results!"

Dr. W. T. Grenfell tells us in his autobiography that he was converted through D. L. Moody's common sense. Moody had asked a minister to lead in prayer at a great meeting. This good man began a long "oratorical effort." Young Grenfell was bored and seized his hat to escape, when Moody cried out, "Let us sing a hymn while our brother finishes his prayer." Grenfell was delighted at the remark. He remained and was won to Christ.

83 a Minute

At a certain mission church (says the Rev. W. W. Martin) I had put over the clock these words: "83 a minute." At last a deputation came to me and said, "Will you kindly take that down? It haunts us." They knew that it meant that eighty-three souls a minute were passing into eternity.

Don't Be Afraid of Failure

Babe Ruth struck out 1330 times, a record in futility unapproached by any other player in the history of baseball. But that isn't what we remember about Babe Ruth. His 714 home runs completely obliterate the 1330 strikeouts.

Even Names Are Significant

Nero lived covetously. History relates that he wore a crown valued at $500,000; he had his mules shod with silver; he fished with golden fishhooks; he traveled with one thousand carriages, and he never wore the same garment twice. Ruling Rome, he was dissatisfied, and is perhaps best known for his act of fiddling while the city burned. He died, and terminated an inglorious career.

Paul, beaten with many stripes, scarred by stones and rods, imprisoned and suffering loss of all earthly things, lived victoriously as Christ's steward. He enjoyed God's peace, was wondrously satisfied in Christ, and looked forward to eternal riches. Many dogs are named Nero; millions of aspiring sons are named Paul.

Evereybody's doing it! so they say,
Everybody's drinking in our day.
Everybody's starting, you'll start, too.
So they say—but it's not true!

Everybody's doing it? No, not yet.
For I'm somebody—don't forget.
Anyone with courage to step aside
    and think
Is sure to be somebody. I don't
    drink!

Many a "somebody" who fell into
    line
Became a "nobody" in almost no
    time.
Anyone can follow what the crowds
    do,
But I'm somebody. H o w about
    you?

Everybody's doing it? No, not yet.
For I'm somebody—don't forget.
Anyone with courage to see what's
    true
Is sure to be somebody. How a-
    bout you?

—*Indian Temperance News*

Take Your Choice:

If you want your father to take care of you, that's *Paternalism*.

If you want your mother to take care of you, that's *Maternalism*.

If you want Uncle Sam to take care of you, that's *Socialism*.

If you want your comrades to take care of you, that's *Communism*.

If you want to take care of yourself, that's *Americanism!*

SPEND NOW—PAY LATER. . . "It is too bad that future generations cannot be here at this time to see the 'wonderful things we are doing with their money."

—The Spendthrift.

HAVE YOU EVER HEARD . . .

Of a man who lost his job because he was a total abstainer?

Of an insurance company that offered reduced premiums to booze addicts?

Of a booze seller who was proud of his finished product, the drunkard?

Of a woman who said: "My husband would be the best husband in the world if only I could get him to start drinking"?

Of a chauffeur who could drive more safely if he had a "snort" of alcohol before starting?

Of a railway employee who stood better with the company if he patronized saloons?

Of parents who were pleased to have their daughter marry a "rummy"?

Of a community that was as proud of a groggery as of a grocery?

Of a murderer on the gallows saying: "If I had spent more time in the tavern I wouldn't be here"?
—W. E. Johnson, Quoted in The Bible Teacher.

TIME AND TIDE . . .

If a man had a bank that credited his account each morning with $86,400, that carried over no balance from day to day, allowed him to keep no cash in his account, and every evening cancelled out whatever part of that amount he failed to use during the day, what would he do?

Draw out every cent, of course! Well, every man does have such a bank and its name is *"time."* Every morning, it credits him with 86,400 seconds. Every night it rules as lost whatever of this he has failed to invest to good purpose! It carries over no balance and allows no overdrafts. If he fails to use the day's deposit, the loss is his. There is no going back, no drawing against tomorrow. So, invest your seconds wisely in an effort to bring forth fruit for the Lord's Kingdom. —Anonymous

---

Little minds are too much wounded by little things; great minds see all, and are not even hurt.— La Rochefoucauld

Be punctual. Some men won't be on time in eternity. As for myself, I never mean to be the LATE Mr. Spurgeon as long as I live.—Spurgeon.

Familiar With Sin?

"Vice is a master of such frightful mein,
    That to be hated needs but to be seen;
But seen too oft, familiar with its face,
    We first endure, then pity, then embrace!"
                                    —Pope

Men Who Stood Alone With God

Probably one of the main reasons why we like to be in the crowd is that we are not men of deep conviction. Occasionally we see an individual coming into a place where he is prepared to receive a broadside of criticism and abuse. That man is one who is held by power of convictions.

Men who have made a great mark for God in the world have generally been those who have had to stand alone. Many leaders had to stand alone with God during their entire lifetimes. Moses was a classic example of this. Few of his fellows understood him and he was often misunderstood and misjudged. His course was a lonely one, and at times he had to depend utterly on God for vindication because of the jealousy of his most immedate associates. Abraham was another who had to walk a lonely pathway if he was to become the father of the faithful. It is less difficult, somehow, if there are others to share an experience with us, but to walk alone is not easy.

Think of David and his lonely vigil with the Lord, awaiting the crowning day in the kingdom. Even though anointed by the Holy Spirit he had to flee from that jealous monster Saul. Who could be more alone with God than Jeremiah, who had to endure the utmost rigors of suffering and persecution in order to be faithful to the commission given him from on high? The names of these men are famous to us now, but at the time the persecution was no romantic experience for them. What romance was there in the prison of Pharaoh where Joseph was held? He could have sympathized with himself, that he was the most oppressed man in creation, but he didn't; he stood in that trying situation as a true witness—*alone with God.* He knew that God understood and was with him. That was enough.

Luther, in the dawning of a new age of Gospel light, had to tread this pathway, and so did Wesley, in the midst of a dead Christianity. Had they not been prepared to stand alone with God they would never have seen the great movements that came as the result of their witness. George Muller has left a great testimony to the world as to what God can do through the man who fully trusts Him, but his was a life that no other man could share fully with him. He had to stand in the sanctuary alone with God. We could continue the list of worthy souls. Livingstone was alone with God in Africa, Hudson Taylor likewise in China, and Judson in Burma. Had these men not gone through this experience there would have been no record to thrill us today.

Perhaps the loneliest man who ever walked this earth was the Lord Jesus Himself. His was not a temporary loneliness. He had to go to death and on the Cross to endure an experience that none of us will ever be called on to undergo, for He was cut off from God His Father.

Do we seek the pathway of greatness? This, then, may be the price we shall have to pay. We shall have to be men with a mission: with great convictions; we shall have to be men who at times may have to stand alone, utterly alone, with God. In this way we shall be led to know Him in a mighty way, and there will be fruitage beyond all expectations.— Gordon Junk.

THE GREAT NEED OF THE HOLY SPIRIT

If we do not have the Spirit of God, it were better to shut the churches, nail up the doors, to put a black cross on them, and say, "God have mercy on us!" If you ministers have not the Spirit of God, you had better not preach, and you people had better stay at home. I think I speak not too strongly when I say that a church in the land without the Spirit of God is rather a curse than a blessing. If you have not the Spirit of God, Christian worker, remember that you stand in somebody else's way; you are as a tree bearing no fruit standing where another fruitful tree might grow. This is solemn work; the Holy Spirit or nothing, and worse than nothing. Death and condemnation to a church that is not yearning after the Spirit, and crying and groaning until the Spirit has wrought mightily in her midst. He is here; He has never gone back since He descended at Pentecost. He is often grieved and vexed, for He is peculiarly jealous and sensitive, and the one sin never forgiven has to do with His blessed person; therefore let us be very tender towards Him, walk humbly before Him, wait on Him very earnestly, and resolve that there should be nothing knowingly continued which should prevent Him dwelling in us, and being with us henceforth and forever. Brethren, peace be unto you and your spirit!

CHARLES SPURGEON

No Time to Complain

On one occasion when young in experience I had written my preacher-father telling him of my troubles and feeling sorry for myself. His reply was something like this:

"Son, by the time you take childhood off one end of your life and old age off the other end, you don't have much time for doing good. Make the best of your time."

That was a gentle yet impressive rebuke I have never forgotten. You don't have time to complain and find fault.—Arthur Ely.

An imaginary story illustrates a heart-searching truth: A millionaire stood at Heaven's gate, waiting to be shown his heavenly home. He was conducted to a small cottage, located in the midst of other tiny, unpretentious homes. He complained, "Can it be that I, who have lived in a palace on earth amidst scenes of luxury and comfort, must now dwell eternally in this small abode?" Replied the conductor, "We built this house out of the material you sent to us while you were on earth. We could have built a palace for you if you had sent us the material with which to build it!"

The Scoffer's Text

In the days of Whitefield, a man named Thorpe, one of his most violent opponents and three others, laid a wager as to who could best imitate and ridicule Whitefield's preaching.

Each man was to open the Bible at random and preach a sermon from the first verse that presented itself. Thorpe's three competitors each went through the game with impious buffoonery.

Then, stepping upon the table, Thorpe exclaimed, "I shall beat you all." They gave him a Bible and, by God's inscrutable providence, his eyes fell first upon this verse:

"Except ye repent, ye shall all likewise perish."—Luke 13:3.

He read the words, but the Sword of the Spirit went through his soul in a moment, and he preached as one who scarce knew what he said.

The hand of God laid hold upon him, and, intending to mock, he could only fear and tremble.

When he descended from the table, a profound silence reigned in the company, and not one word was said about the wager.

Thorpe instantly withdrew, and after a season of the deepest distress, passed into the full light of the Gospel, and became a preacher of the grace of God, that had met him, a sinner in his sins, on the way to Hell, which he felt he richly deserved, and had revealed to him a Saviour, whose blood could cleanse him, and make him fit for the very glory of God.

His message was that the work of Christ was so perfect and complete that the vilest sinner might be saved, who came to Him in repentance and faith.

Remember his text. It is true for you.

"Except ye repent, ye shall all likewise perish."

—from THE BAPTIST ECHO

Do a deed of simple kindness;
Though its end you may not see,
It may reach, like widening ripples,
Down a long eternity.
—Joseph Morris

The Law of Harvest

A man rocked a boat to see if it would tip. It did!

O laborer stepped on a nail to see if it would go through his shoe. It did!

A man looked into the gun to see if it was loaded. It was!

A woman looked into a patent medicine booklet to see if she was sick. She was!

Last June a helper smelled escaping gas and lit a piece of oily waste to find the leak. He found it!

A young girl kept late hours to see if it would really injure her office work. And it did!

A young man tried drinking to see if it would make him act like a fool. It did!

God's Word says, "Whatsoever a man soweth that shall he also reap." You cannot afford to play with sin. If you do, you will reap the terrible results.

—Copied.

Inescapable Date

We celebrate Christ's birth by referring to it in the date placed on our coins, birth certificates, and death certificates. All our records bear that wonderful date. It is inscribed upon metal and written upon parchment and engraved on the cornerstones of great buildings. It is on every newspaper, every cheque, every deed, and it is universally acknowledged as the beginning of a new life.

Every human transaction is related to the birth of Christ. It cannot be avoided or evaded. God has seen to it that this event is more widely advertised than anything on earth that is or that ever has been. He came to save men. He came to defeat Satan. He came to reveal God. Hallelujah, what a Saviour!

—Dr. Walter Wilson

Resurrection

If the Father deigns to touch with divine power the cold and pulseless heart of the buried acorn and to make it burst from its prison walls, will He leave neglected in the earth the . . . man made in the image of his Creator? If matter, mute and inanimate, though changed by the forces of nature into a multitude of forms can never die, will the spirit of man suffer annihilation when it has paid a brief visit like a royal guest to this tenement of clay? No, I am as sure that there is another life as I am that I live today!"—William Jennings Bryan.

Spurgeon's Funeral

At Spurgeon's funeral, Pastor A. G. Brown said—

"Beloved President, faithful Pastor, Prince of Preachers, Brother Beloved, Dear Spurgeon — We bid thee not 'farewell,' but only for a little while 'good-night.' Thou shalt rise soon, at the first dawn of the resurrection day of the redeemed. Yet is not the 'good-night' ours to bid, but thine. It is we who linger in the darkness; thou art in God's own light. Our night, too, shall soon be past, and with it all our weeping. Then, with thine, our songs shall greet the morning of a day that knows no cloud nor close, for there is no night there.

"Hard Worker in the field, thy toil is ended! Straight has been the furrow thou hast ploughed. No looking back has marred thy course. Harvests have followed thy patient sowing, and Heaven is already rich with thine ingathered sheaves, and shall be still enriched through years yet lying in eternity.

"Champion of God, thy battle long and nobly fought is over! The sword, which clave to thine hand, has dropped at last; the palm branch takes its place. No longer does the helmet press thy brow, oft weary with its surging thoughts of battle; the victor's wreath from the Great Commander's hand has already proved thy full reward.

"Here, for a little while, shall rest thy precious dust. Then shall the Well-beloved come, and at His voice thou shalt spring from thy couch of earth, fashioned like unto His glorious body. Then spirit, soul, and body shall magnify thy Lord's redemption. Until then, beloved sleep! We praise God *for* thee; and, by the blood of the everlasting covenant, we hope and expect to praise God *with* thee. Amen."

Keep on Praying

Just keep on praying "Till light breaks through!"
The Lord will answer, will answer you,
God keeps His promise, His Word is true—
Just keep on praying "Till light breaks through!"

Mary Had a Little Boy

Mary had a little boy, His soul seemed white as snow, He never went to Sunday School 'Cause Mary wouldn't go. He never heard the stories of Christ That thrill the childish mind. While other children went to class, This child was left behind. And as he grew from babe to youth, She saw to her dismay; The soul that once seemed snowy white Became a dingy gray. Realizing he was lost She tried to win him back, But now the soul that once seemed white Had turned an ugly black. She even started back to church, And Sunday School too! She begged the preacher, "Isn't there A thing that we can do?" The preacher tried, and failed and said, "We're just too far behind, I tried to tell you years ago, But you would pay no mind." And so, another soul Is lost, That once seemed white as snow. Sunday School would have helped . . . But Mary wouldn't go!—Blue Print.

That Boy Was Dwight L. Moody!

A man stepped up to us one day at the close of a meeting, and said, "I want to tell you a story. Years ago I was teaching a class of boys in a certain city. There were eight boys in the class. It was in the days before the lesson helps were so plentiful as now, and we were confined to the use of the Bible alone. There was but one Bible for the whole class. This was passed from hand to hand in due order. I noticed especially how the second boy in the class acted when the book reached him in turn. He fumbled at the leaves. He hesitated and halted at words of but ordinary difficulty. The big words he skipped entirely. Yet he was most faithful and persistent in it all. My brother," said the speaker, "that boy was Dwight L. Moody."

—James McConkey

Abraham Separates From Lot

"Let there be no strife, I pray thee, between me and thee, and between my herdmen; and thy herdmen; for we be brethren." This is what Abraham said to Lot when a strife had developed between Abraham's herdmen and Lot's herdmen. In this connection God's Word said, "and the Canaanite and the Perizzite dwelled then in the land." Abraham and Lot represented the true God in the land. Any strife in their families or family connections reflected on their testimony. God had chosen Abraham to be the father of a nation—a nation that would be a repository for the truth of the one God and a nation through whose loins the Messiah was to come. It was the responsibility of Abraham to maintain the testimony. He must do it regardless of the cost. Nothing is to interfere with the witness the man of God is supposed to give. So Abraham said, "Lot, separate yourself from me." Abraham was human and like all other men he sinned along life's way. But he stood the test in this hour of crisis. He was true to his responsibility.—Bob Jones, Sr.

Fatherhood

One dad to another: "I'm no model father. All I'm trying to do is behave so that when people tell my son that he reminds them of me, he'll stick out his chest instead of his tongue."—Manchester Oak Leaves.

How few there are who have courage enough to own their faults, or resolution enough to mend them!

—*Benjamin Franklin*

Effects of Enthusiasm

One thing I admire about Garibaldi—his enthusiasm. In 1867, when he went on his way to Rome, he was told that if he got there he would be imprisoned. Said he, "If fifty Garibaldis are imprisoned, let Rome be free!" And when the cause of Christ is buried so deep in our hearts that we do not think of ourselves and are willing to die, then we will reach our fellowmen.

Five years ago I went to Edinburgh, and stopped a week to hear one man speak—Dr. Duff, the returned missionary. A friend told me a few things about him, and I went to light my torch with his burning words. My friend said that the year before he had spoken for some time, and had fainted in the midst of his speech. When he recovered he said, "I was speaking for India, was I not?" And they said he was. "Take me back, that I may finish my speech." And notwithstanding the entreaties of those around, he insisted on returning; and they brought him back. He then said, "Is it true that we have been sending appeal after appeal for young men to go to India, and none of our sons have gone? Is it true, Mr. Moderator, that Scotland has no more sons to give to the Lord Jesus? If true, although I have spent twenty-five years there, and lost my constitution—if it is true that Scotland has no more sons to give, I will be off tomorrow, and go to the shores of the Ganges, and there be a witness for Christ."—Moody

A Mother's Love

By D. L. Moody

The closest tie on earth is a mother's love for her child. There are a good many things that will separate a man from his wife, but there isn't a thing in the wide, wide world that will separate a true mother from her own child. I will admit that there are unnatural mothers, that there are mothers who have gone out of their heads, mothers who are so steeped in sin and iniquity that they will turn against their own children, but a true mother will never, never turn against her own child. I have talked with mothers when my blood boiled with indignation against the sons for their treatment of their mothers, and I have said, "Why don't you cast him off?"

They have said, "Why, Mr. Moody, I love him still. He is my son."

I was once preaching for Dr. G. in St. Louis, and when I got through he said that he wanted to tell me a story. There was a boy who was very bad. He had a very bad father, who seemed to take delight in teaching his son everything that was bad. The father died, and the boy went on from bad to worse until he was arrested for murder.

When he was on trial, it came out that he had murdered five other people, and from one end of the city to the other there was a universal cry going up against him. During his trial they had to guard the court-house, the indignation was so intense.

The white-haired mother got just as near her son as she could, and every witness that went into the court and said anything against him seemed to hurt her more than her son. When the jury brought in a verdict of guilty a great shout went up, but the old mother nearly fainted away; and when the judge pronounced the sentence of death they thought she would faint away.

After it was over she threw her arms around him and kissed him, and there in the court they had to tear him from her embrace. She then went the length and breadth of the city trying to get men to sign a petition for his pardon. And when he was hanged, she begged the governor to let her have the body of her son, that she might bury it. They say that death has torn down everything in this world, everything but a mother's love. That is stronger than death itself. The governor refused to let her have the body, but she cherished the memory of that boy as long as she lived.

A few months later she followed her boy, and when she was dying she sent word to the governor, and begged that her body might be laid close to her son. That is a mother's love! She wasn't ashamed to have her grave pointed out for all time as the grave of the mother of the most noted criminal the State of Vermont ever had.

The prophet takes hold of that very idea. He says, "Can a mother forget her child?" But a mother's love is not to be compared to the love of God.

Raising Billie

Papa said, "Now Billie, don't"
But Billie said, "I will," and did;
And Papa went to get the rod,
But Mama said, "Don't beat the kid."
So Papa laid aside the rod
While Billie smiled at "poor old Dad,"
And Mama stroked "dear Billie's" head
And called him her poor little lad.

The years have passed and Bill is gone—
Buried in a sinner's grave
While Mom and Dad still linger on,
So sad they let him misbehave.
The lesson's clear for all to see:
If you would raise a son for God,
Father and Mother must agree
When Billie needs it, use the rod!

—R. H. Burrows

In the dogmas of modern thought there is not enough mental meat to bait a mousetrap, as to food for a soul, there is none of it, an ant would starve on such small grain. No atonement, as regeneration, as eternal love, no covenant, what is there worth thinking upon?—Spurgeon.

To forget to praise God is to refuse to benefit ourselves; for praise, like prayer, is one great means of promoting the growth of the spiritual life. It helps to remove our burdens, to excite our hope, to increase our faith.

—Spurgeon

THE QUESTION IS

It is not so much *where* you live,
As *how*, and *why*, and *when* you
live
That answers in the affirmative,
Or maybe in the negative,
The question—Are you fit to live?
It is not so much *where* you live,
As *how* you live, and whether good
Flows from you through your
neighborhood.
And *why* you live, and whether
you
Aim high and noblest ends pursue,
And keep life brimming full and
true
And *when* you live, and whether
time
Is at its nadir or its prime,
And whether you descend or climb.
It is not so much *where* you live,
As whether while you live you *live*
And to the world your highest give,
And so make answer positive
That you are truly fit to live.
                        —John Oxenham

THE LITTLE STICK

A little stick
That you can't kick
Has got you, line and sinker.
You "gotta smoke"
And, that's no joke.
Admit it! You're a stinker.

A nose of bone,
A taste of stone,
A heart that pleads for air,
A throat that's sore
But pleads for more
Old nicotine down there.

A burned-out lung,
A dark-brown tongue,
An ash-tray kind of breath;
A coat that stinks,
A soul that shrinks,
An early kind of death.

If you won't pet
That cigarette,
But give up ev'rything,
You're sure to quit
Without a fit
If you let Christ be King.
                        Bill Harvey

A good character is the best tombstone. Those who loved you and were helped by you will remember you when forget-me-nots are withered. Carve your name on hearts and not on marble.—Charles H. Spurgeon.

His Sobering Choice

"As I entered the office of a well-known merchant," said an American writer, "a thrilling temperance lecture confronted me—a placard nailed to the desk."

WHICH?
Wife or Whiskey
The Babes or the Bottles
HEAVEN OR HELL

"The merchant explained, 'I wrote that myself. Sometime ago I found myself falling into the habit of drinking —an occasional glass with a friend. Soon my stomach got bad, my faculties became dulled, and constant craving for stimulants dominated me. I saw tears in my wife's eyes and wonder on the faces of my children. One day I sat down and wrote that card. On surveying it carefully, its awful revelation burst on me like a flash. I nailed it there and read it many times that day. I went home sober that night, and have not touched a drop since.'"
                        —From The Ideal Christian Home
                        by Helen S. Dyer

He that does good, for good's sake, seeks neither praise nor reward; though sure of both at last.—Wm. Penn

Why Is It Necessary to Shoot a Horse When It Breaks Its Leg?

Because a horse is such a poor patient. "He won't be immobilized and he'll constantly bang a cast, or fight a sling, and will just not be calm enough for the broken leg ever to heal. On the other hand, a dog with a broken leg has enough sense and patience to hold it up; but a horse will put his entire weight on it, and it is just impossible to treat it successfully."

"Be not as the horse, or as the mule, which have no understanding" (Ps. 32:9).

Happy is the person who learns to *yield* to God in the time of trials and troubles. He who maintains a rebellious spirit does so to his own destruction; but he does well who submits to God's providence and says, "My Father never makes a mistake: all things that He permits will work out for His glory and my good (Rom. 8:28)—so I will be faithful, praise the Lord, in the midst of my troubles, and 'glory in my tribulations'" (Rom. 5:3). Like Job, he who submits and trusts in the day of trouble will be greatly blessed "in the latter end." (See Job 42:12).

(From *Christian Victory*)

Scruples of Conscience

In Pennsylvania, America, there is a woman who won't allow her children to play with doll-babies. She says it is so much like worshiping graven images. But there was a still more remarkable case of conscientiousness than that in Boston, where a man stole a horse on Saturday night, and on Monday morning the police found him very near where he had stolen the horse on Saturday night, and they said, "How is it you did not get away yesterday? You had all day on Sunday to get away, and have not done it." The man replied, "Oh, I must let you understand that I have conscientious scruples about traveling on Sunday."—Talmage.

In Everything

In everything? In sorrow, pain, and loss?
When some hard lesson racks the weary mind?
When, just before, there looms the threat'ning cross?
When nights are long, and morn brings day unkind?

In everything! Each sorrow and each pain
Is known by One who measures every day;
And lessons hard, well mastered, will make plain
The faithful Teacher planning all the way.

Dost know the cross must come before the crown?
And seed unburied must abide alone?
Dost know the cloud that spreads its sullen frown
Harms not the sun, whose power must be shown?

Then waiting not for that which shall make clear
The tender love in what seems harsh and stern,
O Soul redeemed, look up! Dismiss thy fear!
Now is the time when thanks thou shouldst return!

Author Unknown

From **Inspirational and Devotional Verse**
Compiled by Dr. Bob Jones, Jr.

Henry Grady On Drink

Henry Grady, famed orator and journalist of half a century ago, gave one of the greatest speeches of his brilliant career in opposition to the reopening of the saloons in his home city, Atlanta, Georgia. See how his words fit our situation today:

"My friends, hesitate before you vote liquor back . . . now that it is shut out. Don't trust it. It is powerful, aggressive, and universal in its attacks. Tonight it enters an humble home to strike the roses from a woman's cheeks, and tomorrow it challenges this republic in the halls of Congress.

"Today it strikes the crust from the lips of a starving child, and tomorrow levies tribute from the government itself. There is no cottage humble enough to escape it —no place strong enough to shut it out . . .

"It is the moral enemy of peace and order. The despoiler of men, the terror of women, the cloud that shadows the faces of children, the demon that has dug more graves and sent more souls unshriven to judgment than all the pestilences that have wasted life since God sent the plagues to Egypt, and all the wars since Joshua stood before Jericho . . . .

"No interest can profit by its return. It can uplift no industry, revive no interests, remedy no wrong . . . It comes to destroy, and it shall profit mainly by the ruin of your sons and mine. It comes to mislead human souls and crush human hearts under its rumbling wheels.

"It comes to bring gray-haired mothers down in sorrow to their graves. It comes to turn the wife's love into despair, and her pride into shame. It comes to still the laughter on the lips of little children and to stifle all the music of the home and fill it with silence and desolation. It comes to ruin your body and mind, to wreck your home."

A wealthy man watched a missionary nurse attending to lepers in China. He said to her, "I wouldn't do that for a million." And the nurse quietly replied: "Neither would I. But I do it gladly for the love of God."

Dig the well before you are thirsty.—Chinese.

When God Makes the Bed!

Those who are ill can get strength and comfort from this passage in Psalm 41:3: "The Lord will strengthen him upon the bed of languishing: thou wilt make all his bed in his sickness." The Hebrew indicates, "Thou turnest, or changest his bed in his sickness."

This is most wonderful! God takes a personal interest in His sick saints! He whispers words of comfort to them, and in many ways, makes their "bed" of suffering—whereon they are languishing—easier to lie on. He not only eases the pain, but He assures His children who are enduring affliction that their "light affliction, which is but for a moment, **worketh** for them a far more exceeding and eternal weight of glory." (2 Cor. 4:17). Be encouraged, dear suffering saint, your affliction, if faithfully endured, for His glory, is actually working for you—piling up GLORY!

To get the needed strength, day by day, in the time of testing, it is necessary that we "look **not** at the things which are seen, but at the things which are not seen: for the things which are seen are temporal: but the things which are not seen are eternal." (2 Cor. 4:18).

If we suffer, we shall also reign with him.—2 Tim. 2:12

Does your bitter load of grief,
Tears and pain,
Seem too great for you to bear?
Don't complain;
You are only being made
Fit to reign.

Fit to reign with Christ our Lord;
Destiny
Far beyond imagining!
How could He
Ever use as potentates
You and me?

Surely we are all unfit,
All untaught,
And of wise and kingly lore
Knowing naught.
All the gold of Ophir could
Not have bought.

Private lessons from a King!
Precious pain,
Used of God to teach His child
How to reign! . . .
Taught by very God Himself,—
And we complain!
—*Martha Snell Nicholson*

A Teaser of Curiosity

A teaser of curiosity as well as an incentive to Bible reading was an old seventy-year-old tract—faded, time-yellowed, and broken at the edges—which was shown to me the other day. Here it is. Read it and see if you can resist the impulse to look up the references:

"Dear Reader:

"I once resided with II Timothy 3:4 and walked in Ephesians 2:2, and my continued conversation at that time is still recorded in Ephesians 2:3.

"I heard one day that an inheritance had been purchased for me, and a description of it reached me; you will find it at I Peter 1:4. One who resides in Hebrew 4:14 had purchased it and paid an extraordinary price for it; but, to say the truth, I did not believe this report, as I was entirely unacquainted with the man, and long experience had convinced me that strangers never gave favors through love alone, and friends seldom gave any favors that cost much.

"However, I called at I Timothy 3:16, as my own prospects at Ephesians 2:12 were as bad as they could be. I found the house I sought for at II Corinthians 4:1, and the invitations to it, which you will see put up at Isaiah 55:1 and by John at 7:37, are wonderfully inviting to the poor and needy. The house has only one door, and it was some time before I saw the door at John 10:9.

"My permanent address will be Galatians 5:1, but call any day at Hebrews 4:16; you will meet me and many others—we are daily in the habit of meeting there. If you call, attend to what the servant says at Luke 14:22, and you may depend upon what that servant says."

You know the old story of the boy and the echo. The boy, living on the edge of the woods, heard the echo of his voice and he cried out,

"Halloa there!"

The answer came, "Halloa there!"

"You are a bad boy!"

"You are a bad boy!"

"Come here, and I'll whip you!"

"Come here, and I'll whip you!"

"I am coming!"

"I am coming!"

The little fellow ran into the house and said, "Mother, there is a bad boy out in the woods, and he is going to whip me."

The wise mother said, "No, I don't think he is a bad boy; you didn't talk to him well. If you had spoken to him kindly, I think he would have spoken to you kindly. Go out and try it again."

So the boy went out.

"Halloa!"

"Halloa!"

"You are a good boy!"

"You are a good boy!"

"I love you!"

"I love you!"

He came running into the house and said, "Mother, that is a good boy, after all."

Life is largely an echo. If we go through the world with love in our hearts, we will make people love us; and love is one badge Christ gave His disciples.

Occupation Unchanged

An infidel was introduced by a gentleman to a minister with a remark, "He never attends public worship." "Ah!" said the minister, "I hope you are mistaken." "By no means," said the stranger; "I always spend Sunday in settling my accounts." "Then, alas," was the calm but solemn reply, "you will find, sir, that the day of judgment will be spent in the same manner."

—*Spurgeon's Sermon Notes*

Moody's Look at Death

One day, realizing that he would soon be done with this world, Moody said to a friend, "Someday you will read in the papers that D. L. Moody of Northfield is dead. Don't you believe a word of it. At that moment I shall be more alive than I am now. I shall have gone higher, that is all—out of this old clay tenement into a house that is immortal, a body that sin cannot touch, that sin cannot taint, a body fashioned into His glorious body. I was born in the flesh in 1837; I was born of the Spirit in 1856. That which is born of the flesh may die; that which is born of the Spirit will live forever."

ICELAND'S REAL FREEDOM

Iceland, about half the size of Missouri, has no jail, no penitentiary; there is no court, and only one policeman. Not a drop of alcoholic liquor is made on the island, and its people are total abstainers, since they will not permit any liquor to be imported. There is not an illiterate person on the island, not a child ten years old unable to read, the system of public schools being practically perfect.

—Sunday School Times

A man who wants to lead the orchestra must turn his back on the crowd.

A man can never be a true gentleman in manner until he is a true gentleman at heart.—Dickens.

EVER NEAR

There is an EYE that never sleeps
　Beneath the wing of night;
There is an EAR that never shuts
　When sink the beams of light.

There is an ARM that never tires
　When human strength gives way;
There is a LOVE that never fails
　When earthly loves decay.

That EYE unseen watcheth o'er all;
　That ARM upholds the sky;
That EAR doth hear the sparrow's call;
　That LOVE is ever nigh.

—Author Unknown

HER SPIRIT

Fanny Crosby lost her sight when a little girl, but she was not discouraged. Out of her tribulation came scores of the sweetest songs of the Church. Although she has long ago passed to her reward, her spirit goes marching on. In her blindness she wrote this note of cheer to the discouraged:

Oh, what a happy soul am I!
　Although I cannot see,
I am resolved that in this world
　Contented I will be;
How many blessings I enjoy
　That other people don't!
To weep and sigh because I'm blind
　I cannot, and I won't!

Indispensable Christians

"He is impossible to get along with, because he thinks he's impossible to get along without," was said of a Sunday School worker. No wonder the result was a dismal failure for the would-be indispensable. The worst idea a Christian can have is that he is absolutely necessary to the work in which he is engaged, that his absence would stop the whole undertaking.

—*Sunday at Home*

What the country needs is dirtier fingernails and cleaner minds.　Will Rogers

It is easier and better to build boys than to repair men.

I would I were beside the sea,
　Or sailing in a boat,
With all the things I've got
　to write—
　　wrote.

I would I were away from town
　As far as I could get,
With all the bills, I've got to meet—
　met.

I would I were out on a farm,
　A-basking in the sun,
With all the things I've got
　to do—
　done.

Author Unknown

Southern Loyalty!

A man from the deep South was about to jump from the window of a building, when a passer-by saw him and tried to talk him out of it. "For the sake of your mother, don't do it!" the passer-by pleaded.

"I don't have a mother," the would-be suicide said hopelessly.

"Well, think of your father."

"I don't have a father," the despondent man replied.

"Well, think of your wife!" the passer-by persisted.

"I never married," the dejected fellow said.

"Well then, think of Robert E. Lee!"

"Robert E. Lee! Who's he?"

"Never mind, Yankee. Go ahead and jump."

SEVEN BLESSINGS FROM GOD'S PRESENCE

1. Above you—to guard (Deut. 4:39).
2. Underneath — to support (Deut. 33:27).
3. Behind as a reward (Isa. 52:12).
4. Before—to lead (Isa. 45:2).
5. At your right hand—to protect (Ps. 16:8; 110:5).
6. Round about—to shield (Ps. 125:2).
7. Within — as Companion and Comforter (Ezek. 36:27; Gal. 2:20).

Dr. Bob Jones Says: "It is all right for charity to begin at home; but if it is the right kind of charity, it will call on the neighbors once in a while."

COME! Just as You Are

By Oliver G. Wilson

"JUST AS I AM, WITHOUT ONE
 PLEA,
BUT THAT THY BLOOD WAS SHED
 FOR ME,
AND THAT THOU BIDST ME COME
 TO THEE,
O LAMB OF GOD, I COME, I
 COME."

A tourist's handbook and guide book carried the advertisements of hotels and motels. After describing the advantages of the particular hotel or motel, in easy readable type were the words: "Come in just as you are." That's the Gospel message.

If the wear and tear of daily living tends to get you down; if everybody, including yourself, gets on your nerves; if you are just plain bored and don't know what to do about it, the invitation is "Come as you are."

To those who are bowed down under the weight of a great guilt, tormented by an accusing conscience and shunned by those who stand on their own self-righteousness, come to Jesus as you are.

To those who are frustrated, from whom hope has fled, and who feel that life is a farce, the invitation is "Come as you are."

This is an aspirin age—a day of being half alive. At least, that's the way we act--as if "What we don't feel won't hurt us; what we don't like, put off until tomorrow. Then tomorrow, the real facing of our difficulties, and we sigh for the help of the "Lone Ranger" or "Super Man." The farther we go down that road the more frustrations we meet.

Come to the Lord Jesus Christ. The invitation is given to every weary individual. In every conceivable form of assurance God has called sinners to partake of His salvation. Yet some poor, sinbound, mind-darkened sinner goes on in despair. Christ is the Day Star, the Light of Life, the Water of Life, the Bread of Life, the Hope of a despairing heart. The Spirit of God whispers to the depths of every heart, "Come." The Church, in all her divinely appointed ordinances, cries, "Come." Every believer in the highways and hedges is authorized to say, "Come."

You are invited. Come in just as you are. By delaying you do not ready yourself; by your self-efforts you sink deeper into the mire of sin and shame.

"God has promised forgiveness to your repentance; but He has not promised tomorrow to your procrastination."—St. Augustine.

Come penitently, come believingly, and accept this invitation from the heart of Infinite Love to come to the storehouse of His exhaustless wealth. Your guilt will be removed; your hope will be restored; new life will course through your soul. Come, just as you are; and come now.

—Wesleyan Methodist.

Only One Took an Umbrella

The writer's grandfather, John W. Knight, was a Methodist circuit rider. Before his conversion, he was a notorious, blatant atheist. When God saved him his life was totally changed. It is said that, wherever he went, a revival of "the old-time religion" broke out. Bishop Pierce, in his biography of "Uncle Knight," tells some interesting stories of him. The following incident shows the old circuit rider's faith. A destroying drought had cast its sear mantle over the countryside. Crops were withering and lying in the parched fields. "Uncle Knight" and others wended their way to the little Crawford Church in Putnam County, Georgia, to pray for rain. "Uncle Knight," however, was the *only* one who took an umbrella with him to the prayer meeting. On bended knees the old man began to pray as follows: "O Lord, we need rain. O, Lord, we need much rain. O, Lord, we don't want any drizzly-drazzly rain. We want a gully-washer!" God, as He always does, honored the simple faith of the old circuit rider, and the people soon knew the answer to the ancient question. "Where is the Lord God of Elijah?"—W. B. K.

He Answers Prayer

I believe God answers prayer,
Answers always, everywhere;
I may cast my anxious care,
Burdens I could never bear,
On the God who heareth prayer.
Never need my soul despair
Since He bids me boldly dare
To the secret place repair,
There to prove He answers prayer.

Influence of Books

Benjamin Franklin said that the reading of "Cotton Mather's Essay on Doing Good" moulded his entire life. The assassin of Lord Russell declared that he was led into crime by reading one vicious romance. The consecrated John Ankell James — England never produced a better man—declared in his old days that he had never yet got over the evil effects of having for fifteen minutes once read a bad book. But I need not go so far off. I could come nearer home and tell you of something that occurred in my college days. I could tell you of a comrade who was great-hearted, noble, and generous. He was studying for an honorable profession, but he had an infidel book in his trunk, and he said to me one day, "De Witt, would you like to read it?" I said, "Yes, I would." I took the book and read it only for a few minutes. I was really startled with what I saw there, and I handed the book back to him, and said, "You had better destroy that book." No, he kept it. He read it. He reread it. After a while he gave up religion as a myth.—Talmage.

The best thing to give to your enemy is forgiveness; to an opponent, tolerance; to a friend, your heart; to your child, a good example; to a father, deference; to your mother, conduct that will make her proud of you; to yourself, respect; to all men, charity.
—Lord Balfour

The Other Little Ships

By Bill Harvey

I had a Hardship, but I didn't mind. For sailing that Hardship was a Captain so Kind. He's the Lordship of Hardship and He shall prevail; He is guiding this Hardship He wants me to sail.

Discipleship sails when the billows roll high, So steady the Pilot with His watchful eye. Such fellowship constant I have with my guide, Through peril and terror and treacherous tide.

Sailing with others is Friendship so strong, 'Tis never unfailing when Christ is along. The clouds may well threaten my craft to drown, But, beyond the dark clouds there is waiting a crown!

In Christ we have a love that can never be fathomed; a life that can never die; a righteousness that can never be tarnished; a peace that can never be understood; a rest that can never be disturbed; a joy that can never be diminished; a hope that can never be disappointed; a glory that can never be clouded; a light that can never be darkened; a happiness that can never be interrupted; a strength that can never be enfeebled; a purity that can never be defiled; a beauty that can never be marred; a wisdom that can never be baffled; resources that can never be exhausted.

The ability of God is beyond our prayers, beyond our largest prayers. I have been thinking of some of the petitions that have entered into my supplication innumerable times. What have I asked for? I have asked for a cupful, and the ocean remains! I have asked for a sunbeam, and the sun abides! My best asking falls immeasurably short of my Father's giving. It is beyond that we can ask.—J. H. Jowett.

'Twill Not Be Long

"'Twill not be long our journey here,
Each broken sigh and falling tear
Will soon be gone, and all will be
A cloudless sky, a waveless sea.

Though sad we mark the closing eye
Of those we loved in days gone by,
Yet sweet in death their latest song . . .
"We'll meet again; 'twill not be long!"

Roll on, dark stream,
We dread not thy foam;
The pilgrim is longing
For home . . . sweet home!
—Fanny J. Crosby

A Baby--

That which makes the home happier,
Love stronger,
Patience greater,
Hands busier,
Nights longer,
Days shorter,
Purses lighter
Clothes shabbier,
The past forgotten,
The future brighter.

—Marion Lawrence

WHO SAID THIS?

You cannot bring about prosperity by discouraging thrift. You cannot strengthen the weak by weakening the strong. You cannot help the wage earner by pulling down the wage payer. You cannot keep out of trouble by spending more than you earn. You cannot build character and courage by taking away man's initiative and independence. You cannot help men permanently by doing for them what they could and should do for themselves. (Abraham Lincoln)

A new convert expressed the confidence he had in Christ, "I feel much better now when I feel badly than I used to feel when I felt good."

Don't be squeamish in the pulpit, like one who read, "Jonah was three days and three nights in-- ahem--the society of the fish."
--Spurgeon

It's easy to make a mountain out of a molehill—just add a little more dirt. Anon.

I am standing on the promises, walking in His footprints, leaning on His everlasting arms and drinking from the fountain that never runs dry.
—Bud Robinson

Prayer does not need proof; it needs practice.

The Submissive Dog and Spurgeon

Preachers, this is primarily for you. The prince of preachers, Dr. Charles H. Spurgeon, had this to say about sermon illustrations.

"If you keep your eyes open, you will not see even a dog following his master, nor a mouse peeping up from his hole, nor will you hear even a gentle scratching behind the wainscot, without getting something to weave into your sermons if your faculties are all on the alert. When you go home tonight, and sit by your fireside, you ought not to be able to take up your domestic cat without finding that which will furnish you with an illustration. How soft are pussy's pads, and yet, in a moment, if she is angered, how sharp will be her claws! How like to temptation, soft and gentle when it first cometh to us, but how deadly, how damnable the wounds it causeth ere long!

"I recollect using, with very considerable effect in a sermon in the Tabernacle, an incident that occurred in my own garden. There was a dog which was in the habit of coming through the fence, and scratching in my flower-beds, to the manifest spoiling of the gardener's toil and temper. Walking in the garden, one Saturday afternoon, and preparing my sermon for the following day, I saw the four-footed creature,—rather a scurvy specimen, by-the-by,—and having a walking-stick in my hand, I threw it at him with all my might, at the same time giving him some good advice about going home. Now, what should my canine friend do but turn round, pick up the stick in his mouth, bring it, and lay it down at my feet, wagging his tail all the while in expectation of my thanks and kind words! Of course, you do not suppose that I kicked him, or threw the stick at him any more. I felt quite ashamed of myself, and told him that he was welcome to stay as long as he liked, and to come as often as he pleased. There was an instance of the power of nonresistance, submission, patience, and trust, in overcoming even righteous anger. I used that illustration in preaching the next day, and I did not feel that I had at all degraded myself by telling the story."

Then Mrs. Spurgeon added:

"If my memory does not play me false, there used to be sundry crusts, or even bones, secretly conveyed to that mongrel cur after this memorable encounter."

Salvation—Gain or Loss

"Well, Jack, old fellow!" said one who met a man who had lately been converted, "I hear you have given up all your pleasures." "No! no!" said the friend, "the fact lies all the other way. I have just found all my pleasures and have given up only all my follies."

The heart never grows better by age; I fear, rather, worse. A young liar will be an old one; and a young knave will be a greater knave as he grows older.

—Lord Chesterfield

"What we retain we may lose, but what we give to Christ we are sure to keep."— T. L. Cuyler

A Bible Temperance Catechism

Prepared by Vincent D. Beery

Question: Does the Bible have anything to say about alcoholic drink?

Answer: Yes, the Bible has a great deal to say about it.

Q: What does the Bible say about the folly of drinking?

A: "Wine is a mocker, strong drink is raging: and whosoever is deceived thereby is not wise."— Proverbs 20:1

Q: What does the Bible say about the results of strong drink?

A: "Who hath woe? Who hath sorrow? Who hath contentions? Who hath babbling? Who hath redness of eyes? They that tarry long at the wine."—Prov. 23:29, 30.

Q: What is the safe way to deal with alcoholic drinks?

A: "Look not thou upon the wine when it is red, when it giveth his color in the cup; when it moveth itself aright."—Prov. 23:31.

Q: What happens to a person who gets the liquor habit?

A: "At the last it biteth like a serpent, and stingeth like an adder."—Prov. 23:32.

Q: What does the Bible say about the future of a drunkard?

A: "No drunkard shall inherit the kingdom of God."—I Cor. 6:10.

Q: Is it a good thing to "treat" others to alcoholic liquor?

A: "Woe unto him that giveth his neighbor drink, that puttest thy bottle to him, and makest him drunken also."—Hab. 2:15.

Q: Does drinking lead to success in life?

A: "The drunkard and the glutton shall come to poverty."— Prov. 23:21.

Q: Is it good sense to say, "I can take it or leave it alone"?

A: "Let him that thinketh he standeth take heed lest he fall."— I Cor. 10:12.

Q: Is it wrong to eat or drink anything that harms the body?

A: "Know ye not that ye are the temple of God? . . . If any man defile the temple of God, him shall God destroy. . . ."—I Cor. 3:16, 17.

Q: How should we live and act each day?

A: "Be thou an example of the believers, in word, in conversation, in charity, in spirit, in faith, in purity."—I Tim. 4:12.

Q: What commandment bears against using alcohol as a drink?

A: "Thou shalt not kill."

"Keep The Gate Shut"

Many years ago in England a farmer was one day at work in his fields when he saw a party of horsemen riding about his farm. He had one field that he was especially anxious that they should not ride over. So he sent one of his boys to the field, telling him to shut the gate, and then watch it, and on no account to let it be opened.

The boy went as he was told, but was scarcely at his post before the huntsmen came up and ordered the gate to be opened. This the boy refused to do, stating the orders he had received and his determination not to disobey them.

Threats and bribes were offered alike in vain.

After a while one of the huntsmen said in commanding tones, "My boy, you do not know me. I am the Duke of Wellington, and I command you to open that gate that I and my friends may pass through."

The boy lifted his cap, and stood uncovered before the man whom all England delighted to honor, then answered firmly, "I am sure the Duke of Wellington would wish this gate shut, and not allow anyone to pass but with my master's permission."

Greatly pleased, the old warrior lifted his own hat and said: "I honor the boy or man who can be neither bribed nor frightened into doing wrong," and handing the boy a sovereign, the old Duke put spurs to his horse and galloped away.

Every boy is a gatekeeper, and his Master's command is, "Be thou faithful unto death." Keep the gate of your mouth fast closed, and allow no evil company to enter. When evil companions would tempt you to lie, to deal falsely, to disobey your parents, keep the gate of your ears fast shut against such temptations.   —My Pleasure

A QUEEN'S QUESTION

A beautiful incident in the experience of Queen Victoria is worth remembering. It is unquestionably authentic. The Queen had attended a service in St Paul's Cathedral and had listened to a sermon that interested her greatly; then she asked her chaplain, "Can one in this life be absolutely sure of eternal safety?" His answer was that he "knew of no way that one could be absolutely sure."

This was published in the Court News and fell under the eye of a humble minister of the Gospel, John Townsend. He was an intimate friend of George Muller, whose life of faith led to the founding of his well-known orphanages. This John Townsend was the father of "Sister Abigail," another Christian of extraordinary faith and service.

After reading Queen Victoria's question and the answer she received, John Townsend thought and prayed much about the matter, then sent the following note to the Queen:

To her gracious Majesty, our beloved Queen Victoria, from one of her most humble subjects:

With trembling hands, but heart-filled love, and because I know that we can be absolutely sure even now of our eternal life in the Home that Jesus went to prepare, may I ask your Most Gracious Majesty to read the following passages of Scripture: John 3:16; Romans 10:9, 10?

These passages prove there is full assurance of salvation by faith in our Lord Jesus Christ for those who believe and accept His finished work.

I sign myself, your servant for Jesus' sake. John Townsend.

John Townsend was not alone in praying about his letter to the queen. He took others into his confidence, and much prayer, from many hearts went up to God. In about a fortnight he received a modest-looking envelope containing the following letter:

To John Townsend:

Your letter of recent date received and in reply would state that I have carefully and prayerfully read the portions of Scripture referred to. I believe in the finished work of Christ for me, and trust by God's grace to meet you in that Home of which He said, "I go to prepare a place for you."

(Signed) Victoria Guelph.

Character is what you are in the dark.
—D. L. Moody

Books are friendly things. Do not count as wasted the hours spent in selecting them.
—Johnson

Love sought is good, but given unsought is better.
—Shakespeare

The seller of liquor is the only man who is ashamed of his best customers.
—Herbert W. Thomson

Separated!

"I understand you and your wife are going to be separated," said a friend to a well-known judge.

"How dare you insinuate any such thing?" shouted the judge, his face purple with anger. "My wife and I love each other very much."

"Is that so?" queried the friend. "Well, I heard from your doctor that she has only a short time to live, and since I know she is a Christian she will go to be with her Lord. Where are you going when you die?"

The judge stood awhile quietly thinking. His face began to pale as the words took effect.

He cried out, "My God, save me. All these years I have been turning away from Thee. Forgive me, God, and save me."

—Gospel Herald

The Prospect of Facing the List

William Webb, a butcher of West Worthing, Canada, put up this notice in his window: "This business has been compelled to close owing to bad debts. A list of the names and amounts owing will shortly be shown." Money rolled in; the shop is open again, and business flourishing.

—Regina Leader-Post

A young Christian soldier in the army was often assaulted by his tent-mates while at prayer at night. He sought advice of his chaplain, and, at his advice, omitted his usual habit. His conscience, however, could not endure this. He chose rather to have prayer with persecution than outward peace without it, and resumed his old way. The result was, that, after a time, all his ten or twelve tent-companions knelt with him in prayer. In reporting to his chaplain, he said, "Isn't it better to keep the colors flying?"—Selected.

Alcohol Tragedy

"A liquor store near us sold liquor to a neighbor until he beat his wife and she died as a result. They were both classed as alcoholics at the trial." So wrote a distressed friend.

And, of course, under the new judicial insanity this brutal monster will not have to be punished for this horrible crime. As an alcoholic he will be ruled a "sick" man. They will give him a gentleman's treatment, sober him up, feed him well, dry him out, dress him up, put him on welfare, pay his house rent, give him more money to buy liquor with, and turn him loose on society to go out and commit another murder.

Oh, this Great Society!

"The wicked shall be turned into hell, and all the nations that forget God" (Ps. 9:17).

Beware of Drifting Along!

Rev. Stanley Dokken

"Therefore we ought to give the more earnest heed to the things that were heard, lest haply we drift away from them" (Heb. 2:1, ASV).

There is nothing easier than drifting; but at the same time, there is nothing that can be more dangerous. While this holds true on any sea, it becomes even more serious when we think of life's sea. Where few would ever dare to drift in any boat, many seem unconcerned about drifting along through life. Therefore, we need this warning from God's Word. We need to realize the awful consequences of drifting along.

In the first place, the drifter is always going down. No one ever drifts upstream. The law of gravity applies spiritually too. It is easy to float downstream. Oh, the many that are doing it! To go the way of the world with the crowd is the easy way of the drifter, but it is the way down to Hell itself.

The drifter not only is going down, but even worse is the fact that he is seldom aware of it. For the most part, he does not even realize that he is drifting. The drifter becomes so much like Samson of whom we read, "He wist not that the Lord was departed from him" (Judges 16:20). The currents that cause drifting are often barely perceptible. We drift before we know it. That is why we need to constantly keep our bearings and have our port in view.

The Devil seldom urges a Christian to leave the church or give up his faith in the Lord. His strategy is more subtle than that. He just seeks to cause us to relax—to rest on the oars and drift along in our Christian life.

Are there not many Christians who have drifted into a state of coldness and indifference in this way? They have seemingly forgotten their conversion experience with its sense of guilt concerning sin and subsequent joy in coming to the Lord. The truths of sin and grace which once so strongly gripped their hearts and consciences have become so familiar that they now fall on almost deaf ears. Their "first love" for the Lord and for the souls of men has been largely left, and other things, though good and legitimate, have taken first place.

This is the peril of drifting. We must recognize it. We must beware of its deceitfulness and also realize "it *can* happen to me."

Drifting along is so serious. If we continue drifting along, we will ultimately come to ruin. The waters may still seem placid, but the rapids and finally the falls are sure to come at last. Besides, all the time we are drifting, we are not only ruining ourselves, but we are also endangering the lives of others. Just as derelicts endanger other ships, so aimless, ambitionless, spiritual drifters are often a menace to the spiritual welfare of others.

Are you drifting along? Heed the songwriter's plea: "Drift no longer! Let Jesus save."

—*Faith and Fellowship*

It is a virtue in a woman if she is a one-man woman. Men are proud of a dog if that dog does not run after anybody else's wagon, if he just likes one man. It is good to get settled in your mind that we have a one-Man salvation. Too many people have two-men salvation. They think, "I do half and the Lord Jesus does half." For some people it takes a whole company to get them saved, for they think God has some part of it, Christ has part of it, and the Virgin Mary has part of it, the priest has part of it, all the saints have part of it, and then if they do right and hold out faithful, and if after they die other people pay enough to the priest to pray them out of purgatory, they might get to Heaven. That is too many people to depend on. I am preaching on a *one-Man* salvation.--**Dr. John R. Rice.**

Early Rising to Worship God

ROBERT G. LEE

Abraham rose early to stand before the Lord (Gen. 19:27).

Jacob rose early to worship the Lord (Gen. 28:18).

Moses rose early to give God's message to Pharaoh (Exodus 8:20).

Moses rose early to build an altar to God (Exodus 24:4).

Moses rose early to meet God at Sinai (Exodus 34:4).

Joshua rose early to capture Jericho (Joshua 3:1).

Joshua rose early to take Ai (Joshua 8:10).

Gideon rose early to examine the fleece (Judges 6:38).

Hannah and Elkanah rose early to worship God (I Samuel 1:19).

Samuel rose early to meet Saul (I Samuel 15:12).

David rose early to do as his father bade him (I Samuel 17:20).

Israel rose early, and found their enemies dead (2 Kings 19:35).

Job rose early to offer sacrifices for his children (Job 1:5).

The Son of God rose early, and went to a solitary place to pray (Mark 1:35)

Jesus rose early to go to the Temple to teach (John 8:2).

The people rose early to go to hear Him (Luke 21:38).

The women rose early to go to the sepulchre (Mark 16:2).

As an old writer puts it: "The morning is the gate of the day, and should be well guarded with prayer. The morning is one of the threads on which the day's actions are strung, and should be well knotted with devotion."

If we felt more the majesty of life, we should be more careful of its mornings. He who rushes from his bed to his business and waiteth not to worship in prayer, is as foolish as though he had not put on his clothes, or washed his face, and as unwise as though he dashed into battle without arms or armour.

Be it ours to bathe in the softly flowing river of communion with God before the heat of the wilderness and the burden of the day begin to oppress. How better can we do this than by rising early and being on time at God's house for the study of His Word and for worship?

One day a man went running and puffing into the railroad station to catch a train, but missed it. He looked at his watch and said, "Watch, I had a lot of faith in you." A friend overheard him and said, "Don't you know that faith without works is dead?"

Keeping Christmas

Are you willing to forget what you have done for other people, and to remember what other people have done for you; to ignore what the world owes you, and to think what you owe the world; to put your rights in the background, and your duties in the middle distance, and your chances to do a little more than your duty in the foreground; to see that your fellow men are just as real as you are, and try to look behind their faces to their hearts, hungry for joy; to own that probably the only good reason for your existence is not what you are going to get out of life, but what you are going to give to life; to close your book of complaints against the management of the universe, and look around you for a place where you can sow a few seeds of happiness—are you willing to do these things even for a day? Then you can keep Christmas.

Are you willing to believe that love is the strongest thing in the world—stronger than hate, stronger than evil, stronger than death—and that the blessed life which began in Bethlehem nineteen hundred years ago is the image and brightness of the Eternal Love? Then you can keep Christmas.

And if you keep it for a day, why not always?

But you cannot keep it alone.

—Henry Van Dyke

Our Lord's Seven Invitations

1. "Come unto me, all ye that labor and are heavy laden, and I will give you rest" (Matt. 11:28).

A very precious invitation to every sin-burdened soul. We can come to Him who is the "sin-bearer," and to Him who says, "Cast thy burden on the Lord." There is no load of human care of which He cannot relieve us, and there is no sin too dark for His precious blood to cleanse, thus making us "whiter than snow."

2. "Come and see" (John 1:39). These two disciples were honest seekers after truth. They wanted to know more, and to have converse with Jesus. They had found their true Master, and believed Him to be what He professed to be, "The Son of God." The closer we come to Christ, and the more we look to Him, the more satisfied will our souls be.

3. "Come unto me, and drink" (John 7:37).

Christ knows our human nature. He knows what soul-thirst means and that nothing else but the fountain of life can satisfy the parched soul. David knew this longing, and expressed it in Psalm 42:1,2: "As the hart panteth after the water brooks, so panteth my soul after thee, O God. My soul thirsteth for God; for the living God: when shall I come and appear before God?"

4. "Come and dine" (John 21:11).

He knows the soul's hunger. He is Himself the living bread. He satisfies the hungry soul; He meets our every need. It is indeed a privilege to sit down and dine with Him.

5. "Come, take up the cross, and follow me" (Mark 10:21).

We cannot wear the crown if we will not bear the cross. As followers of Jesus, we must walk in His footsteps, and account it all honor if we are permitted to bear the cross.

6. "Come ye yourselves apart . . and rest awhile" (Mark 6:31).

"He knoweth our frame." He knows our weakness, and just as the body needs periods of rest, so our souls need the same. We want more meditation—more quiet times with the Lord Jesus. Our Father usually calls His servants away for a quiet time before sending them to important work. Moses was sent into the desert for forty years before he began his real life's work. Paul was sent away for three years before his public preaching began. He prospers most in spiritual things who gets most alone with God.

7. "Come ye blessed . . . inherit the kingdom" (Matt. 25:34).

He has not redeemed us to a life of spiritual insignificance. We are born again, made new creatures, heirs, and joint-heirs with Him. We are to be kings and priests, and our position is far above that of angels, pure though they may be. May we never despise our inheritance!—**Christian Union Herald**.

None Like Jesus

When Napoleon Bonaparte was exiled on St. Helena, he was asked by one of his friends, "Who was the greatest warrior the world has ever known?" Without hesitation, Napoleon answered, "Jesus Christ." "But," said his friend, "you have not always talked that way. When you were winning battles, even up to the very time of Waterloo, you left the impression that you were the world's greatest warrior."

This is how Napoleon replied: "Yes, I have always acted as though I thought I was the world's greatest conqueror. I have had lots of time to think since I have been here on this island. The Caesars, Alexander the Great, Hannibal, Charlemagne, and myself—we have fought with blood and tears and swords and iron, and we lost. All of us lost. We lost our scepters, our crowns and our offices. The only sword Christ had was a broken reed: His crown, some twisted thorns: His army, a band of fishermen and farmers: His ammunition, a heart of redeeming love. He lives, and I and my kind die. I stand here and call for the Old Guard to come, but they do not hear me. There are no responding voices. My old soldiers do not hear me. I hear nothing but the waves as they bite at the rock beneath my feet. But after 1800 years have gone into the tomb of time, Christ calls and men answer. If need be, they give their bodies to be burned: if need be, they follow Him into the heart of Africa; but, better still, they live patient and triumphant lives in His name. Yes, the other warriors and I will ride down to dust, but Christ will live forever."

(Excerpt from *And Be Ye Saved*, a book of revival sermons by C. Gordon Bayless.)

"A Torn Leaf"

A clergyman in England asked a dying Christian woman where she found the Saviour; and she gave him a piece of paper torn from an American journal containing part of one of C. H. Spurgeon's sermons. The scrap had been wrapped around a package that came to her from Australia. The words of Spurgeon were read by her and were the means of leading her to Christ.

Commenting on this incident, a writer says, "Think of it; a sermon preached in England, printed in America, in some way coming to Australia, a part of it used as wrapping paper there, coming back to England, was the means of converting this woman."

What an encouragement there is in such an incident for those who preach the Gospel by means of printer's ink! Tracts and religious papers have been wonderfully used of God in the salvation of souls.

—*Church of Christ Advocate*

Resignation, the Root of Peace

"Commit thy works unto the Lord, and thy thoughts shall be established."—Proverbs 16:3.

The habit of resignation is the root of peace.

A godly child had a ring given him by his mother, and he greatly prized it, but on one occasion he unhappily lost his ring and he cried bitterly. But recapturing his composure, he stepped aside and prayed; after which his sister laughingly said to him, "Brother, what is the good of praying about a ring—will praying bring back your ring?" "Perhaps not," said he, "but praying has done this for me; it has made me quite willing to do without the ring if it is God's will; and is not that almost as good as having it?"

Thus faith quiets us by resignation, as a babe is hushed in his mother's bosom. Faith makes us quite willing to do without the mercy which once we prized; and when the heart is content to be without the outward blessing, it is as happy as it would be with it; for it is at rest.

—*Charles H. Spurgeon*

"Humility is to make a right estimate of oneself."
—*C. H. Spurgeon*

Bein' poor is a problem, but bein' rich ain't the answer.

—C. Grant

If God sends us on stony paths He will provide us with strong shoes.—Alexander Maclaren

The Compassionate Heart

"They that sow in tears shall reap in joy."—Ps. 126:5.

Hear these remarkable words, "in tears"! The tears of a broken heart are necessary equipment of the soul winner. The certainty of returning with joy depends, says Holy Writ, on going with tears. There are other requirements for the one who would be a fisher of men. He must go, he must bear precious seed, but the thing so often lacking is the broken heart. Indeed, I make bold to say that the broken heart must come to drive one out, that he go. The broken heart will seek the seed that will bear fruit. Yea, even the same broken heart will make the home-coming joyful. There is joy in the surcease of a broken heart. The broken and compassionate heart, the humble and contrite spirit, pleases God, attracts the sinner, and makes the contact between these two that results in the changed heart and saved soul of the sinner, and brings honor to the Saviour.

See the example of Jesus. Never was there such a compassionate winner of men! He saw the people as sheep having no shepherd, and "had compassion on them." He wept over Jerusalem. He sought the fallen woman to forgive her, and the publican to make him a preacher. His compassion would not let Him eat. He found "meat that ye know not of" in the winning of souls. His compassionate heart would not let Him sleep, for He must needs go into a mountain and pray all night, or rise a great while before day to pray for the lost. His compassionate heart would not let Him die, even, till the repenting thief on the neighboring cross was forgiven and won to Himself and Heaven. The prodigal son was a sinner, and the forgiving, grieving father was like Jesus. Christ was the Shepherd, and the sinner was the poor lost lamb, at the mercy of the cold and the beasts. As the shepherd seeks the sheep until he finds it, rescues it and rejoices over it, so Jesus with the sinner.

They crowned Him with thorns,
He was beaten with stripes;
He was smitten and nailed to the tree.
But the pain in His heart was the hardest to bear,
The heart that was broken for me.

No marvel, then, that when He died on the cross for sinners He loved so well, the soldiers opened His side with a spear and found a heart literally broken. O Saviour, teach us to love sinners, to weep over them, to find pillows hard, food tasteless and life not worth living, if they be not saved! Send us out with compassion and tears to win the lost!

How Paul wept over sinners! Hear him say, "Remember, that by the space of three years I ceased not to warn every one night and day with tears." Night and day! Night and day with tears! Hear him say, "Brethren, my heart's desire and prayer to God for Israel is, that they might be saved." Again he said, "For I could wish that myself were accursed from Christ for my brethren, my kinsmen according to the flesh." A stoning, a shipwreck, a life-and-death fight with lions in the Colisseum, a Philippian jail at midnight, with his bleeding back and shackled feet, could not quench Paul's tears for lost men, nor distract his compassionate heart, till they were saved.

All the great winners of men have been men of compassionate hearts. Moody, Spurgeon, Torrey, Finney—all have been beyond other preachers mainly, if not only, in this. Charles Alexander had showed it in his singing. John Vassar, Bible agent, tract distributor, and soul winner rare, oh, so rare, had this and almost no other equipment by nature, in his personal work. No one will win souls without it. The preacher, the teacher, the everyday Christian, will do well to cultivate this compassionate heart. He may have all else without the broken heart, but will not, cannot, win the lost to a Saviour who died for them.

Once there was a preacher on the streets of a Texas town who strangely stirred and melted the hearts of men in his unlettered street preaching. The people heard him gladly, and you will not marvel when you know that they called him "Weeping Joe." I do not know, nor want to know, his other name, for no name can so well recall the tears and prayers, and the heartbroken, compassionate love of Jesus which he had for a lost world.

O Saviour! give us the broken heart that, going forth weeping, we may come again with rejoicing, bringing precious sheaves!

JOHN R. RICE

(Reprinted from THE SWORD for January 18, 1935.)

Saved in Time

Paul Rader had many a talk with a banker in New York, and the banker would reply that he was too busy for religion. But he over-worked and was sent to a sanatorium for a complete rest. One day God spoke to Paul Rader. The message was quite clear, "Go and speak to the banker." Rader caught a train and went with all speed to the sumptuous sanatorium.

As he drew near he saw the banker standing in the doorway. "Oh, Rader," he said, "I am so glad to see you."

"I received your telegram," said Rader.

"No," said he, "that is impossible. I wrote a telegram begging you to come, but I tore it up. I did not send it."

"That may be so," said Mr. Rader, "but your message came by way of heaven." He found his friend was under deep conviction of sin; and he pointed him to Christ as a perfect Saviour. That man accepted Christ as *his* Saviour, and his heart was filled with joy.

"Rader," he said, "did you ever see the sky so blue or the grass so green?"

"Ah," said Rader, "we sometimes sing:
"Heaven above is softer blue,
Earth around is sweeter green;
Something lives in every hue
Christless eyes have never seen."

Suddenly the banker leaned against Mr. Rader and fell into his arms—dead.---*The Sunday School Times.*

The Giver and the Gift

Over one hundred years ago, Mary I. McClellan, when a schoolteacher, attended the little Pearl River Church in Mississippi and was moved by a missionary sermon. When the offering plate reached her pew, she put in five dollars and a note which read, "I give five dollars and myself, Mary I. McClellan."

John Watson, enlarging on the thought that the Bible is so simple that a wayfaring man or a fool need not err therein, said: "It is shallow enough so that the most timid swimmer may enjoy its waters without fear, and yet deep enough for the most expert swimmer to enjoy it without touching the bottom."

How to Have a Revival

I can give a prescription that will bring a revival to any church or community or any city on earth.

First, let a few Christians (they need not be many) get thoroughly right with God themselves. **This is the prime essential!** If this is not done, the rest I am to say will come to nothing.

Second, let them bind themselves together in a prayer group to pray for a revival until God opens the heavens and comes down.

Third, let them put themselves at the disposal of God for Him to use as He sees fit in winning others to Christ.

That is all.

This is sure to bring a revival to any church or community. I have given this prescription around the world. It has been taken by many churches and many communities and in no instance has it ever failed; and it cannot fail.

—R. A. Torrey

The Extra Sparrow

Two sparrows for a farthing,
And yet, three more for two,
So then, there is an extra one for naught;
So worthless, insignificant,
Even when it flew:
A sparrow, dead, thrown in, not even bought.

Not long ago 'twas flying:
It wasn't noticed much;
So many kept on flying when it fell.
Who could have known its dying
Or be concerned with such:
A sparrow, dead, thrown in that wouldn't sell?

Scrabbling for its food,
Flitting here and there,
Chased from gardens, residences, fruit;
Thought by some as rude,
Who is there to care
For a sparrow, dead, thrown in, t' boot?

Ah, but Someone knows;
Yes, Someone is concerned.
Someone knows a sparrow fell to earth.
The One who made it knows
And says He is concerned
And that alone decides the sparrow's worth.

—Bill Harvey

The Evangelistic Passion

A study of the Christian pulpit reveals the fact that men of outstanding success as soul winners have almost been those with a strong, almost consuming passion for the lost. Jesus said of Himself: "The zeal of thine house hath eaten me up." The Apostle Paul so longed for the salvation of his countrymen that he said: "I could wish that myself were accursed from Christ for my brethren, my kinsmen according to the flesh." Of Samuel Rutherford it was said by a friend: "Many a time I thought he would have flown out of the pulpit when he came to speak of Jesus Christ." It was likewise said of Joseph Alleine that "infinite and insatiable greed for the conversion of souls," possessed him and he preached "with far-reaching voice, flashing eye, and a soul on fire with love."

John Wesley was denied the privilege of preaching from the pulpit in the church; but with true evangelistic fervor took his father's tomb for a pulpit and preached to the people the great truths of full salvation. Whitefield loved field preaching. Returning from a tour he lighted a candle and went upstairs to retire, weary after the journey; but the people gathered in front of the house and filled the street; and there on the stairway with a lighted candle in his hand, he preached his last message, retired and was no more; for God took him. John Knox, who cried out in his earnestness, "Give me Scotland or I die," carried with him this zeal to the close of his ministry. Often he would be supported by attendants in order to reach the pulpit; but when he arose to speak the divine passion so filled his soul that one of his friends said: "So mighty was he in his yearning that I thought he would break the pulpit into bits."

The modern pulpit has suffered from a lack of passion. Back of this lack has been a false psychology which minified the emotional nature and glorified the reason. This pagan psychology maintained that any display of emotion was a weakness; and not only so, but it was a deteriorating element in personality, antagonistic to true intellectuality. It is this underlying pagan element which has produced a dry rot in the churches. False philosophy has had more to do with undermining Christian truth than is apparent to the superficial observer. As a result many sermons of the present time have the same characteristic as Dr. Chalmers attributed to those of his time. He compared them to a fine winter day —short, clear, and cold. "Brevity is good," he says and "clearness is better, but coldness is fatal. Moonlight preaching ripens no harvest."

—Selected

The Holy City...

Thirty men, red-eyed and disheveled, lined up before a judge of the San Francisco police court. It was the regular morning company of "Drunks and disorderlies." Some were old and hardened, others hung their heads in shame. Just as the momentary disorder attending the bringing in of the prisoners quieted down, a strange thing happened. A strong, clear voice from below began singing:

"Last night I lay a-sleeping,
There came a dream so fair."

Last night! It had been for them all a nightmare or a drunken stupor. The song was such a contrast to the horrible fact that no one could fail of a sudden shock at the thought the song suggested.

"I stood in old Jerusalem,
Beside the Temple there,"

the song went on. The judge had paused. He made a quiet inquiry. A former member of a famous opera company known all over the country, was awaiting trial for forgery. It was he who was singing in his cell.

Meantime the song went on, and every man in the line showed emotion. One or two dropped on their knees; one boy at the end of the line, after a desperate effort at self control, leaned against the wall, buried his face against his folded arms, and sobbed, "Oh, mother, mother!"

The sobs, cutting to the very heart the men who heard, and the song, still welling its way through the courtroom, blended in the hush.

At length one man protested, "Judge," said he, "have we got to submit to this? We're here to take our punishment, but this—" He, too, began to sob.

It was impossible to proceed with the business of the court, yet the judge gave no order to stop the song. The police sergeant, after an effort to keep the men in line, stepped back and waited with the rest. The song moved on to its climax:

"Jerusalem, Jerusalem! Sing,
for the night is o'er!
Hosanna in the highest! Hosanna
for evermore!"

In an ecstasy of melody the last words rang out, and then there was silence.

The judge looked into the faces of the men before him. There was not one who was not touched by the song; not one in whom some better impulse was not stirred. He did not call the cases singly—a kind word of advice, and he dismissed them all. No man was fined or sentenced to the workhouse that morning. The song had done more good than punishment could possibly have accomplished.

—Author unknown.

It is not the arithmetic of our prayers; that is, how many. It is not the rhetoric of our prayers; how eloquent. It is not the geometry of our prayers; how long. It is not the music of our prayers; how sweet. It is not the logic of our prayers; how argumentative. It is not the method of our prayers; how orderly. But, how FERVENT and how BELIEVING are our prayers?—Bishop Hall.

"Every man knows something that I do not know. I must probe until I find it, study until I learn it, work until I master it; hence, all men are my teachers."—Jack Hyles.

"God Is Dead!"

A story is told about Dr. Martin Luther, the great Reformation leader. Reportedly, Luther was once discouraged with the cares and trials of life. He had temporarily forgotten the greatness and faithfulness of God, and had become consumed with worry.

One morning Dr. Luther came downstairs to breakfast. His wife greeted him, dressed in black mourning clothes.

"Oh," said Luther, "who has died?"

"Don't you know?" she replied, "God is dead."

"How can you say such a foolish and wicked thing?" he asked. "How can God die? He will live through all eternity. He never changes. He can never die."

"Then," asked the wife, "why are you so discouraged, if God is still alive?"

"Then I saw," said Luther, "what a wise woman my wife was. She was trying to make me see that God is truly the same, and that He loves us and will take care of us, and we do not need to be afraid. He is always the same wonderful God."

There is a law of gravitation in the spiritual world just as there is a law of gravitation in the physical world. The rich man did not go to Hell just because he had money, and the poor man did not go to Heaven just because he was broke. The rich man went to his place and the beggar went to his place. Heaven is a place, and Hell is a place; but these places are what they are because of the people who are there. A sinner would not be happy in Heaven. He would be out of step. He would sing off key. He could not stand the decency. There would be no night in which he could hide to commit sin. I speak reverently. If a drunkard went to Heaven just as he is in this world, he would look for a bootlegger. If a gambler should step off this planet into Heaven just as he is, he would try to get into a poker game. If a godless politician should step out of the underworld of an American city and go to Heaven just like he is, he would not be happy because he could not organize the angels and the redeemed to put over dirty political schemes in God's eternal city.
—Dr. Bob Jones, Sr.

A Tall Enough Preacher

A steward came to the presiding elder and asked for a preacher. "How big a man do you want?" asked the elder. "I do not care so much about his size," said the steward, "but I want him to be tall enough to reach Heaven when he is on his knees."

—Baptist Bulletin Service

As the Twig Is Bent

A little girl with shining eyes,
  Her little face aglow:
Said, "Father, it is almost time
  For Sunday School, let's go:
They teach us there of Jesus' love
  Of how He died for all
Upon the cruel cross, to save
  All those who on HIM call."

"Oh, no," said Father, "not today,
  I've worked hard all this week,
And I must have one day of rest,
  I'm going to the creek;
For there I can relax and rest
  And fishing's fine, they say,
So—run along, don't bother me—
  We'll go to church some day."

Months and years have passed away,
  But Father hears that plea no more:
"Let's go to Sunday School."
  Those childhood days are o'er;
And now that Father's growing old
  When life is almost through,
He finds the time to go to church,
  But what does his daughter do?

She says, "O Father, not today—
  I stayed up most all night,
I've got to have some sleep—
  Besides, I look a fright."

Then Father lifts a trembling hand
  To brush away his tears,
As again he hears the pleading voice
  Distinctly through the years;
He sees the small girl's shining face
  Upturned, with eyes aglow,
As she says: "It's time for Sunday School,
  Please, Father, won't you go?"
              —Selected

Statistical association between smoking and lung cancer is so strong that scientists believe that the annual cancer toll can be reduced from 40,000 to 4,000 if everybody stops smoking.
              —Dr. Earl Ubell

Never a heartache and never a groan,
Never a teardrop and never a moan,
Never a danger but there on the throne
Moment by moment He thinks of His own. —Author Unknown

It is no use to grumble and complain;
It's just as cheap and easy to rejoice,
When God sorts out the weather and sends rain—
Why, rain's my choice.
              —James Whitcomb Riley

Patience

After several hours of fishing the little girl suddenly threw down her pole and cried, "I quit!"

"What's the matter?" her father asked her.

"Nothing," said the child, "except I can't seem to get waited on."

It was said of D. L. Moody that he was as humble as a child before God and as bold as a lion before men.

Can't Work Soul to Save

"I cannot work my soul to save
  For that my Lord has done;
But I can work like any slave
  For love of God's dear Son."
              —Selected

No Fear at Night

A little girl was walking home with her father one night. As they trudged along in the darkness she said, "Take my hand, Papa! I can take only a little piece of yours, but you can take the whole of mine." Later she asked, "Papa, are you afraid?" "No," he replied. "All right! If you isn't, I isn't," she said.

Be always displeased with what thou art if thou desirest to attain to what thou art not; for where thou hast pleased thyself, there thou abidest.—Augustine.

Try these resolutions—Just for Today

Just for today I will be happy. This assumes what Abraham Lincoln said is true, that "most folks are about as happy as they make up their minds to be." Happiness is from within; it is not a matter of externals.

Just for today I will try to adjust myself to what is, and not try to adjust everything to my own desires. I will take my family, my business, and my luck as they come and fit myself to them.

Just for today I will try to strengthen my mind. I will learn something useful. I will not be a mental loafer. I will read something that requires effort, thought and concentration.

Just for today I will exercise my soul in three ways. I will do somebody a good turn and not get found out. I will do at least two things I don't want to do just for exercise.

Just for today I will be agreeable, I will look as well as I can, dress as becomingly as possible, talk low, act courageously, be liberal with praise, criticize not at all, nor find fault with anything and not try to regulate or improve anyone.

Just for today I will try to live through this day only and not try to tackle my whole life problem at once. I can do things for twelve hours that would appall me if I had to keep them up for a lifetime.

Just for today I will have a program. I will write down what I expect to do every hour. I may not follow it exactly, but I will have it. I will eliminate two pests, hurry and indecision.

Just for today I will have a quiet half hour all by myself to relax. In this half hour sometimes I will think of God, so as to get a little more perspective into my life.

Just for today I will be unafraid, especially I will not be afraid to be happy, to enjoy what is beautiful, to love and to believe that those I love, love me.—*Dateline*, reprinted from the *Oakland Bulletin*.

Can You Afford to Delay?

Choose yourself as to which is the best time. Perhaps it is better to put off this matter of religion for ten years. If so, drop the whole subject now. Just as a judge in court sets down a trial for three months ahead, and does not bother himself about the trial until that day comes, so set down a day for your conversion, ten years from now. If you can keep the world all these ten years and at the close of that time can take Christ, will it not be better than to take Him now? Decided, then, let it be that ten years from now you will attend to it. Or, if you be in robust health, and your prospects are very fair, then put it off twenty years. But I hear some one say: "How if an accident should take me off before that? How if I should lose my reason before that? How if my day of grace should end before that? How if the Holy Spirit should leave my soul before that? How if the avalanche of my transgressions should crush me before that? How if I should lift my eyes in Hell before that?" Oh, I see the point you make. You mean to say: "I think that it may be now or never." I think you mean to say that of a million souls lost, 999,999 are lost through procrastination.
—T. DeWitt Talmage

This above all: to thine own self be true,
And it must follow, as the night the day,
Thou can'st not then be false to any man.
—*William Shakespeare*

Man's Work Compared to God's Grace

Longfellow could take a worthless sheet of paper, write a poem on it, and make it worth $6,000 — *that's genius.*

Rockefeller could sign his name to a piece of paper and make it worth a million dollars—*that's capital.*

Uncle Sam can take gold, stamp an eagle on it, and make it worth $20.00—*that's money.*

A mechanic can take material that is worth only $5.00 and make it worth $50.00—*that's skill.*

An artist can take a fifty-cent piece of canvas, paint a picture on it, and make it worth $1,000—*that's art.*

God can take a worthless, sinful life, wash it in the blood of Christ, put His Spirit in it, and make it a blessing to humanity—*that's salvation.*
—Christian Digest.

No candle on the altar of a church will ever substitute for a flame in the heart of the preacher in the pulpit.

It wasn't the Goths that defeated Rome— It was the free circuses

LUXURIES, power, indulgence had made the once-tough Roman people soft. To stay popular, their emperors gave them more and more of the ease they craved—free bread, free circuses, easier living.

So the Romans softened up themselves for the ambitious, hard-working barbarians. And in 410 A.D. the greatest nation the world had ever seen was invaded and destroyed.

The greedy cry of "something for nothing," the stupid whine of "s o m e b o d y else should sacrifice, not me"— could do exactly the same for this nation, NOW.

I reckon him a Christi indeed that is neither ashamed of the Gospel nor a shame to it.
--Matthew Henr

What "Lovingkindness" Means

A mother asked her six-year-old what loving-kindness meant. "Well," he said, "when I ask you for a piece of bread and butter and you give it to me, that's kindness, but WHEN YOU PUT JAM ON IT, THAT'S LOVING-KINDNESS."—Chicago Tribune.

Walking Revival!

Newspapermen went down from London to report at first hand the marvelous happenings of the great Welsh revival at the turn of the century. On their arrival in Wales one of them asked a policeman where the Welsh revival was. Drawing himself to his full height he laid his hand over his heart and proudly proclaimed: "Gentlemen, the Welsh revival is inside this uniform!" He had caught the holy fire.

—Power

Maugham, an Agnostic, Wished to be Buried in Cathedral

It is strange how some people who have no use for God or the church want to be married or buried in the church.

"I have not uncovered any evidence in my ecclesiastical researches to cause me to change my agnostic views. I still neither believe in the existence of God nor in the immortality of the soul." So said the author, Somerset Maugham and yet he requested burial in Canterbury Cathedral.

Maugham frankly admitted "most of my life I've written for money, written what people want to read" and in this he was very successful for it is estimated his writings made him a multi-millionaire.

For the man who once said, "Death gives me the same passionate thrill as years ago was given me by life. I am drunk with the thought of it. It seems to offer me the final absolute freedom," the end came on December 16th, at the age of 91.—Evangelical Baptist.

"I Did Like Mother and It Killed Me!"

What imitators are little children! A small girl watched, with absorbing interest, everything which was happening at mother's card party. She observed how mother was dressed; how she dealt the cards; how the women drank cocktails, and how freely they smoked cigarettes!

Next day, the girl gathered her playmates together to play party. She dressed herself in some of her mother's clothes. Slipping into her mother's room, she got mother's package of cigarettes. Returning to her little playmates, she put a cigarette in her mouth, struck a match, and, in lighting the cigarette, she accidently ignited the over-size dress she was wearing. Instantly, she became a "human torch!" A few hours later, her little charred body lay still in death! As she died, she gasped, "I did like mother, and it killed me!"

Good Cheer

Ain't it fine today?
Sure, this world is full of trouble;
  I ain't said it ain't.
Lord, I've had enough and double
  Reason for complaint:
Rain and storm have come to fret me,
  Skies were often gray;
Thorns and brambles have beset me
  On the road—but, say—
  Ain't it fine today?

It's today that I am livin'—
  Not a month ago.
Havin', losin', takin', givin',
  As time wills it so.
Yesterday—a cloud of sorrow;
  Fell across the way.
It may rain—but, say—
  Ain't it fine today?
—Selected

What's Wrong With Being Old-Fashioned?

In the America of yesterday you paid your debts as quickly as possible, and went without things, to do it.

You disciplined your children—but disciplined yourself, first.

You spent less than you earned, and demanded your government do the same.

You went to church, your children to Sunday School, you held daily prayers—and no court would have dared to interpose any law into your private religion.

You would have been horrified at (and quick to change) men in high places who made "deals."

You expected to prosper by individual initiative—by doing a better and better job.

You obeyed the law—but took active enough part in government to see that the laws were just. You "walked softly but carried a big stick."

And that was the character which brought this country victory in two world wars in your lifetime, built it back from a shattering depression, and fed and saved the civilized world.

If all this is "old hat," so be it. It needs resurrection.
—Idaho Power Company, Reddytorial.

I have known God to use people who never had a chance, but I have never known God to use a person who has had a chance and will not take it.—Dr. Bob Jones, Sr.

Christmas Over There

Perhaps He tells them over there
About His Birthday long ago,
And pictures for the children fair
The happy times He used to know.

Perhaps He Takes them on His knee,
Our babies He has called away
And tells them of the days when He
With earthly children used to play.

I fancy at this Christmas time
He tells them tales to us untold,
Repeats some little nursery rhyme
He spoke when He was six years old.

There were not many then to keep
His birthday as we do today;
The shepherds, watching o'er their sheep,
Had no such happy time of play.

They little knew or dreamed, back then,
Who saw the little boy at play,
Carols of peace, good will to men,
The world would sing for Him today.

Tonight, perhaps, He calls them all,
The little children round His knee,
And tells those eager angels small
Of Christmas days that used to be.

And it may be the one we miss
So sadly at this Christmas time,
Climbs on His Knee His face to kiss
And nestles in His arms sublime.
                              —Edgar A. Guest.

Love of Books

No wonder Cicero says that he would part with all he was worth so he might live and die among his books . . . No wonder Petrarch was among them to the last, and was found dead in their company. It seems natural that Bede should have died dictating, and that Leibnitz should have died with a book in his hand, and Lord Clarendon at his desk. Buckle's last words, "My poor book!" tell a passion that forgot death; and it seemed only a fitting farewell when the tears stole down the manly cheeks of Scott as they wheeled him into his library, when he had come back to Abbotsford to die. Southey, white-haired, a living shadow, sitting stroking and kissing the books he could no longer open or read, is altogether pathetic.—Cunningham Geikie, D.D.

Her Sacrifice of Praise

It is not to the honor of our gracious Master that we should sit under juniper trees, hang our harps upon willows, and walk about the world in the shadow of death and despair. "I won't be unhappy," said a fine old saint; "It is all I have to give to God and I will praise Him and glorify Him by a happy face and a radiant life."

A. B. Simpson, in
Alliance Weekly

Happiness consists in being happy with what we have got and with what we haven't got.
—Spurgeon

Here's a thought

★ Have you ever known a man to lose his job because he drank too little?

★ Have you ever known of a doctor who told his patients that their chances would be better if they would start drinking?

★ Have you ever known of an employer who picked men for responsible positions because they drank constantly?

★ Have you ever heard a wife say: "My husband would be the best husband in the world if he would start drinking"?

★ What insurance company offers reduced rates to drinkers?

★ Did you ever hear of an alcoholic, when he began drinking, to say: "It will happen to me"?

★ Did you ever hear of a coach who encouraged his men to drink before a game?

★ Have you ever heard of children who complain because their daddy never came home drunk?

★ Have you ever heard of parents encouraging their daughter to become a barmaid so as to become popular and successful?

★ Did you ever hear of a drunk who boasted: "I can take a drink or let it alone," who ever did leave it alone?

—Alert

Would you like to test your character? The test of your character is, What would you do if you knew nobody would ever know it? What you would do, you have done in God's sight. A man is not a thief because he steals; he steals because he is a thief already in his heart.—Dr. Bob Jones, Sr.

The Undertaker's Traffic Recipe

One natural born fool; two or three big drinks of bad liquor; one high-powered motor car.

Soak fool in liquor, place in motor car and let go. After due time, remove fool from wreckage, place in black, satin-lined box, and garnish with flowers.

Never -- Never -- Never!

Never compromise with that which you are sure is wrong for the sake of peace. Never compromise principle for the sake of favor, advancement, or position.

Never say "Yes" when the Holy Spirit and the Word of God say an emphatic "No."

God is at eternal enmity with every manifestation of sin. Men soften the name. They say popularity, influence, respectability, and self-interest are harmless amusements, necessary vices. God says they are sin, and those who take delight in them are condemned to eternal perdition.

Men seek for the dividing line between sin and holiness. They seek long and earnestly, through winding and devious ways, and appear with a smile of imagined triumph in the church, with flying banners inscribed "Compromise." Sinai gathers blackness as God's voice thunders in reply, "Separation."

Here is the "great gulf fixed." "Ye cannot serve God and mammon." "He that committeth sin is of the Devil."

Thus God's immutable law separates holiness from all unrighteousness, and in eternity that law of separation prevails; it welcomes holiness to "the joy of thy Lord" but dooms unrighteousness to "everlasting fire."

No place along the way from earth to Heaven does God allow, for one moment. a compromise between them.—V. A. Dake, in **The Burning Bush.**

Feeding the Preacher's Horse
By J. B. Culpepper

Rev. J. B. Culpepper, himself one of the Methodist "circuit riders," says in speaking of their influence upon his life: "These men had visited our house from my earliest childhood. I once thought they came direct from heaven, horse and all. Was I mistaken? I mean those old-time-sure-enough men of God. My! how they awed me, thrilled me, stirred me, 'taught' me. From the age of seven I was feed boy. I never gave the preacher's horse a 'nubbin' in my life. (Should some not be familiar with farm language, a 'nubbin' is a small, scrawny undeveloped ear of corn.) No, sir! He got big, sound corn, and good fodder. I had a sort of undefined, but deeply imbedded notion that I was laying up treasures in Heaven. "Well, those days and those grand men are gone. I find myself a preacher, called to fill the place of one of them. How am I succeeding? Do I pray as they once did around the old family altar, as if the world was coming to an end, and as if sinners were really being lost? Do I ever take fire at morning prayer, so that I scorch my way through breakfast and out into the rising day? Do I often send the children out, glancing up to see if Jesus is not really coming back in bodily shape, as these old Heaven-openers did to me? Do I send the mothers and wives out from morning prayers, as my mother used to go, singing, 'Together let us sweetly live,' 'Together let us die,' because a new star of hope has risen concerning the unsaved members of the family?"

To Young Ministers

Pray every night and shave every morning.

Keep your conscience clean, also your linen.

Let your light shine and shine your shoes.

Press your advantages, your opportunities and your trousers.

Brush the cobwebs from your brain and the dandruff from your collar.

Take liberties with grammar, if you will, but not with women.

Be filled with the Spirit, not with spirits.

Take chances when fighting for principle but not in games of Chance.

Of course you will not break any of the Ten Commandments, but be sure not to break any rules of etiquette.

Beware of a reputation for bad breath or rancid jokes. Both alike offend.

A delinquent debt in a parish is like an addled egg in an omelet.

The polite liar easily becomes a plain liar.

Covet a golden tongue more than a greenback.

Be poor in spirit but not in vocabulary.

Don't mix your metaphors, but nevertheless be a good mixer.

You can't put fire in your sermons unless there is a fire in your heart.

Two things cannot be imitated: God's sunset and man's sincerity.

It is better to establish a good precedent than to follow a bad one.

It is better to lose a good fight than to win a bad one.

Be more kindly to a shabby coat than to a silk hat.

Call in the homes of men if you would have men call in the House of God.

Never allow temporal trivi alities to displace eternal verities.

People would rather listen to lively heresy than dull platitudes.

The approval of God is more to be desired than the patronage of a rich unscrupulous pew-holder.

Always be content with what you have but never with what you are.

(Log of the Good Ship Grace)

LITTLE READINGS (TAKE YOUR TIME & ENJOY THEM)

Calling all Grandmothers

One Sunday, little Johnny went to a new Sunday School and so naturally his parents wondered how he liked it.

"Real good!" he said.

"Who was your teacher?" mother probed.

"I don't know her name, but I think she must have been Jesus' grandmother."

"Why do you say that?" asked the father.

"Well, she sure bragged about Jesus, so she must be his grandmother," he said seriously.

To swear is wicked because it is taking God's name in vain. To murmur is likewise wicked for it takes God's promises in vain.

There is no time lost in waiting if you are waiting on the Lord.—Eternity

"The more we are humbled by grace, the more we shall be exalted in glory."—C. H. Spurgeon.

Record on High!

In Malden, near Boston, in a Baptist church, is a marble tablet thus inscribed:

IN MEMORIAM
Rev. Adoniram Judson,
Born August 9, 1788,
Died April 12, 1850,
Malden his birthplace,
The ocean his sepulchre,
Converted Burmans and
The Burman Bible
His monument.
His record is on High.
—Selected

Trust

How often we trust each other,
And only doubt our Lord.
We take the word of mortals,
And yet distrust His word;
But, oh, what light and glory
Would shine o'er all our days,
If we always would remember
God means just what He says.
A. B. Simpson

MAKING SURE WE DON'T GO BACKWARD!

Two perspiring Irishmen on a tandem bicycle at last got to the top of the steep hill. "That was a stiff climb, Pat," said one.

"It was that," admitted Pat. "And if I hadn't kept the brake on we would have gone backward sure."

Too many in the Lord's work manage to "keep the brake on," so hindering their own advance, and also that of the Lord's people.
—*Christian Victory*

In a time of unusually deep testing and trial while in China, Hudson Taylor received a letter from George Mueller. In part it read:

On Him then reckon, to Him look, on Him depend: and be assured that if you walk with Him, look to Him and expect help from Him, He will never fail you. An older brother, who has known the Lord for 44 years, who writes this, says for your encouragement that He has never failed him; in the greatest difficulties, in the heaviest trials, in the deepest poverty and necessities, He has never failed me; but because I was enabled by His grace to trust in Him, He has always appeared for my help. I delight in speaking well of His Name.

Such is the delight of believing without seeing, and finding that believing is seeing!

PRAYER—PLUS EFFORT

On one of D. L. Moody's journeys across the Atlantic there was a fire in the hold of the ship. The crew and some volunteers stood in line to pass buckets of water.

A friend said to D. L. Moody, "Mr. Moody, let us go to the other end of the ship and engage in prayer."

The common-sense evangelist replied, "Not so, sir. We will stand right here and pass buckets and pray hard all the time we are doing so."

How like Moody that was! He believed that prayer and work should not be separated.

Groanings which cannot be uttered are often prayers which cannot be refused.
—C. H. Spurgeon

A Love Triangle

A young couple on a train were obviously newlyweds off on a honeymoon. A silver-haired gentleman leaned across the aisle and asked, "Is there a third party going with you on your honeymoon?" The couple were bewildered. The old man added, "When Sarah and I were married, we invited Jesus to our marriage. One of the first things we did in our new home was to kneel and ask Jesus to make our marriage a love triangle—Sarah, myself, and Jesus. And all three of us have been in love with each other for all our fifty years of married life."

"ANTS, 'AUNTS' OR LADY UNCLES!!"

A school teacher asked the pupils to write a short essay and to choose their own subjects.

A little girl sent in the following paper:

My subjek is "Ants." Ants is of two kinds, insects and lady-uncles. Sometimes they live in holes and sometimes they crawl into the sugar bole, and sometimes they live with their married sisters. That is all I know about ants.
—Author Unknown

Thank God every morning when you get up that you have something to do that day which must be done, whether you like it or not. Being forced to work, and forced to do your best will breed in you temperance and self-control, diligence and strength of will, cheerfulness and content, and a hundred virtues which the idle never know.
—*Charles Kingsley.*

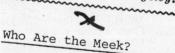

Who Are the Meek?

A missionary in Jamaica was examining his school upon a certain verse. He asked a black boy this question: "Who are the meek?"

The boy answered, "Those who give soft answers to rough questions."

To Please the Master Only

A ragged boy with a violin under his arm once roamed the streets of a great European city. Because he had no home or family, he wandered from place to place for food and shelter.

This urchin had a strange gift for music. He had somehow gotten hold of a violin, and he would stand on the street corners and play for the passing crowd. They were entranced by what they heard and would gather to listen. When he had finished playing, they would toss some coins at his feet. In this way he made an honest but meager living.

In the same city was a famous musician. One day he happened to pass by the place where the ragged boy was playing. His attention was arrested by the unusual quality of the music. He lingered until the crowd had passed on and then said to the little violin player, "Son, to whom do you belong?"

"I don't belong to anybody," the boy answered.

"Well, where do you live?" was the next question.

"I don't have any place to live. I just sleep on the streets and wherever I can."

The man thought for a moment and then said, "How would you like to be my boy and come to live with me? I'll teach you all I know about how to play the violin."

The boy's eyes sparkled through the dirt and grime, and he said, "Mister, I'd love it!"

So the great musician took him to his own home. He had him cleaned up and dressed up, and he became like a father to him. For several years he poured into the eager young mind and heart all that he knew about playing the violin.

Finally the boy was ready for his first public recital, and the word went out that a great new musical prodigy was about to appear on the concert stage. On the night of the performance the house was filled to capacity; even the balcony was packed.

At last the boy came out, put the violin beneath his chin, and began his concert. He played such music as the crowd had never heard before. At every pause there was deafening applause.

For some reason, however, the boy did not seem to pay any attention to the ovation. He kept his eyes turned upward and played on and on. The audience was mystified by his strange manner. Finally one of the persons present said, "I don't understand why he is so insensible to all this thunderous applause. He keeps looking up all the time. I'm going to find out what is attracting his attention!"

Moving about in the concert hall, the observer found the answer. There in the topmost balcony was the old music master, peering over the banister toward his young pupil. He was nodding his head and smiling, as if to say, "You are doing well, my boy; play on!"

And the boy did play on, not seeming to care whether the audience laughed or applauded. He kept his gaze upward. He was playing to please the master only.

Is not this story a vivid reminder that we Christians ought to live so as to please Christ only? He is our Master, the One to whom we should look for approval.

—Baptist Challenge

Just a Few Days

Just a few days—and our tears
    will have ended;
Just a few hours—and our task
    will be done;
    Yet still hear them calling
    From darkness appalling,
While we rest in the light of the
    fast setting sun.

Just a few days—and the gifts
    we've withholden,
Just a few hours—and the call
    we refuse
    Will rush on forever,
    Or return to us never,
And eternity's crown we no longer
    may choose.

Just a few days—and the gifts
    we've withholden,
The thought of the crown that we
    might have won;
    And ah, what the sorrow
    If we miss on the morrow
Our share in that joy, when He
    whispers, "Well done!"

Just a few hours—Our work still
    unfinished,
Just a few moments—to publish
    Thy name.
    In our weakness enfold us,
    Through darkness uphold us,
"Till He come," make us faithful
    Thy love to proclaim.

—*Author unknown*

Divine Guidance

If it were not for my belief in an overruling Providence, it would be difficult for me, in the midst of such complications, to keep my reason on its seat. But I am confident that the Almighty has His plans and will work them out; and, whether we see it or not, they will be the wisest and best for us. I have always taken counsel of Him, and referred to Him my plans, and have never adopted a course of proceeding without being assured, as far as I could be, of His approbation. I should be the most presumptuous blockhead upon this footstool if I for one day thought that I could discharge the duties which have come upon me since I came into this place, without the aid and enlightenment of One who is wiser and stronger than all others.

—Abraham Lincoln

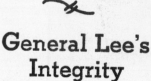

General Lee's Integrity

Robert E. Lee, though poor after the Civil War, refused a salary of $50,000 a year to let an insurance company use his name. He said that if his name was so valuable, he must guard its integrity.

The Full Consequences of Sin

"Keeping mercy for thousands, forgiving iniquity and transgression and sin, and that will by no means clear the guilty; visiting the iniquity of the fathers upon the children, and upon the children's children, unto the third and to the fourth generation."—Exodus 34:7.

Sages of old contended that no sin was ever committed whose consequences rested on the head of the sinner alone; that no man could do ill and his fellows not suffer. They illustrated it thus: "A vessel sailing from Joppa, carried a passenger, who, beneath his berth, cut a hole through the ship's side. When the men of the watch expostulated with him, 'What doest thou, O miserable man?' the offender calmly replied, 'What matters it to you? The hole I have made lies under my own berth.'"

This ancient parable is worthy of the utmost consideration. No man perishes alone in his iniquity. No man can guess the full consequences of his transgressions.

—Charles H. Spurgeon

"The Woods Are Full of Them!"

By Editor John R. Rice

It is said that in the last years of the war between the states, a farmer was drafted into the Confederate army. He did not know the drill manual. He did not know how to keep step on the march, nor how to salute. He knew none of the bugle calls. But he brought his squirrel rifle and when the command was given to attack he charged the Yankee lines, joining in the rebel yell. However, the grey-coated Confederates were outnumbered and were soon driven back. The bugle blew "retreat" and the thin grey line withdrew to safer ground. As the battered soldiers treated their wounded, prepared their camp and threw up breastworks in the late afternoon, some one said, "Poor old Jim! He was either killed or taken prisoner in the first battle he was in! Too bad he didn't know the bugle call to retreat and ran right into that nest of Yankees." But about sundown they saw two tired fellows coming over the hill. The one in front had on a blue uniform and the man behind wore a grey. Somebody had taken a prisoner! As he saw the camp, he prodded his prisoner with a bayonet and somebody shouted, "It is Jim! It is Jim! Jim's got a prisoner! Where did you get him, Jim?" The farmer recruit drew up angrily. He felt they had all deserted him in the first battle! "Where did I get him?" he said. "Why, the woods are full of them! Why don't you get one yourself?" So the world is full of sinners, and you can take them alive for Christ, if you only go after them.

John R. Rice

A Good Book . . .

Is a ship of thought, voyaging to us with precious cargo of truth and beauty.

Is an artist painting the vision splendid in various colors before the dullest eyes—an orator speaking with power—a soloist singing a song that, passing from itself, enters the memory with great transfiguration.

Is an author, writing the literature of godliness on the fleshly tablets of human hearts—a jeweler, adorning the mind with thoughts that give light.

Is a comrade giving instructions, continuing with us on the intellectual road, in mute fidelity, from childhood to the end of life.

Is a tailor, keeping the rustle of divine garments in the ear—a musician, building before the eyes of the soul rhythmic palaces of melody—a pilot, guiding away from the shadows into the deep things of life, of history, of love, of God.

Is a telescope and microscope in one—showing us God's signature, written sometimes hugely large and sometimes very small, on every page of this universe, God's vast autograph album.

—Dr. Robert G. Lee

Looking for Christ

G. Campbell Morgan, distinguished British clergyman, said, "I never begin my work in the morning without thinking that perhaps He may interrupt my work and begin His own. I am not looking for death. I am looking for Him."

Jesus, the Poor Man

Jesus was the poorest man who ever walked the dirt roads of earth. Born in poverty and reared in obscurity, He yet lived to enrich mankind. A stable was His birthplace, a manger His cradle. For twenty years He worked as a carpenter in a poverty stricken and despised village which bore the scorn of man as they asked, "Can any good thing come out of Nazareth?"

He began His ministry at the Jordan River, with no organization to support Him, no patrons to enrich Him. He publicly began a life of poverty that ended at the tomb. He preached without price, and wrought miracles without money. As far as we know, He never possessed the value of one dollar. How pathetic His words "The foxes have holes and the birds of the air their nests, but the Son of Man hath not where to lay His head."

He was an itinerant preacher whose parish was the world. When invited, He entered men's homes for dinner. When unasked, He went hungry. He sought breakfast from the leafing fig tree, but found none. He ate grain from His hands as He walked through fields of corn. His support came from the gifts of a few women, and His treasurer stole part of the pittance put therein. He walked on over the hills of Judea and by the waters of Galilee enriching men, Himself the poorest of all. He slept often under the open sky, in the wilderness without food, by Jacob's well without water, in the crowded city without a home. Thus He lived and loved, toiled and died. His value was thirty pieces of silver when sold—the price of a slave, the lowest estimate of human life.

So poor was He that He needs must carry His own cross through the city until, fainting, He fell. He was nailed to that cross between two thieves, stripped of His robe, the gift of love, for which inhuman soldiers gambled as He died. With no estate with which to endow His weeping and widowed mother, He bequeathed her to the love of the beloved John. Then He gave His peace to the disciples, His pardon to the thief, His life for the world, His body to the cross, and His spirit to God. His burial clothes were the gift of a friend. He was laid at last in a borrowed grave. But He arose again, our Saviour.

Truly, Jesus Christ was the poorest man that ever walked the dirt roads of earth. Though He was rich, yet for our sakes He became poor, that we, through His poverty, might become rich.

—Author Unknown

Rewards

Fourteen-year-old Benjamin Rashkoff, Long Island City, one of two children in his family, found a wallet containing $147. He took it home to ask his mother what to do, and she sent him to Hunters Point Police Station with it.

There Lieutenant William Locke traced it to Lopo De Rosario, a laborer, who was so overjoyed at regaining his entire fortune that he gave the lad a $25 reward.

The subject of reward is always an interesting and profitable one, but never more so than when the Lord is the Rewarder.

Many Rewards Offered

As a reminder of that which the Lord will reward, we give the following Scriptures:

Psalm 19:11—In keeping of the Word is "great reward."

Proverbs 11:18—"To him that soweth righteousness shall be a sure reward."

Matthew 5:12—"Great is your reward in heaven" for persecution.

Matthew 6:4—"Thy Father . . . shall reward thee openly" for secret alms.

Matthew 6:6—"Thy Father . . . shall reward thee openly" for secret prayer.

Matthew 6:18—"Thy Father . . . shall reward thee openly" for secret fasting.

Matthew 10:41—"Receive a righteous man's reward" for receiving a righteous man.

Mark 9:41—"He shall not lose his reward" for a cup of water.

I Cor. 3:8—"Receive his own reward for his own labour."

In addition, patient endurance of trials shall be abundantly rewarded (Jas. 1:12).

There is also a generous reward for the proper investment of "pounds" (Luke 19:17).

There is a divine recompense for practical ministrations to the needy (Luke 14:13, 14).

There is ample reward for the proper running of the Christian race and for fighting the fight of faith (I Cor. 9:24, 25).

There is even a reward for the joyful loser (Heb. 10:34, 35).

Is it not apparent from these and other Scriptures which could be given, that our glorious Lord will reward everything His servants do which gives Him pleasure?

"Therefore, my beloved brethren, be ye stedfast, unmoveable, always abounding in the work of the Lord, forasmuch as ye know that your labour is not in vain in the Lord" (I Cor. 15:58).—Tom M. Olson.

God is before me, He will be my Guide,
God is behind me, no ill can betide,
God is beside me, to comfort and cheer,
God is around me, so why should I fear?

Forty-seven men formed a gang of crooks after the World War. In ten years 4 had reformed, 6 were moderately successful gang leaders, 4 disappeared, 3 are hunted criminals, 3 police-crippled beggars, 6 physical wrecks, 12 in jail and 9 dead! Crime does not pay! Neither does any other branch of SIN.—The Highway.

The Kindness and Love of God Our Saviour Appeared

A farmer had a weather vane on top of his barn on whose arrow occurred the words, "God is love." One asked, "What do you mean by that? Do you mean that God's love is changeable—that it veers about as the arrow turns in the wind?" "Oh, no," said the farmer, "I mean that whichever way the wind blows, God is still love!"

Christian, beware how thou thinkest lightly of sin! Sin a little thing? Who knows its deadliness? It girded the Redeemer's head with thorns, and pierced His heart. It made Him suffer anguish, bitterness, and woe. Look upon all sin as that which crucified the Saviour, and see that it is exceeding sinful!—C. H. Spurgeon

163

ISRAEL—
Beloved of God

"O Israel, thou shalt not be forgotten of me."—Isa. 44:21.

Forgotten! No; that cannot be,
  All other names may pass away;
But thine, My Israel, shall remain
  In everlasting memory.

Forgotten! no; that cannot be,
  Inscribed upon My palms thou
    art,
The name I gave in days of old
  Is graven still upon My heart.

Forgotten! no; that cannot be,
  Beloved of thy God art thou;
His crown forever on thy head,
  His Name forever on thy brow.

Forgotten! no; that cannot be,
  He, Who upon thee named His
    Name,
Assures thee of eternal love,
  A love for evermore the same.

Forgotten! no; that cannot be,
  The oath of Him who cannot lie
Is on thy city and thy land
  An oath to all eternity.

Forgotten! no; that cannot be,
  The grace of ages deep and
    broad,
Is grace without decay, the grace,
  O Israel, of the Lord thy God.

Forgotten! no; that cannot be,
  Sun, moon, and stars may cease
    to shine,
But thou shalt be remembered still,
  For thou art His, and He is
    thine.

Forgotten of the Lord thy God!
No, Israel, no, that cannot be,
He chose thee in the days of old,
  And still His favour rests on
    thee.

—By Horatius Bonar

A Prayer Is Answered – and Fanny Crosby Writes Another Hymn

Among many characteristics of the blind poetess Fanny Crosby, three stand out. She always carried a little American flag. She either held it in her hand or kept it in her bag, and it was buried with her when she died in 1915 at the age of ninety-five. Though blinded in infancy, the petite "Aunt Fanny" (she was Mrs. Alexander Van Alstyne in private life) greeted friends and strangers alike with a cheerful "God bless your dear soul." And, according to her own statement, she never attempted to write a hymn without first kneeling in prayer. If this be true, Fanny Crosby spent considerable time on her knees. She wrote no less than 8,000 songs. So many that critics have said the chief fault with her work lies in that she was too prolific. But none can deny that many "pearls are found among the oyster shells."

Under contract for three hymns a week, Miss Crosby was often under pressure to meet deadlines. It was under such circumstances in 1869 that she tried to write words for a tune Composer W. H. Doane had sent her. But she couldn't write. Then she remembered she had forgotten her prayer. Rising from her knees, she dictated—as fast as her assistant could write—words for the famous hymn, "Jesus, Keep Me Near the Cross."

But one day in 1874 Fanny Crosby prayed for more material things. She had run short of money and needed five dollars—even change. There was no time to draw on her publishers, so she simply prayed for the money. Her prayer ended, she was walking to and fro in her room trying to "get into the mood" for another hymn when an admirer called. Greeting the stranger with "God bless your dear soul," the two chatted briefly. In the parting handshake the admirer left something in the hymn-writer's hand. It was five dollars—even change. Rising from a prayer of thanks the blind poetess wrote:

ALL THE WAY MY SAVIOUR LEADS ME
By Fanny Crosby, 1820-1915

All the way my Saviour leads me;
  What have I to ask beside?
Can I doubt His tender mercy,
  Who through life has been my Guide?
Heavenly peace, divinest comfort,
  Here by faith in Him to dwell!
For I know, whate'er befall me,
  Jesus doeth all things well.

All the way my Saviour leads me,
  Cheers each winding path I tread,
Gives me grace for every trial,
  Feeds me with the living bread.
Though my weary steps may falter,
  And my soul athirst may be,
Gushing from the Rock before me,
  Lo! a spring of joy I see.

All the way my Saviour leads me;
  Oh, the fullness of His love!
Perfect rest to me is promised
  In my Father's house above.
When my spirit, clothed immortal,
  Wings its flight to realms of day,
This my song thro' endless ages;
  Jesus led me all the way.

(From A HYMN IS BORN, by Clint Bonner. Published by Wilcox & Follett Co., Chicago.)

Dr. Charles Mayo met an ancient lady who claimed it was her 108th birthday. The famed surgeon was skeptical but, as ever, cordial. "Well, congratulations," he said. "I hope I'll see you on your 109th birthday."

"You will," the old gal cackled contentedly.

"I will?" he asked.

"Sure," she said. "Very few people die between 108 and 109. Look it up."

The pussyfooters and compromisers never attack modernists; they attack and slander fundamentalists! They are strong for love—that is, love for everybody but the old-fashioned Bible believers who fight for Christ and the Gospel.

—Dr. Bob Jones, Sr.

The further a man goes in lust and iniquity the more dead he becomes to purity and holiness; he loses the power to appreciate the beauties of virtue or to be disgusted with the abominations of vice.— C. H. Spurgeon.

The Watermelon

By WILLIAM JENNINGS BRYAN

I was passing through Columbus, Ohio, some years ago," says William J. Bryan, "and stopped to eat in the restaurant in the depot. My attention was called to a slice of watermelon, and I ordered it and ate it. I was so pleased with the melon that I asked the waiter to dry some of the seeds that I might take them home and plant them in my garden. That night a thought came into my mind—I would use that watermelon as an illustration. So, the next morning when I reached Chicago, I had enough seeds weighed to find out that it would take about five thousand watermelon seeds to weigh a pound and I estimated that the watermelon weighed about forty pounds. Then I applied mathematics to the water-melon. A few weeks before someone, I know not who, had planted a little seed in the ground. Under the influence of sunshine and shower that little watermelon seed had taken off its coat and gone to work; it had gathered from somewhere two hundred thousand times its own weight, and forced that enormous weight through a tiny stem and built a watermelon. On the outside it had put a covering of green, within that a rind of white and within that a core of red, and then it had scattered through the red, little seeds, each one capable of doing the same work over again. What archi-tect drew the plan? Where did that little watermelon seed get its tre-tect drew the plan? Where did it find its flavoring extract and its coloring matter? How did it build a watermelon? Until you can explain a water-melon do not be too sure that you can set limits to the power of the Al-mighty, or tell just what He would do, or how He would do it. The most learned man in the world cannot explain a watermelon, but the most ignorant man can eat a watermelon and enjoy it. God has given us the things that we need, and He has given us the knowledge necessary to use those things, and the truth that He has revealed to us is infinitely more important for our welfare than it would be to understand the mys-teries that He has seen fit to conceal from us.

"So with Christianity; if you ask me if I can understand everything in the Bible, I answer: No. I understand some things that I did not under-stand ten years ago, and if I live ten years longer, I hope some things will be clear that are now obscure. But there is something more important than understanding everything in the Bible,—it is this: if we will only try to live up to the things that we DO understand we will not have time to worry about the things that we DO NOT understand."

NOTE:—One thing is perfectly clear and may be tested by anyone, "To as many as received him (Jesus Christ), to them gave he power to become the sons of God; even to them that believe on his name" (John 1:12).

Life Everlasting

In the fourth century Chrysos-tom was brought before the wicked queen Eudoxia who demanded that he renounce his faith in Christ. She threatened, "If you do not, I will banish you." He replied, "You cannot, for every kingdom and every clime is mine." Then she said, "I will take your goods." But he came back, "Neither can you take my goods, for I have laid them up in Heaven where moth and rust do not corrupt and where thieves like you do not break through and steal." Then the queen threatened his life, and he replied, "Neither can you do that, for mine is life everlasting.

The rich people put money in a collection plate in the temple in Jerusalem. A widow put in two mites. Jesus said in substance, "She put in more than all the rest of them." She put her heart into the treasury. When our hearts are back of our gifts, they give a golden ring to the falling of a copper coin. There is a divine sacredness about everything we do if we have the Christian impulse of a surrendered heart back of our act. A Christian washing dish-es in her kitchen in the name of Jesus Christ is engaged in a work as sacredly divine as preaching the Gospel in a cathedral on the Sabbath morning. It is not how much we give nor how brilliant our gift is. The question is—what is the attitude of the heart? When Jesus washed the disciples' feet, He was just as beautifully divine as when He preached His sermon on the Mount. He made the job of a servant a high calling. He taught that the great ones are servants and that those who would go up must first go down. "Come unto me, all ye that labour and are heavy laden, and I will give you rest. Take my yoke upon you, and learn of me; for I am meek and lowly in heart: and ye shall find rest unto your souls." That is His invitation to tired hearts. We rest not by a cessation of work; we rest when we are willing to "yoke up" with Him in real, hon-est, faithful service to the glory of God.—*Dr. Bob Jones, Sr.*

Danger of Idleness

Master Greenham, a Puritan di-vine, was once waited upon by a woman who was greatly tempted. Upon making inquiries into her way of life, he found she had little to do, and Greenham said, "That is the secret of your being so much tempted. Sister, if you are very busy, Satan may tempt you, but he will not easily prevail, and he will soon give up an attempt." Idle Christians are not tempted of the devil so much as they tempt the devil to tempt them.—Spurgeon.

Early Conversions

Robert Hall, the prince of Baptist preach-ers, was converted at twelve years of age. Matthew Henry, the commentator, who did more than any man of his century for in-creasing the interest in the study of the Scriptures, was converted at eleven years of age; Isabella Graham, immortal in the Christian church, was converted at ten years of age; Dr. Watts, whose hymns will be sung all down the ages, was converted at nine years of age; Jonathan Edwards, perhaps the mightiest intellect that the American pulpit ever produced, was con-verted at seven years of age; and that father and mother take an awful responsi-bility when they tell their child at seven years of age, "You are too young to be a Christian," or, "You are too young to con-nect yourself with the church." That is a mistake as long as eternity.—Talmage.

Will Rogers' Letter to a Departed Friend

Dear Charley:

I bet you hadn't been up there three days until you had out your pencil and was a drawin' something funny. And I bet you that a whole bunch of those great old joshers was just a waitin' for you to pop in with all the latest ones.

And I bet they are regular fellows when you meet em, ain't they? Most big men are.

Well, you will run onto my old Dad up there, Charley, for he was a real cow hand, and I bet he is runnin' a wagon; and you will pop into some well-kept ranch-house, over under some cool shade trees, and you will be asked to dinner, and it will be the best one you ever had in your life. Well, when you are thankin' the women folks you just tell the sweet lookin' little old lady that you knew her boy, back on an outfit you used to rope for, and tell the daughters that you knew their brother, and if you see a cute little rascal runnin' around there with my brand on him, kiss him for me.

Well, can't write any more, Charley, paper's all wet, it must be raining in this old bunk house. Of course we're all just hangin' on here as long as we can. I don't know why we hate to go, we know it's better there.

From your old friend,

WILL

'MID PLEASURE, PLENTY, AND SUCCESS,
　FREELY WE TAKE FROM HIM WHO LENDS:
WE BOAST THE BLESSING WE POSSESS,
　YET SCARCELY THANK THE ONE WHO SENDS.

BUT LET AFFLICTION POUR ITS SMART,
　HOW SOON WE QUAIL BENEATH THE ROD!
WITH SHATTERED PRIDE, AND PROSTRATE HEART,
　WE SEEK THE LONG FORGOTTEN GOD.
　　　　　　　—ELIZA COOK.

There are 365 "Fear Nots" in the Bible, or one for every day of the year.—

I will not permit any man to narrow and degrade my soul by making me hate him.
—Booker T. Washington.

Detective System

"Hey, Bud!" A tall blonde officer placed a delaying hand on the khaki-clad arm of a young soldier as both men turned to leave the mess hall. "You're a Christian, aren't you?" he asked.

"Sure! But how did you know?"

"Oh, I've got my own private detective system that helps me locate other Christians. Every time I've been transferred I've tried it with success."

"Care to tell me about it?" the younger officer asked.

"Certainly," came the quick reply. "You see when I first got into the service, I thought I'd die with loneliness for the kind of young people I knew at home. Then one day I got an idea that changed things. Now, I watch the fellows when they sit down to eat. Before I bow my head to say grace, I keep a sharp eye out for others who do the same. I've found that any fellow who isn't ashamed to bow his head and thank the Lord for his food is usually a pretty good Christian. That's how I found you." (The Lutheran)

What the World Is Looking for

By L. S. Walker

The world is looking for men who are not for sale, men who are honest, sound from center to circumference, true to the heart's core, men with conscience as steady as the needle to the pole; men who will stand for right if the heavens titter and the earth reels; men who will tell the truth and look the world right in the eye; men who neither drag nor run, men who neither flag nor flinch; men who can have courage without shouting it; men in whom courage of everlasting life runs still, deep and strong; men who know their message and tell it; men who know their place and fill it; men who know their business and attend to it; men who will not lie, shirk, or dodge; men who are not too lazy to work, nor too proud to be poor; men who are willing to eat what they have earned and wear what they have paid for; men who are not ashamed to say "no" with emphasis, and who are not ashamed to say, "I can't afford it."—Selected

A man who walks with God always gets to his destination.

Ready to Go

When many of the passengers on a boat in Lake Michigan were very upset because of the danger of a raging storm, D. L. Moody seemed quiet and calm. When he was asked how he could be that way, he replied, "I have a sister in Chicago and one in Heaven; I don't care which I see first."

Beautiful Things

The following article was found in the pocket of Pearley W. Graves:

The beautiful things are the things we do; they are not the things we wear, as we shall find when the journey is over and the roll call is read up there. We're illustrating the latest styles with raiment that beats the band, but the beautiful things are the kindly smiles that go with the helping hand. We burden ourselves with the gleaming gems, that neighbors may stop and stare; but the beautiful things are the diadems of stars that the righteous wear.

There are beautiful things in the poor man's cot, though empty the hearth and cold; if love and service are in each thought that husband and wife may hold. There are beautiful things in the lowest slum where wandering outcasts now grope, when down to its depths they see you come with messages of help and hope. The beautiful things that we mortals buy and flash in the crowded street, will all be junk when we come to die, and march to the judgment seat. When e v e r y t h i n g 's weighed on that fateful day, the lightest thing will be gold. There are beautiful things within reach today, but they are not bought nor sold.

—From **Defender of Faith.**

Frank Word About BOOZE

There probably has never been a franker advertisement in the world than that which was made by one James M. Lawrence, who opened 'The Naked Truth Saloon' in Boise, Idaho, on February 24, 1886, and who ran an advertisement in the Boise Democrat of that date as follows:

"Friends and Neighbors: Having just opened a commodious shop for the sale of liquid fire, I embrace this opportunity of informing you that I have commenced the business of making drunkards, paupers and beggars for the sober, industrious and respectable portion of the community to support. I shall deal in family spirits which will incite men to deeds of riots, robbery and bloodshed, and by so doing diminish the comfort, augment the expenses, and endanger the welfare of the community.

"I will on short notice, for a sum, and with great expectations, undertake to prepare victims for the asylums, poor farms, prisons and gallows.

"I will furnish an article that will increase accidents, multiply the number of distressing diseases, and render those who are harmless incurables.

"I will deal in drugs which will deprive some of life, many of reason, most of property, and all of their peace, which will cause fathers to become fiends, and wives widows, and children to become orphans and all mendicants.

"I will cause many of the rising generation to grow up in ignorance and prove a burden and a nuisance to the nation. I will cause mothers to forget their offspring, and cruelty to take the place of love.

"I will sometimes corrupt the ministers of religion, defile the purity of the Church, and cause temporary spiritual and eternal death, and if any be so impertinent as to ask me why I have the audacity to bring such accumulated misery upon the people, my honest reply is, 'Money.' The spirit trade is lucrative and some professing Christians give their cheerful countenance.

"From the U. S. government I have purchased the right to demolish the character, destroy the health, and shorten the lives and ruin the souls of those who choose to honor me with their custom.

"I pledge myself to do all that I have promised. Those who wish any of the evils before specified brought upon themselves or their dear friends, are requested to meet me at my bar where I will for a few cents furnish them with the certain means of doing so."

If these words applied 67 years ago, they apply equally today.

The Cross

The cross! Poets have sung its praise; sculptors have attempted to commemorate it in marble; martyrs have clung to it in fire; and Christians, dying quietly in their beds, have leaned their heads against it. May all our souls embrace it with an ecstacy of affection! Lay hold of that cross, O dying sinner! Everything else will fail you. Without a strong grip of that you perish. Put your hand on that, and you are safe, though the world swing from beneath your feet. Oh, that I might engrave on your souls ineffaceably the three crosses, and that if in your waking moments you will not heed, then that in your dream tonight you might see on the hill back of Jerusalem the three spectacles—the right-hand cross, showing unbelief and dying without Christ; the left-hand cross, showing what it is to be pardoned; while the central cross pours upon your soul the sunburst of heaven as it says: "By all these would I plead for thy heart. I have loved thee with an everlasting love. Rivers can not quench it. The floods can not drown it."

—DeWitt Talmage

Speak Cheerful Words

Why is it that so many people keep all their pleasant thoughts and kind words about a man bottled and sealed until he is dead, when they come and break the bottle over his coffin, and bathe his shroud in fragrance? Many a man goes through life with scarcely one bright, cheerful, encouraging, hopeful word. He toils hard and in lowly obscurity. He gives out his life freely and unstintedly for others. I remember such a man. He was not brilliant; he was not great; but he was faithful. He had many things to discourage him. Troubles thickened about his life. He was mispresented and misunderstood. Everybody believed that he was a good man, but no one ever said a kindly word or pleasant thing to him. He never heard a compliment, scarcely ever a good wish. No one ever took any pains to encourage him, to strengthen his feeble knees, to lighten his burdens, or to lift up his heart by a gentle deed of love, or by a cheerful word. He was neglected. Unkind things were often said of him.

I stood at his coffin, and then there were many tongues to speak his praise. There was not a breath of aspersion in the air. Men spoke of self denial—of his work among the poor, of his quietness, modesty, his humility, his pureness of heart, his faith and prayer.

There were many who spoke indignantly of the charges that falsehood had forged against him in past years, and of the treatment he had received. There were enough kind things said during the two or three days that he lay in his coffin, and while the company stood around his open grave, to have blessed him and made him happy all his fifty years, and to have thrown sweetness and joy about his soul during all his painful and weary journey. There was enough sunshine wasted about the black coffin and dark grave to have made his whole life-path bright as the clearest day.

But his ears were closed then, and could not hear a word that was spoken. His heart was still then, and could not be thrilled by the grateful sounds. He cared nothing then for the sweet flowers that were piled upon his coffin. The love blossomed out too late. The kindness came when the life could not receive its blessings.

—Anonymous.

The "Usin' and Thummin' "

A young pastor, unduly impressed with his own knowledge of the Bible, was talking with an elderly saint who knew his Bible, but was lacking in formal education. He asked the elderly brother a catch question: "Can you tell me what the Urim and Thummim were?" "No," replied the elderly brother, "I don't think I know exactly, though I understand they were on the breastplate of the High Priest, and that through them the priest could observe the mind of the Lord. But their use suggests to me another way to find the mind of the Lord."

"How is that?" asked the young pastor. "By just changing three letters," said the elder man. "I take this blessed old Book, and by Usin' it and Thummin' it I gain a clear understanding of the will of God!"—*Christian Victory.*

The Sweetest Verse

The old saint was not far from the pearly gates when his minister came to see him, as he had done many times. Looking tenderly down on him, he said, "I'm not going to weary you now, but I'll read to you the sweetest verse in the Bible, and then we'll have prayer together."

He then opened his pocket Testament at the fourteenth chapter of John's Gospel, and read: "In my Father's house are many mansions: if it were not so I would have told you," and was closing the book and kneeling in prayer, when the dying man stretched out a delaying hand, and whispered, "No, that isn't the sweetest verse. Read on."

So the minister read: "And if I go and prepare a place for you, I will come again, and receive you unto myself; that where I am, there ye may be also." At that a seraphic smile spread over the face of the dying saint, "That's it," he whispered. "That's the sweetest verse. It is not the mansions: it is Himself I want."

Prayer Plus Whipping

Bob Jones, D.D., LL.D.

"I cannot see the flowers, but I can still hear the birds sing." These were words on the lips of the mother of Sergeant Alvin York, the great hero of the first World War. Mrs. York has died. She was a woman of rugged Christian character and simple Christian faith. She told her son when he was going off to war, "You fight. I will stay at home and work and pray."

Great men are the sons of great mothers. The world needs mothers of Christian faith and of strong character.

"How did you bring up such manly sons?" a man inquired of a feeble old woman whose sons had gone away from her to bless the world. "I brought them up on prayer and switches," the mother said.

"I am praying for my boy," a woman said one day, "and I am hoping he will be a good boy."

"You can help answer your prayer by giving the boy a good whipping," this writer told her. PRAYER IS NOT A SUBSTITUTE FOR FIRMNESS AND DISCIPLINE. We have some very "soft pray-ers."

The world needs people with great faith in God. Proper faith in God will produce strong character. Abraham believed God and his character grew with the years. The right kind of faith is the best foundation on which character can be built. There is a great deal of sickly sentimentalism that people mistake for Christianity. Peter was impulsive and rather temperamental, but his faith in Jesus Christ turned him into a "Rock-character." GOD CANNOT USE MOTHERS WHO ARE WEAK OR FATHERS WHO HAVE NO CHARACTER, TO BRING UP GREAT SONS AND DAUGHTERS TO BLESS THE WORLD.

The old-time, rugged Christian mothers had something that few mothers have. These mothers had much to do with laying the foundations of our civilization in such a way that the house, in spite of all that has been done to it by modern, superficial women who live for pleasure instead of God, is still standing. "She that liveth in pleasure is dead while she liveth," so Paul said.

The love of pleasure has sapped the spiritual vitality of many mothers. So we need not be surprised that children are out-running these mothers on the road of sinful pleasure and sometimes on the road of moral looseness. God give us rugged, strong Christian mothers who will bring up their children in the nuture and admonition of the Lord!

When there's trouble some folks meet it,
Others pull up stakes and beat it.

The modern child learns at his mother's knee to watch out for hot ashes.

An ex-inmate said that at Sing Sing he couldn't sing because he was behind too many bars and didn't have the right key.

Go ahead and do it. It's easier to succeed than to explain why you didn't.

NONE BUT GOD

By Missionary H. Mel Rutter

The war was over! Now our objective was no longer Tokyo but that beloved place somewhere in the United States called "Home, Sweet Home." We were on the large island of Okinawa just a short distance south of Japan. The island was only a shell of her former self. She had been devastated by bombings, shellings, and weeks of guerilla warfare. Her cities were in shambles. The countryside was laid waste. Most of the populace from the cities had fled to the interior and thousands upon thousands were living in crude makeshift villages.

We were encamped just south of Naha awaiting our return to the States. It was a real opportunity for Satan since "idleness is his workshop." He was not wasting his time; sin was rampant everywhere. Some of us Christians were having nightly Bible study. We were witnessing to the soldiers, but it was difficult as most of them seemed to have two purposes in life; that of pleasure and that of getting home. They were "lovers of pleasure more than lovers of God." The multitudes of Okinawans, who for the most part had not heard the Gospel, presented a real mission challenge, but the language barrier loomed before us.

Then God answered prayer and allowed us to make the acquaintance of a lovely Christian girl called Rose of Sharon. Rose spoke perfect English as well as her own Okinawan dialect and had a real compassion for the souls of her people. She and a friend of hers volunteered to go with us to these makeshift villages in the hills to preach to the people. Another soldier and I were taking turns preaching, and she would interpret for us. (That is, she took our English words and would tell them to her own people in their native tongue.) We emphasized and re-emphasized the need of the new birth (spiritual birth from above) without which, Jesus says, 'no man can see the kingdom of God.'

One day Bob and I arrived at Rose's house to get her to go with us to preach, only to find that she and her friend had already left for the little church in the hills where we had been holding evangelistic services. By the time we arrived services had already begun, and the Christians were singing with all their hearts. The little bamboo church was so packed we could barely get inside. One of the brethren escorted us down to the front. We sat down, and I glanced up to the platform. There stood Rose radiating the love of Christ. She smiled and nodded to us.

Then I noticed the speaker for our service and my heart sank! It was Chaplain _____, a major in the United States Army. Bob and I knew him well. He was a rank modernist! We had heard him declare that the Bible was not the inspired Word of God and that it was full of error. He also said that Jesus was a very good man, surely one of the ten best that had ever lived, but that He was NOT the Son of God. He scoffed at the idea of His shed blood and said his God was a gentleman and would not "bargain" with blood. He said God was love and would never send anyone to Hell, that man was not bad or sinful by nature but good, and if we just brought out the good, the beautiful, and the true, we would make him acceptable to God. You who know your Bible know that these are lies of the Devil!

I was puzzled! How did Rose of Sharon get mixed up with this modernist?

My thoughts were interrupted as a dear old silver-haired Okinawan stood to pray. We knew him to be a real man of God, fervent in spirit, a real soldier of the cross. Although I could not understand his language as he prayed, I realized it to be the language that our Lord understands, the language of His love, and my heart burned within me as I felt the presence of God. Never have I heard anyone pray with such power.

(see next page) ———→

An old lady said she just had two teeth and she thanked God that they met.

Kindness is the language that the dumb can speak and the deaf can hear and understand.

A practical gift this year would be a loose-leaf atlas.--Dan Kidney.

169

"Never get mad at anyone for knowing more than you do. It is not his fault."

* * *

CIRCULATION DEPARTMENT
A Scotchman wrote to the editor of a magazine saying that if he didn't quit publishing Scotch jokes in it that he would quit borrowing the magazine.

After he sat down Rose sang a beautiful song about our wonderful Saviour! Then the chaplain stood to speak (his bony little legs showing beneath his khaki shorts) and I do mean speak, because preaching was foreign to him. He talked about the flowers being beautiful, mentioned the wide ocean that separated us from our homes (never mentioning the Water of Life, or our separation from our heavenly Home), and talked about a book called *A Tree Grows in Brooklyn* (never mentioning the tree of Calvary upon which hung our blessed Saviour). In fact, he only mentioned the name of God twice. He never mentioned the name of Jesus, the cross, sin, Hell, salvation; he just talked and talked. All of this time Rose of Sharon was interpreting; she was talking to her people in the Okinawan dialect.

When the chaplain finished his talk he sat down, and then the unbelievable happened! Rose walked back and forth in front of her people, her cheeks were stained with tears, and she beckoned with her hands for them to come to the altar. The Spirit was strong, people seemed convicted of sin, and many were coming down the aisles weeping and giving every outward evidence of repentance. It was the only time I have ever seen souls being saved when I just could not enjoy it! I was perplexed! How could this be? My soul cried out within me! This man is a modernist, disallows that man is a sinner and needs a Saviour, denies Christ, and yet the people were coming, broken, agonizing, and apparently being saved. He never even mentioned the name of Jesus, and He alone can save!

I could hardly wait until the service was over and at the very first opportunity I said, "Rose, was that real? Were souls really confessing sin? Were people really taking Christ as their personal Saviour?"

She nodded in the affirmative to all of my questions.

"But, Rose, how could this be? That man, that chaplain, is a rank modernist; he does not even believe in our Christ!"

She smiled as she looked up at me and said, "You see, Brother Mel, I did not tell my people what that chaplain said....I just told them about Jesus!"

Well, praise God! I know some preachers who could use an interpreter like her, do you not? Brother, if God has called you to preach, preach! Preach the Book, the blood, and the blessed hope!

When Rose told me that, my soul was flooded with great joy and tears filled my eyes. Again the Holy Spirit took out His auger and bit of love and bored deeply into my soul. He spoke gently, "Mel, back a few years ago (according to Rose's testimony) there was a Baptist missionary who lived in Hawaii. He really knew the Lord, really loved lost souls, and was faithful to witness. He was responsible for Rose of Sharon's coming to know Jesus!" This young Okinawan lady so loved her Saviour that she forfeited her good government job with excellent pay, security, and sunny Hawaii to return to her own war-torn land. She had lived under great privation for months and was faithful to go up and down telling her people about Jesus and His power to save! She lifted Jesus up, and He promised that if He be lifted up, He would draw all men unto Himself! God by-passed a chaplain, who was a major in the United States Army, and spoke through a lowly, faithful girl to the war-ravished people in the hills of Okinawa that day. It was NONE BUT GOD!

Friend, you may be listening to the cultured trash of some educated minister. He may also be a modernist, may deny the verbally inspired Word of God and the atoning power of Christ's shed blood. But no matter how good he may tell you that you are, God says you are a sinner, that the final wages of your sin is to go to Hell. He also tells us that He is not willing that any should perish, and that if you will repent of your sins and trust Jesus, His only begotten Son, as your Saviour, you will have everlasting life!

Will you not repent and trust Him now?

A short time before Christmas the little boy told his father he would like a baby brother for Christmas. His father said, "But, Son, there's not enough shopping days left."

Patience: Ability to count down before blasting off.

Scientists have computed that it takes one-fiftieth of a second to blink an eye and that a person blinks 25 times a minute. Thus, a motorist who averages 55 miles per hour on a 10-hour trip, drives 33 miles with his eyes shut.

Ten Sentence Sermons on Scriptural Giving

Roy F. Miller

1. The Willing Giver—Abraham in the offering of his son.

2. The Big Little Giver — the widow who in giving two mites gave most of all.

3. The Givers Who Were Not Niggardly—the Macedonians, who gave up to their ability and beyond.

4. The Unpretentious Giver—the Good Samaritan, who made no show of his giving.

5. The Sacrificial Giver—David, who in buying the threshing floor of Araunah would not give to the Lord that which had cost him nothing.

6. The Voluntary Giver — Zacchaeus, the man who did not wait to be asked to give.

7. Givers Who Had Nothing to Give—Peter and John: "Silver and gold have I none," but gave themselves.

8. The Covetous Givers—Ananias and Sapphira, who held back a part and suffered dire penalty.

9. The First Givers—the Wise men, who came from the heathen world!

10. The Giver Who Did Not Count the Cost—Mary, who gave lavishly of the gifts of love.

—*Watchman-Examiner*

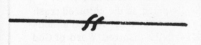

Three "Fifteens"

When Billy Sunday was converted and joined the church, a Christian man put his arm on the young man's shoulder and said, "William, there are three simple rules I can give to you, and if you will hold to them you will never write 'backslider' after your name.

"Take 15 minutes each day to listen to God talking to you; take 15 minutes each day to talk to God; take 15 minutes each day to talk to others about God."

This young convert was deeply impressed and determined to make these the rules of his life. From that day onward throughout his life he made it a rule to spend the first moments of his day alone with God and God's Word. Before he read a letter, looked at a paper or even read a telegram, he went first to the Bible, that the first impression of the day might be what he got directly from God.

—Ashville (N. C.) Church Bulletin

Teen Talks

By Rev. Bud Lyles

Christian Patriotism

It seems that those who will admit it are getting fewer and fewer but our great country was founded by God-fearing men who came here under religious persecution to establish one nation where men might worship God in freedom. The sacred documents of this nation, The Declaration of Independence, The Pledge of Allegiance to the Flag, The National Anthem, all have reference to God. This is a nation that was founded upon faith in God and in His Word. Without doubt this is why this nation has been blessed as has no other nation on the face of God's earth. It is one nation that has publicly and privately honored God.

When we begin to turn our backs upon our heritage of faith, we are headed for trouble. The Bible warns plainly, "The wicked shall be turned into hell, and all the nations that forget God" (Ps. 9:17). The attempts by some to eliminate God from our society may ultimately lead us to the point where God is left with no alternative but to bring judgment against America. It is axiomatic that God honors those who honor Him. It is also true that those who dishonor God and His Word place themselves in position to experience the fierce anger of the Lord. We who are Americans should thank God that we are privileged to live in this land so blessed of God. We could just as easily have been born in Russia or China. We might have been born in Cuba or some other land where we would not enjoy our freedoms and blessings as we do here.

Sure, there are some things we do not like. Taxes keep rising and so do crime rates. We dislike the war and sending our boys across the waters to fight and die. We dislike deficit spending and would like a balanced budget. We dislike government hand-outs that produce generation after generation of dependent people who are too lazy to work to better themselves. But though we may speak out against our faults and do what we can to improve the situation, we should still thank God that we are Americans and we should set out to be loyal and true and patriotic. With all of its faults,

America is the greatest nation and the best place in the world to live.

This week our nation celebrates Independence Day, the 192nd anniversary of the adoption of the Declaration of Independence. On this great anniversary we Christian Americans need to consider again our own dedication to the causes upon which this nation was founded. We are too often inclined to let others be vocal. We need to stand up and speak up for the things in which we believe. We believe the Bible and should say so. We believe in God and should shout it. We believe in the American way of life and should let others know about it. We have let the radicals use the freedoms won by our forefathers to intimidate us. We need to take hold of those freedoms and let the world know that all Americans are not sick. There are a great many of us who still believe this country is worth fighting and dying for today.

Those men who signed the Declaration of Independence pledged themselves in the last sentence of that document: "and for the support of this Declaration, with a firm reliance on the Protection of Divine Providence, we mutually pledge to each other our Lives, our Fortunes and our sacred Honor." Most of the men who signed that Declaration suffered great hardship. Some lost family, home, fortune and some their very lives. They did not count the cost too great. They stood upon principle. Their character was such that they could do no less.

In our present soft, affluent society, we have grown tolerant of draft-card burners and flag desecraters. In our defense of freedom of speech, we have allowed some to stump the land advocating treason. It is time some Christian Americans led some demonstrations of patriotism. Instead of instigating and leading civil disobedience riots, some of our preachers should demonstrate their love and support for a nation that gives them freedom to preach.

Sure, I believe in the principle of separation of church and state. I do not believe that any religion should be forced upon anyone by law or by any other means. But our national constitution guarantees us freedom of religion, not freedom *from* religion.

We Christian Americans need to stand up for our faith. We need to stand up for our country and defend it from those who would try to bring it down whether from within or from outside our borders. God Bless America!!

Suggested New Year's Resolutions

By John R. Rice

Let me earnestly suggest some New Year's resolutions, some changes in your life that very possibly ought to be made now, early in the new year.

1. Do you read the Bible every day? How much of it do you read? Have you ever read it through? You may read the Bible through in less than a year by reading one chapter each day in the New Testament or the Psalms, and three chapters daily in the rest of the Old Testament. Better set a time early in the day when you can read your Bible alone. Do not rush. Read consecutively chapter after chapter through a book. Memorize favorite verses. Pray for God to use the Scriptures in your heart. Read not less than one chapter reverently every day, and you should average at least four chapters daily. Shame on a Christian who has never even read his Bible through!

2. You should have a special time of secret prayer everyday, preferably in the morning. It may be in connection with your Bible reading. Be sure to thank God for His mercies. Take every burden to God, every earnest desire of your heart and keep praying till you have peace. Confess your sins, mistakes and failures daily and have them out of the way, cleansed and forgiven. It is better if possible to have a regular time and a customary place for secret prayer. However, one should pray all through the day, should join in family prayers, etc.

3. Does your home have family worship? It should include reading aloud of the Bible by every member of the family old enough to read. It ought to include prayer by every member of the family who is saved. The family altar ought to be made so important that every member of the family is expected to be present, even more important than being to school on time, or at work on time. If people are late in school or work a time or two, they will learn to co-operate, get up earlier, and expect God's blessing. The family altar will not succeed unless it is counted important, and only on unusual occasion should any member of the family be excused.

In my judgment, the best time for most families is immediately after breakfast. Set breakfast early enough, get everybody ready, have Bibles at hand, push back the plates and read while all are at the table. When my children were at home, we read consecutively two verses each, around the table, through a chapter (or with short Psalms, through two chapters). Mrs. Rice and I still follow this plan. Thus everyone must pay attention, everyone takes part, and children learn to read the Bible and pronounce the words. Then have prayer, each one in order, around the table. Of course, we have thanks before all the meals besides this. Why not establish family worship in your home, for the new year?

4. Do you tithe? That is, do you give one-tenth of your income to the Lord and His cause? God required tithes under the ceremonial law. Surely a Christian under grace should not do less. God blesses those who love Him enough to put Him first on the money question. I thank God for marvelous blessings given in connection with my tithing. Will you give God the first tenth of your income this year? Remember, the tithe is the Lord's, so ask Him where to give every dollar. It does not belong to the deacons, to the finance committee, nor to the nance church but to the Lord. Support your local church in proportion as its work is worthy and other work as God leads.

A Teenager's Code

In submitting her ten commandments the youthful author, Virginia Chose, suggests that "if every teen-ager would follow these simple rules, the world would be a safer place to live in." To which one may add "Amen."

1. Don't let your parents down. They brought you up.
2. Stop and think before you drink.
3. Ditch dirty thoughts fast, or they'll ditch you.
4. Show-off driving is juvenile. Don't act your age.
5. Be smart: Obey. You'll give orders yourself someday.
6. Choose your friends carefully. You are what they are.
7. Choose a date fit for a mate.
8. Don't go steady unless you're ready.
9. Go to church regularly. God gives a week. Give Him back some hours.
10. Listen to the Gospel. The soul you save may be your own.

—From *The Word and Way*

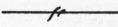

'All I Hear'

"All I hear is money," said the barber. "The church is always asking for money. I think a person should give as he feels like it, instead of tithing."

When the haircut was over the minister got out of the chair and gave the barber a quarter. The barber told him that wasn't enough. The preacher commented, "I thought I would give as I felt like it."

Worry is the advance interest you pay on troubles that seldom come.

A person who "knows everything" has a lot to learn.

It's hard for children to learn manners when they never see any.

The fellow who has the right to boast doesn't have to do it.

The first grader slipped in the hall and skinned his knee.

"Remember, big boys don't cry," called the teacher.

"I'm not gonna cry," the lad replied. "I'm gonna sue."

Over the Hill to the Poorhouse

Over the hill to the poorhouse I'm trudgin' my weary way—
I, a woman of seventy, and only a trifle gray—
I, who am smart an' chipper, for all the years I've told,
As many another woman that's only half as old.

Over the hill to the poorhouse—I can't quite make it clear!
Over the hill to the poorhouse—it seems so horrid queer!
Many a step I've taken, a-toilin' to and fro,
But this is a sort of journey I never thought to go.

What is the use of heapin' on me a pauper's shame?
Am I lazy or crazy? am I blind or lame?
True, I am not so supple, nor so awful stout;
But charity ain't no favor, if one can live without.

I am ready and willin' an' anxious any day
To work for a decent livin', an' pay my honest way;
For I can earn my victuals, an' more too, I'll be bound,
If anybody is willin' to only have me 'round.

Once I was young an' han'some—I was, upon my soul—
Once my cheeks was roses, my eyes as black as coal;
And I can't remember, in them days, of hearin' people say,
For any kind of a reason, that I was in their way!

'Tain't no use of boastin', or talkin' over free,
But many a house an' home was open then to me;
Many a han'some offer I had from likely men,
And nobody ever hinted that I was a burden then!

And when to John I was married, sure he was good and smart,
But he and all the neighbors would own I done my part;
For life was all before me, an' I was young an' strong,
And I worked my best an' smartest in tryin' to get along.

And so we worked together: and life was hard, but gay,
With now and then a baby to cheer us on our way;
Till we had a dozen: an' all growed clean an' neat,
And went to school like others, an' had enough to eat.

With now and then a baby to
cheer us on our way . . .

An' so we worked for the child'rn, and raised 'em every one;
Worked for 'em summer and winter, just as we ought to 've done;
Only perhaps we humored 'em, which some good folks condemn;
But every couple's own child'rn's a heap the dearest to them!

Strange how much we think of our blessed little ones!—
I'd have died for my daughters, I'd have died for my sons;
And God he made that rule of love; but when we're old and gray,
I've noticed it sometimes somehow fails to work the other way.

Strange, another thing: when our boys an' girls was grown,
And when, exceptin' Charley, they'd left us there alone;
When John he nearer an' nearer came, an' dearer seemed to be,
The Lord—of Hosts!—He came one day an' took him away from me!

173

Still I was bound to struggle, an' never to cringe or fall—
Still I worked for Charley, for Charley was now my all;
And Charley was pretty good to me, with scarce a word or frown,
Till at last he went a-courtin', and brought a wife from town.

She was somewhat dressy, an' hadn't a pleasant smile—
She was quite conceity, and carried a heap o' style;
But if ever I tried to be friends, I did with her, I know;
But she was hard and haughty, an' we couldn't make it go.

She had an edication, an' that was good for her;
But when she twitted me on mine, 'twas carryin' things too fur;
An' I told her once, 'fore company (an' it almost made her sick),
That I never swallowed a grammar, or 'et a 'rithmetic.

So 'twas only a few days before the thing was done—
They was a family of themselves, and I another one;
And a very little cottage one family will do,
But I never have seen a mansion that was big enough for two.

An' I never could speak to suit her, never could please her eye,
An' it made me independent, an' then I didn't try;
But I was terribly humbled, and felt it like a blow,
When Charley turned ag'in me, an' told me I could go!

I went to live with Susan: but Susan's house was small,
And she was always a-hintin' how snug it was for us all;
And what with her husband's sisters, and what with child'rn three,
'Twas easy to discover there wasn't room for me.

An' then I went with Thomas, the oldest son I've got:
For Thomas's buildings 'd cover the half of an acre lot;
But all the child'rn was on me—I couldn't stand their sauce—
And Thomas said I needn't think I was comin' there to boss.

An' then I wrote to Rebecca, my girl who lives out West,
And to Isaac, not far from her—some twenty miles at best;
And one of 'em said 'twas too warm there for anyone so old,
And t'other had an opinion the climate was too cold.

So they have shirked and slighted me, an' shifted me about—
So they have well nigh soured me, an' wore my old heart out;
But still I've borne up pretty well, an' wasn't much put down
Till Charley went to the poor-master, an' put me on the town!

Over the hill to the poorhouse —my child'rn dear, good-by!
Many a night I've watched you when only God was nigh;
And God'll judge between us; but I will al'ays pray
That you shall never suffer the half I do today!
                                        —by Will Carleton, in *Farm Ballads*

"So, you're lost, little man," said the lady. "Why didn't you hang onto your mother's skirt?"

Replied the lad: "Couldn't reach it."

"I am afraid doctor," said Mrs. Brown, "that my husband has some terrible affliction. Sometimes I talk to him for hours and then discover that he hasn't heard a word."

"That isn't an affliction, madam," was the weary reply. "That's a gift."

Over the Hill From the Poorhouse

Over the hill to the poorhouse I went, one winter's day:
I—who was always considered a "bad stick" anyway;
I—who was always gettin' in a large assortment of tricks,
And always sure to be quoted as "the worst of the Deacon's six."

Tom was a steady fellow, and saved up all he got;
But when it came to payin' his debts, he'd always rather not;
And Isaac could quote the Scriptures, an' never forgot nor slipped;
But "Honor thy father and mother" was one of the verses he skipped.

An' as for Susan an' 'Becca, their hearts, as one might say,
Was good—what there was of 'em—which wasn't much, anyway;
And all of our little family was good as you'll often see,
Exceptin' one poor fellow—and that 'ere one was me.

All of the rest was steady, an' nice, an' good, an' right;
All of the rest was sober—but I was mainly tight;
An' when I "borrowed" two horses, or helped to, just for fun—
If I hadn't been drunk as blazes, it never would have been done.

But when they sent me to prison, the hardest grief I felt
Was when my poor old mother beside me feebly knelt,
And cried and prayed all 'round me, till I got melted down,
And cried as I wouldn't have cried that day for half the horses in town.

And with my left arm 'round her—my right hand lifted high—
I swore henceforth to be honest, and sober live and die;
And I went and served my term out, although 'twas a bitter pill,
Which many fellows ought to take who probably never will.

And when I had served my sentence, I thought 'twould answer the best
To take the advice of Greeley: "Go West, young man, go West!"
And how I came to prosper there, I never could understand;
For Fortune seemed to like me—she gave me a winning hand!

And year after year I prospered, and kept a-going ahead;
And wrote to a trusty neighbor East, to tell 'em that I was dead;
And died a good straight fellow; for I knew it would please them more
Than if I had lived to a hundred and twelve—the chap that I was
  before!

But when this trusty neighbor—he wrote a line to me—
"Your mother's in the poorhouse, a-pining away," says he:
To keep dead any longer—I knew that it wouldn't be right;
So I'd a private resurrection, and started for her that night.

And when I came in the old town, my first act was to buy
A snug and handsome cottage, which rather seemed to my eye
To look just like the old one; I finished it off the same;
You couldn't have told the difference—if you could, I wasn't to blame!

I swore henceforth to be honest,
and sober live and die . . . . .

175

The same old clock in the corner; the fireplace, wide and high,
Sent up the smoke and cinders, and flung them towards the sky;
From garret down to cellar—'twas all the selfsame thing:
'Twas good enough for the President—'twas fine enough for a king!

Then over the hill to the poorhouse, one blustering winter day,
With two fleet nags and a cutter, I swiftly took my way:
The fleetest nags in the county, and both as black as coal—
They very much resembled the pair of horses I stole.

I hitched in front of the poorhouse—I opened the poorhouse door;
My poor old mother was on her knees, a-scrubbin' the kitchen floor!
I coughed a little, on purpose—she started, in surprise—
Rose up, with scared expression, an' looked me in the eyes.

I slowly walked up to her, an' all her troubles' trace
I saw in the lines of sorrow that marred her dear old face:
"Mother, O Mother!" I shouted; "your poorhouse contract's done;
An' you henceforth are adopted, by your resurrected son!"

She didn't faint nor holloa—but knelt down by my side,
And thanked the Lord for saving her me, till I broke down and cried;
But maybe our ride wasn't merry! and maybe we wasn't gay;
And maybe I didn't wrap her up that blustering winter day!

And maybe, when we had got home, and entered the cottage door,
She didn't start back kind of sudden—as if she'd seen it before!
And maybe it wasn't pleasant—our cozy evening tea—
With her quite often stoppin', and huggin', and kissin' me!

And maybe we didn't live happy, for quite a number of years!
And I gained the respect of my neighbors—in spite of my brother's
sneers,
And spite of my sisters' caution; who said, as I have heard,
That they never could own a brother that had been a prison bird!

But I'll bet, when the great bugle rings out its cheerful notes,
And the good Lord Almighty sorts out His sheep and goats,
However my case is settled. if you are there you'll see
That my old Christian mother will stand right up for me.

—by Will Carleton, in *Farm Ballads*

And maybe we didn't live happy
for quite a number of years . . . .

Emerging from the beauty shop resplendent in a new coiffuer, a woman was confronted by a neighbor.

"Why, Margie," said the neighbor, "what did you do to your hair! It looks like a wig."

"It is a wig," Margie replied.

"Well, my goodness," said the neighbor, "I'd never have known it."

Clearance Rack!

He: "How come your sister married such a halfwit?"

She: "Oh, she's such a bargain-hunter she couldn't resist anything that was fifty per cent off!"

EPITAPHS EXTRAORDINARY...

...seen in Britain's old churches and churchyards:

A husband's seemingly lighthearted farewell to his wife:

Here lies my wife, Samantha
    Proctor,
She ketched a cold and wouldn't
    doctor,
She couldn't stay, she had to go--
Praise God from whom all blessings
    flow.

To be seen at Hertford; takes the form of a rhymed dialogue between husband and wife:

Woman:

Grieve not for me, my husband
    dear,
I am not dead but sleeping here;
With patience wait, prepare to
    die,
And, in a short time, you'll
    come to I.

Man:

I am not grieved, my dearest wife;
Sleep on, I've got another wife.
Therefore I cannot come to thee
For I must go and live with she!

The widow of a certain Jared Bates was evidently thinking of her own future, judging from the inscription on her husband's tombstone:

Sacred to the Memory of Jared
    Bates
Who died August the 6th, 1800
His widow, aged 24, lives at
    7, Elm Street
Has every qualification for
    a good wife
And yearns to be comforted.

So You Think You're Not Capable . . .

The newly hired traveling salesman wrote his first sales report to the home office. It stunned *the brass* in the sales department, for here's what he had written:

"I seen this outfit which ain't never bought a dimes worth of nothing from us and I sole them a cuple hundred thousand dollars of guds. I am now going to Chcawgo."

But before the illiterate itinerant could be given the heave-ho by the sales manager, along came another letter:

"I cum hear un sole them haff a millyon."

Fearful if he did, and fearful if he didn't fire the illiterate peddler, the sales manager decided to dump the problem in the lap of the president.

The following morning the members of ivory tower were flabbergasted to see the two letters posted on the bulletin board and this letter *from the president* tacked above:

"We ben spending two much time trying two spel instid of trying to sel. Let wach those sails. I want everybody should read these liters from Gooch who is on the rode doin a grate job for us, un you shud go out and do lake he done."

MORAL: Many Christians never give a testimony or take part in the calling program for fear they are not capable. It is true that we ought to be our best for God but it is also surely true that God can use whatever we have. Read Acts 4:13 and do accordingly.
—Selected

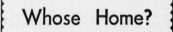

Whose Home?

G. Campbell Morgan says: "My father came into my house soon after I was married, and looked around into every room, and then he said to me, 'Yes, it is very nice, but nobody will know, walking through here, whether you belong to God or the Devil.' I went through and looked at the rooms again, and I thought: 'He is right.' So we made up our minds straightway that there should be no room in our house, henceforth, that had not some message, by picture or wall text, for every corner should tell that we serve the King."—*Selected*.

The God-Called, Blood-Cleansed, Spirit-Filled Preacher

By H. C. Morrison

"We are thinking now of the God-called, blood-cleansed, Spirit-filled preacher, the man of God who is wholly occupied with his concern for and his message to his fellowbeings. We are thinking of the man who is little concerned about other things, but his thought is centered on the salvation of human souls. He is possessed with a burning passion. Nothing can divert him from his one great objective. He is so rich in his own spiritual state, he is so uplifted with the love of Christ in his heart; he is so constrained to seek after the lost; he is so satisfied with the blessings that God gives him as he brings in the lost sheep that he has little concern or thought of material things.

"This preacher we are thinking about is one of the most independent men in the world. Don't misunderstand me. I do not mean he is a rash man or lawless man or a man who rends and tears propriety to pieces, but I do mean that the perfect love of Christ has cast out fear. He feels and knows that God is with him, that his message is not his own. He is not afraid to trust God. Whatever comes or goes, he charges it up to headquarters. 'Thou hast called me, Thou art with me; I am dead to the world; my life is hid with Christ in Thee. All things concerning me are safe for time and eternity. What care I, live or die, so immortal souls are saved and Christ is glorified?'

"It was a privilege to look upon such a man in the pulpit. He is not proud and he is not cowed. He doesn't fear the face of any man. He is filled with the Holy Ghost. He rests while he labors. He feasts while he hungers. His garments may be seedy, but he is clothed with invisible garments of righteousness. The weather may be below zero; his body may be lean and chilled, but his heart is on fire. He is warmed with the sense of the indwelling of the Holy Ghost. He can get on somehow. He eats well of whatever comes to hand. He braves the tempest. He wears out opposition and he sleeps as if he were enfolded in the everlasting arms of Omnipotence. It awakens and stirs and thrills the souls of men to hear him speak. The voice is human, but the truth is divine. His message is a sword to conquer; it is medicine to heal; it is bread to feed us; it is water out of the wells of salvation to slake the burning thirst of our famishing souls. There is no way to describe what this man, who is God-called, blood-cleansed, and Spirit-filled, means to us with his message that is the Gospel of Christ and the power of God unto salvation."

"Because" - - -

A little drop of drink
  Because I am so old;
A little drop of drink,
  Because the weather's cold;
A little drop of drink,
  To make me soundly rest;
  To make my food digest;
Because I am so sad;
Because I am so bad;
Because the weather's warm;
Sure it can do no harm;
Because my neighbor's wed
Because my uncle's dead;
Because 'tis Christmas Day;
Because I can't say "Nay"—
It cures them every one.
Was ever such a remedy
E'er found beneath the sun?

"But" - - -

A little drop of drink
May lead to many more;
And the man become a sot
Ere many months are o'er.
A little drop of drink
Brings many a heartache;
Makes the little child to quake;
May make bright eyes grow dim;
Takes the manhood out of him;
Brings "the wolf" to many a door;
Makes bare the cottage floor;
Takes the money from the bank;
Brings down the highest rank;
Sinks the man below the brute;
Brings forth but sorry fruit—
Ponder it, neighbor, well,
A little drop of drink
Can bring a soul to Hell.

The Essential Difference

The late Dr. Harry Rimmer, while traveling in Egypt, was negotiating with the then Secretary of State who was a refined and cultured Egyptian. In a conversation regarding their respective faiths Dr. Rimmer stated that:

"We believe that God has given to man three revelations of Himself. First, we believe that He has revealed Himself in the work of creation."

"We, too, believe that," interjected the Egyptian.

"We believe that God has revealed Himself in a book, the Bible," continued Dr. Rimmer.

"We, too, believe that God has revealed Himself in a book, the Koran," replied the Egyptian.

"We believe that God has revealed Himself in a Man, and that Man is Jesus Christ," added Dr. Rimmer.

"We also believe that God revealed Himself in a man, and that man is the prophet Mohammed," said the Egyptian.

"We believe that Jesus died to save His followers," said Dr. Rimmer.

"We believe that Mohammed died for his people," replied the Egyptian.

"We believe," continued Dr. Rimmer, "that Jesus is able to substantiate His claims because He rose from the dead."

The Moslem hesitated, then his eyes fell. He had no answer to that statement. Finally he admitted, "We have no information concerning our prophet after death."

Dr. Rimmer was right, he was convinced of the truth of his assertion, because it was founded on the Word of God that has withstood all attacks for over 1,900 years; and there are hundreds of thousands today who would agree with him.

The fact of the resurrection of Jesus Christ is a proven fact of history. The great Apostle Paul states, "For I delivered unto you first of all that which I also received, how that Christ died for our sins according to the scriptures; and that he was buried, and that he rose again the third day according to the scriptures" (I Cor. 15:3, 4). Read the whole chapter, and learn more of what Paul taught about the resurrection. This loving Saviour died and rose again that you might have forgiveness of all your sins; past, present, and future. If you will accept Him today, you will be able to say with Paul, that you serve a risen, living, omnipotent Saviour. This is beautifully expressed by A. H. Ackley in his inspiring hymn:

What Money Cannot Do

Money, no doubt, is a power; but a power of well defined and narrow limits. It will purchase plenty, but not peace; it will furnish your table with luxuries, but not you with an appetite to enjoy them. It will surround your sick bed with physicians, but not restore health to a sickly frame; it will encompass you with flatterers, but never procure you one true friend; it will bribe for you into silence the tongues of accusing men, but not an accusing conscience; it will pay some debt, but not the largest one of all, your debt to the law of God; it will relieve many fears, but not those of guilt—the terrors that crown the brows of Death. He stands as grim and terrible by the dying bed of wealth as by the pallet of the poorest beggar whom pitiless riches has thrust from her door.

—Guthrie.

I serve a risen Saviour, He's in the world today,
I know that He is living, whatever men may say;
I see His hand of mercy, I hear His voice of cheer,
And just the time I need Him, He's always near.

In all the world around me, I see His loving care,
And though my heart grows weary, I never will despair;
I know that He is leading, through all the stormy blast,
The day of His appearing, will come at last.

Rejoice! Rejoice! O Christian, lift up your voice and sing
Eternal hallelujahs to Jesus Christ the King!
The Hope of all who seek Him, the Help of all who find,
None other is so loving, so good and kind.
H. J. Aylwin
in *The Gospel Monthly*

It Has Been Said
"IT IS NO SACRIFICE"

"People talk of the sacrifice I have made in spending so much of my life in Africa. Can that be called a sacrifice which is simply paid back as a small part of the great debt owing to our God, which we can never repay? Is that a sacrifice which brings its own reward in healthful activity, the consciousness of doing good, peace of mind, and a bright hope of a glorious destiny hereafter?

Away with such a word, such a view, and such a thought! It is emphatically no sacrifice. Say rather it is a privilege. Anxiety, sickness, suffering or danger now and then, with a foregoing of the common conveniences and charities of this life, may make us pause and cause the spirit to waver and sink; but let this only be for a moment. All these are nothing when compared with the glory which shall hereafter be revealed in and for us. I never made a sacrifice. Of this we ought not to talk when we remember the great sacrifice which He made who left His Father's throne on high to give Himself for us."—David Livingstone

Mystery of the Roast Meat

More than a century-and-a-half ago there lived near Lowick in Northumberland, England, a man of the name of Thomas Hownham. As far as this world's goods are concerned he was very, very poor, but he was rich in faith. He lived very close to God, and was favoured with many wonderful experiences of definite answers to prayer, and also of God's provision in times of need.

His only means of livelihood, for the support of his wife and two children, was by keeping a donkey, on which he used to deliver coals from the local coal-mine, or by making brooms of heath, which he sold round the country. He often found it hard to make ends meet. After one particularly discouraging day, when he had received no money at all, he came home to find to his great distress that there was no food in the house. His wife and children were hungry, the latter having cried themselves to sleep. Finally his wife fell asleep also from sheer exhaustion and anxiety. Being a fine moonlit night he went out to a sheltered spot some way from the house, a familiar trysting place for him. There he pleaded with the Lord on behalf of his wife and children, asking Him to meet their need in their sore plight. As he did so, a wonderful time of liberty in prayer followed.

He returned to the house, and saw something on a stool beside the bed—chairs they had none—and found it to be a roast of meat, and a loaf of bread. He went to the door to see if he could see anybody, but there was no sign of anyone. He immediately woke his wife and children for a good meal. Where the food came from in the middle of the night was a complete mystery.

Nearby lived a young fellow, who knew Thomas Hownham. They met the following day, when this story was related, but he was able to throw no light on it. Occasionally his parents used to help the Hownham family but they had not done so recently.

Not long after this event the young man left the country. Returning some twelve years later, on a certain evening the conversation took a turn about an old miser, who had lived at Lowick Highstead, but had since died. The young man enquired as to what had become of his property, adding that it did not appear that he had done one generous action in his whole lifetime.

An elderly woman in the company then spoke up, and told him that he was mistaken. She could tell of *one*. She had been with him as a servant, and about twelve or thirteen years ago he had ordered her one day to roast a joint of meat, and to bake two loaves of bread. He then went to Wooler market, taking a bit of bread and cheese in his pocket as usual. He came home later in the day in very bad humour, and went to bed. After a couple of hours or so he called up his man-servant and ordered him to take one of the loaves and the joint of meat to Thomas Hownham's and to leave them there. The man did as he was told, and finding the family asleep he left the loaf and the joint on the stool by the bed and came away.

The following morning her master sent for her and the man-servant. Greatly agitated, he told them that it had been his intention to ask some neighbouring farmers in for supper the night before. They were always taunting him for his meanness. It was for this the food had been prepared. But they left the market early, before he had time to ask them, and so he missed the opportunity. On going to bed he did not rest well. Three times he dreamed that he saw Hownham's wife and children starving. On sudden impulse he sent his servant with the food. He much regretted having been so foolish, but it was too late now to do anything about it. He charged her and the man never to speak of it on threat of instant dismissal. She then added that since he was dead, she felt at liberty to tell the story as a proof that he had done *one generous action,* even though he regretted it afterwards.

The above incident was well authenticated at the time, and illustrates how easy it is for God who feeds the ravens to care for His people even in the most mysterious ways.

—Bright Words

CAUSES OF FAILURE...

I didn't know you were in a hurry for it.

That's not in my department.

No one told me to go ahead.

How did I know this was different?

That's his job, not mine.

Wait till the boss comes back and ask him.

I forgot.

I didn't think it was very important.

I'm so busy I just didn't get around to it.

I thought I told you.

I wasn't hired to do that.

I thought it was good enough.

They will never notice that.

(From The Advance).

Speak Evil of No Man

A godly minister was approached by one of his church members who wanted to repeat to him some of the wrong-doings of others. The pastor said, "Does anybody else know this but you?" "No sir." "Have you told it to anyone else?" "No." "Then," said the good man, "go home and hide it away at the feet of Jesus, and never speak of it again unless God leads you to speak to the man himself. If the Lord wants to bring scandal upon His Church, let Him do it; but don't you be the instrument to cause it."—*Christian Herald* (London).

Where Can I Find Him?

I have seen men find Him where the shepherds did—in the barn; where Paul did—on a journey; where Mary of Magdala did—in the garden; where the jailer did—in the prison. I have seen men find Him on the seas, in the forests, down in the mines and in the most evil places outside of hell.

I saw a man find Him on his knees in a tavern, with his head on the bar over which he had bartered all his life's happiness. There is no spot on earth where Christ will not come to meet us if we will only seek Him with a heart that so thirsts it will go to any length to find Him.

It is not where, it is how we seek. If there is any particular place where we lost Him, there must we go to find Him.

That is why Mary went to the grave. He was not there, but it was there that she had lost Him, and so she came back with her breaking heart to find Him, and He was found of her.

If you know on what part of the journey you lost Him, for what sin you sacrificed Him, it is there you must seek Him, and there you will find Him.

—*Evangeline Booth*

This You Must Believe—

By Evangelist John R. Rice

Men say that some things are "as certain as death." Well, the coming of every condemned sinner to stand in judgment before God is one of the things that is as certain as death. The Scripture links them together. "It is appointed unto men once to die, but after this the judgment" (Heb. 9:27). Man cannot get by with sin. The Scripture says, "Be sure your sin will find you out" (Num. 32:23).

Warning after warning has fallen from the mouth of God to sinners about judgment and the result of sin. We are warned, "Be not deceived; God is not mocked: for whatsoever a man soweth, that shall he also reap" (Gal. 6:7). We well know that man does not do all his reaping in this life. No, God has yet a trump card to play. God will yet call men—unsaved, unrepentant, unregenerate men—to judgment. There they will reap what they sow, receive their just and public sentence and depart to the lake of fire and a Christless, hopeless, peaceless eternity.

This is a striking and terrible thought: sinners must face God and their sins. No wonder the Scripture says, "It is appointed unto men once to die, but after this the judgment"! But thank God, you do not have to wait for that awful day, my sinner friend. If you will trust in Christ, you can escape that judgment, for Revelation 20:6 says:

"Blessed and holy is he that hath part in the first resurrection, on such the second death hath no power, but they shall be priests of God and of Christ, and shall reign with him a thousand years."

God loves you, brother! Trust Him for forgiveness and mercy today and you will not come to this awful judgment. Christ was judged for your sins on the cross. When He cried out just before He died, "It is finished!" He meant that every sin of yours and mine was paid for—every one, thank God! And now He pleads, "Come now, and let us reason together, saith the Lord; though your sins be as scarlet, they shall be as white as snow; though they be red like crimson, they shall be as wool" (Isa. 1:18). You can have mercy instead of justice if you will trust in Christ.

John 5:24 teaches that if you will trust in Christ you will have no judgment, no condemnation, no second death. There Jesus said, as recorded in the American Revised Version: "Verily, verily, I say unto you, He that heareth my word, and believeth him that sent me, hath eternal life, and cometh not into judgment, but hath passed out of death into life."

Cometh not into judgment! That is what I need, and thank God, that is what I have.

Christ will answer in your place, sinner, if you trust Him. He bore your sins. He took your place. He is even now at the right hand of the Father to intercede for those who trust Him. He is one lawyer who never loses a case; one physician who never turns His back on His own.

This brief message is done and God will hold you to account for the way you read and the decision you make. Will you today confess your sins and trust Christ to forgive you? Will you claim Him as your Saviour?

THERE IS A DEADLINE BEYOND WHICH YOU MAY NEVER BE SAVED

The stern facts of life prove that if men and women continue to resist God's Spirit, He will remove His Spirit from them. It is clearly stated in Scripture, "My Spirit shall not always strive with man" (Gen. 6:3). God will strive up to a certain moment. But one day, one fatal hour, one tragic moment, when a sinner is saying, "Go, Spirit, go thy way; some more convenient day on Thee I'll call," God will take that man's refusal as his final answer, and will leave him; the Spirit will cease His striving, His pleading, His entreaty, and that man will be a sinner let alone. And when God decides to let a man alone, that man might as well brace himself against the terrors of the judgment day, for though he might live twenty or thirty years after that, he would be as doomed as though he had already entered the gates of darkness and of Hell.—John Linton.

METHODIST COFFEE

Here is a pleasant story which I will
  tell in rhyme
About a certain preacher who lived in
  recent time.
He was a circuit rider of Mr. John
  Wesley's band,
And he rode the finest circuit in all
  this blessed land.
At one of his good charges, come
  members, not a few,
Became quite sorely troubled about the
  word "INTO."
The Good Book says quite plainly, Acts 8,
  They came unto,
And went down into the waters as Baptist
  people do.
The parson preached a sermon of extra
  power and might,
And to his satisfaction, he set the
  passages right.
"INTO" there don't mean "INTO" but
  "of," or "near," or "by,"
They went to the water, and got a good
  supply.
Now near the place of worship, there
  lived a Sister Jones,
Who, by her splendid cooking had gained
  a great renown.
Her yellow-legged chickens, her luscious
  cakes and pies,
Oft made the Circuit rider roll up his
  weeping eyes.
And her delicious coffee on all the circuit round
The parson oft admitted its like could
  not be found.
So when he preached a sermon of extra
  power and strength,

He landed at Jones' table to rectify his
  strength.
But Sister Jones was a Baptist, the
  stoutest in that land,
And often reproved the Methodist for
  changing God's command.
She heard Brother Smith's sermon, and
  thought the subject o'er,
But asked him up to dinner as she had
  done before.
She ground her good brown coffee, the
  kettle steaming hot,
She put it "at" not "into" the famous
  coffee pot.
She poured Brother Smith a cupful, and
  thought it was no sin,
"Why Sister, you've forgotten to put the
  coffee in."
"No, no, Brother Smith, that's coffee; I
  ground a good, supply;
Then down by the kettle, I put it 'at,'
  or 'near,' or 'by.'
By the logic of your sermon, I thought
  it rather thin
If 'at' or 'near' or 'by' means into, I
  put the coffee in.
If you'll strictly promise no more such
  stuff to teach
Nor dodge God's plain commandments
  when you attempt to preach
I'll make some coffee just to a bible
  dot,
And will put the coffee INTO the
  coffee pot."

                                Author Unknown

Street Scene: Man buying pack
of cigarettes slipping coin
into cancer donation box.

* * *

KEEP YOUR WORDS SWEET--
YOU MAY HAVE TO EAT THEM.

* * *

A successful man keeps looking
for work after he has found a
job.

A Swarm of "Flys"

Fly from self, and fly from sin,
Fly the world's tumultuous din;
Fly its pleasures, fly its cares,
Fly its friendship, fly its snares.
Fly the sinner's hast'ning doom,
Fly and 'scape the wrath to come.
Fly to Jesus, He's the road,
Fly through Him alone to God.
Fly to mercy's gracious seat,
Fly, 'tis sorrow's last retreat;
Fly to Christ in deepest grief,
Fly, and you shall find relief.
Fly and let your wings be love,
Fly and stretch your flight above;
Fly while life and grace are giv'n,
Fly from Hell and fly to Heaven.

                          —Author unknown

Is Evolution Reasonable?

(Excerpt from a tract by the Late Dr. James E. Bennet)

I was teaching in a Bible institute in Brooklyn several years ago, and one of the young ladies said to me:

"Mr. Bennet, you are the first intelligent looking man that I ever heard that did not believe in evolution."

I said to her—"Do *you* believe in evolution?"

Her reply was—"Why, of course. Everybody does."

"Maybe then I'm the exception. Perhaps you never heard of any one against it before," I said.

"No, sir! You are the first intelligent looking man in my experience that did not accept evolution as a fact."

"Tell me, where did you get this conviction about evolution being absolutely correct?" I asked her.

"College."

"Do you go to church? Your minister surely doesn't preach it."

"Oh, yes, he believes in evolution."

"That is very interesting. You are the person I have been looking for," I confessed. "I do not believe in it because I do not know any reasons why I should believe in it. Now here you are, and perhaps you can tell me why I should believe in evolution. Give me one or two simple little reasons so I can think them over during the week."

"Do I have to have a reason?" she parried.

"Yes, ma'am. If you want to convince me, you do. Perhaps you did not need any reason to convince yourself. Most people I have met who believe in evolution have no reason to give. They have a few arguments but no reasons."

"Well, I don't believe I am prepared right now—" and she seemed a bit uncomfortable.

"Dear me, I thought from the way you spoke it was going to be so simple. Can't you hand me out one simple reason?"

"Well," she replied, "I never studied up on it because I did not t h i n k there was any need. I thought EVERYBODY just knew it was so," and her voice trailed off.

"That may be so, but please take a chance and try to convince me on some one of the many points you must know."

"I can't just now but I will ask around and certainly will tell you next week."

And the next week came around, and she said, "You know, I talked it over with the pastor and some others but they did not give me any reason, and now I'm all mixed up myself."

"Maybe they are all just like you. They thought everybody accepted it."

I thought I would help her out and I said, "Do you remember anything about the Venus de Milo?"

"That was a statue," she answered.

"Yes, and since that w a s a statute of a girl, there must have been a girl who was the model."

"Yes, there must have been a model."

"When they dug up the statue they thought t h a t this original was sculptured one thousand years before Christ. Isn't that correct?" I asked her; and she answered:

"Yes, I think that is what they estimate."

"So that now it would be about 3,000 years ago that girl was a model for the statue," I pointed out.

"Yes, sir."

"Now listen carefully. How does the rhythm, the beauty, the symmetry of the physical body of that girl compare with yours?"

"She was supposed to be perfect."

One brief glance was sufficient to show that this girl was not perfect. I let it pass, and continued. "Then you think that she was superior to you in perfection of physical form?"

"Yes," she confessed.

"If evolution is still going on, don't you think you should be more perfect in body than the girl of 3,000 years ago? Unless evolution, of course, is behind time. Maybe it stopped. Maybe evolution ran along up to 1,000 years ago and then discontinued. Do you think evolution is really going on today? Can you show me an instance?"

She rubbed her forehead and said, "I never was so bothered about anything before. Do you suppose there isn't such a thing?"

"As far as I am concerned," I said, "there is no such thing as evolution for no one h a s ever shown me anything concrete to prove it," and she walked away perplexed.

Ask any evolutionist for a simple fact and in a few minutes they have sought the air, and you give them the air, and you go—on your way rejoicing in a God, and a true religion, with a true Biblical record.

You must a l w a y s ask them which form of evolution they believe in and have them give you definitions, and then always go back to the very beginning—always push them back to the beginning.

This reminds me of another girl who said she was a graduate of a college.

"Mr. Bennet," she said—"I have listened to you teach the Bible, but it is so simple to prove the Bible is not true."

After hearing me teach, that was a startling remark and I said meekly, "Is that so?"

With a snap of her fingers she said, "I can disprove it just like that."

I was willing to learn anything, even from a girls' college, and I said, "That's very interesting. Go right ahead and do it."

She hunted around in her brain for an apt example and came out with, "There a r e no apples in Mesopotamia."

"My, that is distressing! What do they have in the way of applesauce?"

"Oh, it isn't that they do not like apples, but they cannot grow them there."

"Do you mind telling me a little more?" I asked her. She virtually expanded as she gave forth this bit of knowledge. "Mesopotamia is where the Garden of Eden is supposed to have been, and therefore that story about Adam eating the apple is not true. There were no apples in Eden."

"Oh, I see. But suppose Adam didn't eat an apple—so what?"

"It was Adam eating the apple which brought sin into the world according to what you teach."

"I have certainly not taught that Adam ate an apple. I have heard of Adam's apple, that is what you speak with or articulate with, but you don't eat it or swallow it. There wasn't any other apple in Adam's life that I know of. He had a wife, and that proved to be enough to ruin the human race. I don't really know what you are talking about."

"Your Bible says that Adam ate an apple," she continued to insist.

"You show me where it says that," and I handed her the Bible.

Evidently that young lady did not know much, if anything, about the Bible. Evolutionists and atheists certainly do not know the Bible or they would not argue. She handled it rather gingerly. She seemed more or less confused, and asked, "Where do I look?"

I hadn't the slightest idea where she would look and I said so. She became impatient b e c a u s e she thought I was making fun of her and said, "You're a Bible teacher. Where will I find that story of Adam and the apple?"

I had only been studying the Bible for fifty years and I must have overlooked that portion, but I turned to the only story of the Garden of Eden that I knew anything about and showed it to her, and pointing with my finger read to her Genesis 2:16:

"And the Lord commanded the man, saying, of every tree of the garden thou mayest freely eat; But of the tree of the knowledge of good and evil, thou shalt not eat of it; for in the day that thou eatest thereof thou shalt surely die."

And then she a s k e d me— "Where's the apple?"

"I don't know where the apple is. The tree, the Bible says, is the tree of the Knowledge of Good and Evil. And that is the 'fruit' which Adam ate. Satan promised him knowledge of evil and he got it, and that is what brought sin into the world."

"Do you mean to say that Adam did not eat an apple?" she demanded.

"No, ma'am, he did not eat an apple. Everything that Adam ate was written down, but apples were not in his menu and had nothing to do with sin."

"Then, where do you suppose the world got the idea? Newspapers, magazines, anything I read referring to sin says that Adam ate the apple." She thought that made a good argument, and she couldn't be contradicted.

I sighed, but I thought I'd try to explain in my feeble way—so I said, "Way back some fools said that Adam ate an apple, and some fool repeated it to another and now it is down to you."

So many things in the Bible are just that way. . . . No one can prove evolution.

Reprinted from Bob Jones Univ. Fellowship News

When a man went to apply for a life insurance policy, the agent inquired, "Do you drive a car?"

"No," replied the applicant.

"Do you fly?"

"No."

"I'm sorry," said the agent, "we no longer insure pedestrians."

Five Minutes After

It may be in a moment, or after months of waiting, but soon I shall stand before my Lord—perhaps even before 1965 is over.

Then, in an instant, all things will appear in a new perspective. The things I thought important—tomorrow's tasks, my success or failure in pleasing those around me —will not matter at all. And the things to which I gave but little thought—the word about Christ to the man next door, the moment (how short it was!) of earnest prayer for the Lord's work in far-off lands, the confessing and forsaking of that secret sin—will stand as real and enduring.

Five minutes after I'm in Heaven, I'll be overwhelmed by the truth I've known but somehow never grasped. I'll realize then that it's what I am in Christ that comes first with God, and that when I am right with Him, I do the things that please Him.

I'll sense that it was not just how much I gave that mattered, but how I gave and how much I withheld.

In Heaven I'll wish with all my heart that I could reclaim a thousandth part of the time that I've let slip through my fingers, that I could call back those countless conversations which could have glorified my Lord, but didn't.

Five minutes after I'm in Heaven I believe I'll wish with all my heart that I had risen more faithfully to read the Word of God and wait on Him in prayer . . . that I might have known Him here on earth as He wanted me to know Him.

A thousand thoughts will press upon me, and, though overwhelmed by the grace which admits me to my heavenly home, I'll wonder at my aimless earthly life: I'll wish . . . (if one may wish in Heaven). . . but it will be too late!

Heaven is real and hell is real, and eternity is but a breath away. Soon we shall be in the presence of the Lord we claim to serve. Why should we live as though salvation were a dream—as though we did not know? "To him that knoweth to do good, and doeth it not, to him it is sin."

There may yet be a little time. God help us to live NOW in the light of that *real* tomorrow.

—*Moody Monthly*

Question Time for the Atheist

A number of open-air meetings were going on in Hyde Park, London. Some of the speakers were preaching the Gospel: some were denying that there is any Gospel to preach. One proclaimed that he was an atheist. He stood on a platform and told a little crowd such things as these: "There is no God." "Jesus Christ wasn't anybody in particular." "The churches are doing no good." They listened without much interest—until a young man livened things up.

"May I ask a question?" he began.

"Go ahead," answered the atheist.

"I want to know the address of the Atheists' Hospital," the young man said. "Now there's St. Bartholomew's Hospital down east, and St. Thomas' across the river. Both are named after great saints. Where is there a hospital named after a great atheist? So far as I can make out," he went on, "practically all the hospitals were founded by people who believed in God, and it seems to be mostly that sort of people who kept them going. What I want to know is, where is there a hospital founded by atheists and maintained by atheist?"

And the atheist growled: "Don't be a fool."

"I take it, then there isn't one," said the young man. "Well, here's another question: Where's the Atheists' Orphanage? Everybody knows Barnardo's, and Spurgeon's, and Muller's, and everybody knows that these men were great Christians. Is there an orphanage anywhere founded by a great atheist?

"Oh, shut up," said the atheist.

"So that's another poser," said the young man. "Just one more question please: Where's your association for uplifting backward races? Christians have many—missionary societies they call them. I have a friend who is working for one in the middle of Africa. Fifty years ago the people were miserable savages: today they are quite decent folk. What has made the difference? Three buildings which the missionaries have put up and are running—a church for their souls, a school for their minds, and a hospital for their bodies. I have another friend in a missionary compound in China," the young man went on, "and I understand it's the same there—and indeed in scores, hundreds of other places. Missionaries are everywhere civilizing and uplifting backward people by those three things—religion, education, and medicine. What are the atheists doing for the elevation of the backward races?"

"Look here, young fellow; I've had enough of your talk," the atheist cried. "Now shut up."

"No," shouted the crowd—for quite a big crowd had now collected. "No" they shouted, "let him go on!"

Then the young man turned to the crowd. "My friends," he began, "we have all learned that in the year 55 B. C., Julius Caesar landed in Britain. What did he find there? A backward race—barbarians. Today we are civilized, and with all our missionaries! They came so long ago that their very names are forgotten, but it was the Christian religion they brought that elevated those British savages, until their children are among the leaders of the world."

"Look," said somebody, "the old chap's gone off." The young man turned to the platform and saw that the atheist was quietly taking his departure.

"Stop!" he cried. "I'm going to offer you my best wishes."

"I hope," said the young man, "that you'll get home safely without any accident. But if you do happen to get knocked down by a car, an ambulance will take you quietly to a hospital—founded by the religion of Jesus Christ. And, if unhappily, you don't recover and your children are left unprovided for, they will be looked after in an orphanage—founded by the religion of Jesus Christ.

"You don't believe in religion, but I am glad to say that won't make any difference to the people who do, if you need their help."

But the atheist was moving off his platform.

"Oh, stop, do stop," shouted the young man. "Why, I'm going to agree with you!"

And the atheist turned back. "Well, it hasn't sounded like it," he said.

"I agree with you that the Christian churches aren't doing anything like the good they should in the world. What's the reason? You—and others like you—are always finding fault with them, and doing your level best to hinder them, instead of lending them a hand. Change your creed! Become a Christian! Join the church! Pull your weight! If only you, and other fellows like you—"

"He's gone," said somebody.

And so the young man had the last word. And this was it, at the top of his voice he shouted:—

"God bless you, sir!"
—Mobray Presbyterian Church Tract

"It's the Driver!"

D. C. Motor Vehicles Director George A. England is carrying the safety poem, "It's the Driver!" on the back of the large paper envelope which carries the 1964 D.C. license tags. It is well worth reprinting by any organization interested in highway safety.

Here it is:

It isn't the car that begins to whine
When forced to stop for an old stop sign—
It's the driver.

It isn't the car that takes a drink,
Then quickly loses its power to think—
It's the driver.

It isn't the car that fails to heed
The dangers of reckless, discourteous speed—
It's the driver.

It isn't the car that steps on the gas
And causes an accident, trying to pass—
It's the driver.

A car may be bent and twisted awry,
But it isn't the car that will have to die—
It's the driver.

The Welfare State

The government is my shepherd: I need not work.

It alloweth me to lie down on a good job;
It leadeth me beside still factories;
It destroyeth my initiative.

It leadeth me in the path of a parasite for politic's sake;
Yea, though I walk through the valley of laziness and deficit-spending,
I will fear no evil, for the government is with me.

It prepareth an economic Utopia for me, by appropriating the earnings of my own grandchildren.

It filleth my head with false security;
My inefficiency runneth over.
Surely the government should care for me all the days of my life,
And I shall dwell in a fool's paradise forever.

—Author Unknown.

How to Handle an Atheist

Some years ago Charles Bradlaugh was the outstanding atheist in England. He was ever challenging the validity of the claims of Christianity. Down in one of the slums of London was a minister by the name of Hugh Price Hughes. He was a real personality and all London was aware of miracles of grace accomplished at his mission.

Charles Bradlaugh challenged Mr. Hughes to debate with him the validity of the claims of Christianity. London was greatly interested. What would Mr. Hughes do? He immediately accepted the challenge, and in doing so added one of his own. He said in substance:

"Since we know, Mr. Bradlaugh, that 'a man convinced against his will is of the same opinion still,' and since the debate as a matter of mental gymnastics will not likely convert anyone, I propose to you that we bring some concrete evidences of the validity of the claims of Christianity in the form of men and women who have been redeemed from lives of sin and shame by the influence of Christianity and by atheism. I will bring one hundred such men and women, and I challenge you to do the same.

"If you cannot bring one hundred, Mr. Bradlaugh, to match my hundred, I will be satisfied if you will bring fifty men and women who will stand and testify that they have been lifted up from lives of shame by the influence of your teachings. If you cannot bring fifty, I challenge you to bring twenty people who will testify with shining faces, as my hundred will, that they have a great new joy in a life of self-respect as a result of your atheistic teachings. If you cannot bring twenty, I will be satisfied if you bring ten. Nay, Mr. Bradlaugh, I challenge you to bring one, just one man or woman who will make such a testimony regarding the uplifting of your atheistic teachings. My redeemed men and women will bring an unanswerable proof to the saving power of Jesus Christ in the lives of those who have been redeemed from the slaveries of sin and shame. Perhaps, Mr. Bradlaugh, this will be the real demonstration of the validity of the claims of Christianity."

Again London was stirred. What would Mr. Bradlaugh do? For answer, Charles Bradlaugh, in great discomfiture and chagrin, publicly withdrew his challenge for the debate and London smiled.

From **Peoples Magazine**

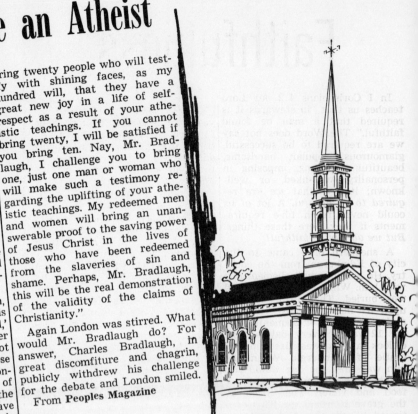

Night Vigils and Days of Fasting

I have been in that old church in New England where Jonathan Edwards preached his great sermon, "Sinners in the hands of an angry God." He had a little manuscript which he held up so close to his face that they could not see his countenance. He went on and on until the people in the crowded church were tremendously moved. One man sprang to his feet, rushed down the aisles and cried, "Mr Edwards, have mercy!" Other men caught hold of the backs of the pews lest they should slip into perdition. I have seen the old pillars around which they threw their arms when they thought the day of judgment had dawned upon them. The power of that sermon is still felt in the United States today. But there is a bit of history behind it.

For three days Edwards had not eaten a mouthful of food: for three nights he had not closed his eyes in sleep. Over and over again, he had been saying to God, "Give me New England! Give me New England!" and when he rose from his knees, and made his way into the pulpit they say that he looked as if he had been gazing straight into the face of God. They say that before he opened his lips to speak, conviction fell upon his audience.

—J. Wilbur Chapman

John Bunyan Saved Through A Tract

Did you know that it was Leigh Richmond, who dropped a tract on the pavement in England and prayed that a bad man would pick it up?

A bad man did pick it up. He carried the tract with him to prison and he was converted, and he wrote "Pilgrim's Progress", which turned millions to righteousness. The book is second only to the Bible in sales.

— Selected

A miser isn't much fun to live with--but he sure makes a wonderful ancestor.

Faithfulness

In I Corinthians 4:2 our Lord teaches us that "in stewards it is required that a man be found faithful." The Word does not say we are required to be successful, glamourous, popular, handsome, beautiful, appealing, imposing in personality, well-liked, or well-known; it says that *we are required to be faithful.* A lot of us could never reach the requirements if they were these things. *But we all can be faithful!*

A shepherd once came to the city of Edinburgh from the country. He had his small obedient dog with him. While there he died and was buried. That little dog lay upon its master's grave—not for a day, a week, or a month, but for 12 years. Every day at one o'clock a gun was fired in the castle of Edinburgh. When the gun was fired the dog would run to the local baker who gave it food and water. Then back to the grave it would go. This continued till the dog died and that was 12 years. *That was faithfulness!*

The owner threw a goose, which had been run over and crushed by a car, into an oil drum. For 7 years the gander, that goose's mate, never went more than 10 feet away from that oil drum. Yes that gander kept watch by the drum till it died and that was 7 years. *That was faithfulness!*

George Muller prayed for 52 years for a certain man to come to Christ. *A pastor* visited an elderly man 21 times before being admitted, but then he befriended the man and led him to Christ. *That was faithfulness!*

A Welsh postman had the British Empire Medal conferred upon him by Queen Elizabeth; he had not missed a day's service in 43 years. A Minneapolis man retired as a high school teacher without having missed a single day on the job for 43 years. Paul Ehrlick, the chemist, performed 605 unsuccessful experiments; the 606th was a success! Thomas Edison made 18,000 experiments before he perfected the arc light. At another time after 50 failures on a project he said, "I have found the 50th way it cannot be done!" *That was faithfulness!*

During the Korean War a man buried himself in the muck and mud of a pig sty (except for his nose and mouth so he could breath) for 8 days and nights rather than betray his buddies and surrender to the enemy. *That was faithfulness!*

Are you not glad that Jesus was faithful in dying for us and that He now lives and is faithful to care for us? *God grant us grace to be faithful!*

—From Maranatha

A canny Scot was engaged in an argument with the train conductor as to whether the fare was to be 25 or 30 cents. Finally the conductor, in disgust, picked up the Scot's suitcase and tossed it off the train just as it was crossing a long bridge. The suitcase landed in the river below with a mighty splash.

"Hoot mon!" screamed the Scot. "First you try to rob me, and now you've drowned my little boy!"

* * *

To do nothing is tiresome because you cannot stop and take a rest.

The normal reactions to a new idea is to think of reasons why it can't be done.

HORSE SENSE

A minister was driving through the country when suddenly his motor stopped. He got out of the car and raised the hood.

All at once a voice behind him said, "The trouble is in the carburetor."

Quickly he turned around in surprise, but saw only an old horse standing on the other side of the fence watching him. Hardly daring to believe his ears, he asked, "Did you say something?"

"Yes, I said you'd better check the carburetor," replied the horse.

Rushing down the road to the nearest farmhouse, the minister excitedly related his experience to the old farmer who answered the door. "Was it an old bay horse with one flop ear?" asked the farmer.

"Yes, yes, that's the one!"

"Well, don't pay any attention to him," the farmer scoffed. "He don't know anything about automobiles anyway."

If your religion cannot get you to Sunday School, don't count too heavily on it getting you to Heaven!

One dad to another: "I'm no model father. All I'm trying to do is behave so that when folk tell my son that he reminds them of me, he will stick out his chest instead of his tongue."

Religion may polish, but only Christ can cleanse.

When swept off your feet — better get on your knees.

We have all heard of people who trusted God too little, but have you ever heard of anyone who trusted Him too much?

An atheist is like a man who builds a house without windows and then blames God because he has to live in the dark.

THE END

Will not the End explain
The crossed endeavour, earnest purpose foiled,
The strange bewilderment of good work spoiled,
The clinging weariness, the inward strain?
Will not the End explain?

Meanwhile He comforteth
Them that are losing patience; 'tis His way.
But none can write the words they hear Him say,
For men to read; only they know He saith
Kind words, and comforteth.

Not that He doth explain
The mystery that baffleth; but a sense
Husheth the quiet heart, that far, far hence
Lieth a field set thick with golden grain,
Wetted in seedling days by many a rain.
The End, it will explain.

—Amy Carmichael
in *Toward Jerusalem*

I'm a Nice Stranger

I never complain. I never create a scene.

When I go to church I never offer an objection if the usher leads me down the long middle aisle to the front seat, while all the members of that church crowd the back seats and fix their curious gaze on my embarrassed march. No—I just take my seat. I'm a nice visitor.

I never growl aloud when I have to push by and walk over the feet of selfish church members who hog the aisle seats and would not move out of their favorite places if it meant the salvation of a soul. Oh, no—I just sit down meekly. I'm the ideal church stranger.

I never reprimand young people who sit behind me chewing gum, talking and making love. Oh, no; I'm too polite for that. I'm a nice person.

At the close of the service as I walk toward the door I never make a scene if nobody speaks to me or shakes my hand. No, they gather in little cliques and don't bother me. I'm the nice visitor to the church.

And I'll tell what else I am. I'm the stranger who never comes back. That's my little revenge for not being welcomed. I know when I'm not wanted. I can sense when church members are cliquish and unfriendly. I can tell when they lack interest in the spiritual welfare of their visitors. I, of course, am too cultured and too nice to say anything. I just go to some other more friendly, more hospitable, more spiritual church—or don't go to church at all.

Much is said in the Bible about hospitality, kindness and concern.

A few years ago I found myself in Chicago on a Sunday morning with a few hours between trains. I decided to visit a large well-known church in the Loop. I went early on purpose and, following the service, lingered just to see. And I saw—and felt! Not one person greeted me on arrival, and no one shook my hand on dismissal. Sunday School was to follow the worship service. I was not invited. I walked out of that cold, formal, wealthy church feeling unwelcomed and unwanted. I have never gone back.

I wouldn't make a complaint—I'm a nice visitor. I just don't go back.

There are millions who could be reached by a little bit of hospitality and warmth.

Are you just a nice, complacent church member, or are you genuinely concerned about the spiritual condition of strangers and visitors?

Remember Paul's admonition, "Be not forgetful to entertain strangers."
—Christian Digest

We Can't Ask God

For help, if we are not making any effort.

For strength, if we have strength we are not using.

For guidance, if we are ignoring the guidance we now have.

For faith, when we are afraid to act on what we already know.

For forgiveness, if we continue hating someone.

For mercy, if we intend to commit the same sin again.—*Dateline*

CLEANING HOUSE!

A little Zulu girl, who had given her heart to Christ, prayed thus:

"O Thou Great Chief, light a candle in my heart that I may see the rubbish, and sweep it out." And along with this little African girl's prayer should go the prayer of William Cowper, the poet:

The dearest idol I have known,
Whate'er that idol be,
Help me to tear it from Thy throne,
And worship only Thee.

—Homiletical Review

Old-Time Dancing

Do I believe in dancing?
Well, I should say I do.
My father used to teach me
To dance a step or two.

'Twas not exactly waltzing,
Nor any fancy swing;
Sometimes I knocked the back-step,
Sometimes the pigeon wing.

My father played the music,
The time was double quick,
He didn't use a fiddle,
But just a limber stick.

And on my back and shoulders
The lively notes would ring,
And then with my hand in his
We'd promenade and swing.

And when the dance was over,
And father'd left the hall,
The other chaps would tell me,
"We'll have a splendid (bawl)."

I know this kind of dancing
Seems rather out of date
To all the modern children
Who go the fancy gait.

But I shall always like it,
For 'twas my father's plan,
And that's the kind of dancing
It takes to make a man.
                    --Selected.

Frogs and Freedom

There's an old story that says you can't kill a frog by dropping him in boiling water. He reacts so quickly to the sudden heat that he jumps out before he's hurt. But if you put him in cold water and then warm it up gradually, he never decides to jump till it's too late. By then he's cooked.

Men are just as foolish. Take away their freedom overnight, and you've got a violent revolution. But steal it from them gradually (under the guise of "security," "peace," or "progress") and you can paralyze an entire generation. Look at the income tax. It started out at a harmless sounding 1%. It would have been easy to jump out of water as tepid as this, but like the frog, we waited while it climbed ever higher. (Try jumping now!)

Worst of all, we never learn. Even today we cannot believe that Medicare is the same warm water that will one day boil us in Socialized Medicine. We see no connection between farm price supports and Nationalized Agriculture. And if we draw a parallel between subsidized teachers' pay and federal control of education, we are called "extremist."

The tragedies of history are always repeated by those who refuse to learn them. To seek guidance from the past is not "turning the clock back" as we are so often told. It is merely a good way to keep out of hot water.

(Courtesy of Blackmere Pump Co.)

CHECK THAT STUB!

A young lady driver was headed downtown when she was flagged down by a police-man, who shouted,

"Lady, pull over." She did. The next day she was fined $25 for speeding. Anxious to keep her husband from knowing of the incident, she marked on the check stub: "One pull over--$25."

When God says, "Come,"
He goes out to meet us.
When He says, "Go," He
goes with us!

Judas

By Dr. Bob Jones
Bob Jones University,
Greenville, S. C.

What a picture of human depravity—Judas Iscariot—who betrayed the Son of Man with a kiss! There is not much said in the Bible about Judas. It is not how much is said about a man that reveals his character. It is what is said about a man, or what the man says, that reveals his character.

"What will you give me?" That is what Judas asked the chief priests when he went to see them to sell the Son of God. These words reveal the heart of Judas Iscariot. They are not many words, but no more wicked words were ever uttered. It does not take many poems to prove a man is a poet. One great poem is sufficient. It does not take many oaths to show a man's heart is black. One foul oath is sufficient to prove the man's heart is wicked and depraved. Judas Iscariot who had been a trusted member of the firm, the one who handled the money—and no doubt had stolen many times some of the money that belonged to all of them, is now selling the Son of God to His enemies. What a tragedy of horrors! Judas had been with Jesus for three years. He had seen Him perform miracles. He had heard Him speak as never man spake. He witnessed what the others witnessed, yet he sold the Lord for thirty pieces of silver! Judas thought he wanted the money until he got it. The thirty pieces of silver mocked his agony, and he threw it down at the feet of the priests and went out and hung himself. After Judas Iscariot sold the Son of God, he knew he was not fit to live. There are modernistic preachers and modernistic educators who have sold Jesus Christ to His enemies as truly as Judas ever sold Him and they have not been decent enough to hang themselves. Some of these preachers continue to stand in pulpits that are supposed to be Christian, and some of these educators are still teaching in colleges and universities that were built with Christian money.

Death Is Loss, But Oh, What Gain!

By C. H. Spurgeon

"For me to live is Christ, and to die is gain." (Philippians 1:21).

Surely death is loss. When I look upon thee, thou cold corpse, and see thee just preparing to be the palace of corruption and the carnival for worms, I cannot think that thou hast gained!

When I see that thine eye hath lost its sight, and thy lip hath lost its joy, and they that looked out of the windows are darkened, the grinders have failed, and no sounds of tabret or harp wake up thy joys, *O clay-cold corpse, thou hath lost, lost immeasurably!*

YET — TO DIE IS GAIN

And yet my text tells me that it is not really so; it says, *"To die is gain."* It looks as if it could not be thus; and certainly it is not, so far as I can see. But put to your eye the telescope of faith, take that magic glass which pierces through the veil that parts us from the unseen. Anoint your eyes with eyesalve, and make them so bright that they can pierce the ether, and see the unknown worlds.

Come, bathe yourself in this sea of light, and live in holy revelation and belief, and then look, and oh, how changed the scene. *Here is the corpse, but there the spirit; here is the clay, but there the soul; here is the carcass, but there the seraph. He is supremely blest; his death is gain.*

WHAT DID HE LOSE?

Come now, what did he lose? I will show that, in everything he lost, he gained far more. He lost his friends, did he? His wife, and his children, his brethren in church-fellowship, are all left to mourn his loss. Yes, he lost them; but, my brethren, what did he gain?

He gained more friends than he lost. He had lost many in his lifetime, but he meets them all again. Parents, brethren and sisters who had died in youth or age, and passed the stream before him, all salute him on the further brink.

There the mother finds her lost infant, there the father meets his children, there the venerable patriarch greets his family to the third and fourth generation, there brother clasps brother to his arms, and husband meets with wife, no more to be married or given in marriage, *but to live together, like the angels of God.*

Some of us have more friends in Heaven than in earth; we have more dear relations in glory than we have here. It is not with all of us, but with some it is so; more have crossed the stream than are left behind. *But if it be not so, yet what friends we have to meet us there!*

Oh, I reckon on the day of death if it were for the mere hope of seeing the bright spirits that are now before the throne; to clasp the hands of Abraham, Isaac, and Jacob, to look into the face of Paul the apostle, and grasp the hands of Peter; to sit in flowery fields with Moses and David, to bask in the sunlight of bliss with John and Mary Magdalene. Oh, how blest! The company of poor, imperfect saints on earth is good; but how much better the society of the glorified! Yes, brethren, *"To die is gain.". . . .*

"They are supremely blest,
Have done with care, and sin, and woe,
And with their Saviour rest."

"Wrong is wrong even if everyone
is doing it;
Right is right even if no one is
doing it."

Even the perfect people
buy pencils with erasers.

190

From My Kitchen Window

By Jessie Rice Sandberg

The Prodigal Son — Modern Version

It was late afternoon and I was hurrying around trying to get last minute things done so that the house would be left neat before the family went off for Wednesday night prayer meeting.

The little boys' bedroom was a mess. Donnie, aged four, had been playing there and there were toys scattered from one end of the room to the other.

"Oh, Donnie," I said, "what a mess you've made in your room! You come up here right now and get these toys put away!"

Donnie came up the stairs fussing as he came. As he passed me in the hall I heard him grumble to himself, "I sure don't like living in a house where I always have to pick up toys."

"Now listen here, young man," I said, "if you don't like the rules at our house you can just find some other place to live."

"Well, I could go and live with Uncle Bill and Aunt Jo. . . ."

"All right," I answered. "You do that; see if you can find out whether they make little boys pick up their toys." On an impulse I reached into the hall closet and pulled out the first suitcase in sight. "Here's something to put your clothes in."

Donnie gave me a sheepish grin as though he were wondering just how far he ought to carry his scheme. Then he went to his dresser and pulled out a pair of pajamas, his new jeans and a pair of tennis shoes—and threw them all into the bag. After that, he put in his whole fortune (one thin dime) and closed the suitcase.

Three-year-old Mark, watching the process, suddenly decided he was about to miss out on the excitement, so he ran quickly to his drawer, pulled out one shirt, and announced he was going too.

When the suitcase was shut, the two little boys stood watching me, to see what I intended to do. "Aren't you going to drive us there?" Donnie asked.

"No," I said, "If you are someone else's little boy, I don't believe I'll have the time to take you anywhere. I guess you will just have to walk."

I watched them go out the front door and start across the yard—Donnie struggling with a suitcase that weighed almost as much as he did, and Mark following, dragging his little shirt by one sleeve.

They got as far as the corner of the lot and then turned around and came on back to the house.

"What's the matter?" I asked. Donnie's reply: "The suitcase was too heavy."

Without a further word he went upstairs to his room and quickly began picking up the toys.

* * *

How like the backslider, running away from God! The erring son decides God's rules are too stiff. He longs for the freedom and fun of some far country—away from God, away from the high standards of Home.

All too often the backslider influences someone else to drift away from the Father too. Like little Mark, who wanted to be like his big brother, there are always others who will be affected and led astray by the sin of a wayward Christian.

Donnie discovered that he simply could not carry the heavy load he had brought upon himself by running away. And so the backslider finds eventually that the burden of guilt and shame that he drags behind him when he runs away from God is too heavy to carry.

Fortunately, Donnie decided, before he got too far, that he preferred the love and comforts of home and favor with his parents, to the dubious pleasures of having his own way.

What about you? Are you tempted to choose your own paths? Is your heart rebelling against the too-strict rules of your Heavenly Father? Don't do it! The burden of sin is heavier than you can carry alone.

"Get my Mother in"

The following is related by the late Dr. J. H. Jowett, as told him by his friend, the late Charles H. Beery, D.D., and abridged from the Homiletic Review.

Dr. Beery received at a very early age the highest honors that the denomination to which he belonged was able to confer. His fame as a preacher was as wide as the English-speaking world. He was a modern theologian when the following incident took place.

"One night there came to me," he says, "a Lancashire girl, with her shawl over her head, and with clogs on her feet."

"'Are you the minister?' she said.

"'Yes.'

"'Then I want you to come and get my mother in.'

"Thinking it was some drunken brawl, I said, 'You must get a policeman.'

"'Oh, no,' said the girl, 'my mother is dying, and I want you to get her into salvation.'

"'Where do you live?'

"'I live so and so, a mile and a half from here.'

"'Is there no minister nearer than I?'

"'Oh, yes, but I want you, and you will have to come.'

"I was in my slippers, and I did all I could to get out of it, but it was of no use. That girl was determined, and I had to dress and go. I found the house, and upstairs I found the poor woman dying. I sat down and talked about Jesus as the beautiful Example, and extolled Him as a Leader and Teacher. She looked at me out of her eyes of death, and said:

"'Mister, that's no good for the likes of me. I don't want an example. I'm a sinner.'

"Jowett, there I was face to face with a poor soul dying, and had nothing to tell her. I had no Gospel but I thought of what my mother had taught me, and I told her the old story of God's love in Christ's dying for sinful men, whether I believed it or not.

"'Now you are getting at it,' said the woman. 'That's the story for me.'

"And so I got her in, and I got myself in. From that night," added Dr. Beery, "I have always had a full gospel of salvation for lost sinners."—*Things New and Old.*

CALEB'S SONG
(I Want that Mountain! It Belongs to Me) Copyright 1968
Joshua 14:9-12

Words and Music
By Bill Harvey

1. I saw the Giant of Prayer-less-ness up-on the moun-tain high; He
2. There was a Giant of La-zi-ness who said I would-n't go and
3. One faith-less Giant up-on the crest of Heb-ron's lof-ty height has
4. Let ev'-ry Gi-ant of Dis-tress and Un-be-lief and Sin get

laughed so hard at my un-bend-ed knee. No long-er in the Wil-der-
wit-ness for the One who set me free. I'll come from out the Wil-der-
vowed that he's the one to make me flee. I'll climb from out the Wil-der-
read-y now to va-cate, for you see: I've come from out the Wil-der-

ness I'll stay, and so I cry:
ness, I'll wit-ness now I know;
ness and trust Je-ho-vah's might!   I WANT THAT MOUNTAIN, It Be-longs to me!
ness! I know I'm going to win!

CHORUS:

I want that moun-tain! I want that moun-tain! Where the milk and hon-ey

flow, Where the grapes, of Es-chol grow. I want that moun-tain! I want that

moun-tain! The Moun-tain that my Lord has giv-en me.

192

JONAH

By the late William A. Fuller

Now listen, dear friends--I'll tell you a tale
How a prophet called Jonah got caught by a whale.
The whale got the prophet and, bless your dear soul!
He not only caught him but swallowed him whole!
This part of the story is awfully sad,
For it tells of a city that went to the bad.
When the Lord saw those people with such wicked ways,
He said: "I'll allow them but forty more days."
He then spoke to Jonah and said, "Go and cry
To that sin-hardened city and tell them just why
I give them six weeks to get well humbled down,
And if they don't yield I will tear up their town."
Jonah heard the Lord speaking and said, "I won't go.
It's against my religion and so I say No.
Those Nineveh people are nothing to me,
And I'm always against foreign missions, you see."
So he went down to Joppa, defiant in face,
And boarded a ship for some faraway place.
But God saw that ship as it sailed and said He,
"I can see Jonah's planning to run off from Me."
There are railroads that run into Nineveh town.
There are "prophets" galore who should flag sinners
      down.
But not many do it; far easier, you see,
To sail on a ship, hoping God cannot see.
So they join a nice church, with a place on the
      board,
And put in much effort by "serving the Lord."
But pointing the lost to the pathway of grace
Is for "others," so to them relinquish their place.
The Lord knows the ship that all dead Christians take,
And He turns to confusion the plans that they make.
A whale's waiting ready though judgment is slow.
How much better to say to the Lord, "I WILL GO!"

193

God set the winds blowing, with squeaks and with squeals,
While the sea became stormy and kicked up its heels;
But when Jonah confessed it was all for his sin,
The crew threw him out and the whale took him in.
The whale said, "Old fellow, now don't you forget
I was sent here to take you in out of the wet;
You're now to be punished, all right, for your sin."
Then he opened his mouth and poor Jonah went in.
'Neath the billows of green did that fish try to rest
As he sought for some sleep that his food could digest;
But he got mighty restless and very disturbed,
As the prayers of the backslidden prophet were heard.
The whale on the third day rose up from his bed,
With his insides aboil and a pain in his head.
He decided to get to the air mighty quick,
For this backsliding preacher was making him sick.
So he stirred up the sea with the flukes of his tail,
Performing his duty as God's prepared whale.
Then he made for the shore and, fast running aground
Put his passenger out on the beach, safe and sound.
Here's where Jonah thanked God for His mercy and grace,
As he saw in His service he still had a place.
His punishment o'er, though reaction was slow,
He repented and answered, "YES, LORD, I WILL GO."

Jonah stepped on the shore with a yawn and a sigh,
Sitting down in the sun for his clothing to dry.
He thought how much better his preaching would be
Since from Whale Seminary he had a degree.
Repentant and rested and dried in the sun,
He started for Nineveh, fast on the run,
Giving thanks to the Father in Heaven above
For His mercy and patience and wonderful love.
Now, this story of Jonah was cut into three,
And the final the best of its sections will be;
For the backsliding prophet, 'neath discipline's rod,
Is obedient now and a witness for God.
So though behind time, three most precious days late,
Jonah preached from the time he reached Nineveh's gate;
Till the men of that city repented and prayed
And the stroke of God's justice and vengeance was stayed.
Now, you backsliding Christian, remember this tale.
When you run from God's call, look out for God's whale!
Or whatever He sends you to help understand
There is no getting off--no way round His command:
            "YE ARE MY WITNESSES."--Isa. 43:10.

                        194

Snakes in His Boots

By the late Dr. H. C. Morrison

I had been called to assist in evangelistic meetings in a beautiful little city in Virginia. The pastor of the Methodist Church was a most delightful Christian gentleman.

Soon after the beginning of the meeting, my attention was called to a young man in the town, the son of an excellent family who had been successful in business, but had taken to drink. He had gone from bad to worse, his business had failed, a good property had been swept away. At the present time, he was having delirium tremens. Some young men were working with him faithfully. They would take him into the woods, on a creek bank, during the day and keep him there—a fine thing by the way; the deep, silent woods, on the bank of a clear, gurgling creek, is a place for calm thought and earnest prayer—a good place for a struggling soul to seek after God. These young friends would bring their fighting victim into church at night and sit with him on the back seat. As the days went forward, he improved a bit. He became less violent. He gradually sobered. On the last night of the meetings, he was happily converted. It was a wonderful transformation.

Before his conversion, I had gone up to his cottage to talk and pray with him. His yard gate was off the hinges and his yard rooted up by the pigs. Weather boarding had been torn off his cottage and it was in great need of repairs and paint. In the house, there were broken chairs and a little dilapidated furniture. His wife, lean and gaunt, in faded dress, sat on a piece of chair with her head down. A little baby sat on the floor with a hard crust in its hand and a swarm of flies about its face. It was a wretched place. The whiskey demon, it seemed, had done his worst.

Some three months afterward, I spent a few days in the same town. I met the pastor in front of his church and after a cordial greeting, he insisted that I should preach in the church on Wednesday evening, which I promised to do. He then said, "Step across the street to that grocery; there is a man there who would like to see you." I went over. A big, handsome, well dressed man rushed from behind the counter, grabbed my hand and squeezed it until the bones ached. He expressed his great joy at seeing me. I confessed that I did not know him. "Why," said he, "I am the fellow who had the snakes in my boots and the monkeys on my bedposts when you were here for your evangelis-

tic meetings. Don't you remember I was converted the last night of the meeting."

I did remember at once and we rejoiced together. He said, "I have not had the slightest appetite or desire for whiskey from that night to this time." He went on, "You must have supper with us Thursday evening. My wife will be delighted to see you." I was glad to accept his invitation. After the preaching in the church on Wednesday evening, many friends came up to greet me, among them a beautiful woman, tastefully dressed, with roses in her cheeks, laughter in her mouth and tears in her eyes. She said, "I want you to have supper with us Thursday evening." I thanked her, but said to her, "I promised to take supper with my friend, Frank," naming this remarkable convert. She answered in laughter, "I am Frank's wife."

I was greatly surprised and a bit displeased. I hardly thought it the proper thing for this new convert to bury the poor wretched looking creature of a wife he had just three months ago and marry this beautiful young woman in so short a time. But on inquiry, I found it was the same woman. The difference was when I saw her the first time, she was the wife of a miserable lost drunkard, jabbering with delirium tremens. When I saw her three months later, she was the wife of a wonderfully saved man, filled with the joy of the Lord, prosperous and happy in his business.

You may be sure I went up to their house for supper the next evening. The gate was on its hinges, the fence had been repaired, the yard was in good order, the cottage had been mended and painted white as snow. When I entered the house, there was a carpet on the floor, well-arranged furniture, books on the shelves and pictures on the wall. When supper came, there was T-bone steak in plenty and a fat rosy-cheek baby sitting in a high chair without a fly on him. I renewed my faith and purpose to preach a Christ who is so mighty and so gracious to save.

Back yonder three months ago, at a late hour in the evening, at the altar of the Methodist Church, there had been a new birth. It was the beginning of a new life. Old things had passed away; all things had become new. This new birth and new life is a powerful and irrefutable evidence of the Godhead and saving power of the Lord Jesus. This is an argument that cannot be answered.

Shortly after this visit to old Virginia, I met one of the distinguished lawyers of old Kentucky, a friend of mine, who was an infidel. We got into a discussion about the inspiration of the Scriptures, the deity of Christ and His power to save sinners. When I had the opportunity I related to him the above incident and he became deeply interested. At the close, I said, "Colonel, all skepticism in all the world has never taken snakes out of a man's boots, monkeys off his bedposts, put into him the power of a new life, planted roses in the cheeks of his wife and frightened the flies off his baby." I said, "Colonel, if I have a lie and you have the truth, my falsehood is worth a million times more to the human race in its sorrow and sin than your truth, for this Gospel that I preach is winning multitudes of lost sinners to Christ, to pardon and peace, to salvation and victory, to happy hearts and joyful homes, while your infidelity is only destroying faith, blighting hope and sending sinners adrift into darkness." I said, "Colonel, I have the truth and you have the falsehood."

He said, "Brother Morrison, if I believed the Bible as you believe it and could preach what you claim to be the Gospel with the faith and joy that you have, I would rather preach the Gospel than be President of the United States." We took a long walk together. He was one of the handsomest and most eloquent men I ever saw or heard. I said, "Colonel, I love you. You have a great soul, but you are in error and you are in darkness. I am going to pray for you and I hope, through the mercy of God, that sometime in the future, somewhere in the grand galleries of God's universe, I may meet you graciously saved and rejoicing in Jesus Christ."

The great lawyer wept, he pressed my hand and said, "I want you to pray for me." Soon afterwards, he died, and in his dying hour, he cried aloud and most earnestly to God for mercy. Who knows but the Christ, whose mighty arms of mercy caught the thief away from the cross to Paradise, may have reached out in answer to prayer and caught this poor man away from the verge of the pit to eternal blessedness?

—*Remarkable Conversions, The Herald Press*

"R U There, Madam?"

A hilarious duel between an affronted woman and an implacable machine

Condensed from Martin Levin's column, "The Phoenix Nest," in SATURDAY REVIEW CONSTANCE L. MELARO

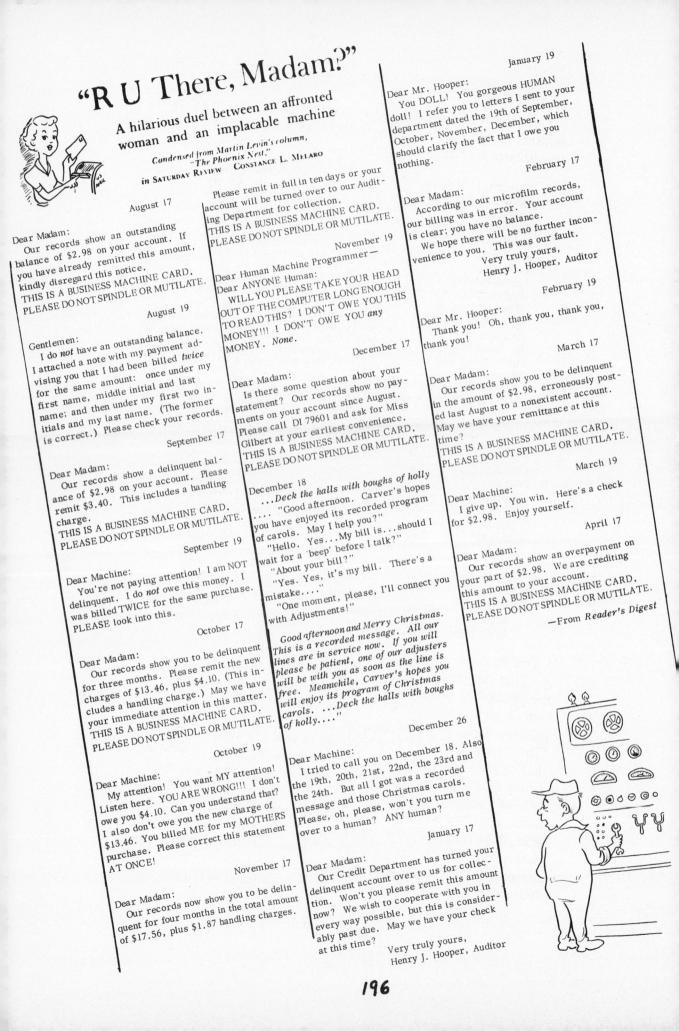

August 17

Dear Madam:
Our records show an outstanding balance of $2.98 on your account. If you have already remitted this amount, kindly disregard this notice.
THIS IS A BUSINESS MACHINE CARD. PLEASE DO NOT SPINDLE OR MUTILATE.

August 19

Gentlemen:
I do *not* have an outstanding balance. I attached a note with my payment advising you that I had been billed *twice* for the same amount: once under my first name, middle initial and last name; and then under my first two initials and my last name. (The former is correct.) Please check your records.

September 17

Dear Madam:
Our records show a delinquent balance of $2.98 on your account. Please remit $3.40. This includes a handling charge.
THIS IS A BUSINESS MACHINE CARD. PLEASE DO NOT SPINDLE OR MUTILATE.

September 19

Dear Machine:
You're not paying attention! I am NOT delinquent. I do *not* owe this money. I was billed TWICE for the same purchase. PLEASE look into this.

October 17

Dear Madam:
Our records show you to be delinquent for three months. Please remit the new charges of $13.46, plus $4.10. (This includes a handling charge.) May we have your immediate attention in this matter.
THIS IS A BUSINESS MACHINE CARD. PLEASE DO NOT SPINDLE OR MUTILATE.

October 19

Dear Machine:
My attention! You want MY attention! Listen here. YOU ARE WRONG!!! I don't owe you $4.10. Can you understand that? I also don't owe you the new charge of $13.46. You billed ME for my MOTHERS purchase. Please correct this statement AT ONCE!

November 17

Dear Madam:
Our records now show you to be delinquent for four months in the total amount of $17.56, plus $1.87 handling charges.

Please remit in full in ten days or your account will be turned over to our Auditing Department for collection.
THIS IS A BUSINESS MACHINE CARD. PLEASE DO NOT SPINDLE OR MUTILATE.

November 19

Dear Human Machine Programmer—
Dear ANYONE Human:
WILL YOU PLEASE TAKE YOUR HEAD OUT OF THE COMPUTER LONG ENOUGH TO READ THIS? I DON'T OWE YOU THIS MONEY!!! I DON'T OWE YOU *any* MONEY. *None.*

December 17

Dear Madam:
Is there some question about your statement? Our records show no payments on your account since August. Please call DI 79601 and ask for Miss Gilbert at your earliest convenience.
THIS IS A BUSINESS MACHINE CARD. PLEASE DO NOT SPINDLE OR MUTILATE.

December 18

...Deck the halls with boughs of holly .... "Good afternoon. Carver's hopes you have enjoyed its recorded program of carols. May I help you?"
"Hello. Yes...My bill is...should I wait for a 'beep' before I talk?"
"About your bill?"
"Yes. Yes, it's my bill. There's a mistake...."
"One moment, please, I'll connect you with Adjustments!"

Good afternoon and Merry Christmas. This is a recorded message. All our lines are in service now. If you will please be patient, one of our adjusters will be with you as soon as the line is free. Meanwhile, Carver's hopes you will enjoy its program of Christmas carols. ...Deck the halls with boughs of holly...."

December 26

Dear Machine:
I tried to call you on December 18. Also the 19th, 20th, 21st, 22nd, the 23rd and the 24th. But all I got was a recorded message and those Christmas carols. Please, oh, please, won't you turn me over to a human? ANY human?

January 17

Dear Madam:
Our Credit Department has turned your delinquent account over to us for collection. Won't you please remit this amount now? We wish to cooperate with you in every way possible, but this is considerably past due. May we have your check at this time?
Very truly yours,
Henry J. Hooper, Auditor

January 19

Dear Mr. Hooper:
You DOLL! You gorgeous HUMAN doll! I refer you to letters I sent to your department dated the 19th of September, October, November, December, which should clarify the fact that I owe you nothing.

February 17

Dear Madam:
According to our microfilm records, our billing was in error. Your account is clear; you have no balance.
We hope there will be no further inconvenience to you. This was our fault.
Very truly yours,
Henry J. Hooper, Auditor

February 19

Dear Mr. Hooper:
Thank you! Oh, thank you, thank you, thank you!

March 17

Dear Madam:
Our records show you to be delinquent in the amount of $2.98, erroneously posted last August to a nonexistent account. May we have your remittance at this time?
THIS IS A BUSINESS MACHINE CARD. PLEASE DO NOT SPINDLE OR MUTILATE.

March 19

Dear Machine:
I give up. You win. Here's a check for $2.98. Enjoy yourself.

April 17

Dear Madam:
Our records show an overpayment on your part of $2.98. We are crediting this amount to your account.
THIS IS A BUSINESS MACHINE CARD. PLEASE DO NOT SPINDLE OR MUTILATE.

—From *Reader's Digest*

HOW A NINE-YEAR-OLD WAS SAVED

Dr. John R. Rice tells of his conversion at the tender age of nine, in his biography, <u>Man Sent From God</u>, by Evangelist Robert L. Sumner. Beginning on page 25, we quote:

Though I was saved so young, I remember a long series of incidents through which God spoke to my heart and convicted me of my sins. I remember the Sunday School lesson when we learned about the baby Jesus' being born in a stable because there was no room for Him in the inn. I was not more than four years old at the time, but I kept that little pictured Sunday School card and felt guilty in my heart that human beings like me had no room for Jesus! When I was not more than five I was deeply moved by a song my mother sang, "Turned Away From the Beautiful Gate." I seemed to have known that it was by their own sinful rebellion and rejection of Christ that men miss Heaven. I remember some unrest of soul about it. About the same time my mother, after I had told her a lie, talked to me with tears of how God hated a lie, and what a sin it was. The occasion was burned on my memory, and I know that I felt I deserved the just condemnation of God. Surely that was God speaking to me through His Holy Spirit! When my mother lay on her deathbed she talked so of the Saviour as she had us all promise to meet her in Heaven that I felt myself under the spell of her dying smile and testimony until the time I trusted Christ as my Saviour. After mother's death I remember the tears and the exhortations of my Sunday School teacher. I remember the godly pastor who told the story of the prodigal son, told how he himself had once been a prodigal, how he ran away from home and came to want and trouble and how he was forgiven on his return. How strange, but it seems that God must have been calling from the first day I knew anything about good and bad, from the first time I ever had a sense of moral responsibility to God.

Dr. Sumner, the biographer, writes:
"That deepening conviction came to a head one Sunday as the young lad sat in the morning service of the First Baptist Church at Gainesville, Texas, and listened to the faithful pastor, Rev. A. B. Ingram, preach a moving message entitled, 'The Prodigal Son.' The realization was strong in his heart that he, too, was a prodigal son who had broken the laws of a holy God and had chosen his own way of sin in preference to God's way of righteousness. At the same time he sensed there would be welcome for him, like the young man of the text, if he would only arise and go to the Father. With holy, determined resolve he slid off his seat and walked down the aisle to take the preacher's hand in an open, public profession of faith in Jesus Christ as his personal Saviour.

"However, when he got to the front the minister was urging others, grown people, to come, and he seated young John to one side. No one showed him any Scripture or gave him any solid foundation on which to rest assurance of his salvation; so it was several years before he came into the definite, sweet, positive conviction that Christ was his and he was Christ's.

"In his booklet for young Christians, Seven Secrets of a Happy, Prosperous Christian Life, Dr. Rice tells about the sad, troubled years from the time he was saved until that positive assurance came."

Here is an excerpt from that booklet:

I sat stricken and silent before my father. I did not know what all those big words meant; *repentance* and *regeneration* and more. I simply knew my father did not think I was saved! Well, I thought, my father was the wisest man in the world and a preacher, besides; and if he thought I was not saved, I supposed I was not. Sadly I gave up the idea of joining the church and hoped the time would soon come when I would be old enough to be saved so my father would know that I was saved.

I wish I could tell you all the sadness and disappointment of the next three years. I often prayed...We moved out to a ranch in west Texas and then to a little cow town. The company was not always the best. My mother had gone to Heaven, and I was a motherless boy. I did not get much instruction in the Word of God. I got no assurance about salvation. Again and again I prayed for God to save me. Once I asked a godly preacher to pray for me and he asked me to pray for myself. So that night when I went home from the little church I went out into the horses' stall and knelt down and asked God to save me. Then I prepared for bed and knelt by the bed as I usually did for a good-night prayer and asked God to forgive my sins and save me. I felt no change. I did not have any glorious experience. I did not see any light shining around about me. I did not hear the flutter of angel wings. No electricity came in at my head or went out at my fingers and toes! So I sadly went to bed without any assurance of salvation. Then I thought, "Well, I had better settle this thing for good someway or other;" so I got out of bed and prayed again. There on my knees I thought how strange it was that when I realized I was a sinner and that there was nothing I could do to earn salvation and when God had promised so plainly that He would save people and that Jesus had died to pay for our sins—how strange, I thought, that God would not save me! I decided I would leave the matter in the hands of God the best I knew how and go to bed.

I offered myself for membership in the church. I could not feel any great conviction for sin, and yet I did not know that I was saved. When, in that little west Texas church, they asked me to stand and give my "experience," give my testimony before being received into the church, I simply said that I had thought about the matter a great deal, that I did not want to be a Methodist so I had decided to be a Baptist! I was a trembling, inexperienced boy, twelve years old. I was frightened at speaking before the people. And they someway had more confidence in my salvation than my testimony would have warranted, and received me in the church as a candidate for baptism!

When I was baptized I was strangely happy. Even yet I could give no clear testimony as to when I was saved or how. Oh, I wished that I knew just how and when I was saved and could know for sure that it was settled for good! But when others gave the very date and place when they were saved and told how happy they had been, I could not give any such experience.

Then one glad day I began reading the New Testament and came upon those wonderful promises in the Gospel of John, like clusters of ripe fruit on a beautiful tree!

"As many as received him, to them gave he power to become the sons of God, EVEN TO THEM THAT BELIEVE ON HIS NAME." John 1:12.

"He that believeth on the Son hath everlasting life."—John 3:36.

"Verily, verily, I say unto you, He that heareth my word, and believeth on him that sent me, hath everlasting life, and shall not come into condemnation; but is passed from death unto life."—John 5:24.

Oh, that last wonderful promise! I found that when I heard the Word of God and put my trust in the God who had sent His Son to save me, I then and there received everlasting life. I had often tried to remember that incident or that experience when I was nine years old and came to claim the Saviour publicly. I could not remember how I felt. I wondered if I had been as deeply moved as one must be to be saved. I recalled that a twelve-year-old boy who came the same day had been weeping and I had shed not a tear! I had thought many a time, "If I were really saved I would not do some of the things I do." But now I saw, praise the Lord, that when I had put my trust in Jesus Christ, then and there I received everlasting life! My doubts and fears were gone; gone, thank God, forever! From that day to this I have never doubted for a moment that I am God's child. I know one thing beyond any doubt: when I trusted Jesus, depended on Him to forgive me, He did! The Word of God says so and that makes it so. On those promises I have hung the eternal welfare of my soul, and how sure, how unchanging is that blessed foundation for my faith!

On page 29 of Man Sent From God, Dr. Robert L. Sumner sums up the experience of this West Texas country boy with these words:

"John Rice was certainly saved at the age of nine. He was saved for certain at the age of twelve."

Index of Authors

Index of Prose Articles

205

Index of Poetry

TITLES OF POEMS ARE IN CAPITAL LETTERS.
Where poem is given no title, first line is used
(in lower case).

Index of Topics

P.118 Politics